Table of Contents

Primary

Fine Arts

Health

Interdisciplinary Studies

Language Arts

Literature

Math

Science

Social Studies

Table of Contents

Intermediate

The purpose of this book is to help people use 4MAT. It was written by teachers for teachers. The instructional plans included are the work of creative professionals. They were chosen for their diversity of content, clarity of concept, generalizable appeal, creative methods of instruction, and incorporation of 4MAT principles. Most importantly, the authors reported that these plans had a positive impact on teaching and learning in their classrooms.

The task of choosing these plans was a most pleasurable one; it is gratifying to see how much we have all learned since the previous editions of 4MAT in Action were published in 1983 and 1990. And it is, indeed, a pleasure to note that this third edition of exemplary 4MAT plans demands two separate volumes: the first for grades K - 6, and the second for grades 7 - 12.

We are indebted to the teachers who contributed to this collection. We gratefully dedicate this book to them.

Susan Morris
Bernice McCarthy
Spring 1995

The 4MAT System

The 4MAT System: A Cycle of Learning

Major premises of 4MAT

1

- Human beings perceive experience and information in different ways.
- Human beings process experience and information in different ways.
- The combinations formed by our own perceiving and processing techniques form our unique learning styles.

2

- There are four major identifiable learning styles.
- They are all equally valuable.
- Learners need to be comfortable about their own unique learning styles.

3

- Type One Learners are primarily interested in personal meaning. Teachers need to create a reason.
- Type Two Learners are primarily interested in the facts as they lead to conceptual understanding. Teachers need to give them facts that deepen understanding.
- Type Three Learners are primarily interested in how things work. Teachers need to let them try it.
- Type Four Learners are primarily interested in self-discovery. Teachers need to let them teach it to themselves and others.

4

- All learners need to be taught in all four ways, in order to be comfortable and successful part of the time while being stretched to develop other learning abilities.
- All learners will "shine" at different places in the learning cycle, so they will learn from each other.

5

- The 4MAT System moves through the learning cycle in sequence, teaching in all four modes and incorporating the four combinations of characteristics.
- The sequence is a natural learning progression.

6

- Each of the four learning modes needs to be taught with both right- and left-brain processing techniques.
- The right-mode-dominant learners will be comfortable half of the time and will learn to adapt the other half of the time.
- The left-mode-dominant learners will be comfortable half of the time and will learn to adapt the other half of the time.

7

- The development and integration of all four modes of learning and the development and integration of both right- and left-brain processing skills should be a major goal of education.

8

- Learners will come to accept their strengths and learn to capitalize on them, while developing a healthy respect for the uniqueness of others and furthering their ability to learn in alternative modes without the pressure of "being wrong."

9

- The more comfortable we are about who we are, the more freely we learn from others.

Teaching to All Four Learning Styles Using Right- and Left-Mode Techniques

Remember,
each of the four learning style types
has a quadrant, or place,
where s/he is most comfortable,
where success comes easily.

The Imaginative Learners, those who fall
in quadrant one,
prefer to learn through a combination
of sensing/feeling and watching.

The Analytic Learners, those who fall
in quadrant two,
prefer to learn through a combination
of thinking through concepts and watching.

The Common Sense Learners, those who fall
in quadrant three,
prefer to learn by thinking through concepts
and trying things out for themselves,
by doing.

The Dynamic Learners, those who fall
in quadrant four,
prefer to learn by sensing/feeling and doing.

The 4MAT System is designed so all four types of learners are comfortable some of the time and challenged some of the time.

We continue to understand the 4MAT cycle in deeper ways.

What follows is the result of our experiences since the first edition of 4MAT in Action.

We continue to make discoveries about 4MAT.

The most important ongoing affirmation is that 4MAT is more difficult than it looks.

and the second is that some steps are more difficult than others.

4MAT requires major attitudinal shifts in the way we think and feel about teaching.

These attitudinal shifts are necessary in order to produce:

- Learning environments where all learners have an equal chance to learn;
- Learning environments where motivation is considered the primary task of the teacher;
- Learning environments where non-trivial concepts form the instructional base;
- Learning environments where the skills that are taught are related to concepts and have immediate usefulness;
- Learning environments where learners are encouraged to speak in their own voices while attending to and honoring the voices of others;
- Learning environments where learners are led to the delight of self-discovery;
- Learning environments where alertness is fostered by teaching to all four learning styles using right and left mode techniques;
- Learning environments where learners are assessed according to the multiple ways knowledge can be represented;
- Learning environments that not only honor but also celebrate the diversities of learners.

Let us begin by going around the circle once again.

Quadrant One: Integrating Experience with the Self

A process from Concrete Experience to Reflective Observation.

Sensing/Feeling to Watching/Reflecting.

All learners go through all of the quadrants, but quadrant one appeals most to Imaginative Learners. The favorite question of the Imaginative Learner is "Why?" You must create an experience through which learners discover their own reasons for learning.

The Type One Imaginative Learner's most comfortable place is the upper right corner of the model.

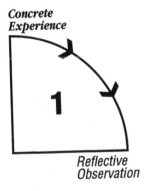

Concrete Experience

Reflective Observation

Teacher's Role - Motivator/Witness
Method - Simulation, Discussion

The goals that are emphasized in the first quadrant are focusing and generating skills, making meaning, observing, visualizing, imagining, inferring, connecting, diverging, listening, interacting, honoring subjectivity, and reflecting. In Quadrant One, students may be engaged in activities such as sharing personal reflections and autobiographic episodes, relational thinking, journal entries, brainstorming, mindmapping, drawings, group discussions, simulations, study teams, exit slips and self-assessment. Teachers may assess student performance through observation of student interest and engagement, level of student excitement, students' abilities to own their own message and acceptance of each other's ideas, individual authenticity and willingness to present ideas they are not yet sure of, the frequency of student initiated ideas, analysis of products resulting from student discussion or the quality of journal entries.

The Quadrant One Steps

Step One

Create An Experience
Type One, Right Mode Learner most comfortable
Teacher's Role - Motivator
Method - Discussion
Question to be answered - Why?
Create a reason

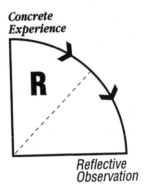

Concrete Experience

R

Reflective Observation

In Quadrant One we create a reason. We answer the question "Why?"

Begin by Creating an Experience. The Right Mode, Quadrant One Step.

The objective is to allow the learners to enter into the experience, to engage them, and to integrate the experience with personal meaning. Remember, the right mode jumps right into the experience, and the left mode stands back and analyzes what happened.

Imbue the experience with meaning so learners are able to see connections from their own experience. Richard Gibboney of the University of Pennsylvania School of Education comments on objectives and meaning: "Objectives must be valuable now, in their own immediate having."

A majority of teachers with whom we have worked report that this step is very difficult. They seem to struggle to create a concrete experience, something that can be apprehended or perceived on a direct and immediate level by the learners, something that connects to the learners' own experience and is therefore valuable to them now.

When we encounter teachers who have this difficulty, and

The 4MAT Steps in Depth

they are in the majority, we begin by asking them what they are teaching. In other words, we go immediately to the Second Quadrant in order to find out the concept they are teaching.

They answer, for example, "Capital letters."

We then ask, "What is the concept underlying capital letters?"

And to our amazement we are usually met by silence, and a most uncomfortable silence.

If capital letters differentiate between generalities and specifics, then one can easily construct experience based on this concept. The students know, for example, that they like to be called by their names, John, Jane, etc., rather than "the girl in the red sweater" or "the boy in the grey shirt." They can understand the concept of generalities versus specifics when you point out to them how they like to be called by their names, how they like to be specified. Tell them there is a method for specifying in written form, and it is capital letters.

In addition, you can give the students the experience of a world where capital letters are not used, and have them discuss and with luck discover the reason for capital letters, a reason that connects to their own experience.

But the more serious question remains: how can the teacher help learners make the connection to meaning, the purpose and usefulness of the underlying concept, the glue that holds it together, the reason that makes sense, if the teacher does not know what it is?

In order to "Create a Concrete Experience," you must understand the concept.

Jerome Bruner speaks to this:

"When we try to get a child to understand a concept . . . the first and most important condition, obviously, is that the expositors themselves understand it. I make no apology for this necessary point. To understand something well is to sense wherein it is simple, wherein it is an instance of a simpler general case. . . to understand something is to sense the simpler structure that underlies a range of instances, and this is notably true in mathematics."

We teach skills in boxes. Somehow these skills have become ends in themselves, isolated entities, and have become separated from their meaning.

Without meaning, there is no understanding. It is like

memorizing words in a foreign language without knowing what they mean, a frustrating and foolish task.

In order to Create an Experience, you must know the concept.

The problem graphically illustrated is this:

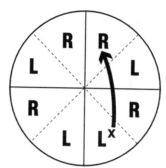

The Concept is the Key!

Our system has taught us to break things down, to look at the parts.

We must return to the whole picture.

Teachers need to motivate their learners to want to learn what they are about to teach. We felt the difficulty we would encounter in Quadrant One was that some teachers would not agree that motivation was their primary task.

In some cases that has been true. The following conversation took place during the first break in one of our workshops. The speaker was a high school science teacher on a faculty in a Midwestern city. He moved in quickly and with great intensity.

"Motivating students is not my job. That's an outrageous notion."

I replied, "Then whose job is it?"

He answered, "It's their job, the students, I mean. It's their responsibility to be motivated when they come to my class. And it's their parents' job to make sure they stay that way."

I asked, "Then what is your responsibility?"

He answered, "To give them information."

I replied, "Then they don't need you. A good text, a good computer program could do just as well."

So we continue to meet some teachers who operate under

The 4MAT Steps In Depth

the assumption that they are only required to teach motivated learners, learners who enter their classrooms excited and curious about the content to be taught. These teachers do not accept the idea that the art of teaching is arousing curiosity, creating excitement, answering the question "Why?" Motivation is the purpose of the Concrete Experience, the Right Mode Step of Quadrant One.

But, in order to design the Concrete Experience, a teacher needs to know the concept to be taught. Without the proper grasp of the concept, one cannot create a meaningful Concrete Experience. Somehow it takes the knack of grasping the idea of something in a way that connects to meaning. It is the core idea formed by mentally combining all the characteristics and particulars into a useful construct.

We are convinced this process is whole-brained, simply because we must analyze the parts while seeing the whole.

The Measurement unit presented in this book (see page 255) is a perfect example of this grasping. The Quadrant One, Right Mode experience created by the author constitutes the essence of why we have standards for measurement, the objective of this multi-cycle unit. The students are asked to trace their own hands and feet, and compare the variation in their own sizes. This activity goes to the heart of why standard measurement was created in the first place, and the students are engaged in a task which creates a very real reason for such standards.

It is the simplicity inherent in the meaning that connects the concept to understanding. Note that the Bruner quote ends with the statement, "to understand something is to sense the simpler structure that underlies a range of instances, and this is notably true in mathematics."

When the teacher truly understands the concept, the creation of the concrete experience simply becomes a matter of translating the concept into the language of the students, the language the students would use if they were attempting to explain the same thing.

In Literature, it is particularly important for the teacher to identify the concept which is exemplified by the literary work being studied. In other words, the teacher is not just teaching the literary work which the learners will read, but rather a significant concept is identified which all of the learners can relate to their own lives. Laurie Kelly uses the concept of "Friendship" when her students read the book, Charlotte's Web. (See page 87) She engages

them through the sharing of a special story in an activity where they think of themselves as friends, and how they themselves experience growth when they are being a good friend. This creates an immediate connection between her students life experiences and the theme of the book they will read and study in this unit.

The Concrete Experience must embody the essence of the concept at a simpler level, in order to prepare the students for the complexities that lie ahead as they move around the circle. Herein lies the right mode aspect - the concept gestalt coupled with the personal experience, the experience that connects to the self.

The right mode seems to engage the sense of relationship. It seems to embody a natural, intuitive way of thinking. We need to encourage intuitive ways of thinking, as "our left brains have become too stiff with technique, far from the scanning eye."

We believe one of the biggest stumbling blocks in designing the Quadrant One, Right Mode Step is the inability to translate the concept into a simple structure, in language learners can understand and relate to, and in a manner that connects to their personal lives.

We now move on to Step Two.

Step Two

Reflecting on Experience
Type One, Left Mode Learner most comfortable
Teacher's Role - Witness
Method - Discussion
Question to be answered - Why?
Create a reason

Concrete Experience

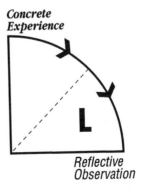

Reflective Observation

The left mode aspect of reflecting on experience lies in the quality of analysis. Now the learners examine the experience. The method is discussion, which is the method in the first quadrant, but the focus has changed. The learners are now asked to step outside the experience and look at its parts.

Teachers do not seem to encounter much difficulty with this step, although there are two things to guard against: one, getting too technical in the analysis, and two, attempting to introduce new material. It appears when teachers construct a meaningful concrete experience, they have no difficulty helping learners to reflect on that experience. The experience itself flows into the quality of the reflection.

Notice this ease of operation when you read the lesson units included in this book. Teachers have made creative use of cooperative learning strategies, mindmapping, classification charts, and teacher-led discussion to enable their learners to reflect on their personal feelings and experiences.

Quadrant Two: Concept Formulation

A process of learning from Reflective Observation to Abstract Conceptualization.

Reflecting/Watching to Developing Concepts.

All of the students go through this process, but Quadrant Two appeals most to the Analytic Learners.

The Type Two Learner's most comfortable place is the lower right corner of the model.

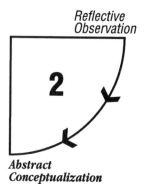

Reflective Observation

2

Abstract Conceptualization

Teacher's Role - "Teacher"
Method - Informational

The first quadrant is "create a reason" and the second is "teach it to them."

The second quadrant and those that follow are also divided into right- and left-mode techniques. The development of both right- and left-mode functioning continues throughout the learning cycle. Some of our students are right-mode dominant, some are left-mode dominant, but all need to develop both types of processing skills.

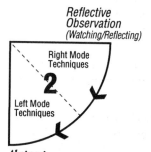

Reflective Observation (Watching/Reflecting)

Right Mode Techniques

2

Left Mode Techniques

Abstract Conceptualization (Thinking/Developing Concepts)

The goals that are emphasized in Quadrant Two are reflecting, seeing relationships, developing idea coherence, conceptualizing, defining, patterning, classifying, comparing, contrasting, being objective, discriminating, planning, constructing theoretical models, and acquiring knowledge. In the second quadrant, students may be engaged in activities such as non-verbal representations of connections, essays, spatial non-representations; creating analogs, metaphors, and clusters; outlining; using fish, venn and tree diagrams; discussions; oral exams and research; constructing theoretical models; objective tests, exit slips, and self-assessment. Teachers may assess student progress by checking for concept congruence (oral or written), quality of concept maps showing linkages between ideas, descriptions of reasoning; quality of planning steps; identification of criteria; ability to break into parts; evidence of theoretical understanding; and essays showing understanding of knowledge presented.

Quadrant Two has been discussed above in the context of the relationship between the Concrete Experience and the concept to be taught, but we need to examine concept formulation more carefully, as it is the essence of Quadrant

The 4MAT Steps In Depth

Two, as well as the core of the entire unit plan. It leads directly to practice and personalization in Quadrant Three, and on to Self-Discovery in Quadrant Four. The degree to which the "Why?" of the first quadrant is answered affects the understanding of the "What?" of the second quadrant; so also the "What?" of the second quadrant has an impact on the success of the third and fourth quadrants.

As we move into Quadrant Two, we are leading students from the specific personal reality to the theoretical conception. We now need to deepen student understandings of how the concept can be examined in the abstract, at the theoretical level. We are integrating the Concrete Experience (Right Mode, Quadrant One) and the analysis of the experience (Left Mode, Quadrant One) into a deeper understanding of the concept.

If Steps One and Two in Quadrant One have embodied the essence of the concept, then the students are ready to move to Quadrant Two.

You begin with the Right Mode step, possibly the most critical step in the learning process.

The Quadrant Two Steps

Step Three

Integrating Observations into Concepts
Type Two, Right Mode Learner most comfortable
Teacher Role - "Teacher"
Method - Informational
Question to be answered - What?
Teach it to them

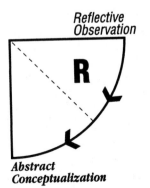

Reflective
Observation

R

Abstract
Conceptualization

The right mode step of Quadrant Two attempts to deepen reflection; it is an integrating step. We have come to see this step as the key to the learners' internalization of their need for further understanding of the concept at hand. It is the place where they link their personal, subjective experience with the objective, analytic world of the content at hand.

In Molly Merry's plan using Whales as the theme to teach the Concept of Size, (see page 138) she has her students imagine they are whales as they view a non-verbal film taken by underwater photographers. The film is followed by a reflective drawing and writing activity as the children imagine their feelings about their size compared to the creatures of the deep. John Wolf, on the other hand, begins his Democracy unit with a "game with no rules." In this third step, his students are asked to create visuals which depict what a "place with no rules" looks like. All of these Step Three activities enable the learners to tap into and deepen the richness of what they already know about the concepts being studied.

When you design Step Three, Quadrant Two, the Right Mode Step, look for another medium, another way of looking at the concept that engages the senses while simultaneously affording the opportunity for more reflection. Remember you are moving the learners from the concrete to the abstract, and Reflective Observation is the gateway. You want to create an activity that causes them to mull over the experience and reflection just completed in Quadrant One and assists them in formulating and deepening their understanding of the concept, the purpose of Quadrant Two.

The 4MAT Steps in Depth

Step Four

Developing Theories and Concepts
Type Two, Left Mode Learner most comfortable
Teacher Role - "Teacher"
Method - Informational
Question to be answered - What?
Teach it to them

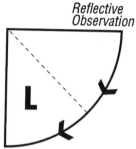

Reflective
Observation

L

Abstract
Conceptualization

The left mode step of Quadrant Two takes your learners to the heart of conceptual information. Be sure "the subject matter does not swamp the learner with information easily available elsewhere, but rather information is given selectively to assist in learner inquiry." We are not interested in rote memory, the antithesis of thinking. We are stressing information that relates to the core of the concept. Many of the unit plans in this book demonstrate Step Four activities in which creative teachers have gone beyond traditional lecture accompanied by the text to teach content to their learners.

In Don Weber's social studies unit on Local History (see page 354) the teacher invites local senior citizens into the classroom to be interviewed by the students and a guest speaker from the historical society presents the mini-lecture.

The Fourth Step is to "teach it to them." The choices of content must be related to the concept and engender further learner inquiry.

Quadrant Three: Practice and Personalization

A process of learning from Abstract Conceptualization to Active Experimentation.

Thinking/Developing Concepts to Doing/Trying it Themselves.

All of the students continue on through this process, but Quadrant Three appeals most to the Common Sense Learners.

The Type Three Learner's most comfortable place is the lower left corner of the model.

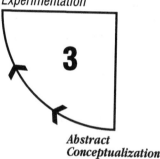

Active
Experimentation

3

Abstract
Conceptualization

Teacher's Role - Coach
Method - Facilitation

Common Sense Learners rely heavily on kinesthetic involvement to learn, using body senses as a focus for understanding. They need to try it. They are concerned with finding out the answer to the question, "How does this work?" They are anxious to try it themselves. They edit reality. The teacher's role is to provide the materials and the encouragement necessary for a "trying things out" environment.

Abraham Maslow speaks of growth as taking place subjectively "from within outward." He comments on the healthy child as follows:

"... (s)he tends to try out his (her) powers, to reach out, to be absorbed, fascinated, interested, to plan, to wonder, to manipulate the world. Exploring, manipulating, experiencing, being interested, choosing . . .

(This) lead(s) to Becoming through a serendipitous way, fortu-

itously, unplanned, unanticipated. Spontaneous, creative experience can and does happen without expectations, plans, foresight, purpose or goal."

In commenting on the relationship between safety and growth, Maslow goes on to say:

"Apparently growth forward customarily takes place in little steps, and each step forward is made possible by the feeling of being safe, of operating out into the unknown from a safe home port (emphasis ours) of daring because retreat is possible... Now, how can we know when the child feels safe enough to dare to choose the new step ahead? Ultimately the only way in which we can know is by his choice which is to say only he can ever really know the right moment when the beckoning forces ahead overbalance the beckoning forces behind, and courage outweighs fear. Ultimately the person even the child must choose for himself. Nobody can choose for him too often, for this itself enfeebles him, cutting his self-trust, and confusing his ability to perceive his own internal delight in the experience, his own impulses, judgments, and feelings, and to differentiate them from the interiorized standards of others."

Maslow speaks eloquently of choices encouraged by a safe environment. We emphatically agree. We do not believe learning can take place without learners being allowed to make choices, to explore, to manipulate, to experience. These activities are often found in primary schools, but exploration, manipulation, and experimentation in the higher grades and post-secondary learning environments is frequently limited to reading another book or writing another essay, activities that appeal to only a small percentage of our learners.

The four quadrants in the 4MAT System move from teacher-initiated to learner-initiated activities. In Quadrant One (Steps One and Two), the teacher is the initiator, the primary actor. S/he plans and implements the experience as well as the reflective discussion that follows the experience. In Quadrant Two, the teacher is the information giver; first in Step Three by linking the experience and the reflection into the concepts to be taught, and second (Step Four) by teaching the material and skills.

"Apparently growth forward customarily takes place in little steps, and each step forward is made possible by the feeling of being safe, of operating out into the unknown from a safe home port..."

This changes as we move into Quadrant Three. The third quadrant is where the learners become active, more self-initiating. Learners become the primary actors even more in Quadrant Four.

In the first quadrant the teacher creates a reason.

In the second quadrant the teacher teaches it to them.

In the third quadrant the teacher lets them try it themselves.

The teacher's role in the third quadrant is one of coach/facilitator. The crucial teaching skill in this quadrant is organizational, to gather the materials needed for manipulation and to set up the encouraging environment needed so the learners can try it themselves. Without the active involvement of the learners, schooling at all levels is a sterile overlay, an externally applied act, satisfying the teacher perhaps (after all, s/he's working), but not involving the students in any meaningful way.

So, the emphasis in the third quadrant (and the fourth) is on learner activity.

The learners take the concepts and skills that have been taught and try them. The goals that are emphasized in Quadrant Three include resolving contradictions, managing ambiguity, computing, collecting data, inquiring, predicting, recording, hypothesizing, tinkering, measuring, experimenting, problem-solving, and making decisions. Students may be engaged in activities such as field work and lab work, adapting new knowledge for personal usefulness, conversations with teacher and peers, demonstrations, worksheets, chapter questions, and essays; puzzles, diagrams, computer experiments, interviews, exit slips, and self-assessment. Teachers may assess student progress by looking for evidence of learner authenticity, student ability to integrate knowledge into life (usefulness), flexi-

The 4MAT Steps in Depth

bility of thought, contingency logic and reasoning, manageability and timelines for projects, project choice parameters, reflective notes about content, essays or problems requiring multiple methods of solution, accuracy and thoroughness.

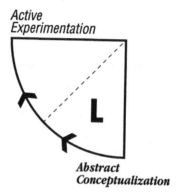

Active Experimentation

Right Mode Techniques

3

Left Mode Techniques

Abstract Conceptualization

The third quadrant is also divided into Left and Right Mode Techniques.

Note that Left Mode techniques come first in the third quadrant.

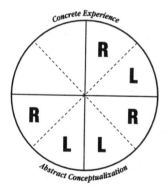

Concrete Experience

R

L

R

R

L

L

Abstract Conceptualization

This is because of the proximity to the Abstract Conceptualization dimension. As we move into Quadrant Three (Step Five) the learners react to the "givens" presented in Quadrant Two, but in a more fixed, prearranged way than in Step Six.

Quadrant Three: Practice and Personalization

Step Five

Working on Defined Concepts
(Reinforcement and Manipulation)
Type Three, Left Mode Learner most comfortable
Teacher Role - Coach
Method - Facilitation
Question to be answered - How does this work?
Let them try it

Active Experimentation

L

Abstract Conceptualization

Comments on Step Five

In Step Five, the students react to the givens. They do worksheets, use workbooks, try fixed lab experiments, etc. These materials are used to reinforce the concepts and skills taught in Quadrant Two. A good workbook of prepared exercises can be used in Step Five. This is a traditional step, as is Step Four. Sad to say, Steps Four and Five in the 4MAT Model constitute the bulk of what transpires in many traditional learning environments and what is recommended in many teacher's manuals.

Note that these two steps, Steps Four and Five, are left-mode techniques. Step Four appeals to the Analytic left-mode learners, and Step Five appeals to the Common Sense left-mode learners. One can easily see the value of these two steps for all learners, but exclusive teaching in this way handicaps all learners. Schools must stop teaching exclusively in these two steps if we are to individualize in any meaningful way.

The 4MAT Steps In Depth

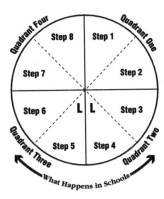

Good unit plans have learners really practice what they are learning. For example, in the unit on Natural Selection/ Animal Hiding Places (page 129), after answering traditional questions and filling in worksheets, the students must look outside at home, find and sketch possible real animal hiding places, an immediate application and field-testing of classroom learning.

The left-mode characteristic of Step Five lies in the reaction to givens. The learners have been taught a skill or a concept, and now they are asked to manipulate materials based on those skills/concepts. They are still adapting to experts; they are still working on prescribed materials. They have begun. But the creative stepping out, the adding something of their own, the applying their own uniqueness to the material, comes in Step Six, the right mode step of Quadrant Three.

Step Six

Messing Around
(Adding Something of Themselves)
Type Three, Left Mode Learner most comfortable
Teacher Role - Coach
Method - Facilitation
Question to be answered - How does this work?
Let them try it

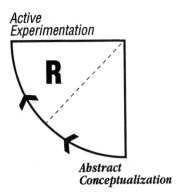

Real integration begins with Step Six.

The learners are "adding something of themselves," "messing around," and making the material theirs.

The right mode characteristic of Step Six is in the integration of the material and the self, the personal synthesis, as well as in the opportunity for learners to approach the content in their own most comfortable way. The right mode Common Sense Learners are most comfortable in Step Six.

To return to Maslow:

"If the child can choose the experiences which are validated by the experience of delight, then he can return to the experience, repeat it, savor it to the point of repletion, satiation or boredom. At this point he shows the tendency to go on to more complex, richer experiences and accomplishments.

. . . Such experiences not only mean moving on, but have a feedback effect on the Self, in the feeling of certainty (This I like; that I don't for sure); of capability, mastery, self-trust, self-esteem."

The skills materials given in Step Five should afford learners the opportunity to practice what they have learned, to try it themselves. Workbook pages can never be substituted for conceptual learning; rather they complement and reinforce the concepts. We are concerned about the amount of workbook pages being used in the schools we visit. It appears that many times they are used to teach the concepts, rather than to reinforce the concepts. If this is true, it indicates that teachers are bypassing Quadrant Two and going directly to skills and drills without the conceptual underpinnings so necessary for understanding.

We ask the reader to ponder any classroom learning situation in which learners are required to complete workbook pages as the major emphasis of the class. Our experience indicates that this is the case in a great many classrooms. The workbook has become the concept lesson.

To return to Gibboney again:

"... skills and drills must be related to thought. Information is never severed from thoughtful doing. And thinking and doing are inseparable."

Creative teachers provide their learners with the opportunity to extend what they have learned through making project choices and individualizing their own experimentation. In good lesson plans, the teacher may keep in mind individual learning style characteristics when planning activities for the learners to select. Good teachers also require their learners to maintain ownership over the quality of the work they choose to do; Step Six of a 4MAT unit is the ideal place for the teacher and students to agree upon the rubrics that will be used to assess the final product created by the learners. Likewise, learners may appreciate the opportunity to choose either to work cooperatively in a team or to work alone on a project to be shared later with the group.

There are a number of excellent examples of creative Step Six options in the units in this volume. For instance, in Victoria Tennant's science unit on the Life Cycle of a Butterfly (see page 123), her primary grade students participate in an array of learning center activities which involve creative use of multiple modalities as they further extend and integrate what they have learned. The Friendship unit contributed by Juanice Hayslip (page 237) allows for multiple forms of learner representation. Her students creatively apply their understanding of Friendship by making posters, interviewing the characters from "Charlotte's Web," role playing scenes from the story with props and scenery, creating a "friendship quilt," or writing descriptive poems about their favorite characters.

In other words, the drills you design must prepare the stu-

dents to move from the Abstract Conceptualization of Quadrant Two to the Active Experimentation of Quadrant Three. "Without testing, ideas do not flow from the abstract to the real (the equally important realm of experience.)"

Step Six begins to move the students into Self-Discovery. Maslow speaks of delight, *"experiences which are validated by ...delight."* The word describes Self-Discovery beautifully.

Actor-director Richard Benjamin, speaking of his experience at La Guardia Performing Arts School, epitomizes the delight of learning in this mode:

It was . . . the luckiest thing that ever happened to me. It was a longer (school) day, but they couldn't get the kids out of there."

This is active thinking. This is learning by doing, and its essence is problem solving.

"We solve a problem or make a discovery when we impose a puzzle form on a difficulty to convert it into a problem that can be solved in such a way that it gets us where we want to be. That is to say, we recast the difficulty into a form that we know how to work with - then we work it. Much of what we speak of as discovery consists of knowing how to compose a workable kind of form on various kinds of difficulties. A small but crucial part of discovery of the highest order is to invent and develop effective models or puzzle forms. It is in this area that the truly powerful mind shines. But it is surprising to what degree perfectly ordinary people can, given the benefit of instruction, construct quite interesting and what, a century ago, would have been considered greatly original models.

Of only one thing am I convinced: I have never seen anybody improve in the art and technique of inquiry by any means other than engaging in inquiry."

We cannot lead our learners to inquiry by using workbook pages as the major thrust of our lessons. We must motivate them by answering the question "Why?"; we must teach it to them by answering the question "What?"; we must lead them from the abstract to the real by answering the question "How does this work?"; and we must allow them the delight of self-discovery by building in the question "If?"

"Much of what we speak of as discovery consists of knowing how to impose a workable kind of form on various kinds of difficulties."

Quadrant Four: Integrating Application and Experience

A process of learning from Active Experimentation to Concrete Experience.

Doing/Trying It Themselves to Sensing/Feeling.

All of the learners go through this process, but Quadrant Four appeals most to the Dynamic Learners.

The Type Four Dynamic Learner's most comfortable place is the upper left corner of the model.

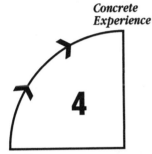

Teacher's Role – Evaluator/Remediator/Co-Learner
Method – Self-Discovery

The goals that are emphasized in Quadrant Four are creating, identifying constraints, revising, creating models, coming to closure, editing, summarizing, verifying, synthesizing, re-presenting, reflecting anew, re-focusing, and evaluating. Students are actively engaged in editing processes (revising, refining); error analyzing; concluding; taking a position; assessing the quality of their evidence; creating, collaborating, verifying, and summarizing; syntheisizing original performances; preparing and presenting exhibitions and/or publications; exit slips, and self-assessments. Teachers may be assessing students by reviewing portfolio selections, student products, field notes, exhibits, first and second drafts, their use of "best" experts, the quality of oral/visual presentations (appropriateness, sensitivity to feedback, originality, relevance to a larger audience), quality of new insights and questions, willingness to push limits, and ability to extend concepts and ask new questions.

Quadrant Four Steps

Step Seven

Analyzing for Usefulness or Application
Type Four, Left Mode Learner most comfortable
Teacher's Role - Evaluator/Remediator/Co-Learner
Method - Self-Discovery
Question to be answered - If?
"Let them teach it to themselves and to someone else"

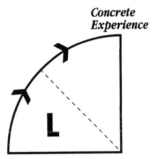

Now we move into Quadrant Four, where the learners deepen the initiative they began in Step Six. Here they refine the uniquely personal things they have done. If we have done our job well, the impetus to explore, to manipulate, to choose now comes from them. They have been freed to go beyond the objectives themselves. The teacher can now evaluate and remediate; and the learners can evaluate themselves, their learning, and refine and edit their own work. The students are truly learning from each other.

Comments on Step Seven

This is the step where the learners are asked to analyze what they have planned as their "proof" of learning. The left-mode characteristic of Step Seven lies in the analysis of the planning. This analysis should be based on:

1. Relevance to the content/skills

2. Originality

3. Excellence

Step Seven requires the learners to apply and refine in some personal, meaningful way what they have learned. As you will see in the lesson plan samples in this book, there are many different ways to achieve this step. The students (as well as peers and the teacher) will be

The 4MAT Steps in Depth

involved in editing and refining the work that has been done so far, analyzing for strengths and weaknesses, taking a position, and productive self-assessment. Many kinds of choices are possible.

Teachers should move their students to usefulness, and it is immediate usefulness. Students are now capable of going beyond the objectives themselves to personal interest based on the combined experience in Quadrant One, the knowledge in Quadrant Two, and the practice leading to personalization in Quadrant Three. The learning is being extended outward into their lives.

Step Eight

Doing It Themselves and Sharing What They Do With Others

Type Four, Right Mode Learner most comfortable

Teacher's Role - Evaluator/Remediator/Co-Learner

Method - Self-Discovery

Questions to be answered - How can I apply this? What can this become?

Let them teach it to themselves and to someone else

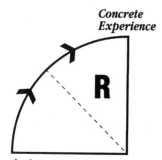

Concrete Experience

R

Active Experimentation

In the last step of the lesson unit, Step Eight, the learners share what they have learned with each other, and perhaps with the wider community at large. This is the place where students truly are asked to stand and speak in their own voices as they share in their own best way what it is they each have learned from the cycle of the unit they experienced. So we return to synergy, where we began. But there is a difference, a great difference (if we have done our job). We have given our learners the skills to discover for themselves whether or not what we have taught is worth knowing.

"We may well ask of any item of information that is taught or that we lead a child to discover for (her) himself whether it is worth knowing. I can think of only two good criteria and one middling one for deciding such an issue: whether the knowledge gives a sense of delight and whether it bestows the gift of intellectual travel beyond the information given, in the sense of containing within it the basis of generalization. The middling criterion is whether the knowledge is useful. It turns out, on the whole, that useful knowledge looks after itself. So I would urge that we as school (wo/men) let it do so and concentrate on the first two criteria. Delight and travel, then.

. . . It seems to me that the implications of this conclusion are that we opt for depth and continuity in our teaching, rather than coverage, and that we re-examine afresh what it is that gives a sense of intellectual delight to a person who is learning."

And so. . .
we move our students
from the usefulness
of Quadrant Three,
to the delight
of Quadrant Four.

We lead them to Self-Discovery;
we take them
back around the circle
in ever-increasing complexity.

The cycle begins again with energy generated by the cycle just completed.

The 4MAT Steps In Depth

It seems to me that good teachers do four things well:

They instill a love of learning,
They make the difficult easy,
They help us believe in ourselves—
 that the impossible is possible,
 that we can help change our world.
And they give us an awareness of the need to honor each other.

So go forth and teach.
And most of all, teach your students to celebrate diversity.

For our culture has a way of giving us ladders when we need trees,
reason when we need myth, and separateness when we need unity.
In the music of the universe, there is harmony.

For when you teach your students to celebrate diversity,
you will give the gift of grace.
The grace to blend all that is, was, and shall be.

And God will go with you.

Bernice McCarthy based on Bob Samples[12]

Footnotes:

1. McCarthy, Bernice, *The 4MAT System: Teaching to Learning Styles with Right/Left Mode Techniques.* Barrington, IL: Excel, Inc., 23385 Old Barrington Road, 60010. 1980, 1987.

2. Gibboney, Richard A., *Toward Intellectual Excellence: Some Things to Look for in Classrooms and Schools (TIE),* Graduate School of Education, University of Pennsylvania, 3700 Walnut Street, Philadelphia, PA 19104-3688. 1982. Page 10.

3. Bruner, Jerome S., *On Knowing: Essays for the Left Hand.* Belknap Press of Harvard University Press, Cambridge, MA. Second Printing, 1980. Paperback, pages 105-106.

4. *ibid.*, page 8.

5. Gibboney, Richard A., *op. cit.* page 14.

6. Maslow, Abraham H., *Toward a Psychology of Being.* Second Edition. NY: Von Nostrand Reinhold Company. 1968. Chapter Four.

7. *ibid.*

8. Gibboney, Richard A., *op. cit.* page 23.

9. Atwater, Carol, "Special Schools," *USA Today,* Wednesday, April 13, 1983. Section 3D.

10. Bruner, Jerome S., *op. cit.*, page 94.

11. *ibid.*, pages 108-109.

12. Samples, Bob, *Mind of Our Mother.* Reading, MA: Addison-Wesley Publishing Company. 1981.

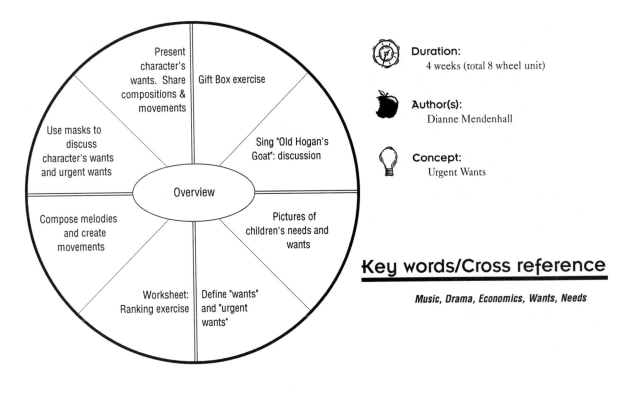

Duration:
4 weeks (total 8 wheel unit)

Author(s):
Dianne Mendenhall

Concept:
Urgent Wants

Overview
Present character's wants. Share compositions & movements
Gift Box exercise
Use masks to discuss character's wants and urgent wants
Sing "Old Hogan's Goat": discussion
Compose melodies and create movements
Pictures of children's needs and wants
Worksheet: Ranking exercise
Define "wants" and "urgent wants"

Key words/Cross reference

Music, Drama, Economics, Wants, Needs

Overview

Author's notes:

In this eight-wheel series of lessons designed for the primary music classroom, I use music to teach basic economic concepts to young children. People have wants and urgent wants. Those wants consist of goods and services. Everyone's wants cannot always be fulfilled due to limited resources. To facilitate getting one's wants, people bartered or traded goods and services. Money was created to make bartering more practical.

Objective:

Students will learn that people want things for different reasons.

About the author:

At the time this unit was first published, Dianne Mendenhall taught elementary music for Indianapolis Public Schools, Indianapolis, IN. She is a certified 4MAT trainer.

Required resources:

Empty gift box, drawing paper, crayons, song: "Old Hogan's Goat," bell sets and mallets, recorders, masks for different characters: nurse, knight, clown, witch, farmer, etc.

Bibliography:

Songs in these "wheels" were found in the Silver Burdette series, World of Music.

Davison, Donald G. *Strategies for Teaching Economics, Primary Level,* New York: Joint Council on Economics, 1977.

Day, Harlan R. *Playdough Economics,* Indianapolis, IN: Indiana Department of Education, Center for School Improvement and Performance, Office of School Assistance, 1988.

Gilliard, June V. *Economics: What and When, Scope and Sequence Guidelines,* K-12, Joint Council on Economics, 1989.

Jennings, Lynne *Try on My Shoe,* 281 E. Millan St., Chula Vista, CA 91910.

Katzman and King *Economy Size,* Santa Monica, CA: Good Year Publishing, 1978.

Saunders, Phillip *A Framework for Teaching the Basic Concepts,* 2nd edition, New York: Joint Council on Economics, 1977.

Skeel, Dorothy J. *Small-Size Economics: Lessons for the Primary Grades,* Glenview, IL: Scott, Foresman and Company, 1988.

Quadrant 1—Experience

 Right Mode—Connect

Gift Box exercise.

Objective

To create connections to the things children want, but may not need.

Activity

Pass small empty gift box from student to student, seated in circle formation. Each student will imagine what they would want in the box. The box is Magical and can change sizes and shapes enabling the students to have whatever they want. Tell children that whenever they hear the word "want" or "wants," they should touch their head and toes as quickly as possible.

Assessment

Quality of brainstorming and contribution to the activity.

 Left Mode—Examine

Sing "Old Hogan's Goat." Discussion.

Objective

To look at the idea of wants and needs through the example in a song.

Activity

Sing "Old Hogan's Goat" (an echo song). After singing, ask students the following:
Who is the song about? (Old Hogan and his goat)
What did the goat do to upset Old Hogan? (Ate 3 red shirts off the line)
What happened to the goat? (Hogan tied him to the railroad track)
What did the man want from the goat? (His shirt)
What did the goat want when he was tied to the track? (His life!)

Assessment

Students level of understanding of what Old Hogan wanted and the goat needed!

Quadrant 2—Concepts

 Right Mode—Image

Pictures of children's needs and wants.

Objective

Children will make images of wants and urgent wants.

Activity

Students draw pictures of things they think children want and things children have to have in order to survive.

Assessment

Quality of student pictures and discussion.

 Left Mode—Define

Define "wants" and "urgent wants."

Objective

To teach the concept of human wants and needs.

Activity

Explain the difference between "wants" and "urgent wants." Make reference to the goat song. Teach the "Gimme" chant:

"Gimme, gimme, gimme, gimme, gimme, gimme, gimme,
gimme, this and gimme that!
Gimme, gimme, gimme, gimme, gimme, gimme, gimme,
gimme this and gimme that!

Assessment

Students' attention to the lesson and involvement and enjoyment in the chant.

Quadrant 3—Applications

Left Mode—Try

Worksheet: Ranking exercise.

Objective:
Guided practice and checking for understanding.

Activity:
Students name four things they want and four things they need. Rank the four items in order of preference. Discuss why they made their choices.

Assessment
Students' ability to discriminate wants and needs.

Right Mode—Extend

Compose melodies and create movements.

Objective:
To give students an opportunity to express the concepts learned.

Activity:
1. Give each child a bell set and mallet. Students create melodies representing wants and urgent wants. Pose the question to them: "What would wants and urgent wants each sound like?"
2. Have students create movement patterns to express wants and urgent wants.

Assessment
Students' attention to task.

Quadrant 4—Creations

Left Mode—Refine

Use masks to discuss character's wants and urgent wants.

Objective:
Students will add to their application.

Activity:
Give masks to students. They are now actors and actresses and may be the character on the mask. Have the students pantomime their characters and explain their character's wants and urgent wants.

Assessment
Involvement and comments from the children.

Right Mode—Integrate

Present character's wants. Share compositions & movements.

Objective:
To celebrate and portray the learning.

Activity:
Students will put on a small show for each other including their movements and melodies, in character if they wish.
Sing the parody, "Happy and You Know It" and review the "Gimme" chant.

Assessment
Enjoyment of the children.

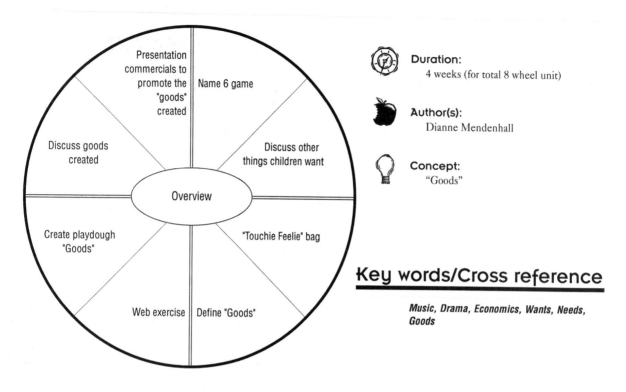

Duration:
4 weeks (for total 8 wheel unit)

Author(s):
Dianne Mendenhall

Concept:
"Goods"

Key words/Cross reference

Music, Drama, Economics, Wants, Needs, Goods

Overview

Author's notes:
See Author's Note in the Overview in Wheel 1 of 8.

Objective:
Students will be able to names three to five "goods" as a result of this lesson.

About the author:
At the time this unit was first published, Dianne Mendenhall taught elementary music for Indianapolis Public Schools, Indianapolis, IN. She is a certified 4MAT trainer.

Required resources:
Small bean bag, a key, a ball, and a few other items which can be passed around and circle; "touchie feelie" bag with items such as cotton, pencil, eraser, small toy, etc.; playdough; crayons and paper.

Bibliography:
See Overview in Wheel 1 of 8.

Quadrant 1—Experience

 ### Right Mode—Connect

Name 6 game.

Objective

To connect students to the idea of "goods" in their lives.

Activity

Seat children in a circle, with one player standing in the center. The center player closes his/her eyes while the others pass a small object around the circle (key, bean bag, or some other similar object). When the center player claps his/her hands, the player holding the object must keep it. The center player gives the person with the object a letter of the alphabet. The player with the object sends it around the circle again and must name six objects that begin with the letter named. Six objects must be named before the object makes it around the circle. If the player doesn't succeed in naming the six objects, he changes places with the person in the center. If he or she names six objects successfully, the game continues with the same player in the center. The teacher records the objects named on the chalkboard.

Assessment

Involvement and enjoyment of the game.

 ### Left Mode—Examine

Discuss other things children want.

Objective

To recognize the items named as "goods."

Activity

Teacher conducts discussion based on the "goods" named during the circle game. *Add to the list the names of other things children would like to have.* Close with the children echoing the following chant:

Hamburgers, teddy bears
pizza and rocking chairs
toys and videos
baby dolls and Legos
fancy cars and big guitars
I want them, I want them
These are goods, get them if you could!
These are goods, get them if you could!

Assessment

Contribution to discussion, involvement in the chant.

Quadrant 2—Concepts

 ### Right Mode—Image

"Touchie Feelie" bag.

Objective

To use another medium to reinforce the concept of "goods."

Activity

Show students the Touchie Feelie Bag and explain that when they put their hand inside, they will describe what they feel and try to guess what it is. Pass the bag around the circle until everyone has had a chance.

Assessment

Children's ability to touch, feel and describe.

 ### Left Mode—Define

Define "goods."

Objective

To teach the concept of "goods."

Activity

Define "goods" as being objects that we can touch and feel. Teacher conducts discussion on what is a "good" and what is not.

Assessment

Teacher verbal checking for understanding of the concept.

Quadrant 3—Applications

 ## Left Mode—Try

Web exercise.

Objective
To reinforce the understanding of "goods" as presented in the previous lesson.

Activity
Using a mindmap or webbing technique, the teacher will create a web around the idea of "goods," Students will brainstorm as many "goods" as possible for the mindmap.

Assessment
Children's ability to contribute to the task.

 ## Right Mode—Extend

Create playdough "goods."

Objective
Students will have the opportunity to create "goods."

Activity
Using playdough, children will sculpt their own "goods" for "sale" and display.

Assessment
Enthusiasm for the project.

Quadrant 4—Creations

 ## Left Mode—Refine

Discuss "goods" created.

Objective
To evaluate and refine the "goods" created from Playdough.

Activity
Working with partners, students will define and discuss their sculpted "goods."

Assessment
Teacher will observe student partner discussions for understanding of the concept.

 ## Right Mode—Integrate

Presentation: commercials to promote the "goods" created.

Objective
To celebrate the "goods" created.

Activity
Using crayons and drawing paper, students will create logo posters for their sculptured "goods." If time allows, give them an opportunity to "sell" their "goods" via their own commercial using their posters.

Assessment
Enjoyment and sharing of projects.

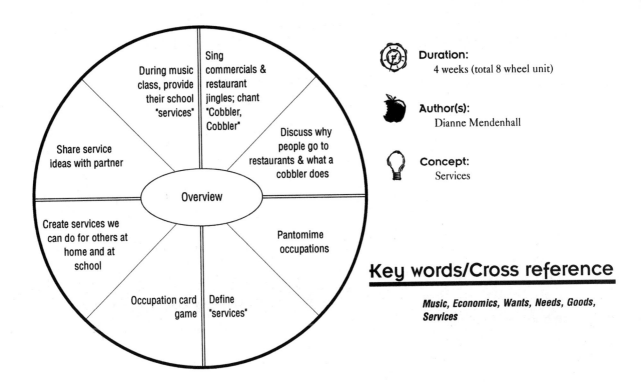

Duration:
4 weeks (total 8 wheel unit)

Author(s):
Dianne Mendenhall

Concept:
Services

Key words/Cross reference

Music, Economics, Wants, Needs, Goods, Services

Overview

Author's Notes
See Overview in Wheel 1 of 8.

Objective
Students will learn that a "service" is something that someone does for someone else.

About the Author
At the time this unit was first published, Dianne Mendenhall taught elementary music for Indianapolis Public Schools, Indianapolis, IN. She is a certified 4MAT trainer.

Required Resources
Teacher-created "services" worksheet; occupation cards (visual).

Bibliography
See Overview in Wheel 1 of 8.

Quadrant 1—Experience

 ## Right Mode—Connect

Sing commercials & restaurant jingles; chant "Cobbler, Cobbler."

Objective

Students will recognize "services" which they regularly enjoy or use.

Activity

Students brainstorm restaurant commercials they hear on TV and sing their jingles. Chant the following:
Cobbler, cobbler, mend my shoe
give it one stitch, give it two,
Give it three, give it four,
And if it needs it, give it more.

Cobbler, cobbler, mend my shoe,
get it done by half past two,
Stitch it up and stitch it down,
then I'll pay you half a crown.

Assessment

Enjoyment and participation in the jingles and chant.

 ## Left Mode—Examine

Discuss why people go to restaurants & what a cobbler does.

Objective

To enable children to realize the "services" they use regularly.

Activity

Discuss why we go to restaurants instead of eating at home, and discuss what a cobbler does. Have students identify other "services" they and their families use.

Assessment

Contribution to the discussion.

Quadrant 2—Concepts

 ## Right Mode—Image

Pantomime occupations.

Objective

Students will imagine "services."

Activity

The teacher needs a stack of pictorial occupation cards (mailman, fireman, doctor, teacher, etc.) Have students select a card and pantomime that occupation while the others guess what it could be.

Assessment

Participation in the pantomime and ability to guess the "services."

 ## Left Mode—Define

Define "services."

Objective

To define "services" as opposed to "goods"

Activity

Teacher conducts lesson to define a "service" as something someone does for someone else.

Assessment

Teacher verbal checking for understanding.

Quadrant 3—Applications

 ### Left Mode—Try

Occupation card game.

Objective

Students will distinguish "goods" from "services."

Activity

Distribute teacher prepared worksheet with pictures of "services" (barber, doctor, etc.) mixed with pictures of "goods" (e.g., child combing hair, child riding bike, etc.) Children will label the Pictures "S" or "G."

Assessment

Students' ability to identify goods and services.

 ### Right Mode—Extend

Create "services" we can do for others at home and at school.

Objective

To plan "services" that children can perform for others.

Activity

Students will each brainstorm "services" they may do for those at home and a "service" they could provide at school. Distribute paper and markers for them to illustrate one which they will choose to do at home, and one which they will do at school.

Assessment

Quality of brainstormed lists.

Quadrant 4—Creations

 ### Left Mode—Refine

Share "service" ideas with partner.

Objective

To evaluate the "services" chosen for practicality and "do-ability."

Activity

Students will share their planned "services" with a partner and with the teacher. They will contract with the teacher for the "service" they will perform at home.

Assessment

Quality of "services," and enthusiasm of children.

 ### Right Mode—Integrate

During music class, provide their school "services."

Objective

Students will share their school "services" with each other.

Activity

Hold a "Service Day" celebration during music class. Prearrange with other teachers for "services" which children are providing in their home classrooms or cafeteria. Students will sign-up for when their "services" will be performed. Give students certificates to celebrate their good "services!"

Assessment

Students' follow-through on performance, and students' enjoyment of providing "service" to others.

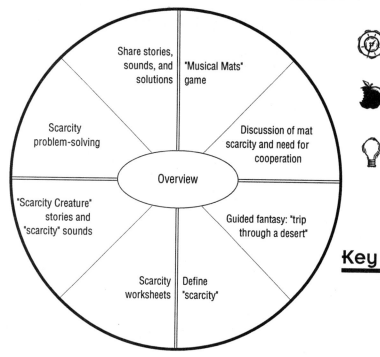

Share stories, sounds, and solutions

"Musical Mats" game

Scarcity problem-solving

Discussion of mat scarcity and need for cooperation

Overview

"Scarcity Creature" stories and "scarcity" sounds

Guided fantasy: "trip through a desert"

Scarcity worksheets

Define "scarcity"

 Duration:
4 weeks (total 8 wheel unit)

 Author(s):
Dianne Mendenhall

 Concept:
Scarcity

Key words/Cross reference

Music, Economics, Scarcity, Goods, Wants, Services

Overview

 Author's Notes
See Overview in Wheel 1 of 8.

 Objective
Students will learn the concept of scarcity and how it affects them: we cannot always have everything we want.

 About the Author
At the time this unit was first published, Dianne Mendenhall taught elementary music for Indianapolis Public Schools, Indianapolis, IN. She is a certified 4MAT trainer.

 Required Resources
Carpet sample "mats" and music; teacher-prepared worksheets; bells and mallets; crayons and drawing paper.

 Bibliography
See Overview in Wheel 1 of 8.

Quadrant 1—Experience

 ### Right Mode—Connect

"Musical Mats" game.

Objective

To involve children in a scarcity experience leading to understanding of why we can't always have what we want.

Activity

Play "musical mats": a cooperative version of "musical chairs". Distribute a carpet sample mat to each child. When music begins to play, children leave their mats and walk in a circle, while the teacher removes one mat. When the music stops, they each must get on any mat as quickly as possible. Continue with the game, until as many children as safely possible on are one mat.

Assessment

Enjoyment of the game.

 ### Left Mode—Examine

Discussion of mat scarcity and need for cooperation.

Objective

Children will discuss their mat-scarcity experience.

Activity

Teacher-led discussion on what happened as the mats were removed, and how the children learned about the need for teamwork and cooperation.

Assessment

Contribution to the discussion.

Quadrant 2—Concepts

 ### Right Mode—Image

Guided fantasy: "trip through a desert."

Objective

To use another medium for the children to imagine "scarcity".

Activity

Conduct a teacher-prepared imaginary trip to a desert. While on the trip through the desert, the bus breaks down and we are all stranded for two days. Include in the imagery all the things that would be scarce in such a situation. Discuss with the children how scarcity can be situational.

Assessment

Student involvement in the imaginary trip and contribution to the discussion.

 ### Left Mode—Define

Define "scarcity."

Objective

To reinforce and define "scarcity."

Activity

Teacher-directed lesson defining "scarcity."

Assessment

Verbal check for understanding.

Quadrant 3—Applications

 ### Left Mode—Try

Scarcity worksheets.

Objective
Students will be able to identify situational scarcity.

Activity
Teacher prepared worksheet with items, such as, "Mary has three erasers" and "Jose has no crayons". Students will identify the scarce items in each situation.

Assessment
Student performance on worksheets.

Right Mode—Extend

"Scarcity Creature" stories and "scarcity" sounds.

Objective
To enable students to extend their understanding of "scarcity".

Activity
Application choices:
Students may choose to create and illustrate the story of the "Scarcity Creature," or they may choose to use the bells and mallets to compose original music to portray what scarcity "sounds" like.

Assessment
Student attention to project choices.

Quadrant 4—Creations

 ### Left Mode—Refine

Scarcity problem-solving.

Objective
To evaluate understanding of scarcity.

Activity
Students will share their projects with their partners. Teacher conducts a brainstorming exercise to identify ways to reduce scarcity. Begin with things in the classroom and extend to the greater world.

Assessment
Students' contribution to the mindmapping/brainstorming activity.

Right Mode—Integrate

Share stories, sounds, and solutions.

Objective
To share what has been learned.

Activity
Students either read their scarcity stories to their group, or perform their scarcity sounds for the class.

Assessment
Enjoyment of performances.

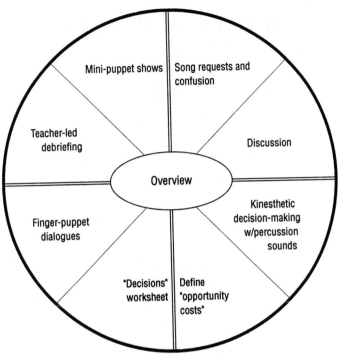

 Duration
4 weeks (total 8 wheel unit)

 Author(s)
Dianne Mendenhall

 Concept
Decision-making

Key words/Cross reference

Music, Economics, Goods, Services,
Decision-making, Choices

Overview

 Author's Notes
See Overview in Wheel 1 of 8.

 Objective
Students will learn that every economic decision has
a cost.

 About the Author
At the time this unit was first published, Dianne
Mendenhall taught elementary music for
Indianapolis Public Schools, Indianapolis, IN. She is
a certified 4MAT trainer.

 Required Resources
Song books; teacher-prepared "Decisions" worksheet; finger puppets for each child.

 Bibliography
See Overview in Wheel 1 of 8.

Quadrant 1—Experience

Right Mode—Connect

Song requests and confusion.

Objective

To create an experience of confusion when sensible decisions are not made.

Activity

Give each child a songbook and have them each select their favorite song. After each child has his/her song identified, tell the children that we will ALL sing our favorite songs at the same time! Try this for about one-minute, or as long as it takes for confusion to reign.

Assessment

Student involvement in singing and confusion.

Left Mode—Examine

Discussion.

Objective

To analyze the experience of confusion and its causes.

Activity

Teacher-led discussion of the experience. Ask students how the confusion could have been avoided. Why do we choose one song at a time? What happens to the other songs when we are singing the one we have chosen?

Assessment

Student involvement in discussion.

Quadrant 2—Concepts

Right Mode—Image

Kinesthetic decision-making w/percussion sounds.

Objective

To use bodily movement to represent "decision-making."

Activity

Working with partners, have child portray what someone looks like who is trying to make a decision.

Assessment

Quality of student pantomimes.

Left Mode—Define

Define "opportunity costs."

Objective

To teach the concept of opportunity costs and decision-making.

Activity

Teacher will present a lesson defining opportunity costs and the relationship to decision-making. Emphasize that there are costs every time a decision is made.

Assessment

Verbal check for understanding.

Quadrant 3—Applications

 ### Left Mode—Try

"Decisions" worksheet.

Objective
To check for understanding of the concept of
"opportunity costs."

Activity
Students work through a teacher-prepared worksheet on
which they have to demonstrate decision-making and
the cost of their decisions. Students must choose
between pairs of options, such as, "Doing homework"
or "Washing the dishes;" "Rent a movie" or "Play with
a friend," and the like. They should circle each decision
that they believe would be the best. Have students
share their worksheets and decisions with a partner and
tell why their decisions are best for them, and what the
opportunity cost is for each decision.

Assessment
Quality of student performance on worksheets and sharing with partners.

 ### Right Mode—Extend

Finger-puppet dialogues.

Objective
To extend what children have learned about "scarcity"
and "opportunity costs".

Activity
Distribute finger puppets to each child. Working in
partners, one child will be Sally or Sam Scarcity, and the
other child will be Mr. or Miss Opportunity Cost. Guide
the children into creating their own dialogue between
their characters, with prompting such as:
What would Sally (Sam) say to Mr/Miss Opportunity
Cost?
How does Sam (Sally) feel about always being scarce?
Does Mr/Miss Opportunity Cost like having to make
choices?
How can Sally (Sam) and Mr/Miss O.C. work together?

Assessment
Teacher observation of student dialogues.

Quadrant 4—Creations

 ### Left Mode—Refine

Teacher-led debriefing.

Objective
Learners will evaluate their learning.

Activity
Teacher-led discussion eliciting new insights or ideas
children had during their puppeteering.

Assessment
Quality of contributions from the children.

 ### Right Mode—Integrate

Mini-puppet shows.

Objective
Students will share what they have learned.

Activity
Solicit volunteers to perform their finger puppet dialogues for the class.

Assessment
Enjoyment of all the children.

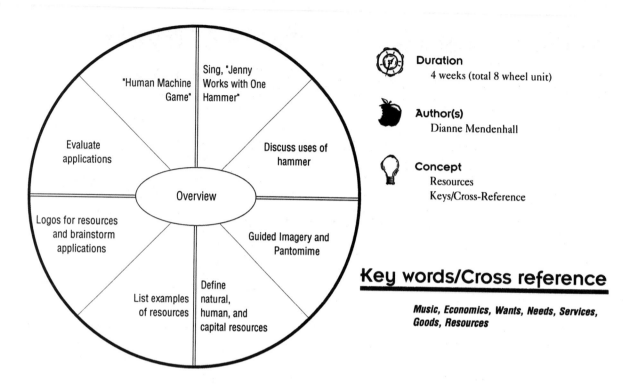

Duration
4 weeks (total 8 wheel unit)

Author(s)
Dianne Mendenhall

Concept
Resources
Keys/Cross-Reference

Key words/Cross reference

Music, Economics, Wants, Needs, Services, Goods, Resources

Overview

Author's Notes
See Overview in Wheel 1 of 8.

Objective
Students will understand that human resources are the people who work in jobs to produce goods and services. Nature provides many things used to produce goods and services. Some goods are used to make other goods or to provide services, i.e. machines.

About the Author
At the time this unit was first published, Dianne Mendenhall taught elementary music for Indianapolis Public Schools, Indianapolis, IN. She is a certified 4MAT trainer.

Bibliography
See Overview in Wheel 1 of 8.

Quadrant 1—Experience

 ### Right Mode—Connect

Sing, "Jenny Works with One Hammer."

Objective
To connect students to the idea of tools (machines) as resources.

Activity
Have students sing and pantomime the hammer song:
"Jenny works with one hammer,
One hammer, one hammer.
Jenny works with one hammer,
Then she works with two ...
Jenny works with five hammers,
Five hammers, five hammers.
Jenny works with five hammers,
Then she goes to sleep!

Assessment
Students' enjoyment of the hammer song.

 ### Left Mode—Examine

Discuss uses of hammer.

Objective
Children will see Jenny as a human resource and her hammer as the product of human resource.

Activity
Teacher-led discussion of Jenny and all the things she could make or do with her hammers. Focus on services and goods—Is the hammer a service or a good?

Assessment
Children's interest in the discussion.

Quadrant 2—Concepts

 ### Right Mode—Image

Guided Imagery and Pantomime.

Objective
To use imagery and pantomime to help children experience resources in other ways.

Activity
Have children imagine and act out the following scenarios:

1. "You are a tiny seed far under the earth. The sun and water are helping you grow. You sprout out from the ground. You slowly grow into a tiny tree with only a few limbs. You continue growing into a big beautiful tree. Your branches are very big now and they reach way out and grow way out. Now a big storm comes and the wind blows your leaves and branches around. The rain pours down hard. Now the storm leaves and the sun comes out and you can relax and dry off. You are a big, beautiful tree.

2. You are running a relay race at school. You are running hard and fast. Next, you go through an obstacle course. You have to crawl, jump, pull yourself across the monkey bars, and swim to complete the course. [Embellish this further.]

3. You are a train going up a big hill. [Develop this, as done above.]

Assessment
Student participation in pantomime.

 ### Left Mode—Define

Define natural, human, and capital resources.

Objective
Students will learn about three kinds of resources.

Activity
Define Natural Resources (the tree growing from nature); Human Resources (the energy we use when we work our bodies); and Capital Resources (machines which are used to make goods or provide services).

Assessment
Check for understanding by having students pantomime each kind of resource.

Quadrant 3—Applications

 ### Left Mode—Try

List examples of resources.

Objective
To provide quick guided practice on the three types of resources.

Activity
Teacher-led practice: Using the chalk board, make a column for each kind of resource. Elicit volunteers to give examples of each. Follow with a teacher-made worksheet.

Assessment
Contribution to brainstorming and performance on worksheet.

Right Mode—Extend

Logos for resources and brainstorm applications.

Objective
To give students an opportunity to extend what they have learned.

Activity
Distribute paper and crayons. Have each student design a logo for the resource of their choice. Have them answer the question, "How could your resource be used to make our classroom a better place for living and learning?"

Assessment
Student attention to task.

Quadrant 4—Creations

Left Mode—Refine

Evaluate applications.

Objective
To evaluate the quality of learning.

Activity
Teacher-led feedback and discussion on student work with each kind of resource. How can we actually put to use what we have learned?

Assessment
Student projects and ideas.

Right Mode—Integrate

"Human Machine Game."

Objective
To celebrate the learning.

Activity
Students will play the "Human Machine" game: Machines are useless unless each part is functioning properly. In this activity groups of players become machines, each playing the role of one machine part. Each group of 8 or 10 selects a machine to portray. One by one, each player pretends to be a machine part and joins the machine. For example if everyone decides to be a car, one chugs and shakes to become the engine, another bends over to be the trunk, another stretches to be a windshield, and becomes windshield wipers, and so forth. After the machine is complete, have each part add a sound, and then operate at different speeds. After each group has a turn at sharing their machine, have them become a totally nonfunctional invention!

Assessment
Enjoyment and participation!

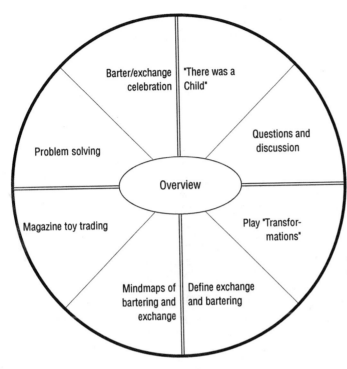

Barter/exchange celebration

"There was a Child"

Problem solving

Questions and discussion

Overview

Magazine toy trading

Play "Transfor-mations"

Mindmaps of bartering and exchange

Define exchange and bartering

 Duration
4 weeks (total 8 wheel unit)

 Author(s)
Dianne Mendenhall

 Concept
Exchange & Bartering

Key words/Cross reference

Music, Economics, Needs, Wants, Bartering, Exchange

Overview

 Author's Notes
See Overview in Wheel 1 of 8.

 Objective
Students will understand that trading goods and ser-vices is synonymous with bartering.

 About the Author
At the time this unit was first published, Dianne Mendenhall taught elementary music for Indianapolis Public Schools, Indianapolis, IN. She is a certified 4MAT trainer.

 Required Resources
Old magazines; newspaper ads for toys; teacher prepared worksheet.

 Bibliography
See Overview in Wheel 1 of 8.

Quadrant 1—Experience

 ## Right Mode—Connect

"There was a Child."

Objective
To provide children with an experience through song of trading.

Activity
Sing "There Was a Child" to the tune of "There Was a Man"

There was a child who had a duck and he traded it for a pickup truck.

The pickup truck, it moved too slow, so he traded it for some play dough.

The play dough, it got so hard, so he traded it for a big red car.

The big red car, it went too quick, so he traded it for some pick-up-sticks.

The pick-up-sticks, they were too small, so he traded them for a baby doll.

The baby doll, it had no hat, so he traded it for a furry cat.

Assessment
Enjoyment of the song.

 ## Left Mode—Examine

Questions and discussion.

Objective
To engage students in a discussion of trading.

Activity
Teacher-led discussion of the trading in the song. Elicit from children their own experiences with trading: were their own trades always fair (equal merchandise exchanged)?

Chant the "Bartering Chant"
Bartering means trading
trading means exchange
If I have something
and you have something
we're both willing to trade.
That's bartering, that's bartering,
let's barter and exchange.

Assessment
Student involvement in discussion and enjoyment of chant.

Quadrant 2—Concepts

 ## Right Mode—Image

Play "Transformations."

Objective
To use another medium to reinforce the idea of trading.

Activity
Play "transformations." Students stand in a circle. Each student makes up a movement and/or sound. Students begin trading their movements/sound with other students. Whichever movement/sound makes it completely around the circle is the winner.

Assessment
Students' contributions to the game.

 ## Left Mode—Define

Define exchange and bartering.

Objective
To define bartering.

Activity
Teacher lesson defining bartering as trading. Discussion with students as to when bartering works and when it does not. If available locally, play excerpts from a radio "swap shop" program.

Assessment
Verbal checking for understanding and student contributions to the lesson.

Quadrant 3—Applications

 ### Left Mode—Try

Mindmaps of bartering and exchange.

Objective
To identify personal experiences with trading (bartering) and when it is used.

Activity
Teacher-led listing of Students' experiences (including those of their parents) with trading personal and household items. Put a "*" next to those experiences which worked and a "-" next to those which did not.

Assessment
Teacher checking for understanding.

 ### Right Mode—Extend

Magazine toy trading.

Objective
To extend students' concept of bartering.

Activity
Using magazine or newspaper ads for toys, have students cut out pictures of toys they would like to have. Then pretend these toys are real. Have them attempt to trade with other students. Reinforce the idea that a trade is not made unless both parties agree.

Assessment
Involvement in bartering game.

Quadrant 4—Creations

 ### Left Mode—Refine

Problem solving.

Objective
To evaluate the experience of the bartering game.

Activity
Discuss the problems students encountered in the bartering activity. Does everything have the same value? What problems did you have when you were trading? How did you solve them?
Assignment: Bring candy or cookies to our next class!

Assessment
Participation in discussion.

 ### Right Mode—Integrate

Barter/exchange celebration.

Objective
To put together everything learned about bartering and trading.

Activity
Barter Day! Students set up personal stations in the classroom and practice good bartering/trading skills with the treats they brought to school.

Assessment
Student enjoyment and success as traders.

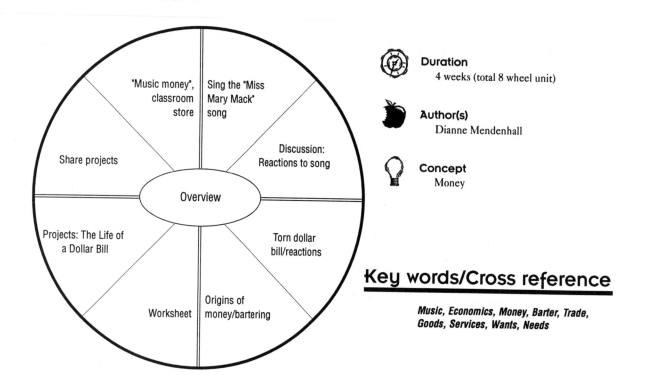

Duration
4 weeks (total 8 wheel unit)

Author(s)
Dianne Mendenhall

Concept
Money

Key words/Cross reference

Music, Economics, Money, Barter, Trade, Goods, Services, Wants, Needs

Wheel contents:
- "Music money", classroom store
- Sing the "Miss Mary Mack" song
- Discussion: Reactions to song
- Torn dollar bill/reactions
- Origins of money/bartering
- Worksheet
- Projects: The Life of a Dollar Bill
- Share projects
- Overview

Overview

Author's Notes
See Overview in Wheel 1 of 8

Objective
Money makes bartering easier.

About the Author
At the time this unit was first published, Dianne Mendenhall taught elementary music for Indianapolis Public Schools, Indianapolis, IN. She is a certified 4MAT trainer.

Required Resources
Coin; mats to sit on; dollar bill; scotch tape

Bibliography
See Overview in Wheel 1 of 8.

Quadrant 1—Experience

 ### Right Mode—Connect

Sing the "Miss Mary Mack" song.

Objective
To connect to the experiences children have had with money.

Activity
Have students seated in a circle and sing the "Miss Mary Mack" song.

Assessment
Enjoyment and involvement of the children.

 ### Left Mode—Examine

Discussion: Reactions to song.

Objective
To use Miss Mary Mack as a vehicle for discussing experiences with money.

Activity
Teacher-led discussion: what did Mary Mack barter in the song? What did she buy? What is the difference between the two transactions? How are they the same? How are they different?

Assessment
Quality of student responses.

Quadrant 2—Concepts

 ### Right Mode—Image

Torn dollar bill/reactions.

Objective
To help students understand what money stands for.

Activity
Present the class with a paper dollar bill. Point out that it is only a piece of paper, and dramatically rip it in half. Discuss their reactions. What really is money and what does it stand for?

Assessment
Student reactions and discussion.

 ### Left Mode—Define

Origins of money/bartering.

Objective
To teach students that money is used to buy things and makes bartering easier.

Activity
Teach students why money was developed, how it is used, and what it represents. Read "Paper and Coins:"
What is money
Paper and coins

But what can it bring
A toy, a book, a puzzle
An object, or a thing.

What is Money
Paper and coins

But what can it buy
An art or music lesson or
A plane ride in the sky

Money has no value
Except for what it brings

Like many kinds of services
And different kinds of things.

Assessment
Teacher observation of student interest and participation in activity.

Quadrant 3—Applications

 ## Left Mode—Try

Worksheet.

Objective
To provide practice in discriminating the use of money vs. bartering for goods and services.

Activity
Check for understanding with a teacher-prepared worksheet.

Assessment
Student performance on worksheet.

 ## Right Mode—Extend

Projects: The Life of a Dollar Bill.

Objective
To extend students' understanding of money and its use.

Activity
Student projects: working in small teams, give students drawing paper and markers and ask them to draw the life of a dollar bill from beginning to end. Where all could your dollar go? Who and what could it be exchanged for? Where would it live?

Assessment
Students' contribution to the task.

Quadrant 4—Creations

 ## Left Mode—Refine

Share projects.

Objective
To critique each group's Life of a Dollar project.

Activity
Student groups will share their posters for comments from the teacher and the class.

Assessment
Students ability to share and critique.

 ## Right Mode—Integrate

"Music money," classroom store.

Objective
A final celebration of what we have learned.

Activity
Students are each given "music money." We set up our classroom store and students have the opportunity to purchase goods and services from each other.

Assessment
Enjoyment of the activity.

Kachina Dolls

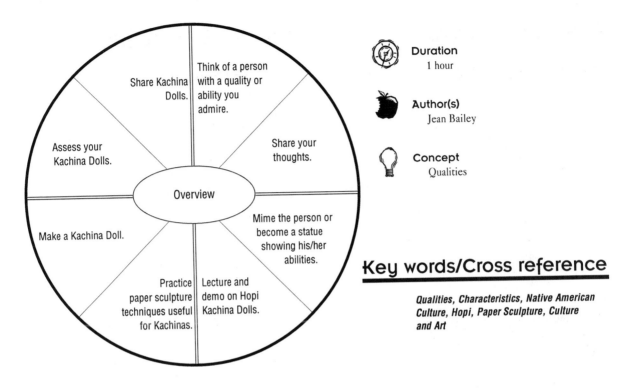

Share Kachina Dolls.

Think of a person with a quality or ability you admire.

Assess your Kachina Dolls.

Share your thoughts.

Overview

Make a Kachina Doll.

Mime the person or become a statue showing his/her abilities.

Practice paper sculpture techniques useful for Kachinas.

Lecture and demo on Hopi Kachina Dolls.

Duration
1 hour

Author(s)
Jean Bailey

Concept
Qualities

Key words/Cross reference

Qualities, Characteristics, Native American Culture, Hopi, Paper Sculpture, Culture and Art

Overview

Objective
Students will learn how artists create works of Art to express the qualities they see in others.

About the Author
Jean Bailey is an art teacher in Hamilton-Wenham School District, Hamilton, MA. She is is a certified 4MAT System trainer and has served as the Project Leader for the Hamilton-Wenham 4MAT Implementation Project.

Required Resources
Sample Hopi dolls for students to examine; toilet paper rolls and other materials for paper sculptures.

Kachina Dolls

Quadrant 1—Experience

 ### Right Mode—Connect

Think of a person with a quality or ability you admire.

Objective
Establish personal connections with the concept.

Activity
Students think of a person who has an ability or quality they admire. Teacher models a personal example first.

Assessment
Student involvement.

 ### Left Mode—Examine

Share your thoughts.

Objective
To share and express thoughts and experiences.

Activity
Students tell a partner about the qualities of their chosen person. Then, share with the larger group.

Assessment
Detail and personal investment in the stories.

Quadrant 2—Concepts

 ### Right Mode—Image

Mime the person or become a statue showing his/her abilities.

Objective
For students to "feel" what it might be like to become a work of art embodying the special quality.

Activity
Students mime the person they have chosen demonstrating the special quality, or they become a "statue" of the person.

Assessment
Student involvement.

 ### Left Mode—Define

Lecture and demo on Hopi Kachina Dolls.

Objective
Introduce an art form related to previous experiences.

Activity
Lecture and Demonstration: Hopi Kachina Dolls: What they are. How and why they are made. Qualities they represent. Review and Demonstrate: Paper sculpture techniques.

Assessment
Student interest, attention, comments.

Kachina Dolls

Quadrant 3—Applications

 ### Left Mode—Try

Practice paper sculpture techniques useful for Kachinas.

Objective
Review and practice skills.

Activity
Practice trying various paper sculpture techniques useful in making Kachina dolls.

Assessment
Ability to use techniques.

 ### Right Mode—Extend

Make a Kachina Doll.

Objective
Use paper sculpture techniques to express their feelings about their special person.

Activity
Students make a Kachina Doll of their special person using toilet paper rolls as a base and paper sculpture techniques.

Assessment
Use of techniques. Quality of product.

Quadrant 4—Creations

 ### Left Mode—Refine

Assess your Kachina Dolls.

Objective
Student assessment of their own work.

Activity
Students look at their own Kachina Doll and think about its special qualities and about the technique.

Assessment
Student involvement and interest.

 ### Right Mode—Integrate

Share Kachina Dolls.

Objective
For students to benefit from each others' ideas and to have an opportunity to share their own ideas.

Activity
Students pair up with a new partner to share the Kachina's qualities and the techniques they used to create it. Insights and ideas are shared with the whole group.

Assessment
Quality of insights, conversations.

Feelings

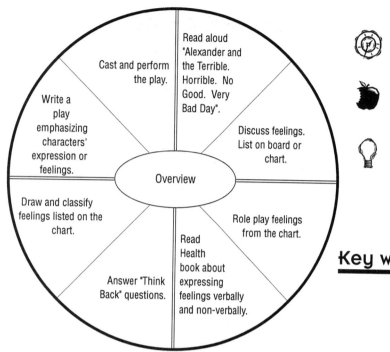

Cast and perform the play.

Read aloud "Alexander and the Terrible. Horrible. No Good. Very Bad Day".

Write a play emphasizing characters' expression or feelings.

Discuss feelings. List on board or chart.

Overview

Draw and classify feelings listed on the chart.

Role play feelings from the chart.

Answer "Think Back" questions.

Read Health book about expressing feelings verbally and non-verbally.

 Duration
4-5 days

Author(s)
Donna J. Balderson

 Concept
Expression of Feelings

Key words/Cross reference

Feelings, Verbal and Non-verbal communication, Classification

Overview

 Objective
Students will learn about different feelings and how we express them.

 About the Author
Donna Balderson is a teacher at Widewater Elementary School, Stafford County Public Schools, Fredericksburg, VA. She is a participant in the Stafford County 4MAT Implementation Project led by Alix Pearce and Donna Krueger.

Required Resources
"Think Back" questionnaire for students to focus on own feelings

Bibliography
Viorst, Judith. *Alexander and the Terrible Horrible No Good Very Bad Day.* New York: Scholastic, Inc., 1972. *Health for Life.* Glenview, IL.: Scott, Foresman and Co., 1987.

Feelings

Quadrant 1—Experience

 ### Right Mode—Connect

Read aloud "Alexander and the Terrible Horrible No Good Very Bad Day".

Objective

To create an experience that causes students to focus on the feelings of others.

Activity

Students listen as teacher reads *Alexander and the Terrible Horrible No Good Very Bad Day.*

Assessment

Student attentiveness and enthusiasm.

 ### Left Mode—Examine

Discuss feelings. List on board or chart.

Objective

To cause students to relate the character's feelings to their own feelings.

Activity

Students discuss Alexander's feelings and similar feelings they've experienced. Teacher lists feelings on chalkboard or chart.

Assessment

Teacher observation for participation.

Quadrant 2—Concepts

 ### Right Mode—Image

Role play feelings from the chart.

Objective

To see the connection between their feelings and their behaviors.

Activity

Students role play feelings that were discussed and listed on chart. This can be done as a game of charades.

Assessment

Student enthusiasm and participation.

 ### Left Mode—Define

Read Health book about expressing feelings verbally and non-verbally.

Objective

To teach how feelings are commonly expressed.

Activity

Students read an appropriate excerpt from their Health book which discusses different feelings and how people express them verbally and non-verbally.

Assessment

Teacher verbally checks for understanding during instruction.

Quadrant 3—Applications

 ## Left Mode—Try

Answer "Think Back" questions.

Objective
To provide students with guided practice.

Activity
Students answer some "Think Back" questions in which they identify feelings they have had.

Assessment
Quality of responses to questions.

 ## Right Mode—Extend

Draw and classify feelings listed on the chart.

Objective
To apply what they have learned about expressing feelings.

Activity
Students draw and classify the feelings listed on the chart. Students must decide how to classify the feelings.

Assessment
Students expression of ideas and feelings and students application of knowledge.

Quadrant 4—Creations

 ## Left Mode—Refine

Write a play emphasizing characters' expression or feelings.

Objective
To extend what has been learned.

Activity
Students work in groups to write a play emphasizing characters' feelings. These feelings should be expressed verbally and non-verbally.

Assessment
Ability to work with peers and incorporate what they've learned into their plays.

 ## Right Mode—Integrate

Cast and perform the play.

Objective
To share their new knowledge with others.

Activity
Students cast and perform their plays for the class.

Assessment
Quality of completed plays, participation, expression of feelings.

Farm Animals (1 of 3)

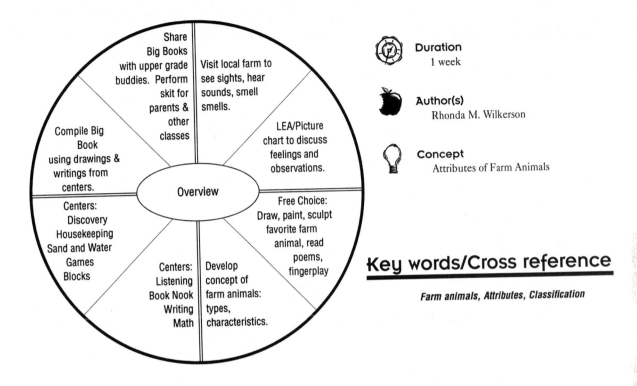

Share Big Books with upper grade buddies. Perform skit for parents & other classes

Visit local farm to see sights, hear sounds, smell smells.

Compile Big Book using drawings & writings from centers.

LEA/Picture chart to discuss feelings and observations.

Overview

Centers:
Discovery
Housekeeping
Sand and Water
Games
Blocks

Free Choice:
Draw, paint, sculpt favorite farm animal, read poems, fingerplay

Centers:
Listening
Book Nook
Writing
Math

Develop concept of farm animals: types, characteristics.

Duration
1 week

Author(s)
Rhonda M. Wilkerson

Concept
Attributes of Farm Animals

Key words/Cross reference

Farm animals, Attributes, Classification

Overview

Objective
Children will develop an understanding of the concept of farm animals — different types and the characteristics of each type.

About the Author
Rhonda Wilkerson, Ph.D. is a professor at the University of North Carolina at Chapel Hill. She teaches methods courses and supervises student teachers during their student teaching practicum. She taught 15 years in the public schools in North Carolina. She is a member of the Excel Consultants Group.

Bibliography
Weaning of the Calf, Art Print, North Carolina Museum of Art, Raleigh, North Carolina.

Quadrant 1—Experience

Right Mode—Connect

Visit local farm to see sights, hear sounds, smell smells.

Objective

To connect to previous experiences of visits to farms or create an experience for children who have not visited a farm.

Activity

Class visits a local farm to see the sights, hear the sounds, and smell the smells of the farm. Teacher takes Polaroid pictures of animals, buildings, equipment seen at the farm.

Assessment

Level of interest as determined by comments and questions asked by the children.

Left Mode—Examine

LEA/Picture chart to discuss feelings and observations.

Objective

To discuss what they experienced at the farm.

Activity

Teacher leads discussion of visit to farm using a language experience or picture chart.

Assessment

Level of participation, quality of responses, individual student interest in sharing and listening to others.

Quadrant 2—Concepts

Right Mode—Image

Free Choice: Draw, paint, sculpt favorite farm animal, read poems, fingerplay.

Objective

To recall an animal seen at the farm so the focus can be shifted from the farm experience to the concept to be developed—farm animals.

Activity

Children have choices of drawing a favorite animal seen at the farm, painting the animal, making a 3-D animal using clay or materials from the scrap box. Teacher reads aloud poems about farm animals; teaches finger plays. Children play charades, pretending to be their favorite animal. Photos taken at farm are posted on bulletin board.

Assessment

The quality, accuracy, and level of interest shown in completing each activity.

Left Mode—Define

Develop concept of farm animals: types, characteristics.

Objective

To develop the concept of farm animals: types, characteristics—size, shape, sounds, coverings, habitats, baby animal names.

Activity

Teacher reads aloud to the children, shows filmstrips and videos to develop these concepts, play Farm Animal Bingo.

Assessment

Number of correct responses to questions asked during and at end of each activity. Attentiveness of the children.

Quadrant 3—Applications

Left Mode—Try

Centers: Listening, Book Nook, Writing, Math.

Objective

To provide hands-on opportunities for children to experience/extend what they learned in Step 4.

Activity

Centers: Listening, book nook, writing, math.

Listening: Children will listen to books on tape about farm animals; listen to tape of animal sounds and match sounds to pictures of animals; listen to farm animal songs and respond to taped riddles about farm animals.

Book Nook: Read books and magazines about farm animals.

Writing Center: Write/dictate about favorite animal—this will be used in the Big Book that will be completed in Step 7. Unscramble letters to make farm words; write a description of what was seen at the farm; respond to why you would or wouldn't like to live on a farm; add labels or sentence strips to Polaroid pictures on bulletin board.

Math: Sequence animal pictures by size; sort animal pictures by size, shape, color, coverings; count and graph farm animals; complete math worksheets on addition and subtraction; write word problems.

Assessment

Quality of student participation and worksheets.

Right Mode—Extend

Centers: Discovery, Housekeeping, Sand and Water, Games, Blocks.

Objective

To provide hands-on opportunities for children to experience/extend what they learned in Step 4.

Activity

Centers: Discovery, Games, Blocks, Housekeeping, Sand & Water, Art.

Discovery: Match silhouettes of farm animals to realistic pictures of farm animals; using pictures of farm animals describe the coverings; match animal pictures to piece of wool, fur, and feathers; match baby animals to pictures of mother animals; hatch baby chicken or duckling using incubator—record number of days before hatching on calendar and pictorial timeline of development once hatched.

Sand/Water: Float ducks and fish in water; create farm scenes in the sand using buckets, shovels, hoes, and other plastic tools.

Art: Draw, paint, sculpt using play-doh; make puppets, mobiles; look at art prints and find farm animals, e.g., Homer's Weaning of the Calf.

Blocks: Build a farm with the blocks and plastic farm animals.

Games: Puzzles of farm animals and farm scenes; Farm Feely Box—feel for matching pairs of animals in large covered box; worksheet for matching mother to her baby; match plastic farm animals and other things found on farm to appropriate beginning sound basket.

Housekeeping: Set up as a farm house and role play life on a farm; make haystack cookies.

Assessment

Quality and accuracy of work products; level of participation at each center.

Quadrant 4—Creations

 ## Left Mode—Refine

Compile Big Book using drawings & writings from centers.

Objective

To use the knowledge and skills developed thus far to create Big Books and develop a script for a farm animal puppet show.

Activity

Children combine animal drawings and written descriptions to compile several Big Books. The class develops a skit using the puppets made in the art center.

Assessment

Quality and accuracy of drawings and written descriptions and puppets; individual participation in the planning and practicing of the skit.

 ## Right Mode—Integrate

Share Big Books with upper grade buddies. Perform skit for parents & other classes.

Objective

To share what was learned with others in the school and with parents.

Activity

Children read their Big Books to their partners in the upper grades. The farm animal skit is presented to any interested audience.

Assessment

Individual interest and participation in sharing knowledge with others.

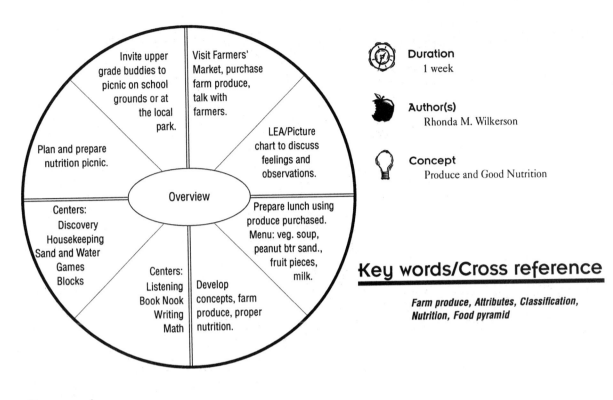

Overview

- Invite upper grade buddies to picnic on school grounds or at the local park.
- Visit Farmers' Market, purchase farm produce, talk with farmers.
- LEA/Picture chart to discuss feelings and observations.
- Prepare lunch using produce purchased. Menu: veg. soup, peanut btr sand., fruit pieces, milk.
- Develop concepts, farm produce, proper nutrition.
- Centers: Listening, Book Nook, Writing, Math
- Centers: Discovery, Housekeeping, Sand and Water, Games, Blocks
- Plan and prepare nutrition picnic.

Duration
1 week

Author(s)
Rhonda M. Wilkerson

Concept
Produce and Good Nutrition

Key words/Cross reference

Farm produce, Attributes, Classification, Nutrition, Food pyramid

Overview

Objective
Children will develop the concepts of farm produce and its relationship to proper nutrition.

About the Author
Rhonda Wilkerson, Ph.D. is a professor at the University of North Carolina at Chapel Hill. She teaches Methods Courses and supervises student teachers during their student teaching practicum. She taught 15 years in the public schools in North Carolina.
She is a member of the Excel Consultants Group.

Bibliography
Berensten, Stan and Jan. (1971) *Berensten's Bear Book*. Random House.

Ebertso, Marjorie and Gisler, Margaret. (1984) *Pancakes, crackers, pizza: Book of shapes*. Childrens Publisher.

Johnson, Hannah. (1977) *From Appleseed to Applesauce*. New York: Lothrop, Lee, Shepard.

Kelley, True. (1989) *Let's Eat*. Dutton Children's Books.

Krasilousky, Phyllis. (1991) *The man who cooked for himself*. New York: Parents Magazine Press.

McGovern. (1970) Stone Soup. Scholastic.

McPhail, Davud. (1979) *Grandfather's Cake*. New York, Scribner.

My First Dictionary. (1980) Houghton Mifflin.

Parkes, Brenda and Smith, Judith. (1985) *Little Red Hen*. Hong Kong South China Printing.

Quadrant 1—Experience

 ## Right Mode—Connect

Visit Farmers' Market, purchase farm produce, talk with farmers.

Objective
To stimulate an interest in the various produce provided by farms. To connect to what they already know about farm produce.

Activity
Class visits a local farmers' market talking to the farmers and purchasing produce, fruits and vegetables, to be used in classroom. Teacher takes Polaroid pictures of food stalls and children and farmers interacting.

Assessment
Level of interest as determined by comments and questions asked by the children and enthusiasm of children as they explore the various farmers' stalls.

 ## Left Mode—Examine

LEA/Picture chart to discuss feelings and observations.

Objective
To discuss what they experienced at the farmers' market.

Activity
Teacher leads discussion of visit to farmers' market using a language experience or picture chart. They discuss sights, smells, sounds, feelings about the visit.

Assessment
Level of participation, quality of responses, individual student interest in sharing and listening to others, level of language development.

Quadrant 2—Concepts

 ## Right Mode—Image

Prepare lunch using produce purchased. Menu: veg. soup, peanut btr sand., fruit pieces, milk.

Objective
To connect the farmers' market experience to concepts of farm produce and proper nutrition.

Activity
Children examine the fruits and vegetables purchased at the farm and discuss the size, shape, color, texture of each (concept of matter). They categorize fruits and vegetables using various attributes. They make bar graphs indicating favorite vegetables and fruits. They use their produce to prepare their lunch: vegetable soup, fruit pieces, peanut butter sandwiches, and milk. Photos taken at farmers' market and during preparation of lunch are posted on bulletin board.

Assessment
Level of familiarity with the names of various fruits and vegetables, ability to sort the produce by various attributes; the understanding of a bar graph to show results of polls; interest in and level development of fine motor skills needed to prepare lunch; enthusiasm for eating their prepared lunch.

 ## Left Mode—Define

Develop concepts, farm produce, proper nutrition.

Objective
To develop the concepts of farm produce and proper nutrition.

Activity
Teacher reads aloud to the children, shows filmstrips and videos to develop the concept of proper nutrition using the food group pyramid. Compare produce used in preparing lunch to food pyramid and determine if nutritious. Analyze school lunches over several days to determine if nutritious when compared to food pyramid.

Assessment
Number of correct responses to questions asked during and at end of each activity. Attentiveness of the children. Selections children make at lunch time.

Quadrant 3—Applications

Left Mode—Try

Centers, Listening, Book Nook, Writing, and Math.

Objective

To provide hands-on opportunities for children to experience/extend what they learned in Step 4.

Activity

Centers: Listening, book nook, writing, and math.

Listening: Listen to books-on-tape about foods: *Grandfather's Cake, The Man Who Cooked for Himself, Let's Eat, Little Red Hen;* Listen to songs—*The Breakfast Song, Ten Green Apples.*

Book Nook: Read books and magazines about various types of food and nutrition, e.g., *The Berenstein Bears, Pancakes, Crackers, and Pizza, From Apple Seed to Applesauce, Stone Soup.*

Writing Center: Draw pictures and write/dictate a description of favorite foods; match words to pictures of foods or artificial foods—record these on paper; use *My First Dictionary* to look up vocabulary words, e.g., vegetable, rice, fruit, banana, write labels or sentence strips for Polaroid pictures on bulletin board.

Math: Graph favorite breakfast foods; using egg cartons, match numeral with correct number of beans; sort artificial foods by various attributes; use pretzel sticks for addition and subtraction problems; complete math worksheets.

Assessment

Quality of involvement in centers and quality of student work.

Right Mode—Extend

Centers, Discovery, Housekeeping, Sand and Water, Games, and Blocks.

Objective

To provide hands-on opportunities for children to experience/extend what they learned in Step 4.

Activity

Centers: Discovery, Blocks, Housekeeping, Sand & Water, and Art.

Discovery: Each child contributes to Favorite Foods Mural by cutting two favorite foods from magazines and pasting them onto mural; using paper plate, the children select nutritious foods for their plate from a series of pictures of nutritious foods and junk foods; dry some fruits to be eaten later; plant a garden at school (concepts of plant growth and needs).

Sand/Water: Float plastic foods in the water; play in sand pretending to plant crops.

Art: Show several still life art prints—children become artists arranging fruits and vegetables and then painting own pictures of a still life which are framed in black poster frames and displayed in room and hall; make potato prints (concept of patterning); make necklaces using different shapes and colors of pasta.

Blocks: Build a farmers' market with all the stalls and surrounding buildings; build a grocery store.

Housekeeping: Set up as a grocery store and sort can goods and artificial produce on shelves and role play being a storekeeper.

Assessment

Quality and accuracy of work products; level of participation at each center; ability to follow directions and complete assigned work.

Quadrant 4—Creations

 ## Left Mode—Refine

Plan and prepare nutrition picnic.

Objective
To use knowledge and skills gained to plan and prepare a picnic to be shared with upper grade buddies.

Activity
The children will plan a nutritious picnic. Working in cooperative groups they will prepare the food, package the food, write and send invitations to their buddies asking them to join them for a picnic on the school grounds or in a nearby park (concept of division of labor).

Assessment
The selection of nutritious foods for the picnic rather than junk foods; cooperativeness in groups; quality of food items prepared; quality of invitations; interest and enthusiasm shown during the picnic.

Right Mode—Integrate

Invite upper grade buddies to picnic on school grounds or at the local park.

Objective
To share what was learned with others.

Activity
Children will participate in a picnic with their upper grade buddies sharing with them what they have learned about nutritious foods.

Assessment
Individual interest and participation in sharing knowledge with others.

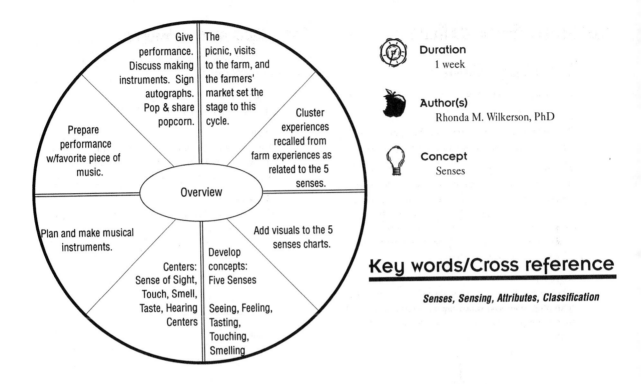

Give performance. Discuss making instruments. Sign autographs. Pop & share popcorn.

The picnic, visits to the farm, and the farmers' market set the stage to this cycle.

Prepare performance w/favorite piece of music.

Cluster experiences recalled from farm experiences as related to the 5 senses.

Overview

Plan and make musical instruments.

Add visuals to the 5 senses charts.

Centers: Sense of Sight, Touch, Smell, Taste, Hearing Centers

Develop concepts: Five Senses

Seeing, Feeling, Tasting, Touching, Smelling

Duration
1 week

Author(s)
Rhonda M. Wilkerson, PhD

Concept
Senses

Key words/Cross reference

Senses, Sensing, Attributes, Classification

Overview

Objective
Children will develop the concept of the 5 senses: seeing, feeling, tasting, touching and smelling.

About the Author
Rhonda Wilkerson, Ph.D. is a professor at the University of North Carolina at Chapel Hill. She teaches Methods Courses and supervises student teachers during their student teaching practicum. She taught 15 years in the public schools in North Carolina. She is a member of the Excel Consultants Group.

Bibliography
Richardson, Joy. (1986) *What Happens When You...* Gareth Stevens, Inc.
Showers, Paul. (1961) *Listening Walk.* New York: Harper and Row.
Winston, George. *Autumn.* (Audio tape)

Quadrant 1—Experience

 Right Mode—Connect

The picnic, visits to the farm, and the farmers' market set the stage to this cycle.

Objective

To connect the previous experience, the class picnic, to the concept of senses—seeing, hearing, speaking, tasting, touching, smelling.

Activity

The class picnic (Step 8). During the picnic, the children will observe and discuss what they are tasting, the texture of the foods they prepared, smell the smells outdoors, see the surroundings, hear the sounds in the environment.

Assessment

The level of interest shown by individual children, the quality of language development, the use of vocabulary developed during the unit, knowledge of senses used in the previous units.

 Left Mode—Examine

Cluster experiences recalled from farm experiences as related to the 5 senses.

Objective

To focus the children's attention on the five senses used during the previous two units—the visits to the farm and the farmers' market, as well as the picnic.

Activity

Teacher posts five charts, each with a large picture of one of the senses in the center: an eye, a mouth, hands, ear, tongue. The children brainstorm what they recall from their visits to the farm, farmers' market, and picnic. Their statements are clustered on each chart according to the sense used.

Assessment

Ability to recall experiences that relate to each of the five senses; quality of language—vocabulary development using words introduced in previous units.

Quadrant 2—Concepts

 Right Mode—Image

Add visuals to the 5 senses charts.

Objective

To use another medium to reinforce the experiences each child had at the farm and at the farmer's market.

Activity

Students will add visuals (pictures from magazines) to add a collage effect to the 5 senses charts.

Assessment

Quality of contributions to the collages.

 Left Mode—Define

Develop concepts: Five Senses. Seeing, Feeling, Tasting, Touching, Smelling

Objective

To develop the concept of senses: sight, hearing, touch, smell, taste and the body part used.

Activity

Teacher reads aloud to the children, shows filmstrips and videos to develop each concept, e.g., What Happens When You Look? What Happens When You Hear? What Happens When You Touch? What Happens When You Smell? What Happens When You Taste? Fingerplays and poems about the senses.

Assessment

Number of correct responses to questions asked during and at end of each activity. Attentiveness of the children. Level of participation in the activities.

Quadrant 3—Applications

Left Mode—Try

Centers: Sense of Sight, Touch, Smell, Taste, Hearing Centers

Objective

To provide hands-on opportunities for children to experience/extend what they learned in Step 4.

Activity

Centers: Sense of Smell, Sense of Touch, Sense of Taste, Sense of Sight, Sense of Hearing.

Sense of Hearing Center: Children listen to a tape of common household sounds and identify each sound; trace large ear pattern, cut out ear, write/draw pictures of favorite sounds on the ear; match containers with the same sounds by shaking the containers; listen to books-on-tape regarding sound, e.g., *The Listening Walk;* make tin can telephones to use to talk to friend; listen to George Winston's *Autumn* and color while listening.

Sense of Sight Center: Read books and magazines about the five senses; look in a mirror and draw eye the size and shape of own eyes, paste eyes on the Senses Mural; play "eye doctor" using eye chart to check "patient's" vision; look at various still life prints and identify the flowers, fruits, vegetables and insects in the paintings; visit an art museum or museum of natural history with parents or as a class and look for plants and animals in art or on display.

Sense of Touch Center: Feely Box with objects of various textures to be felt and identified by child; finger paint making a design of choice; place objects of varying textures in the sand table, use straws and bubble blowers in the water table to create bubbles—feel the texture; create sense of dirt, mud, worms by mixing chocolate pudding (mud) and crushed oreo cookies (dirt) and placing gummy worms into mixture—explore the worms in the mud with hands and eat own creations.

Sense of Smell Center: Children smell small film canisters filled with objects of varying fragrances and determine the smell; describe favorite smells at home; using black paper and different smelling soaps, draw a picture or design of choice; describe the smell of a fresh bouquet of flowers; go on smells walk around the school.

Sense of Taste Center: Children taste foods with four different tastes—salty, sweet, sour, bitter—and record responses on worksheet; make own snack—put peanuts, chocolate chips, coconut, sunflower seeds, and raisins in small brown bag and shake; write or draw pictures of favorite foods on large tongue.

Assessment

Quality and accuracy of work products, level of participation at each center, ability to follow directions and work cooperatively.

Right Mode—Extend

Plan and make musical instruments.

Objective

To use all senses to plan and make musical instruments.

Activity

Children will develop plans for making musical instruments to be used to accompany favorite records or for sound effects with favorite stories or original stories. Regular household objects will be used, e.g., coffee cans, oatmeal cartons, shoe boxes, coffee cans, aluminum plates, etc. The music teacher and art teacher will assist.

Assessment

Enthusiasm of students as they plan their instruments.

Quadrant 4—Creations

 ### Left Mode—Refine

Prepare performance w/favorite piece of music.

Objective

To use instruments in performances.

Activity

The art teacher and music teacher will help students refine their instruments as students practice and plan their performance.

Assessment

Quality of the instruments, ability to describe senses used in making instruments, individual participation in the planning and practicing of the performances.

Right Mode—Integrate

Give performance. Discuss making instruments. Sign autographs. Pop & share popcorn.

Objective

To share what was learned with others in the school and with parents.

Activity

Children invite other classes to their performances. After the performance, each child explains to someone how the instrument was made and how to play it and signs autographs if asked. Popcorn is popped prior to the performance to set the stage and is distributed in small brown bags to guests.

Assessment

Individual interest and participation in sharing knowledge with others.

Paragraphs

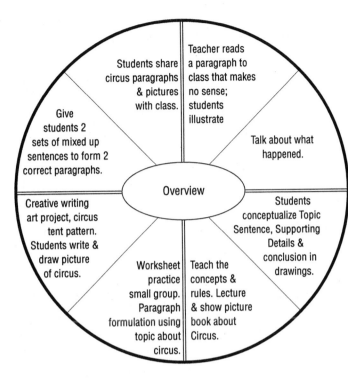

- Teacher reads a paragraph to class that makes no sense; students illustrate
- Talk about what happened.
- Students conceptualize Topic Sentence, Supporting Details & conclusion in drawings.
- Teach the concepts & rules. Lecture & show picture book about Circus.
- Worksheet practice small group. Paragraph formulation using topic about circus.
- Creative writing art project, circus tent pattern. Students write & draw picture of circus.
- Give students 2 sets of mixed up sentences to form 2 correct paragraphs.
- Students share circus paragraphs & pictures with class.

Overview

Duration
6-8 days

Author(s)
Laurie J. Kelly

Concept
Topic Sentences, Supporting Details and Conclusion

Key words/Cross reference

Circus, Paragraphs, Topic Sentences,
Supporting Details, Conclusion Sentences

Overview

Objective
Students will learn how to write complete paragraphs using Topic, Supporting Details and Conclusion sentences.

About the Author
Laurie Kelly is a 2nd grade teacher at Paterson Public Schools in Paterson, NJ. She is a certified 4MAT trainer for her district.

Required Resources
Paragraphs - sentence cards, circus book, teacher-made jumbled paragraph, practice worksheets, oak tag, glitter, magic markers, movie or field trip to a circus.

Bibliography
Barnum and Bailey Circus Book/School System Selected Language Book.

Insights Gr. 2 workbook - Unit 6 - Topic Turtle/Detail Duck, Charlesbridge Publishing Company - Watertown, MA, 1987.

World of Language - workbook - Gr. 2 - Silver Burdett and Ginn, 1990.

Paragraphs

Quadrant 1—Experience

 ### Right Mode—Connect

Teacher reads a paragraph to class that makes no sense; students illustrate.

Objective

To show the students the need for Topic Sentence, Supporting Details and a Conclusion sentence in order to comprehend written language paragraphs.

Activity

Teacher-made nonsense paragraph that begins correctly, but does not stay with the topic and does not allow students to follow the thoughts expressed in order to listen and illustrate on drawing paper.

Assessment

Student reactions and responses.

 ## Left Mode—Examine

Talk about what happened.

Objective

To analyze the problem that occurred and why the task could not be completed.

Activity

Students show incomplete drawings and discuss why their illustrations don't have meaning.

Assessment

Students ability to communicate their feelings and reactions.

Quadrant 2—Concepts

 ### Right Mode—Image

Students conceptualize Topic Sentence, Supporting Details & Conclusion in drawings.

Objective

To teach the concept of paragraph writing by visual imagery of a topic, details and conclusion.

Activity

Instruct student to fold large piece of drawing paper into eight boxes. Number the boxes 1-8. A) In the first box, draw a picture of something you enjoy doing. b) In boxes 2-7, draw pictures of how you learned to do it. C) In the last box, draw a picture that shows you have learned the activity.

Assessment

Quality of visual in understanding the concepts. (Illustration can be limited to fewer boxes depending on age level of students.)

 ## Left Mode—Define

Teach the concepts & rules. Lecture & show picture book about the Circus.

Objective

To further student knowledge and understanding of how to write good paragraphs and give background about a topic to motivate increases in skill development.

Activity

1) Teacher instructs students in proper use of Topic Sentences, Supporting Details and Conclusion sentences by using school selected text and overhead projector for illustrations. 2) Teacher reads and teaches students about the parts of a circus - picture illustrations from book.

Assessment

Student involvement and teacher-made assessment.

Paragraphs

Quadrant 3—Applications

Left Mode—Try

Worksheet practice small group. Paragraph formulation using topic about circus.

Objective

To practice and gain skill in use of Topic, Supporting Details and Conclusion sentences.

Activity

1) Workbook pages from text. 2) Teacher-made worksheets. 3) Small Groups: formulate a group paragraph using a topic about the circus. Read to class and critique for accuracy with class.

Assessment

Quality of completed work. Teacher check for accuracy.

Right Mode—Extend

Creative writing art project, circus tent pattern. Students write & draw picture of circus.

Objective

Give students the opportunity to add something of themselves.

Activity

To give further practice in use of Topic Sentence, Supporting Details and Conclusion sentences, personalizing the learning. 1) Students are instructed to fold a large piece of oak tag in half and cut a circular shape out of one side forming a circus tent frame on paper. Draw a picture inside frame of one exciting event at a circus. Decorate with glitter and markers. 2) Students write a paragraph about their picture (using correct form in writing a paragraph).

Assessment

Quality of completed work and correct use of skills taught.

Quadrant 4—Creations

Left Mode—Refine

Give students 2 sets of mixed up sentences to form 2 correct paragraphs.

Objective

To evaluate understanding of elements needed to write a good paragraph and remediate where necessary.

Activity

Teacher makes several short paragraphs by writing each sentence on a separate card. Students should then work in groups to sort sentences and form two correct paragraphs. Students are them paired to work together to edit and retrieve their paragraphs about the circus.

Assessment

Accuracy in creating paragraphs that have a Topic Sentence, Supporting Details and a Conclusion.

Right Mode—Integrate

Students share circus paragraphs & pictures with class.

Objective

To share their paragraphs and pictures with each other and celebrate their mastery of the skill.

Activity

1) Students show circus tent pictures and read their paragraphs to the class. 2) Students take a field trip to a circus or watch a movie about the circus. 3) Share ideas and experiences in groups. Each group formulates a paragraph about the trip or movie. Read to class.

Assessment

Enjoyment, involvement, enthusiasm - participation and accuracy.

Action Verbs

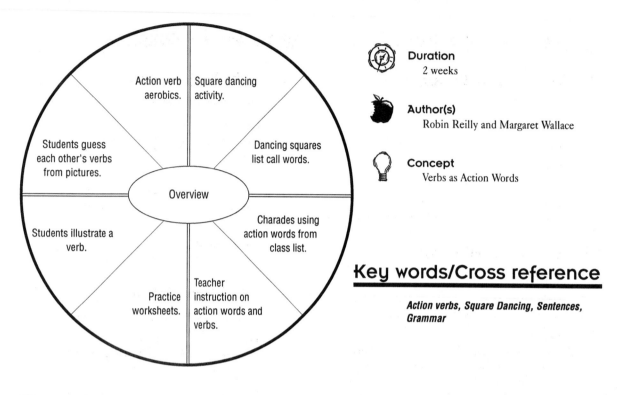

Action verb aerobics.

Square dancing activity.

Students guess each other's verbs from pictures.

Dancing squares list call words.

Overview

Students illustrate a verb.

Charades using action words from class list.

Practice worksheets.

Teacher instruction on action words and verbs.

Duration
2 weeks

Author(s)
Robin Reilly and Margaret Wallace

Concept
Verbs as Action Words

Key words/Cross reference

Action verbs, Square Dancing, Sentences, Grammar

Overview

Objective
Students will use kinesthetic movement activities to understand the concept of action verbs.

About the Authors
Robin Reilly teaches third grade at Mary Fisk School in Salem, New Hampshire. She has been teaching for nine years. Margaret Wallace also teaches third grade at Mary Fisk School. She has been a classroom teacher for fourteen years. They are participants in the Salem 4MAT Implementation project led by their Principal, Jane Batts.

Required Resources
Square dancing music and poster board and markers;

Bibliography
Filmstrips:
"Basic Language Skills Part I," Learning Tree Filmstrips, P.O. Box 4116, Englewood, CO 80155, 1977.

"Developing English Skills Part I," Bears Films, 1974.

"Fundamentals of Grammar, Parts of Speech," Eyegate Media, 3333 Elston Avenue, Chicago, IL 60618, 1976.

"Word Analysis Skills, Part II, Word Forms," Learning Tree Filmstrips, 1981.

Action Verbs

Quadrant 1—Experience

 ### Right Mode—Connect

Square dancing activity.

Objective
To create an experience using action verbs.

Activity
Children participate in square dancing activity.

Assessment
Involvement, participation, and enjoyment of students.

 ### Left Mode—Examine

Dancing squares list call words.

Objective
To analyze the calls used in the dancing.

Activity
Students form cooperative learning groups formed from their dancing square. Each square is given a poster board and markers for listing the call words which directed the action. The teacher creates a master list from contributions of each group of squares.

Assessment
Teacher evaluation of student discussion and participation.

Quadrant 2—Concepts

 ### Right Mode—Image

Charades using action words from class list.

Objective
To see the wider application of the action words already used.

Activity
Two groups of squares form two teams. Each team will participate in charades using the action words from the class list.

Assessment
Student participation and enjoyment.

 ### Left Mode—Define

Teacher instruction on action words and verbs.

Objective
To introduce the word "verb" and to expand student understanding of verbs as action words.

Activity
Teacher provides instruction connecting action words and verbs. Students read text and teacher shows teaching filmstrip. Using overhead projector and a list of words which are action verbs and nouns, teacher checks for understanding, using "thumbs up, thumbs down" for student internalization of concept.

Assessment
Teacher observation of student understanding.

Action Verbs

Quadrant 3—Applications

 ### Left Mode—Try

Practice worksheets.

Objective
To provide guided practice on action verbs.

Activity
Students use practice worksheets accompanying text.

Assessment
Quality of work sheets.

Right Mode—Extend

Students illustrate a verb.

Objective
To extend what has been learned about action verbs.

Activity
Students select their own example of an action verb. They draw a picture illustrating their verb. On a separate piece of paper, they write a sentence using their verb.

Assessment
Student ability to complete the task assigned.

Quadrant 4—Creations

 ### Left Mode—Refine

Students guess each other's verbs from pictures.

Objective
To evaluate and share student drawings.

Activity
In cooperative learning groups, students share their drawings without showing their sentences. They guess each other's action verbs correctly, and evaluate each other's sentences.

Assessment
Student contribution to the group, and student sensitivity to the work of others.

 ### Right Mode—Integrate

Action verb aerobics.

Objective
To take delight in using action verbs.

Activity
Children participate in aerobics exercises demonstrating as many as possible of the action verbs used by them throughout the unit.

Assessment
Student participation and enthusiasm.

Adjectives

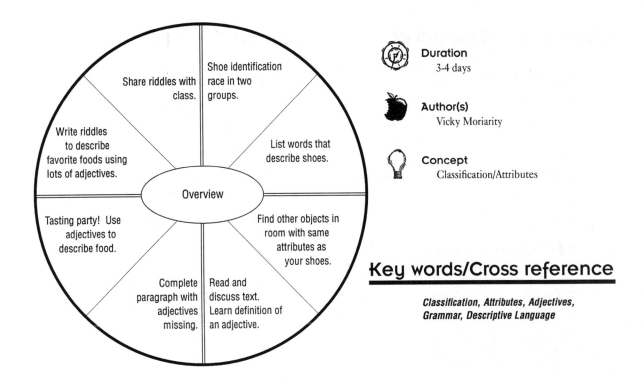

Duration
3-4 days

Author(s)
Vicky Moriarity

Concept
Classification/Attributes

Overview

Shoe identification race in two groups.

List words that describe shoes.

Find other objects in room with same attributes as your shoes.

Read and discuss text. Learn definition of an adjective.

Complete paragraph with adjectives missing.

Tasting party! Use adjectives to describe food.

Write riddles to describe favorite foods using lots of adjectives.

Share riddles with class.

Key words/Cross reference

Classification, Attributes, Adjectives, Grammar, Descriptive Language

Overview

Objective
Students will learn to identify and write adjectives.

About the Author
Vicky Moriarity teaches second grade at Riverview Elementary School, Marion Community Schools, Marion, IN.

Required Resources
English text; tape of square dance music.

Adjectives

Quadrant 1—Experience

 ## Right Mode—Connect

Shoe identification race in two groups.

Objective

To develop an awareness of adjectives.

Activity

Divide class into two groups. All students take off their shoes and put them into a "group" pile. Race to see which group can identify their shoes and get them back on without talking.

Assessment

Students' enjoyment.

 ## Left Mode—Examine

List words that describe shoes.

Objective

To list words that describe their shoes.

Activity

In groups, make a list of words that describe each students' shoes. What attributes helped you to recognize your shoes?

Assessment

Completion of list of adjectives.

Quadrant 2—Concepts

 ## Right Mode—Image

Find other objects in room with same attributes as your shoes.

Objective

To deepen students' awareness of adjectives.

Activity

Using list of adjectives that describe shoes, find other objects in the room with same attributes. Find objects in room with two or more of the same attributes. Share findings.

Assessment

Ability to recognize similar attributes in different items.

 ## Left Mode—Define

Read and discuss text. Learn definition of an adjective.

Objective

To learn the definition of an adjective and be able to identify them.

Activity

Read and discuss text dealing with adjectives.

Assessment

Teacher verbally checks for understanding during instruction.

Adjectives

Quadrant 3—Applications

 ### Left Mode—Try

Complete paragraph with adjectives missing.

Objective
To identify adjectives in written form.

Activity
Read a paragraph and fill in the blanks with adjectives.

Assessment
Correct use of adjectives.

 ### Right Mode—Extend

Tasting party! Use adjectives to describe food.

Objective
To provide an opportunity to extend prior learning about adjectives.

Activity
Have a tasting party. Have several types of similar foods, i.e., four different kinds of apples, chocolate chip cookies, BBQ chips, pickles, etc. Divide students into small groups and let each group taste test a different food. Generate adjectives to describe each food.

Assessment
Verbal interaction with students and the number of adjectives generated.

Quadrant 4—Creations

 ### Left Mode—Refine

Write riddles to describe favorite foods using lots of adjectives.

Objective
To use adjectives in written material.

Activity
Students write riddles using lots of adjectives to describe favorite foods.

Assessment
Use of adjectives in riddles.

 ### Right Mode—Integrate

Share riddles with class.

Objective
To provide an opportunity to share riddles with class.

Activity
Students will share their riddles with the class.

Assessment
Enjoyment and participation of class.

Being a Friend

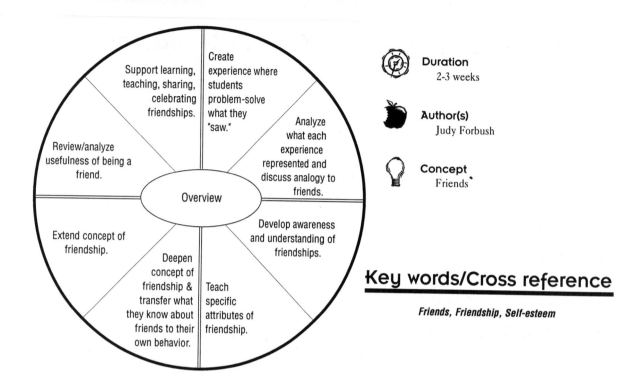

Support learning, teaching, sharing, celebrating friendships.

Create experience where students problem-solve what they "saw."

Analyze what each experience represented and discuss analogy to friends.

Review/analyze usefulness of being a friend.

Overview

Develop awareness and understanding of friendships.

Extend concept of friendship.

Deepen concept of friendship & transfer what they know about friends to their own behavior.

Teach specific attributes of friendship.

Duration
2-3 weeks

Author(s)
Judy Forbush

Concept
Friends

Key words/Cross reference

Friends, Friendship, Self-esteem

Overview

Objective
To connect learners to the qualities of good friends.

About the Author
Judy E. Forbush is Principal of Johnston Elementary School, Cabell County Schools, Huntington, WV.

Required Resources
Two live plants; "Windows on Science" video on symbiotic relationships; library books on friendship

Being a Friend

Quadrant 1—Experience

 ### Right Mode—Connect

Create experience where students problem-solve what they "saw." Prior to unit beginning: bring two plants (one gets care, one does not)

Objective
Create an experience where students problem-solve what they "saw" and "why" it might be good or bad.

Activity
A) Compare/contrast plants. B) Watch "Windows on Science" video on symbiotic relationships. NO SOUND OR EXPLANATION.

Assessment
Participation/engagement of students.

 ### Left Mode—Examine

Analyze what each experience represented and discuss analogy to friends.

Objective
Analyze what each experience represented and discuss analogy to friends.

Activity
A) Discuss in cooperative groups what they saw in video clip and what happened to plants. Infer what was beneficial and what was not beneficial. B) Come to consensus and list five characteristics they want in a friend. C) Create attribute chart designating "events" and "traits". Create "Be A Friend" poster.

Assessment
Participation charts/posters.

Quadrant 2—Concepts

 ### Right Mode—Image

Develop awareness and understanding of friendships.

Objective
Develop awareness and understanding of friendships.

Activity
A) Read to the class *"Fox and the Hound."* Teacher leads discussion about characteristics that each character had and those they had in common. B) Groups of children read the same book to make similar comparisons (e.g., *Charlotte's Web, Bridge to Terabithia, Where the Red Fern Grows,* etc.). C) Create skit, mime or dance to represent how they feel as a best friend.

Assessment
Participation/discussion.

 ### Left Mode—Define

Teach specific attributes of friendship.

Objective
Teach specific attributes of friendship.

Activity
Utilize Health test, Science test and *"Windows on Science"* video used in Q1R with full sound and explanations.

Assessment
Accuracy of outline/web provided by teacher.

Quadrant 3—Applications

Left Mode—Try

Deepen concept of friendship & transfer what they know about friends to their own behavior.

Objective

Deepen concept of friendship and begin to transfer what they know about friends to their own behavior.

Activity

Compare text info and literature experiences by making "Believe It Or Not Chart" separating real experiences from fantasy and looking at how they personally demonstrate being a friend.

Assessment

Participation and charts.

Right Mode—Extend

Extend concept of friendship.

Objective

Extend concept of friendship.

Activity

Groups of three discuss responsibility of each attribute and why it is important. Make group collage showing the positive attributes of group member or role play being a good friend and not being a good friend and the consequences.

Assessment

Participation/quality of work.

Quadrant 4—Creations

Left Mode—Refine

Review/analyze usefulness of being a friend.

Objective

Review/analyze usefulness of being a friend.

Activity

Use collage and skits to share with other classes. Begin journal for self-evaluation of whether or not student is exhibiting friendship qualities.

Assessment

Participation/quality of work.

Right Mode—Integrate

Support learning, teaching, sharing, celebrating friendships.

Objective

Support learning, teaching, sharing, celebrating friendships.

Activity

A) Plant pansy to care for with partner. B) Create family journals on ways to incorporate what they have learned in their family life. C) Encourage "friendship plant" in neighborhood.

Assessment

Participation/willingness to carry info/material into personal home settings.

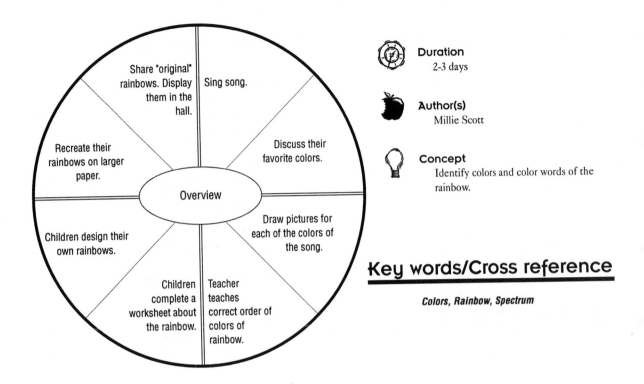

Duration
2-3 days

Author(s)
Millie Scott

Concept
Identify colors and color words of the rainbow.

Key words/Cross reference

Colors, Rainbow, Spectrum

Overview

Objective
To learn to identify colors and the color words of the rainbow.

About the Author
Millie Scott is a primary EMH teacher at Sheridan School in District #87, Bloomington, IL

Quadrant 1—Experience

Right Mode—Connect

Sing song.

Objective
To learn and sing a song about colors.

Activity
Sing the song, "I Like Red" (to the tune of "Three Blind Mice").

I LIKE RED Lyrics by Rozanne Williams
I like red, I like red.
Do you like it too? Do you like it too?
Red is the color of lollipops,
A setting sun and a pair of socks.
Did you ever see such a color, my friend
As red, red, red?

I like blue, I like blue.
Do you like it too? Do you like it too?
Blue is the color of oceans and skies,
Brand-new jeans and my grandmother's eyes.
Did you ever see such a color so true
As blue, blue, blue?

I like yellow, I like yellow.
Do you like it too? Do you like it too?
Yellow is sunny and yellow is bright.
Yellow's the color of the moon at night.
Yellow can shine and yellow can glow.
It's yellow, yellow, yellow.

I like green, I like green.
Do you like it too? Do you like it too?
Green is the grass and the leaf of a tree,
A bright green sweater made just for me.
Green is the color of vines filled with beans.
It's green, green, green.

I like orange, I like orange.
Do you like it too? Do you like it too?
A carrot is orange, a popsicle too,
An apricot and the sun I drew,
A fruit tree drawn with an orange or two
Is orange, orange, orange.

I like brown, I like brown.
Do you like it too? Do you like it too?

Brown is the color of new leather shoes,
Toast in the morning, a cow that moos.
What do you think of the color I found?
It's brown, brown, brown.

I like purple, I like purple.
Do you like it too? Do you like it too?
Purple's the color of grapes and a plum,
The color I see when I bruise my thumb.
Name all the things you know that are purple,
Purple, purple, purple.

Assessment
Did the children learn the song?

Left Mode—Examine

Discuss their favorite colors.

Objective
To talk about their favorite colors.

Activity
Discuss their favorite colors and why they like that color or colors.

Assessment
Did everyone share with the group?

Quadrant 2—Concepts

Right Mode—Image

Draw pictures for each of the colors of the song.

Objective

To demonstrate their ability to color using different colors.

Activity

Review song *I Like Red*. Brainstorm things that are each of the different colors. Make a list of the ideas under each of the color names or a splotch of each color. Make a book by cutting out verses of song, glue them on separate blank sheets of paper, and draw pictures using the color on the page. Students design a cover and combine the pages into their personal book of colors.

Assessment

Are the pictures the children's own ideas? Did they complete the book?

Left Mode—Define

Teacher teaches correct order of colors of rainbow.

Objective

To learn the sequence of colors of the rainbow and color words of rainbow.

Activity

Teacher teaches the correct sequence of the colors of the rainbow. Teacher uses the color words, as well as the actual colors of rainbow. Teacher uses decoding skills, such as beginning and ending sounds, to help teach color words.

Assessment

Can the children sequence the rainbow both in colors and color words?

Quadrant 3—Applications

Left Mode—Try

Children complete a worksheet about the rainbow.

Objective

To sequence the colors of the rainbow by themselves. To sequence the color words of the rainbow by themselves.

Activity

Color a worksheet containing a picture of a rainbow or have them arrange the colors of the rainbow in the correct sequence. Match color words to the colored rainbow.

Assessment

Can the children sequence the colors of the rainbow? Can the children match the color words to a colored rainbow?

Right Mode—Extend

Children design their own rainbows.

Objective

To make up their own rainbow (any shape, they can use the correct sequence of colors or create their own sequence).

Activity

Given a variety of media to work with, such as colors, markers, paints, construction paper, etc., design their own rainbow. Encourage them to use any shape and they can sequence the colors or make up their own sequence of colors.

Assessment

Their rainbows will be their evaluation.

Quadrant 4—Creations

Left Mode—Refine

Recreate their rainbows on larger paper.

Objective
To transfer their personal rainbows to larger paper.

Activity
Give each child a 18" by 24" paper and have each one enlarge their "original" rainbow on this large sheet of paper.

Assessment
Can they transfer their "original" rainbow to the large paper?

Right Mode—Integrate

Share "original" rainbows. Display them in the hall.

Objective
To share their creations with each other and then display in hall outside of room.

Activity
Let each child show and tell their rainbow. Hang them up in the hall outside of room for the rest of the school to enjoy.

Assessment
Did everyone show and tell? The display will show our talent.

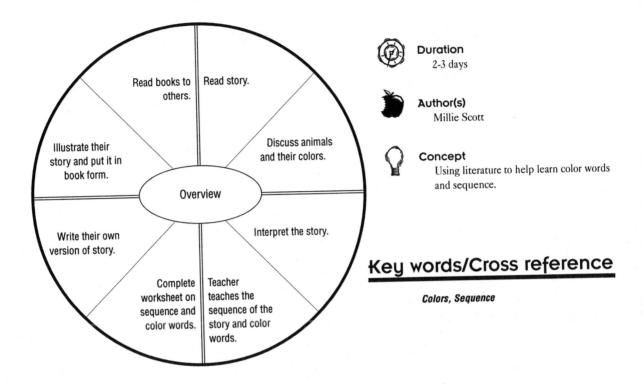

Duration
2-3 days

Author(s)
Millie Scott

Concept
Using literature to help learn color words and sequence.

Key words/Cross reference

Colors, Sequence

Overview

Objective
To learn color words and practice sequence using literature.

About the Author
Millie Scott is a primary EMH teacher at Sheridan School in District #87, Bloomington, IL.

Bibliography
Brown Bear, Brown Bear, What Do You See?
By Bill Martin, Jr.

Quadrant 1—Experience

 ## Right Mode—Connect

Read story.

Objective

To listen to story and to act out the story.

Activity

Read the story *Brown Bear, Brown Bear, What Do You See?* By Bill Martin, Jr. Let the children act out the story by sequencing the animals. They may want to use the animal noises or talk the way they think the animals did—in a quiet voice, a loud voice, a gruff voice, etc.

Assessment

Can the students tell the story back? Can they answer simple questions about the story?

 ## Left Mode—Examine

Discuss animals and their colors.

Objective

To have the children relate what they know about animal and their colors.

Activity

Discuss the color of animals that the children know about: personal pets, zoo animals, forest animals, farm animals.

Assessment

Did everyone participate? Can they tell you the colors of some animals?

Quadrant 2—Concepts

 ## Right Mode—Image

Interpret the story.

Objective

To explore ways to sequence the story.

Activity

Divide the class into three groups. Each group will interpret this book in a different way.

Group 1—Recite the words of the book along with the teacher.
Group 2—Pantomime the way each animal in the book moves.
Group 3—Make soft background noises that are appropriate to the action.

Here's an example:

Group 1—"Goldfish, goldfish, what do you see?"
Group 2—(Pantomimes a fish swimming)
Group 3—(Makes soft water noises, Splash, splish, swish!)

Give them a chance to make up their way of interpreting the book. Give each group a chance to recite, pantomime, and make sound effects.

Assessment

Did the children participate in the interpretation of the book? Could they come up with some ideas other than the teacher's?

 ## Left Mode—Define

Teacher teaches the sequence of the story and color words.

Objective

To learn the sequence of the story and color words.

Activity

The teacher teaches the sequence of animals in story and uses color word flash cards instead of saying the color of the animals.

Assessment

Can the children repeat the animals in sequence? Can they read the color words?

Quadrant 3—Applications

 ### Left Mode—Try

Complete worksheet on sequence and color words.

Objective
To color animals the correct colors and then sequence the animals.

Activity
Given a worksheet with the pictures of the animals from the story, the children color the animals according to the color words on them. They then cut the animals apart, and arrange them in the correct sequence. They can retell the story to someone using their pictures.

Assessment
Did they read and color the animals correctly? Did they arrange them in the correct sequence? Can they retell the story using their pictures?

 ### Right Mode—Extend

Write their own version of story.

Objective
To rewrite the story in their own way.

Activity
Using the text of *Brown Bear, Brown Bear, What Do You See?* as a guide, the children write their own version of the story. Those that have trouble writing can tell their story into a cassette player for the teacher or an older child to write it out later. Maybe the children can work in pairs.

Assessment
Were they able to create another story?

Quadrant 4—Creations

 ### Left Mode—Refine

Illustrate their story and put it in book form.

Objective
To put together a book.

Activity
Using their version of the story, create illustrations to go with their story. Make a cover and put it together as a book.

Assessment
Did they complete their book?

 ### Right Mode—Integrate

Read books to others.

Objective
To share their books with others.

Activity
The children read their books to each other. Then put them on display in the room so they can be read by each other at a later date.

Assessment
Can they read their books?

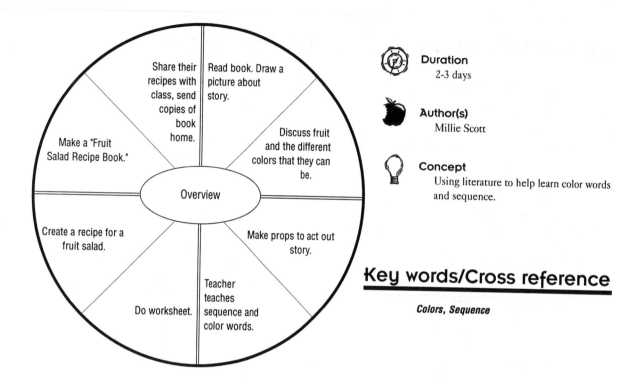

Overview

- Share their recipes with class, send copies of book home.
- Read book. Draw a picture about story.
- Discuss fruit and the different colors that they can be.
- Make a "Fruit Salad Recipe Book."
- Create a recipe for a fruit salad.
- Make props to act out story.
- Do worksheet.
- Teacher teaches sequence and color words.

Duration
2-3 days

Author(s)
Millie Scott

Concept
Using literature to help learn color words and sequence.

Key words/Cross reference

Colors, Sequence

Overview

Objective
To learn color words and practice sequencing using literature.

About the Author
Millie Scott is a primary EMH teacher at Sheridan School in District #87, Bloomington, IL.

Bibliography
Mr. Rabbit and the Lovely Present,
by Charlotte Zolotow.

Quadrant 1—Experience

 ### Right Mode—Connect

Read book. Draw a picture about story.

Objective

To listen to story and draw a picture about what they heard.

Activity

Read book *Mr. Rabbit and the Lovely Present*, by Charlotte Zolotow. The children then draw a picture about something in the story.

Assessment

Does their picture reflect a situation in the story?

 ### Left Mode—Examine

Discuss fruit and the different colors they can be.

Objective

To have children relate their experiences with fruit and different colors and to discuss if they have ever given a present to their mother.

Activity

Discuss how fruit are different. Have them name a color and a fruit of that color. Have them tell if they have given their mother a present, if so, what was it and what color was it?

Assessment

Do they know the color of any fruit? Have they given their mother a gift? If so, can they tell you about it and the colors involved?

Quadrant 2—Concepts

 ### Right Mode—Image

Make props to act out story.

Objective

To make props to act out story using correct sequence of gifts and to use color word flash cards to show color.

Activity

Children make a list of presents. Then the children make props by drawing pictures of all the presents, except the fruit. Bring in some red apples, bananas, green pears, blue grapes, and a basket. Read the story again. This time, have selected children act out the story as you read, using the children-made props as well as the fruit and the basket. Give several children a chance to play the little girl and Mr. Rabbit. Have them hold up the correct color word flash card for each present.

Assessment

Can they tell you the correct sequence? Can they find the correct flash card?

 ### Left Mode—Define

Teacher teaches sequence and color words.

Objective

To learn the correct sequence and to learn the correct color words.

Activity

The teacher teaches sequence of the story emphasizing the color words and correct sequence.

Assessment

Are the children listening to what is being taught?

Quadrant 3—Applications

Left Mode—Try

Do worksheet.

Objective
To complete worksheet on sequencing and color words.

Activity
Complete a worksheet on color by numbers. Children color pictures of the presents correctly (to match the numbers and color words). Cut apart and sequence pictures. Retell story in correct order using their pictures.

Assessment
Did they match the numbers to the correct color words? Did they retell the story in the correct sequence using their pictures? (This can be done using a tape recorder for an adult to listen to at a later time.)

Right Mode—Extend

Create a recipe for a fruit salad.

Objective
To create a recipe for fruit salad using fruit from story.

Activity
The children write a recipe for a fruit salad using the fruit from story. As the recipe is written stress the use of color words. Make a salad for the children to enjoy.

Assessment
After writing the recipe, how did the salad come out? Were there too much of one fruit and not enough of another kind?

Quadrant 4—Creations

Left Mode—Refine

Make a "Fruit Salad Recipe Book."

Objective
To make a book from the children's recipes.

Activity
Each child writes their own recipe as they vision their "perfect fruit salad." Emphasize the use of color words in the recipe. They are free to add other fruits to their recipes. Put each child's page into a book and then let each child create their own cover.

Assessment
Did their recipes make sense? Did they create a cover for their book?

Right Mode—Integrate

Share their recipes with class, send copies of book home.

Objective
To share their recipes with class and home.

Activity
Each child shares their recipes with the class. Then let each child take a copy of their book home to their parents.

Assessment
Can they read their recipes? The reaction of the parents would help evaluate their work.

Colors 4/5

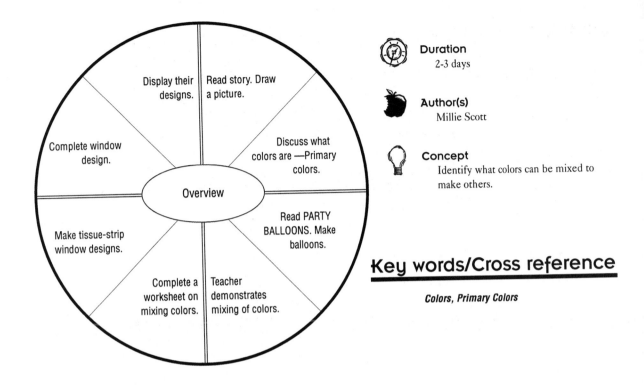

Duration
2-3 days

Author(s)
Millie Scott

Concept
Identify what colors can be mixed to make others.

Key words/Cross reference

Colors, Primary Colors

Overview

Objective
To learn which colors can be mixed to make other colors.

About the Author
Millie Scott is a primary EMH teacher at Sheridan School in District #87, Bloomington, IL.

Bibliography
The Mixed-Up Chameleon, by Eric Carle.

Quadrant 1—Experience

 ## Right Mode—Connect

Read story. Draw a picture.

Objective
To listen to story, then create their own chameleon.

Activity
Read *The Mixed-Up Chameleon*, by Eric Carle. Then the children can create their version of the chameleon.

Assessment
Did they get the idea to use lots of colors?

 ## Left Mode—Examine

Discuss what colors are —Primary colors.

Objective
To see if the children can name the primary colors and which ones you can mix to make new ones.

Activity
Ask the children if they can name the three primary colors. Ask them if they can tell you which ones when mixed together make orange, green, purple, brown, and black.

Assessment
Did they name the primary colors? Could they name any of the mixtures used to create new colors?

Quadrant 2—Concepts

 ## Right Mode—Image

Read Party Balloons. Make balloons.

Objective
To listen to a poem and then design a balloon of their own. Stress the color words.

Activity
Read *Party Balloons.*

Party balloons, party balloons.
It's my birthday today!
I have balloons for all my friends,
When they come over to play.

Here is a pretty round blue balloon.
Blue as the bluest skies.

Here is a shiny red balloon,
Just about your size.

Here is a happy yellow balloon,
Yellow as bright sunshine.

Here is a lovely purple balloon,
Like purple grapes on a vine.

Here is a little orange balloon,
Like oranges from a store.

I have one more green balloon and I don't have anymore.

Let children explore with one or more of the following activities:

Bubbling Balloons
Pour 1/4 cup of dish washing liquid into a container. (An empty cottage cheese carton works great.) Add small amounts of water and tempera paint until the color is intense.

Place a straw in the paint mixture and blow carefully until the bubbles start to overflow.

Gently place the paper over the bubbles, then lift carefully. The broken bubbles leave a beautiful design.

Repeat the procedure with several colors, overlapping the designs.

Spin Designs

Sprinkle a small amount of three colors of dry tempera paint near the center of a piece of paper.

Place another piece of paper over the paint. Press down firmly, turning the top sheet one complete circle. Lift the top sheet. Both pieces of paper will have circular designs. Spray them with fixative or hair spray.

Powder Painting

Put various colors of dry tempera powder in small containers. (Empty margarine tubs work well.) Paint a sheet of paper with liquid starch. Using a slightly damp paintbrush, pick up the paint powder and dab it onto the starch-covered paper. Repeat with other colors. An interesting textured painting will result.

Assessment

Did they participate in any of the projects?

Left Mode—Define

Teacher demonstrates mixing of colors.

Objective

To show the children how two or more colors mixed together can create another color.

Activity

Teacher shows the children how to mix two or more colors to create a new color. Materials needed: three large jars; water; red, blue, and yellow food coloring; large spoons or sticks for stirring.

1. Fill the jars with water. Put a few drops of yellow food coloring in the first jar. Take your time doing this. Students will enjoy the swirl design the food coloring makes as it mixes with the water.
2. Add red food coloring to the yellow water a few drops at a time until the water is colored orange.
3. Repeat the steps above mixing red and blue food coloring to make purple, and yellow and blue coloring to make green.
4. If the group is mature enough to handle mixing colors to make brown or black, the teacher can show them how to create these colors.

Assessment

Can the children name the colors that can be mixed together to create a new color?

Quadrant 3—Applications

Left Mode—Try

Complete a worksheet on mixing colors.

Objective

To check the children's ability to mix colors.

Activity

The worksheet could have color words on it. Have the children choose two color words and use those colors (with markers) to color with. Have them overlap the colors to demonstrate what colors create a new color. They could use colored cellophane shapes (such as circles, squares, rectangles, etc.) to show the teacher how to overlap two colors to create a new color. Be sure to include the colors that they will need to overlap to show the mixing.

Assessment

Can they demonstrate, show or illustrate the mixing process?

Right Mode—Extend

Make tissue-strip window designs.

Objective

To make their own design using tissue paper—overlapping the paper to create new colors in their design.

Activity

Tissue-Strip Window Designs Materials needed: waxed paper, liquid starch or watered-down white glue, large paintbrushes, thin strips of tissue paper in primary colors.

Directions:

1. Cut waxed paper into sheets about 16" in length. Two sheets are needed for each design.
2. Place one sheet of waxed paper on a sheet of newspaper and paint with a thin coat of liquid starch.
3. Place strips of tissue paper on top of liquid starch before it dries. Arrange the red, yellow, and blue strips in an overlapping design. The strips do not have to lie flat.
4. When the design is complete, place the other sheet of waxed paper on top and press to seal completely. Let dry.
5. Point out the new colors made by overlapping tissue strips. (The children could do this.)

Assessment

Did their design show new colors due to the overlapping of tissue strips?

Quadrant 4—Creations

Left Mode—Refine

Complete window design.

Objective
To complete the window design.

Activity
The children will trim the edges and then make a frame from construction paper strips to put around the design. They can put a hanger on the frame. If time, they can write or dictate a simple description to be added to the design.

Assessment
Did they make the frame? Can they give a simple description of their design?

Right Mode—Integrate

Display their designs.

Objective
To share their work with others.

Activity
The children can display their window designs in the windows in the hallway or in their rooms. If there are not enough windows, they may be hung from the ceiling in a hallway where there is a lot of light.

Assessment
How do their designs look?

Colors 5/5

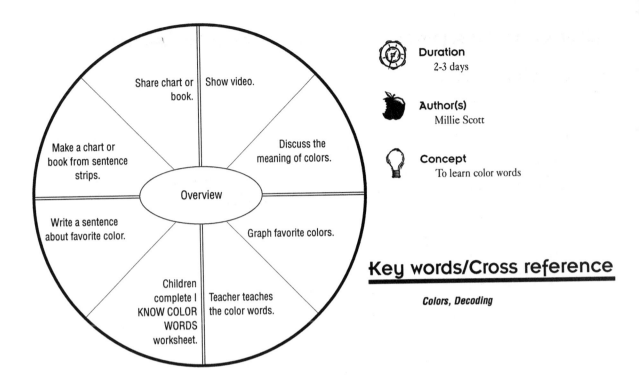

Duration
2-3 days

Author(s)
Millie Scott

Concept
To learn color words

Key words/Cross reference

Colors, Decoding

Overview

Objective
To learn the color words.

About the Author
Millie Scott is a primary EMH teacher at Sheridan
School in District #87, Bloomington, IL.

Required Resources
Video *Wee Sing in Sillyville*

Quadrant 1—Experience

 Right Mode—Connect

Show video.

Objective
To see a video about colors.

Activity
Show the video *We Sing In Sillyville.*

Assessment
Did the children get involved in the video?

 Left Mode—Examine

Discuss the meaning of colors.

Objective
To connect the children's feelings about colors.

Activity
Discuss colors and what meaning they have for us.
What would it be like if we only had black and white?
Why do we want colors?

Assessment
Did they freely participate in the discussion?

Quadrant 2—Concepts

 Right Mode—Image

Graph favorite colors.

Objective
To make a graph of their favorite colors.

Activity
Graphing Favorite Colors (emphasize the color words).
Make a simple color graph on a large sheet of bulletin
board paper. Cut out small squares from construction
paper that match the colors named on the chart. Have
each student come up and paste a square of his or her
favorite color on the chart.

When the chart is complete, discuss the results: Which
color is most popular? Which color is least popular?
Which color(s) is not liked by anyone? How many people like each of the colors? How many more people like
_____ than _____? How many people are represented
on the chart? Does it match the number of people in
the room? If the numbers do not match, why do you
think this is so?

Assessment
Can they answer the questions?

 Left Mode—Define

Teacher teaches the color words.

Objective
To learn the color words.

Activity
Teacher teaches the color words using the words from
the graph. The teacher (using the color words from the
graph) explains decoding of the words: beginning
sounds, ending sounds, configuration of words, shape of
words and number of letters.

Assessment
Are the children into the lecture?

Quadrant 3—Applications

 ## Left Mode—Try

Children complete I KNOW COLOR WORDS worksheet.

Objective
To demonstrate their knowledge of color words.

Activity
Using a worksheet I KNOW COLOR WORDS, color the page by themselves. This page would have outline shapes of crayons with the words written below or on them. The children using the decoding skills that were taught in 2L, should decide what colors to use.

Assessment
Is the worksheet completed correctly?

 ## Right Mode—Extend

Write a sentence about favorite color.

Objective
To write a sentence about favorite color.

Activity
Have the students write a sentence or two on a crayon shaped sentence strip. They could describe their favorite color and give their reasons for choosing that color. They can then decorate their sentence strip with a border design in their favorite color.

Assessment
Did they write (or for younger ones dictate) a sentence and decorate their sentence strip?

Quadrant 4—Creations

 ## Left Mode—Refine

Make a chart or book from sentence strips.

Objective
To combine the children's sentence strips on a chart or in a book.

Activity
Children complete sentence strips and decorating. Then they can be put on a chart together or into a book to be shared.

Assessment
Did everyone complete a page?

 ## Right Mode—Integrate

Share chart or book.

Objective
To share their work with others.

Activity
Have each child share his/her sentence strip with the class.

Assessment
Did they all have a turn to share?

Concept Mapping

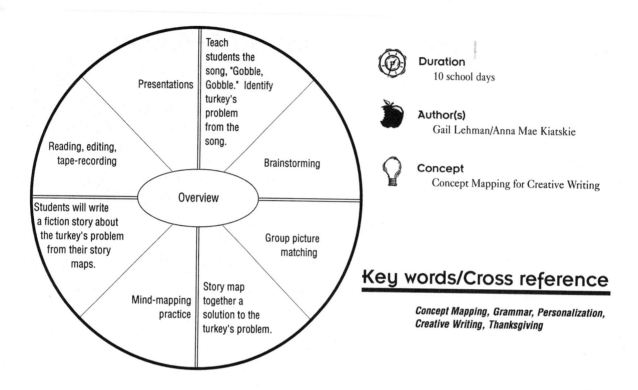

Duration
10 school days

Author(s)
Gail Lehman/Anna Mae Kiatskie

Concept
Concept Mapping for Creative Writing

Key words/Cross reference

Concept Mapping, Grammar, Personalization,
Creative Writing, Thanksgiving

The concept map circle contains:
- Overview (center)
- Presentations
- Teach students the song, "Gobble, Gobble." Identify turkey's problem from the song.
- Brainstorming
- Reading, editing, tape-recording
- Group picture matching
- Students will write a fiction story about the turkey's problem from their story maps.
- Story map together a solution to the turkey's problem.
- Mind-mapping practice

Overview

Objective
Students will enhance their abilities to use story mapping in creative writing.

About the Authors
Gail Lehman and Anna Mae Kiatski are teachers at Beck Elementary School, Shikellamy School District, Northumberland, PA. They are participants in the Shilkellamy 4MAT Implementation Project led by Tim and Trudy Shannon.

Required Resources
Teacher prepared paper "turkey tails" for student practice writing; tape recorders and tapes for student's stories

Bibliography
Norton, June M., *"Gobble, Gobble, Gobble," Singing and Rhyming*, New York: Ginn and Company, 1959.

Concept Mapping

Quadrant 1—Experience

 ### Right Mode—Connect

Teach students the song, "Gobble, Gobble." Identify turkey's problem from the song.

Objective

To help students truly believe that reading is fun. To help students feel empathy for the age old turkey's problem of being served for Thanksgiving dinner.

Activity

Teach students the song, "Gobble, Gobble." Identify the turkey's problem in the song.

Assessment

Listening, enjoying, being engaged.

 ### Left Mode—Examine

Brainstorming.

Objective

To encourage brainstorming for solutions to the turkey's problem.

Activity

To help the students share their feelings about their problem solutions. Brainstorm solutions to the turkey's problem and write these solutions on the chalkboard. Discuss the solutions.

Assessment

Teacher observation of depth of thinking in brainstorming and discussion.

Quadrant 2—Concepts

 ### Right Mode—Image

Group picture matching.

Objective

To connect the problem solutions to a story mapping concept taught in previous lesson.

Activity

Divide the classroom into groups. Put story map signs on one group of children. Label them who, what, when, where, and how. The other group is given the story solutions and answers to the who, what, when, where, and how elements. The two groups are to move to their match.

Assessment

Teacher observes students making the connection between the turkey problem solutions and the story map elements (who, what, when, where, how).

 ### Left Mode—Define

Story map together a solution to the turkey's problem.

Objective

To begin a serious study of story mapping by involving students in a classroom model of a story map.

Activity

The teacher will elicit responses from the class for a story map involving the turkey's problem and solution. The mapping can be done on the chalkboard or on an overhead.

Assessment

Teacher observes quality of work and participation.

Concept Mapping

Quadrant 3—Applications

 ### Left Mode—Try

Mind-mapping practice.

Objective
To give practice in writing their own story map.

Activity
The students will choose their solution to the turkey's problem and create a story map for that solution. The students will write in sentence form the solution on pre-cut multicolored turkey tails.

Assessment
Teacher checks for appropriate responses to the story map elements (who, what, when, where, how). Teacher checks for proper sentence structure on paper tail.

 ### Right Mode—Extend

Students will write a fiction story about the turkey's problem from their story maps.

Objective
To provide students an opportunity to create original story.

Activity
Using the student's story map (created in 36 sections), the student will write a fiction story about a turkey at Thanksgiving time.

Assessment
Teacher checks for sentence structure and appropriate solution to turkey problems. Teacher also checks for paragraph structure.

Quadrant 4—Creations

 ### Left Mode—Refine

Reading, editing, tape-recording.

Objective
To have students edit and refine written stories.

Activity
Working in shared-pairs, the students will read their stories to each other and check for correct grammar. The pairs will tape record their finished product.

Assessment
Listening to the tape, teacher will check for oral expression and check grammar.

 ### Right Mode—Integrate

Presentations.

Objective
To celebrate the sharing of the story mapping experience.

Activity
1) Videotape students reading their solution tail and story to the class. Tail is then attached to the huge classroom bulletin board turkey. 2) Tape recordings and written stories are made available in the school library.

Assessment
Teacher observes students reaction to classmates' solutions and stories.

Shadow and Mystery

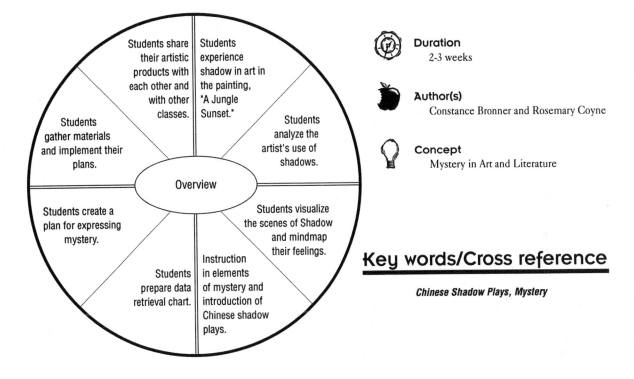

Students experience shadow in art in the painting, "A Jungle Sunset."

Students share their artistic products with each other and with other classes.

Students gather materials and implement their plans.

Students create a plan for expressing mystery.

Overview

Students analyze the artist's use of shadows.

Students visualize the scenes of Shadow and mindmap their feelings.

Students prepare data retrieval chart.

Instruction in elements of mystery and introduction of Chinese shadow plays.

Duration
2-3 weeks

Author(s)
Constance Bronner and Rosemary Coyne

Concept
Mystery in Art and Literature

Key words/Cross reference

Chinese Shadow Plays, Mystery

Overview

Objective
Students will learn the concept of mystery through its portrayal in both literature and art.

About the Author
At the time this plan was first published, Constance Bronner taught second grade at Belle View Elementary School, Fairfax County Schools, Alexandria, VA. Rosemary Coyne was teaching third grade for two years at Belle View Elementary School. She has over thirty years of teaching experience.

Required Resources
Music, large print of *"A Jungle Sunset,"* and a cloth to hide it from the children.

Bibliography
Brown, Marcia. *Shadow.* (Illus.) New York: Charles Scribner's Sons, 1982.

Kettlekamp, Larry. *Shadows.* (Illus.) New York: Morrow & Co., 1957.

Shadow and Mystery

Quadrant 1—Experience

 ### Right Mode—Connect

Students experience shadow in art in the painting, "A Jungle Sunset."

Objective
To stimulate interest in how the use of shadow creates mysterious effects.

Activity
While playing "Carnival of the Animals" by Saint-Saens for background music, the librarian displays a large print of the painting," A Jungle Sunset," by Henri Rousseau, which is hidden by a large piece of fabric. She uncovers the painting in stages, while asking students to describe what they see. The lower center portion is uncovered last, and students discover the shadow.

Assessment
Students' active involvement, curiosity, and contribution to the group.

 ## Left Mode—Examine

Students analyze the artist's use of shadows.

Objective
To stimulate student reflection on the painting.

Activity
The teacher leads a verbal analysis of the painting, "A Jungle Sunset," focusing on the artist's use of shadow. Repeated patterns, overlapping, mood, color, lines, shape, space and texture are discussed insofar as they heighten the shadow's effect.

Assessment
Level of participation in class discussion and willingness to share ideas.

Quadrant 2—Concepts

 ### Right Mode—Image

Students visualize the scenes of Shadow and mindmap their feelings.

Objective
To integrate the concept of shadow and mystery in art and literature.

Activity
Students relax and visualize the scenes as the librarian reads the book, *Shadow*, by Marcia Brown. Students mindmap their feelings which were generated by the story.

Assessment
Students' abilities to express what they imaged during the reading.

 ## Left Mode—Define

Instruction in elements of mystery and introduction of Chinese shadow plays.

Objective
To convey the elements of mysterious expression in art and literature.

Activity
The librarian teaches the elements of mystery which were evidenced in the painting and in the story. Using the book, *Shadows*, by Larry Kettlekamp, she explains Chinese shadow plays as an additional way to express mystery.

Assessment
Verbal checking for understanding during instruction with a focus on the children's internalizing the concepts of mystery and shadow.

Shadow and Mystery

Quadrant 3—Applications

 ### Left Mode—Try

Students prepare data retrieval chart.

Objective
To reinforce and review the elements of mystery.

Activity
In small learning groups, students prepare a data retrieval chart summarizing the key ideas presented by the librarian. All charts are shared with whole group. Librarian creates collective chart displaying all student data.

Assessment
Completeness and quality of group charts.

 ### Right Mode—Extend

Students create a plan for expressing mystery.

Objective
To collaborate on a plan to express mystery.

Activity
Students form small learning groups. Each group will collaborate on a plan to express mystery creatively in an art form or in a Chinese Shadow Play.

Assessment
Quality of individual group plans.

Quadrant 4—Creations

 ### Left Mode—Refine

Students gather materials and implement their plans.

Objective
To extend the internalized concepts of mystery.

Activity
Students gather materials and create their unique mystery expression which they planned in the previous activity.

Assessment
On-task behavior of students.

 ### Right Mode—Integrate

Students share their artistic products with each other and with other classes.

Objective
To share what was learned and created.

Activity
The students share with other classes their artistic products or Chinese Shadow Play. As appropriate, "Carnival of the Animals" is again used as background music.

Assessment
Student participation and enthusiasm.

Group Cooperation

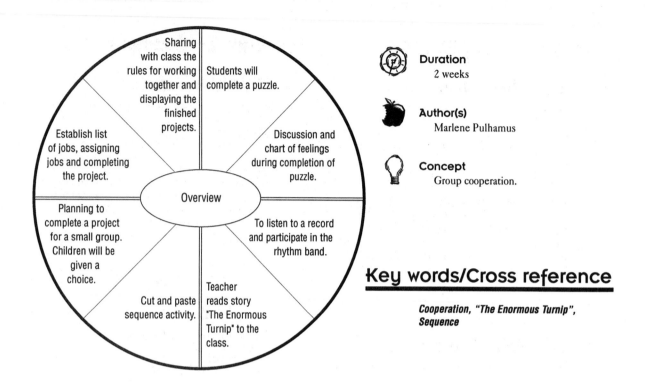

Sharing with class the rules for working together and displaying the finished projects.

Students will complete a puzzle.

Establish list of jobs, assigning jobs and completing the project.

Discussion and chart of feelings during completion of puzzle.

Overview

Planning to complete a project for a small group. Children will be given a choice.

To listen to a record and participate in the rhythm band.

Cut and paste sequence activity.

Teacher reads story "The Enormous Turnip" to the class.

Duration
2 weeks

Author(s)
Marlene Pulhamus

Concept
Group cooperation.

Key words/Cross reference

Cooperation, "The Enormous Turnip",
Sequence

Overview

Objective
To learn to work together to achieve a common goal rather than to work independently.

About the Author
Marlene L. Pulhamus has taught in the Primary grades 21 years. She is presently a Chapter Basic Skills Instructor assigned to Grade 1 at School #3, Paterson, NJ. She works on an in-class model that is a Preventative/Remedial Program.

Required Resources
Story *"The Enormous Turnip."* Record of children's nursery rhymes or other music that lends itself to rhythm instructions. Set of rhythm instructions.

Quadrant 1—Experience

Right Mode—Connect

Students will complete a puzzle.

Objective
To have students work together to complete a 50-piece puzzle.

Activity
Begin with a piece of a picture and have children decide what it is. Continue to add pieces a few at a time until the large picture is seen. Discuss puzzles they have done. Then split the group into threes and have them complete a puzzle. Do not give any directions other than to put this puzzle together.

Assessment
Completed puzzle.

Left Mode—Examine

Discussion and chart of feelings during completion of puzzle.

Objective
To have students discuss their feelings when they worked together.

Activity
Students will discuss and chart those things they liked, agreed with or did not like when they put the puzzle together. Was there only one leader or did they all make suggestions on how to do the puzzle?

Assessment
Charts and participation in the discussion.

Quadrant 2—Concepts

Right Mode—Image

To listen to a record and participate in the rhythm band.

Objective
To play instruments in a class rhythm band.

Activity
Children will listen to music playing nursery rhymes they are familiar with. They will then select the rhythm instruments and play along with the music. Children will realize what it sounds like when instruments work together.

Assessment
The "concert" that the children produce.

Left Mode—Define

Teacher reads story "The Enormous Turnip" to the class.

Objective
To listen to a story and decide how cooperation is important.

Activity
Read the story *"The Enormous Turnip."* Discuss: What was the problem? How was it solved? Sequence the story. Do they need help with something that is "Enormous."

Assessment
Students' knowledge when they contribute to the discussion.

Group Cooperation

Quadrant 3—Applications

 ### Left Mode—Try

Cut and paste sequence activity.

Objective
To be able to sequence a story or a set of pictures showing a project from beginning to completion.

Activity
Children will cut and paste a series of five pictures and write a sentence to tell what is happening in the project.

Assessment
Completed worksheets.

 ### Right Mode—Extend

Planning to complete a project for a small group. Children will be given a choice.

Objective
Children will work together to plan a small project.

Activity
Various projects will be presented to the students.
1) A covered pencil box. 2) A roll movie. 3) Poetry cube.
4) Planting a seed. Children will pick a project and decide on the steps they need to do to complete the project. Children will form groups of three to work on the projects.

Assessment
Students' interaction with each other.

Quadrant 4—Creations

 ### Left Mode—Refine

Establish list of jobs, assigning jobs and completing the project.

Objective
To complete the project that their cooperative group has decided on.

Activity
Children will work in small groups to complete their projects.

Assessment
Completed projects.

 ### Right Mode—Integrate

Sharing with class the rules for working together and displaying the finished projects.

Objective
To share with their classmates the completed projects and what they learned by working together.

Activity
Children will give seeds they planted to their classmates. Will share roll movie with the class. Pencil boxes will be kept in their desks. Students will tell their peers how they decided it was better to work together. They will share how they assigned jobs to different people and how that made the tasks easier to complete.

Assessment
Participation of students as they listen to their classmates describe how they learned to work together.

Measurement/Calendar

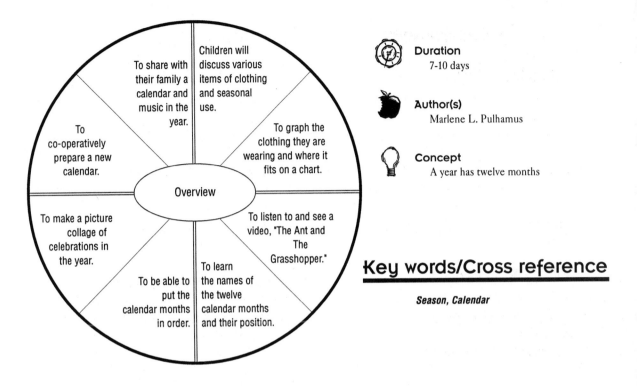

Children will discuss various items of clothing and seasonal use.

To share with their family a calendar and music in the year.

To co-operatively prepare a new calendar.

To make a picture collage of celebrations in the year.

To be able to put the calendar months in order.

To learn the names of the twelve calendar months and their position.

To listen to and see a video, "The Ant and The Grasshopper."

To graph the clothing they are wearing and where it fits on a chart.

Overview

Duration
7-10 days

Author(s)
Marlene L. Pulhamus

Concept
A year has twelve months

Key words/Cross reference

Season, Calendar

Overview

Objective
To have the children learn that there are twelve months in a year and the seasons are in the different months.

About the Author
Marlene L. Pulhamus has taught in the Primary grades for 21 years. She is presently a Chapter 1 Basic Skills Instructor assigned to grade one at School #3 in Paterson, NJ. She works in a class Preventative/Remedial program.

Required Resources
Graphic Learning, *"The Ant and The Grasshopper"* video, *"The Ant and The Grasshopper"* 12-month calendar.

Quadrant 1—Experience

Right Mode—Connect

Children will discuss various items of clothing and seasonal use.

Objective
To have children decide in which season of the year/month various articles of clothing are worn.

Activity
Present children with raincoat, boots, hat, shorts, mittens, scarf, gloves, bathing suit, sweater, jacket. Children will discuss when items of clothing are worn and how they are used. Children may dress up in the clothing.

Assessment
Student participation.

Left Mode—Examine

To graph the clothing they are wearing and where it fits on a chart.

Objective
To chart the clothing that the children are wearing on the particular day and to contrast it to the seasons.

Activity
Chart the clothing that the children have on. Contrast it to the four seasons clothing chart to see where they fit in. List vocabulary words next to the various items of clothing.

Assessment
Charts, graph and the children's participation.

Quadrant 2—Concepts

Right Mode—Image

To listen to and see a video, "The Ant and The Grasshopper."

Objective
To listen to a story and see a video of the story.

Activity
Children will listen and see the video of *"The Ant and The Grasshopper."*

Assessment
Attention of the children while watching and listening to the video.

Left Mode—Define

To learn the names of the twelve calendar months and their position.

Objective
To present a twelve-month calendar to the children and have them learn the names of the months.

Activity
Present the large calendar to the students. Write the names of each month on the top of each page while pointing out a wall calendar that shows the whole year. Count the number of days in the months, noting those that have 30, 31 and February. Graph their birthday months. Notice which are longest, shortest months. Recite poem "Thirty Days."

Assessment
Student participation, teacher checking on birth dates.

Measurement/Calendar

Quadrant 3—Applications

 ### Left Mode—Try

To be able to put the calendar months in order.

Objective
To have students match names of month with position on the calendar. To put holidays in the proper month.

Activity
Children will cut and paste names of the month and add a holiday picture in the proper month.

Assessment
Completed worksheets.

 ### Right Mode—Extend

To make a picture collage of celebrations in the year.

Objective
To have children find pictures of holidays and form a collage with them.

Activity
Children will find pictures of different celebrations in the magazine pile and a song from the music they know. They will form a collage with these things.

Assessment
Finished collages. Children's participation.

Quadrant 4—Creations

 ### Left Mode—Refine

To cooperatively prepare a new calendar.

Objective
Children will cooperatively prepare a calendar for the new year.

Activity
Children will be given twelve empty grids. They will label them with the proper month name and decide on a picture that represents the month. They may list any occasion they feel is important to them. They will put the proper numbering in the grids by looking at another calendar.

Assessment
Student participation, teacher questioning where needed, or help that is given or asked for.

 ### Right Mode—Integrate

To share with their family a calendar and music in the year.

Objective
To produce the calendar that they will take home to share with their family and another grade one class.

Activity
Children will complete the calendar. They will then share it, and the songs they selected for the months, with their classmates and their family. Copies of the calendar will be given to another grade one class.

Assessment
Completed calendars.

Cause and Effect in Emotions

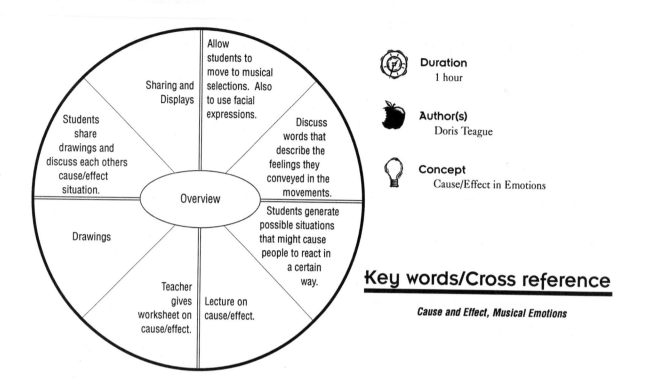

Sharing and Displays

Allow students to move to musical selections. Also to use facial expressions.

Students share drawings and discuss each others cause/effect situation.

Discuss words that describe the feelings they conveyed in the movements.

Overview

Students generate possible situations that might cause people to react in a certain way.

Drawings

Teacher gives worksheet on cause/effect.

Lecture on cause/effect.

Duration
1 hour

Author(s)
Doris Teague

Concept
Cause/Effect in Emotions

Key words/Cross reference

Cause and Effect, Musical Emotions

Overview

Objective
The concept of cause and effect relationships is explored through various activities.

About the Author
Doris Teague is an instructional specialist in Special Education/Gifted and Talented Education for the Region V Educational Service Center, Beaumont, TX. She is a certified 4MAT Trainer.

Required Resources
Musical selections for kinesthetic activity; facial expression pictures from magazines

Cause and Effect in Emotions

Quadrant 1—Experience

 ### Right Mode—Connect

Allow students to move to musical selections. Also to use facial expressions.

Objective
To create the experience of moods/feelings through music and movement.

Activity
Play a variety of musical selections (marches, jazz, rock, etc.). Allow students to move with the music. Guide them to use body language and facial expressions to convey the ways music inspires various emotions.

Assessment
Observe students and movements/expressions.

 ### Left Mode—Examine

Discuss words that describe the feelings they conveyed in the movements.

Objective
To discuss the various types of emotions felt by students when music was playing.

Activity
Allow certain students to demonstrate movement and facial expressions when musical selections are playing. Discuss words which describe the feelings . . . worried, happy, scared, furious, gloomy, etc.

Assessment
Quality of responses and ability to describe feelings.

Quadrant 1—Concepts

 ### Right Mode—Image

Students generate possible situations that might cause people to react in a certain way.

Objective
To generate possible situations that might cause someone to react in a certain manner.

Activity
As students demonstrate various movements and facial expressions related to music. Allow them to describe a possible event that could cause such a reaction.

Assessment
Group participation and comprehension of concepts.

 ### Left Mode—Define

Lecture on cause/effect.

Objective
To explain the concept of cause and effect.

Activity
Lecture and demonstrate examples of ways in which events can have an effect on other things/people/ideas. Use examples from student readers or from previously generated scenarios (see Activity 3).

Assessment
Teacher designed worksheet. Students identify cause and effect relationships.

Quadrant 3—Applications

 ## Left Mode—Try

Teacher gives worksheet on cause/effect.

Objective
To reinforce and practice taught concepts.

Activity
Discuss worksheet. Give feedback/correction as needed.

Assessment
Quality and accuracy of student responses.

 ## Right Mode—Extend

Drawings.

Objective
To provide an opportunity for students to create own cause/effect situations.

Activity
Give each student a cut-out picture from a magazine of a person whose face has a certain expression. Teacher cuts out picture (cut only head and upper shoulders). Students glue pictures on their paper and complete the drawing by adding rest of body and including something in drawing that shows why person is reacting.

Assessment
Students' illustrations and interaction.

Quadrant 4—Creations

 ## Left Mode—Refine

Students share drawings and discuss each others cause/effect situation.

Objective
To explain and respond to drawings.

Activity
Students share drawings and write explanations for their cause/effect situation. Other students listen and give feedback about cause/effect relationships illustrated.

Assessment
Quality of students' explanations and reactions.

 ## Right Mode—Integrate

Sharing and Displays.

Objective
To share illustrations and provide a teaching tool for the classroom.

Activity
Display student work on bulletin board and add words around the examples such as: happy, sad, anxious, etc. Keep word cards handy so students can continue to add to the collection of words and refer to them as needed.

Assessment
Participation and quality of answers. Participation over extended time.

Friendship

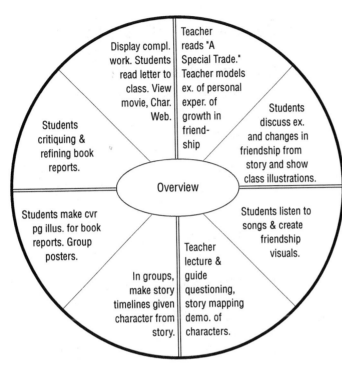

Display compl. work. Students read letter to class. View movie, Char. Web.

Teacher reads "A Special Trade." Teacher models ex. of personal exper. of growth in friend-ship

Students discuss ex. and changes in friendship from story and show class illustrations.

Students critiquing & refining book reports.

Overview

Students listen to songs & create friendship visuals.

Students make cvr pg illus. for book reports. Group posters.

Teacher lecture & guide questioning, story mapping demo. of characters.

In groups, make story timelines given character from story.

 Duration
4-6 weeks

 Author(s)
Laurie J. Kelly

 Concept
Growth and Changes, In Friendships

Key words/Cross reference

Friendship, Change, Farm Life, Fiction, Survival, Fantasy, Interdependence, Literature, Life Cycle, Farm Animals, Book Reports, Story Mapping, Charlotte's Web

Overview

 Objective
The students will gain knowledge and skill in build-ing stronger friendships by understanding how rela-tionships grow and change throughout life.

 About the Author
Laurie Kelly is a 2nd grade teacher with Paterson Public Schools, Paterson, NJ. She is a certified 4MAT trainer for her district.

 Required Resources
1) Video - Movie Charlotte's Web, 2) Friendship songs, 3) Teacher-made worksheets and activity cards, 4) White yarn, construction paper, posterboard and magic markers.

 Bibliography
E.B. White. *Charlotte's Web*
Sally Wittman. *A Special Trade*

Friendship

Quadrant 1—Experience

 ### Right Mode—Connect

Teacher reads "A Special Trade." Teacher models examples of personal experiences. of growth in friendship.

Objective
To connect the students with the concept through past personal experience and literature.

Activity
1) Read the class the story, *A Special Trade*, by S. Wittman. 2) Teacher models a personal friendship and discusses how it has grown stronger through growth and changes through the years. 3) Students reflect on a strong personal friendship and illustrate how it has grown since the friendship began.

Assessment
Student involvement and listening attentiveness.

 ### Left Mode—Examine

Students discuss examples and changes in friendship from story and show class illustrations.

Objective
To share and express thoughts and experiences.

Activity
1) Analyze *A Special Trade* and discuss how the friendship grew stronger between the characters through the years. Discuss how the needs of the two friends changed. 2) Students show the class their personal friendship illustrations and discuss growth and changes. 3) Small groups: list qualities that help friendship grow. Make a class master list from group responses.

Assessment
Quality of student responses and group lists.

Quadrant 2—Concepts

 ### Right Mode—Image

Students listen to songs & create friendship visuals.

Objective
To bridge from direct experience to abstract concept.

Activity
1) Students listen to songs about friendship and create group visuals expressing actions and qualities that help friendships grow. 2) Each group displays their visual and role plays the illustration for the class. 3) Teacher introduces the special friendship between characters in the story *Charlotte's Web* and reads the story to the class, (one or two chapters daily) until story is completed.

Assessment
Quality of group visuals and role playing demonstration. Interaction, enthusiasm and attention to all activities.

 ### Left Mode—Define

Teacher lecture & guide questioning, story mapping demonstrations of characters.

Objective
To teach students how to structure and organize key ideas and meanings in the story *Charlotte's Web* or any story.

Activity
1) Teacher lecture using board demonstration (story Web) about how the animals in the story depended on each other for survival. 2) Teacher lecture and demonstrate on chart paper or board a story mapping timeline of character's growth in friendships in the story. 3) Using the story *A Special Trade*, teach how to write a book report.

Assessment
Student interest, attention and comments.

Friendship

Quadrant 3—Applications

Left Mode—Try

In groups, make story timelines given character from story.

Objective
To review and practice skills.

Activity
1) Small groups — teacher gives each group the name of a main character from the story *Charlotte's Web*. The group makes a character timeline of important events in the life of that character. 2) Teacher made comprehension worksheets. 3) Each student writes a book report for story *Charlotte's Web*. 4) Based on story *Charlotte's Web*, in groups, students make question cards and others answer the questions.

Assessment
Sharing of completed activities with the class. Quality and ability using taught skills and comprehension check.

Right Mode—Extend

Students make cover page illustrations for book reports. Group posters.

Objective
Students are given activities that begin the link from the concept to personal application.

Activity
1) Draw a cover page that illustrates your favorite part of story *(Charlotte's Web)*. 2) Small groups - make posters that show the deep friendship that developed between Charlotte and Wilbur and how they helped each other. 3) Using white yarn, cut out letters and a dark colored piece of construction paper. Each student creates a web and glues an adjective on the web that describes an important quality for building stronger friendships. 4) Creative writing letters. 5) 3R — using a character from Charlotte's Web story, write a letter to another character thanking him/her for their friendship.

Assessment
Quality of completed assignments. Student responses and interaction.

Quadrant 4—Creations

Left Mode—Refine

Students critiquing & refining book reports.

Objective
Student assessment of their own work. Students will edit, refine and where needed, rework their written book reports and analyze the thank you letters for relevance, originality and effectiveness.

Activity
1) Students will work with a partner helping each other to analyze the accuracy and effectiveness of their work. 2) In small groups, students write four questions about growth and changes in friendship. Game style - - - Answers - - - Question and answer session.

Assessment
Student involvement and quality/accuracy in assessment.

Right Mode—Integrate

Display completed work. Students read letter to class. View movie, Charlotte's Web.

Objective
To build strong emotional involvement with the concept by sharing and refocusing.

Activity
1) Display all completed work. 2) Display book reports with cover page illustrations. 3) Read creative writing character friendship letters to the class. (Each student will read his letter.) 4) Invite another class to join in Celebrating Growth in Friendship by viewing the movie, *Charlotte's Web* with your class and answering student-made questions on story and friendship. 5) Each student brings in pictures from magazines to make a class collage showing living creatures displaying growth and changes in friendship.

Assessment
Student enthusiasm, responses and demonstration of what they have learned. Sharing with others and celebrating their new learnings with others.

Classification

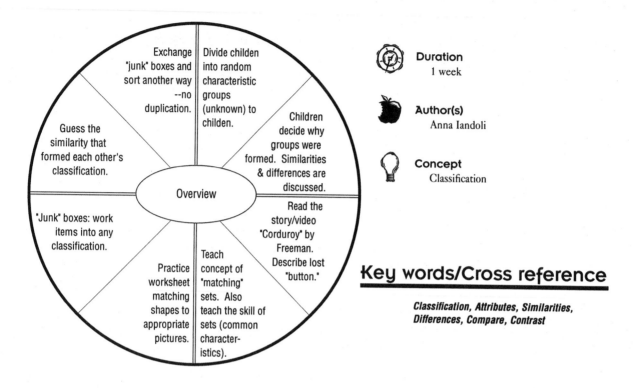

Exchange "junk" boxes and sort another way --no duplication.

Divide childen into random characteristic groups (unknown) to childen.

Children decide why groups were formed. Similarities & differences are discussed.

Guess the similarity that formed each other's classification.

Overview

"Junk" boxes: work items into any classification.

Read the story/video "Corduroy" by Freeman. Describe lost "button."

Practice worksheet matching shapes to appropriate pictures.

Teach concept of "matching" sets. Also teach the skill of sets (common character-istics).

Duration
1 week

Author(s)
Anna Iandoli

Concept
Classification

Key words/Cross reference

Classification, Attributes, Similarities, Differences, Compare, Contrast

Overview

Objective
This is a primary unit to develop the concept of similarities needed to classify (people/objects).

About the Author
Anna Iandoli has been teaching (kindergarten and 1st grade) for over 20 years in Paterson, New Jersey. She is a certified 4MAT trainer for Paterson Public Schools.

Required Resources
Various items to prepare assorted "junk" boxes.

Bibliography
Corduroy by Don Freeman.

Classification

Quadrant 1—Experience

 ### Right Mode—Connect

Divide children into random characteristic groups (unknown to children.)

Objective
Students will be able to follow directions in order to allow introduction to classification skills.

Activity
Assign each child to a specific group by an undisclosed similar characteristic (ex. all those wearing a specific color, or all those wearing glasses, etc.).

Assessment
Students' positive reaction to the classification process.

 ### Left Mode—Examine

Children decide why groups were formed. Similarities & differences are discussed.

Objective
To decide similarities/differences—analyze the classification process.

Activity
Students decide why each group was formed (identification of common characteristic/similarity).

Assessment
Students' ability to take part in the process of identification.

Quadrant 2—Concepts

 ### Right Mode—Image

Read the story/video "Corduroy" by Freeman. Describe lost "button."

Objective
To take part in an imaginative problem solving activity.

Activity
Teacher reads the story *Corduroy* by Don Freeman. Have students decide how Corduroy could describe his lost button in order to allow help in finding the match.

Assessment
Students' approach to the problem/process.

 ### Left Mode—Define

Teach concept of "matching" sets. Also teach the skill of sets (common characteristics).

Objective
To teach the concept of "sameness" (similarity).

Activity
Present students with letter cards, shape cards, or picture cards. Show what "twin" cards look like. Do several examples of "modeling" for group.

Assessment
Students will be able to divide cards into twin sets.

Quadrant 3—Applications

 ## Left Mode—Try

Practice worksheet matching shapes to appropriate pictures.

Objective

To provide a "doing" hands-on practice with similarities and differences (classification).

Activity

Students will be presented with a practice worksheet showing various pictures and shapes. Students instructed to color specific shapes/pictures assigned colors (ex. color all circles and those pictures looking most like circles—red, etc.).

Assessment

Students' successful completion of worksheet.

 ## Right Mode—Extend

"Junk" boxes: work items into any classification.

Objective

To further extend concept of similarities, differences— classification through manipulation.

Activity

Give small groups of children "junk" boxes and ask them to sort the items into any common characteristic grouping. Play background music during this activity.

Assessment

Students' ability to find a common characteristic of items presented in order to form sets.

Quadrant 4—Creations

 ## Left Mode—Refine

Guess the similarity that formed each other's classification.

Objective

To give students the opportunity to share their groupings with the rest of the class.

Activity

The class, as a whole, will have the task of deciding how each group of students sorted their "junk" (macaroni, keys, buttons, beans, etc.).

Assessment

Students' correct classifications will enable the rest of the class to decipher the similarity.

 ## Right Mode—Integrate

Exchange "junk" boxes and sort another way —no duplication.

Objective

To "re" group "junk" from another group—choose alternative similarity.

Activity

Have groups exchange "junk" boxes, and have them now classify items using another common characteristic. This cannot duplicate previous group's characteristic.

Assessment

Students' ability to find alternative similarities in order to further classify items presented to them.

Classification by Attributes

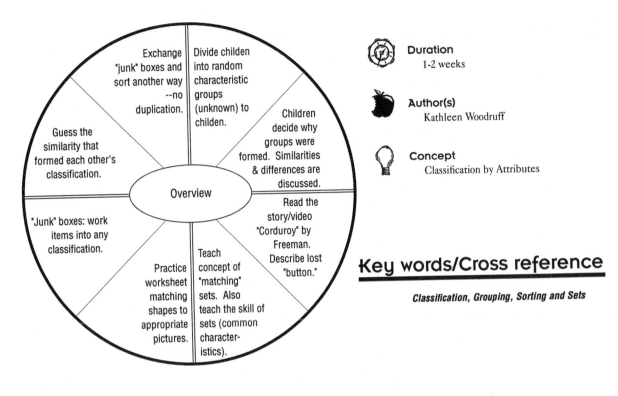

Exchange "junk" boxes and sort another way --no duplication.

Divide childen into random characteristic groups (unknown) to childen.

Guess the similarity that formed each other's classification.

Children decide why groups were formed. Similarities & differences are discussed.

Overview

"Junk" boxes: work items into any classification.

Read the story/video "Corduroy" by Freeman. Describe lost "button."

Practice worksheet matching shapes to appropriate pictures.

Teach concept of "matching" sets. Also teach the skill of sets (common characteristics).

Duration
1-2 weeks

Author(s)
Kathleen Woodruff

Concept
Classification by Attributes

Key words/Cross reference

Classification, Grouping, Sorting and Sets

Overview

Author's Notes

Sorting, Grouping, Classifying are skills which use and strengthen logical thinking. We use logistical skills constantly in life, often without being aware of it. Grouping involves awareness of attributes, which are observed and then isolated. Students need development of this skill to help them make order and sense out of problems and situations, which become increasingly complex as they grow. In this unit, we start with single opposite groupings, which lead to a more complex classification of 8-16 groupings. Materials are simple and instruction uses lots of thinking, questioning and discussion.

Objective

To teach students the decision-making thinking skills involved in classification.

About the Author

Katie Woodruff is a member of the Excel Consultants Group. Her company, "Drum Beats," is located in Waitsfield, VT, where she resides. She has been involved in education for over twenty-five years, with ten years experience in school adminis-tration.

Required Resources

Chart paper and markers for "What's My Rule?" game; attribute blocks and people pieces; large vari-ety of loose buttons; assorted objects for sorting.

Classification by Attributes

Quadrant 1—Experience

Right Mode—Connect

Teacher and students play "What's My Rule?"

Objective

To initiate Classification by personally involving students in sorting themselves into groups based on their physical attributes.

Activity

Teacher initiates game, "What's My Rule?", by explaining that s/he is thinking of a rule and the class must figure it out. The teacher begins to separate the children into two groups. Example: "Joan go to the front of the room. John go to the back. Sam to the back. Linda to the front. I wonder where Jim will go?" Children respond, but teacher does not share the rule until all children have been sorted. Then discuss other ways they can sort themselves.

Children play "What's My Rule?" Send 3-4 children out of the room. The remaining decide on a rule for sorting themselves into groups. Outside children return and can ask any questions to determine the rule. Example: "Would I go into this group or that group?" After they have finished questioning, they may make only one guess at the rule. Continue playing several more times with different children going outside the room.

Assessment

Student participation through questions, guesses, and their enthusiasm.

Left Mode—Examine

Teacher charts rules from game showing opposites.

Objective

To focus student attention on specific attributes used in the game experience. To state opposite attributes, e.g., "blue eyes/brown eyes."

Activity

Using large chart paper, list single word rules used in the "What's My Rule?" game. Then regroup these words into opposite pairs.

Assessment

Student participation and understanding in listing and pairing attributes.

Quadrant 2—Concepts

Right Mode—Image

Students manipulate Attribute Blocks and People Pieces.

Objective

To observe objects and see the attributes. To compare two objects and understand similarities and differences.

Activity

Using Attribute Blocks, hold up one at a time. Solicit responses from students as to characteristics/attributes of each block (color, shape, etc.). Hold up two blocks for comparison of differences and similarities. Allow students to work in pairs, manipulating attribute blocks to solve problems stated by teacher. Example: "Sort by shapes." "How many groups?" "Sort by colors." "How many groups?" Using People Pieces, students continue to practice sorting through teacher direction. "Make 2 groups. What rule did you use for your groups?" With each new direction, children create rules and results.

Assessment

Students' understanding through verbal responses and manipulation of Attribute Blocks and People Pieces.

Left Mode—Define

Instruction in classification by sorting buttons.

Objective

To teach classification using several attributes. To sort objects successively leading to the smallest possible grouping.

Activity

Use large chart paper and real or cardboard buttons (including two shapes, two sizes, two colors, two/four holes). State lesson Objective:"Today we are going to learn how to sort a large amount of buttons into the smallest possible group." At the top of the chart, place all buttons in a circle and label "Buttons." Teacher keeps sorting the buttons into smaller groups by size, then color, then shape and finally number of holes. At each different sorting, make a circle and label the attribute. Take another sheet of paper and sort the buttons again, but change the order of sorting (Buttons: holes, shape, color, size). Continue a third time, letting children respond. Give each student a prepared worksheet to fill in for the fourth and final method of sorting.

Classification by Attributes

Assessment
Quality of children's responses and understanding through the worksheet.

Quadrant 3—Applications

Left Mode—Try

Worksheets; bags of objects are sorted by students.

Objective
To practice and reinforce knowledge of sorting objects by their attributes.

Activity
Prepared worksheets and bags of objects for sorting (People Pieces, Attribute Blocks, marbles, 15 dried beans, soup mix, etc.). Give each student one bag of objects to sort. As they sort the objects, have them record their groupings on the worksheet prepared for that set. When finished with one set, trade with another student until all worksheets are completed.

Assessment
The quality of their recordings on each worksheet. The ease with which they completed their tasks.

Right Mode—Extend

Students create collections for sorting.

Objective
To reinforce and personalize the students' learning by collecting their own objects for sorting.

Activity
Give each student a bag for collecting objects. Ask them to think of one type of object to collect (leaves, stones, twigs, grass/weeds, pencils, crayons, etc.). They should build their own collection of objects either within the classroom, out of the classroom, or for homework, making their own decisions about what goes in their bag.

Assessment
Enthusiasm and quality of each student's collection. Do they have a reasonable sortable collection of objects?

Quadrant 4—Creations

Left Mode—Refine

Students sort own objects and classify them.

Objective
To allow each student the opportunity for creative and personal application of their understanding of classification by attributes.

Activity
Give each child a large sheet of cardboard and have her/him separate the collected objects into smaller and smaller groups, until s/he can sort no further. Record the sorting step by step on a prepared worksheet.

Assessment
The quality and originality of their grouping and the recording on their worksheet.

Right Mode—Integrate

Students lead class in "What's My Rule?" with own collections.

Objective
To share their collection and system of classification with the other students.

Activity
"Guess My Rule?" Have each student demonstrate her/his method of sorting. S/he will sort step by step, using her/his worksheet as necessary. At each step of the sorting, the other students will try to guess "The Rule." Continue until all children have shared projects.

Assessment
The quality of rules for sorting and student responses. The ability to share, to lead, and to participate with others.

The Concept of Size

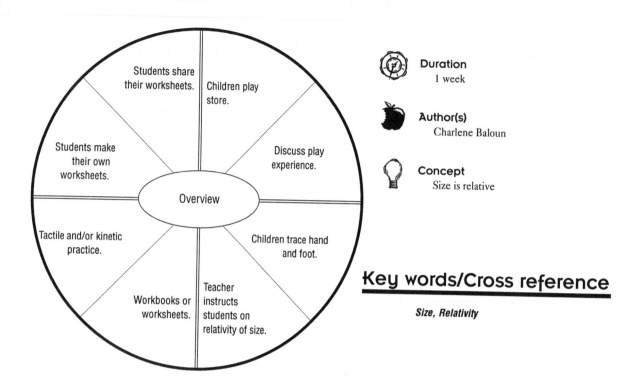

Duration
1 week

Author(s)
Charlene Baloun

Concept
Size is relative

Overview

Children play store.

Discuss play experience.

Children trace hand and foot.

Teacher instructs students on relativity of size.

Workbooks or worksheets.

Tactile and/or kinetic practice.

Students make their own worksheets.

Students share their worksheets.

Key words/Cross reference

Size, Relativity

Overview

Objective
To introduce or reinforce children's understanding of the concept of size.

About the Author
At the time this plan was written, Charlene Baloun was a kindergarten teacher at Oliver Wendell Holmes School District #97, Oak Brook, IL.

Required Resources
Variety of clothing items in various sizes for "clothing store" activity; grab bags and a variety of objects for experimentation; a variety of magazines and catalogs for picture projects.

The Concept of Size

Quadrant 1—Experience

 ### Right Mode—Connect

Children play store.

Objective
To introduce/reinforce the concept of size.

Activity
Set up a play clothing store. Include such items as: hats, mittens, gloves, jackets, shirts, dresses and shoes. All items "for sale" are too large or too small for the children. Give students time to "go shopping."

Assessment
Children's interest and engagement.

 ### Left Mode—Examine

Discuss play experience.

Objective
To increase the children's vocabulary for describing size.

Activity
Discuss the experience. Questions for the children: Did you "buy" anything in our store? Did it fit? Do you know anyone it might fit? Do you think you could have worn it when you were a baby? Do you think it will fit you tomorrow? Do you think you could wear it when you are older?

Assessment
Children's interest.

Quadrant 2—Concepts

 ### Right Mode—Image

Children trace hand and foot.

Objective
To teach the concept that size comparisons are relative.

Activity
Give each child two sheets of drawing paper. Ask the children to place one hand on one of the sheets with fingers outspread, and draw an outline around it. Next, have the children trace an outline of one of their feet on the other piece of paper. Have them compare the two; then compare their hand outline with one of the other children: then a foot with one of the other children. Tracing of the teacher's hand and foot should also be compared. (Or any other significant adult.)

Assessment
Meaningful participation in the activity.

 ### Left Mode—Define

Teacher instructs students on relativity of size.

Objective
To reteach and reinforce the concept that size comparisons are relative.

Activity
Teacher instructs the children in relativity of size following the content of the teacher's manual for mathematics and/or science.

Assessment
Quality of workbooks, worksheets, etc.

The Concept of Size

Quadrant 3—Applications

 ### Left Mode—Try

Workbooks or worksheets.

Objective

To provide additional practice in recognizing and describing the relativity of size.

Activity

Workbook accompanying text or worksheet devised by teacher.

Assessment

Quality of above.

 ### Right Mode—Extend

Tactile and/or kinetic practice.

Objective

To personalize the learning and provide tactile and kinetic practice.

Activity

Put a small collection of objects in a drawstring bag. Ask the children to reach in and find the largest, smallest, something larger than my ring, something smaller than your hand, something longer than your finger, etc. Add kinetic practice by asking the children to stand tall, make yourself taller, make yourself shorter.

Assessment

Students' understanding.

Quadrant 4—Creations

 ### Left Mode—Refine

Students make their own worksheets.

Objective

Students' understanding.

Activity

Have children make up worksheets to try on each other. They may draw simple pictures of objects of different sizes or pictures may be cut from magazines or catalogs and pasted on art paper. Drawings or pasted pictures should be arranged by size.

Assessment

Quality of worksheets.

 ### Right Mode—Integrate

Students share their worksheets.

Objective

To share their "series" with each other.

Activity

To share their "series" with each other.

Assessment

Participation and sharing.

Intro. to Fractions

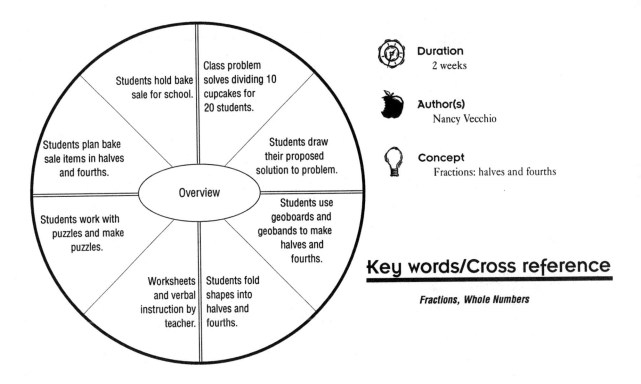

Students hold bake sale for school.

Class problem solves dividing 10 cupcakes for 20 students.

Students plan bake sale items in halves and fourths.

Students draw their proposed solution to problem.

Overview

Students work with puzzles and make puzzles.

Students use geoboards and geobands to make halves and fourths.

Worksheets and verbal instruction by teacher.

Students fold shapes into halves and fourths.

Duration
2 weeks

Author(s)
Nancy Vecchio

Concept
Fractions: halves and fourths

Key words/Cross reference

Fractions, Whole Numbers

Overview

Objective
Students will learn that fractions are parts of a whole.

About the Author
At the time this plan was first published, Nancy Vecchio was a Curriculum Specialist in New Haven, CT, a position she had held for two years. Previously she served as Instructional Associate in Social Studies, Hamden Public Schools, Hamden, CT, a position she held for three years. She has been involved in education for over twenty years.

Required Resources
Cupcakes for the class; geoboards, geobands, and crayons and paper; teacher-prepared construction paper shapes and worksheets; magazine picture puzzles.

Intro. to Fractions

Quadrant 1—Experience

 ### Right Mode—Connect

Class problem solves dividing 10 cupcakes for 20 students.

Objective

To introduce the concept of dividing wholes into equal parts.

Activity

Teacher presents 10 cupcakes to be shared among 20 students. Children problem-solve and dramatize how to divide cupcakes evenly.

Assessment

Enjoyment and participation of students.

 ### Left Mode—Examine

Students draw their proposed solution to problem.

Objective

To allow students to examine the problem and discuss what they did to solve it.

Activity

Students will draw how they proposed to share cupcakes equally. Teacher-directed class discussion will focus on the concept of equal parts.

Assessment

Student participation and understanding of the concept.

Quadrant 2—Concepts

 ### Right Mode—Image

Students use geoboards and geobands to make halves and fourths.

Objective

To have the students see the relationship between wholes and parts.

Activity

Children use geoboards and one color geobands to create shapes (circles, squares, rectangles). These shapes are then divided equally into halves and fourths, using geobands of a different color. Children use paper and crayons to draw what they understood from the geoboard exercises, on ditto representations of geoboards.

Assessment

Ability of children to create shapes and demonstrate halves and fourths.

 ### Left Mode—Define

Students fold shapes into halves and fourths.

Objective

To teach the concept of halves and fourths and the vocabulary used to identify each part.

Activity

Teacher gives students pre-cut construction paper shapes. The students are instructed to fold and label shapes as one-half or one-fourth. Each part is identified and labeled by the students, with the help of the teacher. Children share with the group the different ways they found to make halves and fourths.

Assessment

Quality of participation and comprehension of activity and concepts.

Intro. to Fractions

Quadrant 3—Applications

 ### Left Mode—Try

Worksheets and verbal instruction by teacher.

Objective
To provide guided practice for the concept of fractions.

Activity
Students complete teacher-prepared worksheets on halves and fourths. Some of the activities are directed verbally by the teacher. Example: "Color one half of the circle." Other activities require students to follow written directions, including writing 1/2 and 1/4.

Assessment
The quality of their worksheet activities. The ease with which they completed their tasks.

 ### Right Mode—Extend

Students work with puzzles and make puzzles.

Objective
To personalize students' learning in fractions and to reinforce the concepts learned.

Activity
Puzzles are created by the teacher from magazine pictures backed by construction paper and cut into halves and fourths. Each student chooses one puzzle part; students then find matches to make their puzzles complete. Next, students are placed in cooperating groups of two or four, depending on their completed puzzle. They create two original drawings. They cut one into halves and one into fourths. Students exchange their own puzzles with each other for reassembling.

Assessment
Students' accuracy and enjoyment.

Quadrant 4—Creations

 ### Left Mode—Refine

Students plan bake sale items in halves and fourths.

Objective
To transfer students' learning of fractions into planning an individual fraction activity.

Activity
Children plan a bake sale. They cut cakes, cookies, and cupcakes (baked by the class or donated by parents) into halves and fourths to be sold. They label boxes as halves or fourths and prepare posters advertising the sale items and prices. The signs should be designed in halves or fourths.

Assessment
Enjoyment and understanding as evidenced by the accuracy of posters.

 ### Right Mode—Integrate

Students hold bake sale for school.

Objective
To give students the opportunity to share what they learned.

Activity
Children display bake sale posters and sell baked goods to other students in school.

Assessment
Participation and cooperation.

Intro. to Geometry

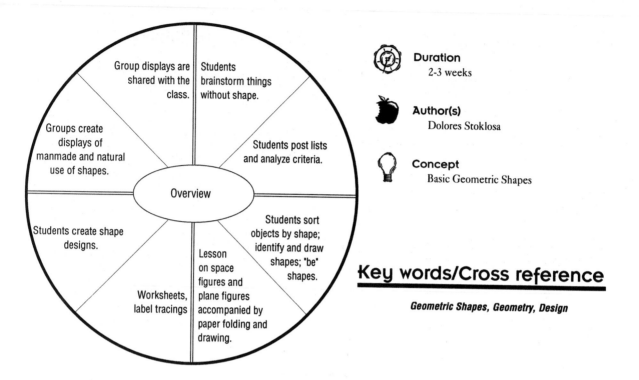

Overview

- Students brainstorm things without shape.
- Students post lists and analyze criteria.
- Students sort objects by shape; identify and draw shapes; "be" shapes.
- Lesson on space figures and plane figures accompanied by paper folding and drawing.
- Worksheets, label tracings
- Students create shape designs.
- Groups create displays of manmade and natural use of shapes.
- Group displays are shared with the class.

Duration
2-3 weeks

Author(s)
Dolores Stoklosa

Concept
Basic Geometric Shapes

Key words/Cross reference

Geometric Shapes, Geometry, Design

Overview

Objective
Students will learn to recognize and name basic geometric shapes.

About the Author
Dolores Stoklosa is a resource room teacher at Mary Fisk School in Salem, New Hampshire. She has been a classroom teacher for over fifteen years. She is a participant in the Salem 4MAT Implementation Project led by her principal, Jane Batts.

Required Resources
Geometric shaped materials for sorting activity and "mystery box" paper for students' shape-folding activity; magazines with pictures.

Bibliography
Addison Wesley Grade 3 Math, Addison Wesley Publishing, Co., Redding, MA, 1987. Carrie F. Barnett, Randall I. Charles, Robert E. Eicholz, Charles R. Fleenor, Phares G. O'Datter, Sharon Young.

Intro. to Geometry

Quadrant 1—Experience

Right Mode—Connect

Students brainstorm things without shape.

Objective

To engage students in the awareness that geometry is all around us.

Activity

Working in cooperative learning groups, students are challenged first to brainstorm examples of all things in our natural world that are not basically shaped in the form of cylinders or circles, cubes or squares, pyramids or triangles, or formed from either curved or straight connecting lines. Second they are challenged to brainstorm a list of all things made by man that do not have the same criteria.

Assessment

Participation and contribution to group activity.

Left Mode—Examine

Students post lists and analyze criteria.

Objective

To analyze the world of geometry based on their own experience.

Activity

Students post lists based on their collective brainstorming. The class as a whole decides if all items meet the set criteria. Their lists will be all liquids or gases; they will discover that all solids have a basic geometric shape or combination of shapes.

Assessment

Quality of group lists and student understanding of concept.

Quadrant 2—Concepts

Right Mode—Image

Students sort objects by shape; identify and draw shapes; "be" shapes.

Objective

To broaden student understanding of basic geometric shapes.

Activity

A. Working in small groups, students are given a set of boxes, each of which has one of the basic shapes represented on it. Given a variety of everyday objects, students will decide each item's basic shape and place it in the correct box.

B. Students will place hands inside several "mystery boxes" each of which contain an item with a basic geometric shape. Students will identify and draw, and label each shape they identify.

C. Working in small groups, students will kinesthetically "Be" each shape.

Assessment

Ability to complete each activity.

Left Mode—Define

Lesson on space figures and plane figures accompanied by paper folding and drawing.

Objective

To provide necessary information and teach new vocabulary.

Activity

Using the text, teacher will introduce space figures and plane figures. Teacher will instruct students in folding paper and drawing on graph paper to better understand concepts of space figures and plane figures.

Assessment

Teacher's verbal checking for understanding during instruction. Students' ability to recognize and define basic shapes.

Quadrant 3—Applications

 ## Left Mode—Try

Worksheets, label tracings

Objective
To provide guided practice for vocabulary and concepts presented.

Activity
A. Students complete review worksheets from the text working with space figures and plane figures.
B. Students take pictures from magazines and coloring books. They trace and label the basic shapes or combination of shapes they see for all items in the picture.
C. Students complete challenge worksheets containing designs with many overlapping shapes. Their task is to identify as many as they can.

Assessment
The quality of their worksheet activities.

 ## Right Mode—Extend

Students create shape designs.

Objective
To provide students with an opportunity to "tinker" creatively with geometric shapes.

Activity
Students will use cut-outs of basic shapes from magazines pasted on construction paper to create their own designs. Their task is to combine as many different shapes as possible while maintaining some artistic integrity.

Assessment
Quality of student projects.

Quadrant 4—Creations

 ## Left Mode—Refine

Groups create displays of manmade and natural use of shapes.

Objective
To extend what has been learned about geometric shapes.

Activity
Working in cooperative groups, each group will be assigned a specific geometric shape. The group task is to create a display of man-made and natural items which are composed of this shape. Large items may be represented by miniature models or pictures.

Assessment
Student on-task behavior and contributions to group efforts.

 ## Right Mode—Integrate

Group displays are shared with the class.

Objective
To share what has been learned.

Activity
The final group display will be shared with the class.

Assessment
Quality of group display, participation, cooperation, and delight in the learning.

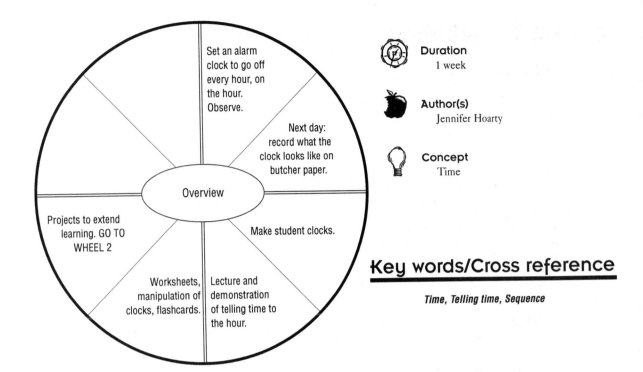

Set an alarm clock to go off every hour, on the hour. Observe.

Next day: record what the clock looks like on butcher paper.

Overview

Projects to extend learning. GO TO WHEEL 2

Make student clocks.

Worksheets, manipulation of clocks, flashcards.

Lecture and demonstration of telling time to the hour.

Duration
1 week

Author(s)
Jennifer Hoarty

Concept
Time

Key words/Cross reference

Time, Telling time, Sequence

Overview

Objective
Telling time to the hour and half-hour.

About the Author
Jennifer Hoarty graduated from University of Northern Iowa in 1989. She has taught first grade in Geneva, Nebraska for four years. She received her 4MAT training in the Masters program at Doane College taught by Sue Burch and Sue Rasmussen.

Required Resources
Alarm clocks — one with hands, one digital, butcher paper, paper plates, student clocks, TV schedule, misc. supplies for students to make posters, games, and charts.

Quadrant 1—Experience

 ## Right Mode—Connect

Set an alarm clock to go off every hour, on the hour. Observe.

Objective
To make students aware of the clock and develop an interest in its movement.

Activity
Set an alarm clock to go off every hour, on the hour. Have students notice the clock. They will begin predicting what the clock will look like the next time the alarm goes off.

Assessment
Observation of student interest, anticipation, and predictions.

 ## Left Mode—Examine

Next day: record what the clock looks like on butcher paper.

Objective
To make observations of what the clock looks like and how the hands change during the day.

Activity
The next day, have the clock go off again—today recording what the clock looks like on butcher paper. At the end of the day, have the students discuss and make observations.

Assessment
Student comments on the clock mural.

Quadrant 2—Concepts

 ## Right Mode—Image

Make student clocks.

Objective
To further student interest and knowledge of what a clock face looks like.

Activity
Students make clocks with paper plates.

Assessment
Evaluate student products.

 ## Left Mode—Define

Lecture and demonstration of telling time to the hour.

Objective
To give students information on telling time to the hour.

Activity
Lecture and demonstration on telling time to the hour.

Assessment
Observation of students, checking for understanding.

Telling Time (1 of 2)

Quadrant 3—Applications

Left Mode—Try

Worksheets, manipulation of clocks, flashcards.

Objective
To practice the concept of telling time to the hour.

Activity
Worksheets, manipulation of student clocks, flashcards.

Assessment
Accuracy of worksheets, observation of students with clocks.

Right Mode—Extend

Projects to extend learning. GO TO WHEEL 2

Objective
To extend the learning by having students apply the concept to a new situation.

Activity
1) Work with a partner to create a skit to show what you might do at certain times of the day. Use a clock in your play. 2) Make a chart showing all the things in your house use to tell time (oven timer, clock, metronome, microwave). 3) Make your own clock using materials other than 2R. 4) Make a game that will help the class practice telling time.

Assessment
Quality and accuracy of student projects.
GO TO WHEEL TWO

Telling Time (2 of 2)

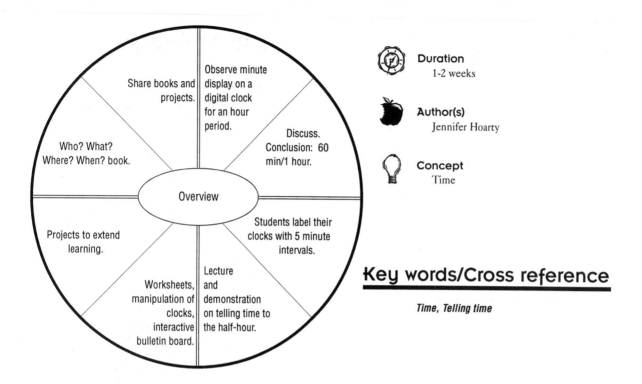

Duration
1-2 weeks

Author(s)
Jennifer Hoarty

Concept
Time

Key words/Cross reference

Time, Telling time

Overview

Objective
Telling time to the hour and half-hour.

About the Author
Jennifer Hoarty graduated from University of Northern Iowa in 1989. She has taught first grade in Geneva, Nebraska for four years. She received her 4MAT training in the Masters program at Doane College taught by Sue Burch and Sue Rasmussen.

Required Resources
Alarm clocks — one with hands, one digital, butcher paper, paper plates, student clocks, TV schedule, misc. supplies for students to make posters, games, and charts.

Quadrant 1—Experience

 ## Right Mode—Connect

Observe minute display on a digital clock for an hour period.

Objective
To further student interest in telling time.

Activity
Bring in a digital clock. At different intervals during a one hour period, have kids predict what the minute part of the clock will be.

Assessment
Observation of student interest and enthusiasm when making and checking predictions.

 ## Left Mode—Examine

Discuss. Conclusion: 60 min/1 hour.

Objective
Reflect on movement of the clock and analyze what happened.

Activity
Have a discussion about what happened. Why did the clock go back to 00 after "59"? Conclusion: 60 minutes in one hour.

Assessment
Student comments and participation in discussion.

Quadrant 2—Concepts

 ## Right Mode—Image

Students label their clocks with 5 minute intervals.

Objective
To get students to see on their clock that 60 minutes is equal to one cycle around the clock and that the 30 minutes comes at the 6 on the clock.

Activity
Students take their student clocks made from previous wheel and label the minutes by counting by 5's around the clock.

Assessment
Accuracy of student clocks now marked with 5 minute intervals.

 ## Left Mode—Define

Lecture and demonstration on telling time to the half-hour.

Objective
To give students information on telling time to the half-hour.

Activity
Lecture and discussion on telling time to the half-hour.

Assessment
Observation of students, checking for understanding.

Quadrant 3—Applications

 ### Left Mode—Try

Worksheets, manipulation of clocks, interactive bulletin board.

Objective
To practice concept of telling time to the half-hour.

Activity
Worksheets, manipulation of student clocks, interactive bulletin board, flash cards.

Assessment
Accuracy of written work and clock manipulation.

 ### Right Mode—Extend

Projects to extend learning.

Objective
To extend the learning by having students apply the concept to a new situation.

Activity
1) Create a chart showing what other classes are doing at half-hour intervals. 2) Use a TV schedule (maybe Saturday mornings) to answer questions about different programs, the times they're on, what the clock would look like, etc. 3) Students make a poster showing daily class schedule including clock faces and time when different things are done. 4) Create a game, or add to one started from the previous wheel, that will help the class practice telling time.

Assessment
Quality and accuracy of student projects.

Quadrant 4—Creations

 ### Left Mode—Refine

Who? What? Where? When? book.

Objective
To get students to apply their learning to their own lives.

Activity
Make a Who? What? Where? When? book. Students keep a record of their activities for one day.

Assessment
Accuracy and quality of student books.

 ### Right Mode—Integrate

Share books and projects.

Objective
To celebrate the students' learning to tell time.

Activity
Share books and projects with the class.

Assessment
Student enthusiasm in sharing their books and projects.

Twoness

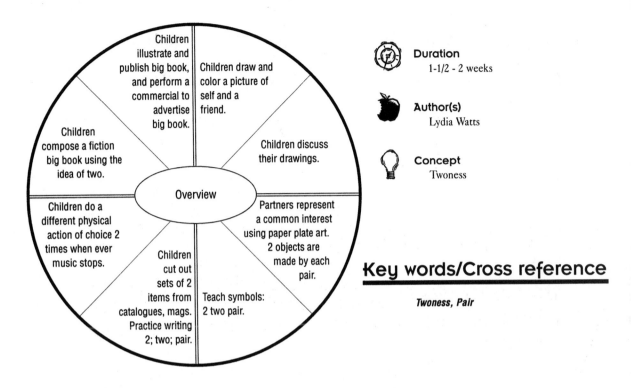

Duration
1-1/2 - 2 weeks

Author(s)
Lydia Watts

Concept
Twoness

Overview

Children illustrate and publish big book, and perform a commercial to advertise big book.

Children draw and color a picture of self and a friend.

Children compose a fiction big book using the idea of two.

Children discuss their drawings.

Children do a different physical action of choice 2 times when ever music stops.

Partners represent a common interest using paper plate art. 2 objects are made by each pair.

Children cut out sets of 2 items from catalogues, mags. Practice writing 2; two; pair.

Teach symbols: 2 two pair.

Key words/Cross reference

Twoness, Pair

Overview

Objective

The property of two consists of one and one more. Twoness can be represented in words: two; pair. Two can be represented using the numeral symbol 2.

About the Author

Lydia Watts teaches first grade at Jefferson Elementary in Kenmore, NY.

Required Resources

Book: *One, Two, One Pair!*, by Bruce McMillan, 1991, Scholastic Inc.

Bibliography

McMillan, B. (1991). *One, Two, One Pair!*, New York: Scholastic Inc.

Twoness

Quadrant 1—Experience

 ### Right Mode—Connect

Children draw and color a picture of self and a friend.

Objective

Children use personal experience to show intuitive knowledge of the property of two.

Activity

Each child draws and colors a picture of self and one friend having fun together.

Assessment

Note the number of people represented in the drawings.

 ### Left Mode—Examine

Children discuss their drawings.

Objective

To acknowledge each child's experience as important. To be aware of language children use to denote numbers.

Activity

Each child talks to a partner about the drawing. Volunteers share drawings with whole class. Post all drawings on a classroom bulletin board.

Assessment

Teacher values each drawing by comments made to children. Informally, teacher circulates and writes down language used to talk about number of people in drawings.

Quadrant 2—Concepts

 ### Right Mode—Image

Partners represent a common interest using paper plate art. 2 objects are made by each pair.

Objective

To find a common interest shared with a classmate. Each pair will use paper plate art to make 2 items representing the common interest shared.

Activity

Children work in pairs to think of an activity both enjoy. As they talk, they are to think of a single object that best represents the activity (for example, soccer/soccer ball). Each child uses art scraps to depict the object on a paper plate background.

Assessment

Each pair makes 2 objects, one on each paper plate. Post decorated paper plates on classroom bulletin board after discussion of how artwork is similar among different pairs of children.

 ### Left Mode—Define

Teach symbols: 2-two-pair.

Objective

To introduce the numeral symbol 2. To emphasize the words two and pair as ways to talk about the idea of two in number.

Activity

Teacher reads aloud the book, *One, Two, One Pair!* Post two word cards "two;" "pair" on chalkboard. Emphasize both words by pointing to posted words during reading. Write numeral 2 on chalkboard. Explain that 2 is a symbol to show two. Be clear that pair describes two in speech. Children say words as teacher points to them, and respond as teacher points to numeral.

Assessment

Attentiveness of children. Children's verbal responses.

Twoness

Quadrant 3—Applications

 ### Left Mode—Try

Children cut out sets of 2 items from catalogues, mags. Practice writing 2; two; pair.

Objective

Children distinguish sets of two. Children practice writing numeral 2 and word two.

Activity

Children cut out sets of two similar items from magazines, worksheets and/or catalogues. Children paste cutouts onto construction paper. Provide worksheets for tracing and writing the numeral 2. Children write the numeral 2 and the word two on their construction paper.

Assessment

Number of items pasted onto construction paper. Resemblance of written work to numeral 2 and word two.

 ### Right Mode—Extend

Children do a different physical action of choice 2 times when ever music stops.

Objective

More practice in internalizing the idea of two in number.

Activity

As an instrumental music tape plays, children listen. Each time the music stops, children think of and do a visible physical action twice (jump 2 times, clap twice).

Assessment

Number of physical motions made.

Quadrant 4—Creations

 ### Left Mode—Refine

Children compose a fiction big book using the idea of two.

Objective

To compose words for a class big book.

Activity

Children compose a fiction big book using the idea of two in a major way in the story. The teacher scripts.

Assessment

Each child contributes ideas as co-authors.

 ### Right Mode—Integrate

Children illustrate and publish big book, and perform a commercial to advertise big book.

Objective

To illustrate and publish the big book. To create a commercial to persuade others to read the book.

Activity

Children decide on page breaks, then illustrate each page, front and back covers. Volunteers compose and perform commercial. Teacher scripts. Children read completed book to parents, others in school.

Assessment

Each child contributes as illustrator, reader, or actor.

Corn Harvest

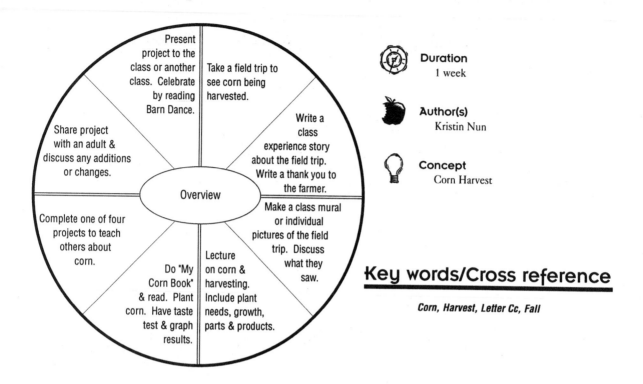

Present project to the class or another class. Celebrate by reading Barn Dance.

Take a field trip to see corn being harvested.

Write a class experience story about the field trip. Write a thank you to the farmer.

Share project with an adult & discuss any additions or changes.

Overview

Make a class mural or individual pictures of the field trip. Discuss what they saw.

Complete one of four projects to teach others about corn.

Do "My Corn Book" & read. Plant corn. Have taste test & graph results.

Lecture on corn & harvesting. Include plant needs, growth, parts & products.

Duration
1 week

Author(s)
Kristin Nun

Concept
Corn Harvest

Key words/Cross reference

Corn, Harvest, Letter Cc, Fall

Overview

Objective
This is a primary unit to develop the concept of corn harvest as one of the fall changes that we see. It also emphasizes the letter "Cc".

About the Author
Kristin Nun is a kindergarten teacher in Geneva, Nebraska.

Required Resources
The Letter Person, Mr. Cotton Candy C, by Alpha-time is optional, a chart with "Little Boy Blue" on it, "My Corn Book" booklets, seed corn, corn products and various art supplies.

Bibliography
The books *Corn is Maize* by Aliki and *Barn Dance* by Bill Martin, Jr. and John Archambault. The song, "Corner Grocery Store" by Raffi.

Corn Harvest

Quadrant 1—Experience

Right Mode—Connect

Take a field trip to see corn being harvested.

Objective

To connect with previous farm and food experiences and to create an experience with corn harvesting.

Activity

Sing "Corner Grocery Store" by Raffi. Recite "Little Boy Blue" and act out. Draw out field trip. Take a field trip to see corn being harvested.

Assessment

Participation in song & rhyme. Level of interest and questions asked during field trip.

Left Mode—Examine

Write a class experience story about the field trip. Write a "thank you" note to the farmer.

Objective

To use the written word to recall what was learned on the field trip and introduce the letter "Cc".

Activity

Write a class experience story about the field trip and practice choral reading. Have students find and mark "Cc's" in the story. Write a class "thank you" note to the farmer.

Assessment

The level of participation and quality of input for story. Student interest.

Quadrant 2—Concepts

Right Mode—Image

Make a class mural or individual pictures of the field trip. Discuss what they saw.

Objective

To reflect on the field trip personally and further develop an awareness of the use of the letter/sound "Cc".

Activity

Make a class mural or individual pictures of the field trip. Discuss what they saw. Note "Cc" words as mentioned in discussion.

Assessment

The level of student participation, quality of product and interest in discussion.

Left Mode—Define

Lecture on corn & harvesting. Include plant needs, growth, parts & products.

Objective

To develop the concept of corn harvesting, plant parts, growth and products, as well as developing the concept of the letter "Cc".

Activity

Lecture on corn harvest. Include plant needs, growth, parts and samples of products made from corn. Read *Corn is Maize* by Aliki. On a second day, introduce *The Letter Person, Mr. Cotton Candy C.* Let students describe him. Discuss the sound a "Cc" makes. Show how to make that letter using a hand sign. Demonstrate how to write "Cc's". Have students make "Cc'ks" with their bodies.

Assessment

Participation in discussion, attentiveness and accuracy of responses.

Corn Harvest

Quadrant 3—Applications

 ### Left Mode—Try

Do "My Corn Book" & read. Plant corn. Have taste test & graph results.

Objective

To practice using the information received about corn and the letter "Cc".

Activity

Complete "My Corn Book" & read. This is about corn parts and plant needs. Plant corn seeds. Participate in a corn product taste test & graph results. On a second day, write "Cc" words on a large corn plant and practice writing "Cc's" as a group on palms, floor, chalkboards, etc.

Assessment

The quality of student work and participation.

 ### Right Mode—Extend

Complete one of four projects to teach others about corn.

Objective

To extend and practice what has been learned about corn in a self-chosen project.

Activity

Complete 1 of 4 projects to teach others about corn: 1) Work in groups to write a song about corn harvest or make a poster about corn parts & products. 2) Write a report about the importance of corn using pictures, own writing or dictation. 3) Survey another class to find out their favorite corn products & report results. 4) Create a corn field/harvest scene in the classroom including as many components as possible. Also, practice writing "Cc's" at the writing center during the week.

Assessment

The level of participation and interest in project chosen.

Quadrant 4—Creations

 ### Left Mode—Refine

Share project with an adult & discuss any additions or changes.

Objective

To evaluate one's work by sharing with others.

Activity

Share project with an adult and discuss any additions or changes.

Assessment

Student's ability to help evaluate their work and willingness to make needed additions or changes.

 ### Right Mode—Integrate

Present project to the class or another class. Celebrate by reading Barn Dance.

Objective

To share what was learned with others at school.

Activity

Present project to the class or another class. Celebrate what has been learned by reading *Barn Dance* by Bill Martin, Jr. and John Archambault and making a classroom scarecrow for the corn field.

Assessment

Interest in sharing and quality of ideas shared. Attentiveness.

Eggs

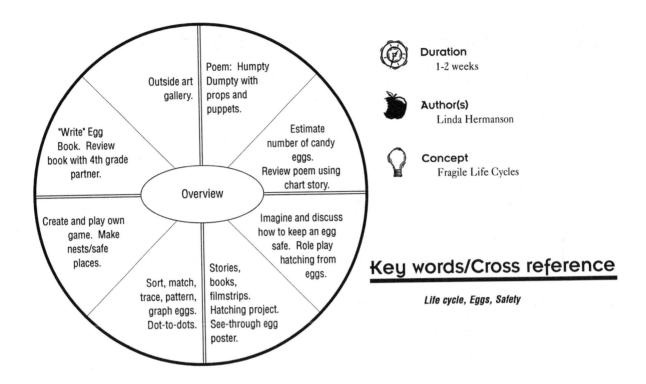

Outside art gallery.

Poem: Humpty Dumpty with props and puppets.

"Write" Egg Book. Review book with 4th grade partner.

Estimate number of candy eggs. Review poem using chart story.

Overview

Create and play own game. Make nests/safe places.

Imagine and discuss how to keep an egg safe. Role play hatching from eggs.

Sort, match, trace, pattern, graph eggs. Dot-to-dots.

Stories, books, filmstrips. Hatching project. See-through egg poster.

Duration
1-2 weeks

Author(s)
Linda Hermanson

Concept
Fragile Life Cycles

Key words/Cross reference

Life cycle, Eggs, Safety

Overview

Objective
Eggs are laid by many animals; they need to be safe; there are many kinds of eggs.

About the Author
Linda Hermanson has been a Kindergarten teacher for 25 years. Her family lives in Minnesota and she teaches in Wisconsin.

Required Resources
Assorted books, audio-visual materials, assorted Kindergarten classroom equipment and supplies, an incubator set-up.

Quadrant 1—Experience

Right Mode—Connect

Poem: Humpty Dumpty with props and puppets.

Objective

To introduce egg unit; to assess knowledge of the nursery rhyme Humpty Dumpty.

Activity

Exploration of room, decorations, books; class shares the poem Humpty Dumpty with props and individual finger puppets.

Assessment

Does child know and say poem? Does child show enthusiasm and excitement?

Left Mode—Examine

Estimate number of candy eggs.
Review poem using chart story.

Objective

To estimate and write estimation; to retell poem with props; to break and examine fresh eggs; to write broken-egg observations in class log book.

Activity

Estimate number of candy eggs and write estimations; review Humpty Dumpty using chart story; decorate blown out eggs to look like Humpty Dumpty; retell Humpty Dumpty using their own Humptys and examine broken shells (save shells); break fresh eggs, examine, and "write" observations in class log; make scrambled eggs using recipe chart.

Assessment

Does child appear confident in estimating? Can child retell the poem? Does child "write" own observation?

Quadrant 2—Concepts

Right Mode—Image

Imagine and discuss how to keep an egg safe. Role play hatching from eggs.

Objective

To encourage children to visualize; to work cooperatively in groups to problem-solve; to pretend.

Activity

Wearing egg headbands, children imagine and discuss in pairs how they would keep an egg from hatching; children pretend they are hatching from eggs.

Assessment

Does child work well with partner? Does child show knowledge of hatching process?

Left Mode—Define

Stories, books, filmstrips. Hatching project. See-through egg poster.

Objective

To teach these concepts: 1) eggs are places for new life, 2) birds and some animals come from eggs, 3) some eggs are protected by shells, 4) eggs need to be safe, 5) the baby from the egg will be the same animal as the mother, 6) eggs can be food, 7) a dozen equals twelve.

Activity

Reading of fiction and non-fiction books, viewing of films and filmstrips, observing chick-hatching project, discussion of photos, posters and charts.

Assessment

Does child attend to and contribute to discussions?

Eggs

Quadrant 3—Applications

 ### Left Mode—Try

Sort, match, trace, pattern, graph eggs. Dot-to-dots.

Objective
To use readiness skills to explore information about eggs; to work cooperatively.

Activity
Sort, match, trace, pattern, and graph eggs; number and alphabet dot-to-dots; number, fill (with that number of objects), and sequence take-apart plastic eggs to make a dozen; learn the poem "5 Baby Chicks" from chart; keep records on hatching project; sequence themselves (with help) according to candy egg estimation cards; count candy eggs by 10's and 1's; "read" sidewalk chalk recipe with 4th grade partner/make chalk.

Assessment
Does child participate in the self-selected activities, working carefully? Does child interact with older partner?

 ### Right Mode—Extend

Create and play own game. Make nests/safe places.

Objective
To work cooperatively; to use unit information to create projects.

Activity
Create and play own game using nests, tongs, markers, spinners, dice, generic game board; make nests or safe places in small groups around the room; decorate oval-shaped paper using various media; draw any egg and its nest environment with older partner.

Assessment
Does child work well with classmate? Can small group plan and play their game? Does child use unit information to complete activities?

Quadrant 4—Creations

 ### Left Mode—Refine

"Write" Egg Book. Review book with 4th grade partner.

Objective
To use unit information to "write" own book; to work with older partner; to review chalk drawing, if necessary; to edit their egg book.

Activity
Write "egg book" in writing center using unit information; child/partner team edit egg book; teams also revise/change the chalk drawing plan and then draw pictures outside.

Assessment
Does child put thoughts into written form? Does Kndg./4th grade team work together to complete the project?

 ### Right Mode—Integrate

Outside art gallery.

Objective
To share projects with others.

Activity
Outdoor art gallery for classmates and parents.

Assessment
Does child show pride in her/his work?

Fall Trees

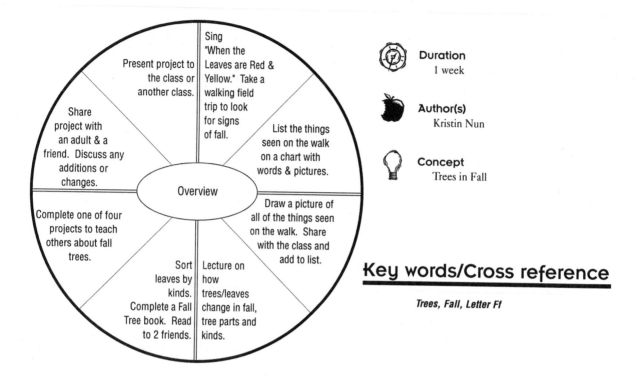

Present project to the class or another class.

Sing "When the Leaves are Red & Yellow." Take a walking field trip to look for signs of fall.

Share project with an adult & a friend. Discuss any additions or changes.

List the things seen on the walk on a chart with words & pictures.

Overview

Complete one of four projects to teach others about fall trees.

Draw a picture of all of the things seen on the walk. Share with the class and add to list.

Sort leaves by kinds. Complete a Fall Tree book. Read to 2 friends.

Lecture on how trees/leaves change in fall, tree parts and kinds.

Duration
1 week

Author(s)
Kristin Nun

Concept
Trees in Fall

Key words/Cross reference

Trees, Fall, Letter Ff

Overview

Objective
This is a primary unit to develop the concept of fall trees as one of the fall changes we see. It also emphasizes the letter "Ff".

About the Author
Kristin Nun is a kindergarten teacher in Geneva, Nebraska.

Required Resources
The Letter Person, Mr. Feet F, by Alpha-time is optional, a variety of leaves, "Fall Tree Book" booklets including tree parts and fall tree colors, and various art supplies.

Bibliography
The books *Red Leaf, Yellow Leaf* by Lois Ehlert, *It Could Still Be A Tree* by Allan Fowler, *Changing Seasons* by Rose Greydanus, *How Leaves Change* by Sylvia A. Johnson and *The Leaf Book* by Anne Orange.

Fall Trees

Quadrant 1—Experience

 ### Right Mode—Connect

Sing "When the Leaves are Red & Yellow." Take a walking field trip to look for signs of fall.

Objective

To connect with previous experiences with trees and create an experience with fall changes.

Activity

Sing "When the Leaves are Red & Yellow." Read *Changing Seasons* by Rose Greydanus and discuss fall changes. Draw out walking field trip. Take a walking field trip to look for signs of fall. Gather leaves or other signs of fall that are found on the ground. Take pictures.

Assessment

Participation in song and interest in book. Attentiveness and questions asked during field trip.

 ### Left Mode—Examine

List the things seen on the walk on a chart with words & pictures.

Objective

To use the written word to recall what was seen on the walk and introduce the letter "Ff".

Activity

List the things seen on the walk on a chart with words & pictures. Have students find and mark "Ff's" on the list.

Assessment

The level of participation during brainstorming and quality of responses.

Quadrant 2—Concepts

 ### Right Mode—Image

Draw a picture of all of the things seen on the walk. Share with the class and add to list.

Objective

To reflect personally on what was seen on the walk and further develop an awareness of the letter/sound "Ff".

Activity

Draw individual pictures of all of the things seen on the walk. Share with the class and add any new items to the list. Note "Ff" words as mentioned in discussion.

Assessment

The level of student participation, quality of product and interest in discussion.

 ### Left Mode—Define

Lecture on how trees/leaves change in fall, tree parts and kinds.

Objective

To develop the concept of trees and how they change in fall, as well as developing the concept of the letter "Ff".

Activity

Lecture on how trees/leaves change in fall, tree parts and kinds. Read such books as *Red Leaf, Yellow Leaf* by Lois Ehlert, *It Could Still Be A Tree* by Allan Fowler and parts of *How Leaves Change* by Sylvia A. Johnson and *The Leaf Book* by Anne Orange. On a second day, introduce Letter Person, Mr. Funny Feet F. Let students describe him. Discuss the sound an "Ff" makes. Show how to make that letter using a hand sign. Demonstrate how to write "Ff's". Have students make "Ff"s" with their bodies.

Assessment

Attentiveness and accuracy of responses. Participation in discussion.

Quadrant 3—Applications

Left Mode—Try

Sort leaves by kinds. Complete a Fall Tree book. Read to 2 friends.

Objective

To practice using the information received about fall trees and the letter "Ff".

Activity

Sort leaves by kinds individually or in small groups. Complete a Fall Tree Book including parts of trees and colors of fall leaves. Read it to two friends. On a second day, write "Ff" words on a large fall tree and practice writing "Ff's" as a group on palms, floor, chalkboards, etc.

Assessment

The quality of student work and participation.

Right Mode—Extend

Complete one of four projects to teach others about fall trees.

Objective

To extend and practice what has been learned about fall trees in a self-chosen project.

Activity

Complete one of four projects to teach others about fall trees: 1) Work in groups to make a book about tree types using leaf rubbings, tracings, etc. 2) Write a report about fall trees using pictures, own writing or dictation. 3) Make a diagram of a fall tree, its parts and colors. 4) Create a fall tree display in the classroom. Also, practice writing "Ff's" at the writing center during the week.

Assessment

The level of participation and level of interest in chosen project.

Quadrant 4—Creations

Left Mode—Refine

Share project with an adult & a friend. Discuss any additions or changes.

Objective

To evaluate one's work by sharing with others.

Activity

Share project with an adult and a friend. Discuss any possible additions or changes.

Assessment

Student's ability to help evaluate their work and the work of others and willingness to make needed additions or changes.

Right Mode—Integrate

Present project to the class or another class.

Life Cycle of a Butterfly

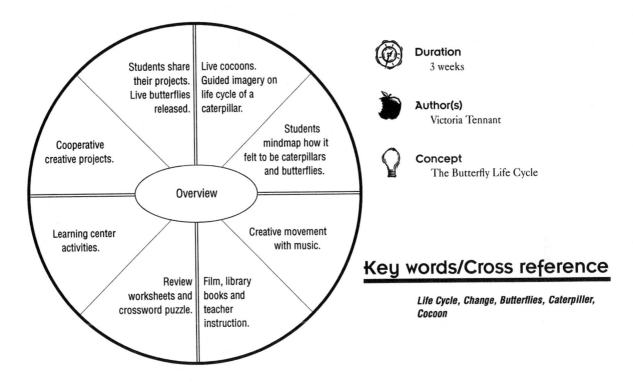

Students share their projects. Live butterflies released.

Live cocoons. Guided imagery on life cycle of a caterpillar.

Cooperative creative projects.

Students mindmap how it felt to be caterpillars and butterflies.

Overview

Learning center activities.

Creative movement with music.

Review worksheets and crossword puzzle.

Film, library books and teacher instruction.

Duration
3 weeks

Author(s)
Victoria Tennant

Concept
The Butterfly Life Cycle

Key words/Cross reference

Life Cycle, Change, Butterflies, Caterpiller, Cocoon

Overview

Objective
Using a variety of modalities, students will learn the stages of development of butterflies.

About the Author
Victoria Tennant is an educational consultant and president of Victoria Tennant Associates. In addition, she has eight years experience as a primary level classroom teacher. She lives in Olympia, WA, and is a certified 4MAT System trainer.

Required Resources
Live cocoons; teacher-prepared guided fantasy of butterfly life cycle; variety of colored scarves and music for students' movement exercise; appropriate film on butterfly life cycles; rice, green paper "leaves," glue, egg cartons, felt tip pens, yarn, paper and other art supplies for butterfly pictures

Bibliography
Carle, Eric. *The Very Hungry Caterpillar.* New York: Philomel Books, Division of Putnam Publishing Group, 1969.
Stevenson, James. Monty. New York: Greenwillow, division of William Morrow & Co., Inc., 1979.
Cocoons for Painted Lady butterflies are available from:
Insect Lore Products, Inc.
P.O. Box 1535
Shafter, CA 93263
1-800-LIVE-BUG

Life Cycle of a Butterfly

Quadrant 1—Experience

 ### Right Mode—Connect

Live cocoons. Guided imagery on life cycle of a caterpillar.

Objective

To create an experience enabling children to imagine the life of a caterpillar.

Activity

At the beginning of this unit, bring in cocoons to hatch for students' observation. (Hatching time is about 3 weeks.) Have the children close their eyes and imagine they are a caterpillar. Conduct a guided imagery that leads them through its life cycle.

Assessment

Enjoyment and engagement of students.

 ### Left Mode—Examine

Students mindmap how it felt to be caterpillars and butterflies.

Objective

To enable students to analyze their feelings while "being" a caterpillar.

Activity

Teacher-led discussion with accompanying mindmap of children's reactions to how it felt to be a caterpillar outside and inside the cocoon and how it felt to be a butterfly. Ask each student to share which phase they liked best and graph student responses. Discuss feelings about changes.

Assessment

Student contributions to the group and individual responses.

Quadrant 2—Concepts

 ### Right Mode—Image

Creative movement with music.

Objective

To deepen students' awareness and understanding of the butterfly life cycle.

Activity

Teacher reads *The Very Hungry Caterpillar*, by Eric Carle. Teacher leads students through a creative movement exercise with colored scarves and music (Pachelbel Canon in D works well here). Students act out being caterpillars with lights on, being in the cocoon with lights out, and emerging as butterflies with lights on again.

Assessment

Student participation in the activity and whether or not their movements "make sense."

 ### Left Mode—Define

Film, library books and teacher instruction.

Objective

To teach the specific stages and attributes of the butterfly life cycle.

Activity

Students view a film on the cycle of a butterfly. Students check out library books on the subject of caterpillars and butterflies. Teacher provides important information and key vocabulary words.

Assessment

Teacher verbally checks for understanding during instruction.

Quadrant 3—Applications

 ### Left Mode—Try

Review worksheets and crossword puzzle.

Objective

To provide guided practice for life cycle stages and vocabulary.

Activity

Students complete review worksheets sequencing the butterfly life cycle and reinforcing the vocabulary words through a crossword puzzle and matching activity.

Assessment

The quality of their worksheet activities.

 ### Right Mode—Extend

Learning center activities.

Objective

To further expand and reinforce student understanding of life cycle concepts.

Activity

Students participate in the following sequenced learning center activities designed to reinforce each life cycle phase:

1. Create caterpillar eggs from rice glued onto green construction paper leaves.
2. Select a picture of a caterpillar from a book. Reproduce it using egg carton pieces and felt-tipped pen.
3. Create a cocoon from 2 egg carton cups wrapped with yarn.
4. Make the butterfly which emerges from that cocoon. Copy its picture from the book and draw an outline of its wings and body. Design its wing patterns with chalk and outline it with a thin line of Elmer's glue. Let dry thoroughly. Color with oil pastels. Cut out finished butterfly.
5. Display butterflies on large bulletin board and/or hang from ceiling.

Assessment

Quality of student projects.

Quadrant 4—Creations

 ### Left Mode—Refine

Cooperative creative projects.

Objective

To review and synthesize all previous lessons.

Activity

Assign students to cooperative learning groups. Each group plans how they will complete one of the following:

1. Write a factual book which will be donated to the school library.
2. Demonstrate the life cycle of a butterfly through a skit presented to another class.
3. Create and perform a puppet show portraying the butterfly life cycle.

Assessment

Enjoyment and understanding as evidenced by the accuracy of student projects.

 ### Right Mode—Integrate

Students share their projects. Live butterflies released.

Objective

To give students an opportunity to share what they learned.

Activity

Children either share their book with others, or perform skits and puppet shows. Invite another class to view the now-hatched live butterflies. Release butterflies outside. Read Monty, by James Stevenson, a story of the life cycle of a butterfly that is a metaphor for our own life changes.

Assessment

Participation, cooperation, and delight in the learning.

Magnetism

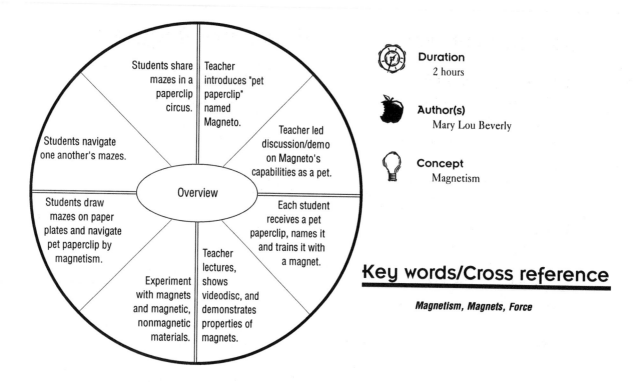

Duration
2 hours

Author(s)
Mary Lou Beverly

Concept
Magnetism

Key words/Cross reference

Magnetism, Magnets, Force

Overview

Objective
To develop an understanding of the properties of magnets.

About the Author
Mary Lou Beverly is a teacher of K-2 gifted resource students at Webster Elementary Model Technology School, St. Augustine, FL.

Required Resources
Paper clips and string, magnets, paper plates.

Bibliography
M.I.S.T. videodisc series.

Magnetism

Quadrant 1—Experience

 ### Right Mode—Connect

Teacher introduces "pet paper clip" named Magneto.

Objective
To encourage students' interest and imagination.

Activity
Teacher walks around room, pulling a paper clip on a string. When a child asks about it, the teacher explains that this is her pet paper clip named Magneto.

Assessment
Engagement and enjoyment of the experience.

 ### Left Mode—Examine

Teacher led discussion/demo on Magneto's capabilities as a pet.

Objective
To reflect on the possibilities of having a magnetic substance for a pet.

Activity
The teacher explains the many advantages of having a paper clip for a pet, as opposed to a dog, cat or hamster. She then mentions that Magneto is also capable of many tricks, especially when he is around a magnet. She demonstrates Magneto's tricks by bringing a magnet close by him when the paper clip is lying on top of a table.

Assessment
Student involvement in the demo/introduction.

Quadrant 2—Concepts

 ### Right Mode—Image

Each student receives a pet paper clip, names it and trains it with a magnet.

Objective
To personally engage the student in his own experience with a magnet.

Activity
Each student receives his own pet paper clip complete with "leash," names it, and "trains" it to do tricks with a magnet.

Assessment
Student participation and enjoyment of the experience.

 ### Left Mode—Define

Teacher lectures, shows videodisc, and demonstrates properties of magnets.

Objective
To teach the properties of magnets.

Activity
Teacher lectures and demonstrates magnetic properties. Showing of videodisc such as M.I.S.T.: Magnetism and discussion.

Assessment
Teacher makes verbal checks to ensure student understanding.

Quadrant 3—Applications

 ## Left Mode—Try

Experiment with magnets and magnetic, nonmagnetic materials.

Objective
To reinforce understanding of magnetic properties.

Activity
Students experiment with magnets and magnetic/non-magnetic materials.

Assessment
Accuracy of conclusions drawn from experiments.

 ## Right Mode—Extend

Students draw mazes on paper plates and navigate pet paper clip by magnetism.

Objective
To extend what has been learned.

Activity
Students draw mazes on a paper plate and have pet paper clips navigate the maze while being guided by a magnet underneath.

Assessment
Completion of maze and its navigation.

Quadrant 4—Creations

 ## Left Mode—Refine

Students navigate one another's mazes.

Objective
To evaluate one another's mazes.

Activity
Students will navigate at least two other students' mazes, using the pet paper clips.

Assessment
Completion of navigation.

 ## Right Mode—Integrate

Students share mazes in a paper clip circus.

Objective
To share what has been learned.

Activity
Students will put on a "Paper Clip Circus" for other, younger class, to demonstrate amazing properties of magnets.

Assessment
Completion of presentation and participation in presentation.

Natural Selection

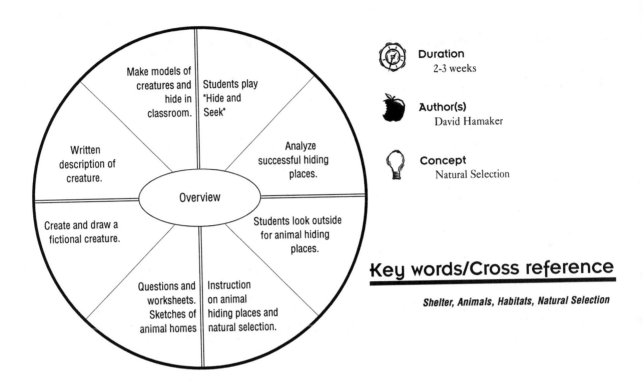

Duration
2-3 weeks

Author(s)
David Hamaker

Concept
Natural Selection

Key words/Cross reference

Shelter, Animals, Habitats, Natural Selection

Overview

Objective
Students will learn the characteristics of animal habitats.

About the Author
David Hamaker teaches fourth grade at Riverview Elementary School, Marion Community Schools, Marion, IN. He has been a classroom teacher for seven years. He is a participant in the Marion 4MAT Implementation Project led by Carol Secttor.

Required Resources
Illustrations for direct instruction; drawing materials and sculpture materials for student projects.

Quadrant 1—Experience

 ## Right Mode—Connect

Students play "Hide and Seek"

Objective

To create an experience which will lead students to an understanding of what they know instinctively about good hiding places.

Activity

Students play "Hide and Seek" either indoors or outdoors. Students are selected to "find" hidden students.

Assessment

Students active involvement and enjoyment of the game.

 ## Left Mode—Examine

Analyze successful hiding places.

Objective

To analyze the game in regard to elements of successful hiding places.

Activity

Students work in small groups to answer the following questions:
1. Why were students found last more successful in hiding than the others?
2. What makes a good hiding place?
3. What are common features of good hiding places?
4. How are these features important and beneficial to animals seeking shelter?

Assessment

Teacher observation of individual student contributions to small group effort.
Quality of group reports.

Quadrant 2—Concepts

 ## Right Mode—Image

Students look outside for animal hiding places.

Objective

To see the connection between what the students know and how animals instinctively apply the same criteria for survival.

Activity

Students go outside and work in small teams. Each team will use what they know about good hiding places to find spots which would be good hiding places for specific creatures, including insects, as well as larger animals such as squirrels, rabbits, and other larger animals.

Assessment

Student participation and observation.

 ## Left Mode—Define

Instruction on animal hiding places and natural selection.

Objective

To teach how animal hiding places contribute to the process of natural selection.

Activity

Teacher provides information and illustrations on the necessary concepts, including introduction of necessary vocabulary. Students read appropriate textbook chapter(s).

Assessment

Verbal checking for understanding during instruction.

Natural Selection

Quadrant 3—Applications

 Left Mode—Try

Questions and worksheets. Sketches of animal homes.

Objective
To provide guided practice on the concept of natural selection and new vocabulary.

Activity
Students will answer questions from the textbook and complete teacher prepared worksheets. Students will go home and find animal hiding places in their own yards. They will make a list of what they find and sketch their findings. They will have an opportunity to share their findings with the rest of the class.

Assessment
Quality of students' written work. Quality of reported findings to the class.

 Right Mode—Extend

Create and draw a fictional creature.

Objective
To extend what has been learned.

Activity
Students are to create a drawing of a fictional creature which can be easily hidden in the classroom. The drawing should represent a "life-size" model of the creature.

Assessment
Student enthusiasm for project.

Quadrant 4—Creations

 Left Mode—Refine

Written description of creature.

Objective
To expand fictional creature project and use what was learned about natural selection.

Activity
Students will develop written descriptions of their creatures. The description should include the creature's name, size, shape, color, special features, etc. Students will work in groups of four to predict how successful each group member's creature would be hiding in the classroom environment.

Assessment
Quality of written descriptions and contributions to other members of the group.

 Right Mode—Integrate

Make models of creatures and hide in classroom.

Objective
To evaluate and test what was learned.

Activity
Students will create paper models of their creatures. Have them hide their creatures in the classroom while members of the class try to find them. Discuss why or why not each creature was easy or difficult to find. Then hide the creatures and try again. Finally, invite another class in to try to find the hidden creatures.

Assessment
Student participation and enthusiasm.

Our Environment

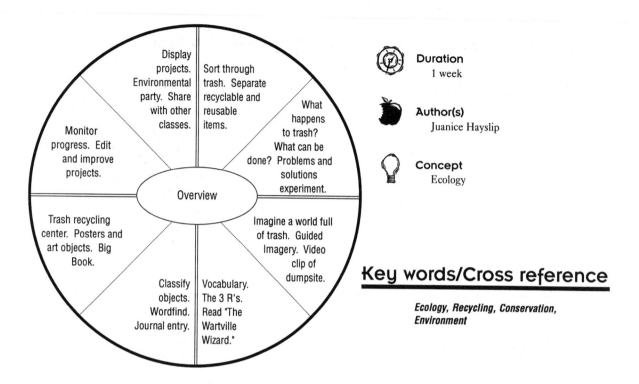

Monitor progress. Edit and improve projects.

Display projects. Environmental party. Share with other classes.

Sort through trash. Separate recyclable and reusable items.

What happens to trash? What can be done? Problems and solutions experiment.

Overview

Trash recycling center. Posters and art objects. Big Book.

Classify objects. Wordfind. Journal entry.

Vocabulary. The 3 R's. Read "The Wartville Wizard."

Imagine a world full of trash. Guided Imagery. Video clip of dumpsite.

Duration
1 week

Author(s)
Juanice Hayslip

Concept
Ecology

Key words/Cross reference

Ecology, Recycling, Conservation, Environment

Overview

Objective
To make first-graders aware of the importance of recycling, reusing, and reducing trash. To help them realize how it affects their future and what they can do to make the world a better place.

About the Author
At the time this plan was first published, Juanice Hayslip was a first grade teacher at El Jardin Elementary School, Brownsville, TX. She is now an elementary teacher in Irving, TX. She is a certified 4MAT trainer.

Required Resources
Assorted trash such as empty boxes, containers, aluminum cans, paper, newspaper, plastic items, etc. Any visuals such as newspaper clippings that relate to the environment. Four containers with garden soil. (I used 3-liter plastic soft-drink containers.)

Bibliography
"The Wartville Wizard" by Don Madden. *"Save The Animals, Save The Earth"* a musical cassette. Any other literature or magazines that can be found that relate to the environment. Thematic unit "Our Environment" and "Ecology." (CTCM)

Our Environment

Quadrant 1—Experience

 ### Right Mode—Connect

Sort through trash. Separate recyclable and reusable items.

Objective
Children will realize how trash affects their lives.

Activity
Collect the trash in the classroom for a couple of days before beginning the unit. Dump the trash in the floor and have the students (in small groups) sort through it and decide what may be used again and what may be recycled. Let the children come up with innovative ideas on how the trash can be reused (box puppets, box cars, etc.).

Assessment
Degree of engagement of children.

 ### Left Mode—Examine

What happens to trash? What can be done? Problems and solutions experiment.

Objective
To have children reflect on their experience with trash. Develop listening skills and group discussion techniques. Use all senses to describe trash.

Activity
Whole group discussion about how trash looks, smells, and feels. Where does trash go? What happens to it? What can we do about the amount of trash? Have several containers with moist garden soil. Bury different items such as aluminum foil, plastic, paper and food scraps. This is an experiment to see what is bio-degradable. Check results at the end of the unit.

Assessment
Participation in discussion.

Quadrant 2—Concepts

 ### Right Mode—Image

Imagine a world full of trash. Guided Imagery. Video clip of dumpsite.

Objective
Integrate material being taught by using music and another medium.

Activity
The teacher will take the students on a guided imagery trip to the beach (or any other popular locale). Have the students close their eyes and listen to soft music in the background as they use their imaginations. After building up their excitement in spending a day at the beach, they arrive but there is a "Closed" sign at the entrance. Imagine what the world would look like if we keep throwing our trash everywhere. Where would they play? What would happen to the beaches? Show a clip of "Letters to the Earth" video or any other video that depicts the shortage and problems of dump sites.

Assessment
Children's engagement in activity.

 ### Left Mode—Define

Vocabulary. The 3 R's. Read "The Wartville Wizard."

Objective
Teach students how they can make a difference in their environment. Introduce vocabulary.

Activity
Lecture using flashcards. Give examples using actual trash. Trace the path of a piece of trash. Where does it go? Make a flow chart. Vocabulary: recycle, reuse, reduce. Read *"The Wartville Wizard"* and discuss the story.

Assessment
Student feedback. Oral questions.

Quadrant 3—Applications

 ## Left Mode—Try

Classify objects. Wordfind. Journal entry.

Objective
Practice what has been learned.

Activity
Classify objects as to how they can be recycled and reused by making a list using the trash from the activity in 1R. Give examples. Wordfind using vocabulary. Draw and color the recycle symbol. Journal entry: "What I can do for the Earth."

Assessment
Quality of work and correct examples given for vocabulary.

 ## Right Mode—Extend

Trash recycling center. Posters and art objects. Big Book.

Objective
To create, using what has been learned.

Activity
Students create art objects using trash such as a paper mache globe, environmental glasses using egg cartons and a litter bug using small pieces of trash. Be creative and invent things. (Refer to the ideas given in 1R.) Write books retelling the story of the *"Wartville Wizard."* Make posters to promote the 3R's. Set up a recycling center in the room.

Assessment
Quality of effort put into project and degree of student enthusiasm in developing their ideas.

Quadrant 4—Creations

 ## Left Mode—Refine

Monitor progress. Edit and improve projects.

Objective
To teach children to refine and edit each others work in a positive way.

Activity
In small groups, students will revise their books, improve their art objects and polish up their posters. They will help each other in coming up with the best results possible.

Assessment
Degree of cooperation and ability to accept criticism to improve projects.

 ## Right Mode—Integrate

Display projects. Environmental party. Share with other classes.

Objective
To share completed projects and be able to explain what has been learned. To be able to integrate into their lives.

Activity
Display art and posters. Read books to a kindergarten class. Have an Earth Day celebration in April or make Earth Day any day. Have healthy snacks, tropical fruit juice, etc. Go home and share with their families what they have learned about their environment and the responsibility each person has to help save the Earth.

Assessment
Quality of completed projects and enthusiasm in presentation.

Sunshine and Shadows

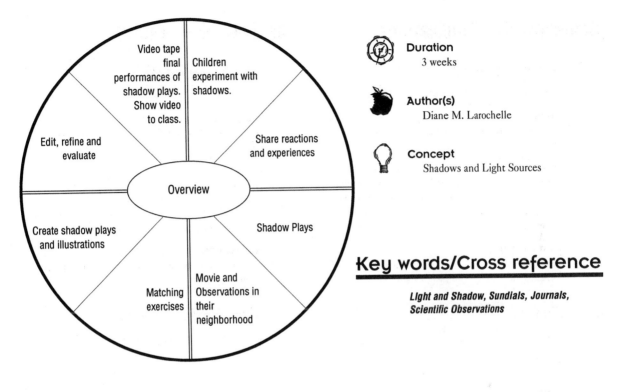

Video tape final performances of shadow plays. Show video to class.

Children experiment with shadows.

Edit, refine and evaluate

Share reactions and experiences

Overview

Create shadow plays and illustrations

Shadow Plays

Matching exercises

Movie and Observations in their neighborhood

Duration
3 weeks

Author(s)
Diane M. Larochelle

Concept
Shadows and Light Sources

Key words/Cross reference

Light and Shadow, Sundials, Journals, Scientific Observations

Overview

Objective
Students will learn the characteristics of how light produces shadows.

About the Author
Diane M. Larochelle is an elementary teacher at Pierce School, Brookline Public Schools, Brookline, MA. She is a participant in the Brookline 4MAT Implementation Project led by Nona Bock and Bob Bates.

Required Resources
Film projector for shadow exploration; other portable light sources and art paper; sundials for display and examination.

Bibliography
Delta Science Modules on Sunshine, Shadows, Seasons, and Sky.

Sunshine and Shadows

Quadrant 1—Experience

 ### Right Mode—Connect

Children experiment with shadows.

Objective
To have the children experiment with light sources and discover their own observations about shadows.

Activity
Using a light source (film projector works best), allow the children to experiment making their own shadows. Allow for ample time for each child to be able to freely explore the light source as well as the results of their bodies interacting with the light source.

Assessment
Observe the children and their responses to use in next activity.

 ### Left Mode—Examine

Share reactions and experiences.

Objective
To accumulate and share the children's responses and discoveries during the initial exploratory activity.

Activity
Make an information chart about what the children discovered during their explorations. Ask the children how they felt about making the shadows. Ask the children how shadows make them feel.

Assessment
Keep the information chart displayed around the room so children can add on to it as the unit progresses.

Quadrant 2—Concepts

 ### Right Mode—Image

Shadow Plays.

Objective
To have the children experience what it would be like to be a shadow and to introduce them to the experience of shadows being related to themselves.

Activity
Have the students pair. One child will be the leader and the other child will be the shadow. The children take turns leading their respective shadows around the room.

Assessment
Observe the children in each of their roles and watch how they enact how the shadow would act.

 ### Left Mode—Define

Movie and Observations in their neighborhood.

Objective
To deliver information to the children about how shadows are made and how they are formed by interactions between an object and a light source.

Activity
a) Have the children bring their science journals outside and have them observe neighborhood shadows and the objects that form them.

b) Watch a film on shadows.

c) Introduce the concepts of sundials and the way they work.

Observe how the children arrange light sources to make and draw their own shadows. Assess drawings to be sure they include the light source, the object, and the shadow.

Assessment
Student engagement and demonstration of understanding of the concept.

Sunshine and Shadows

Quadrant 3—Applications

 ### Left Mode—Try

Matching exercises.

Objective

To reinforce information given in the second quadrant activities. To give more practice to children in making shadows.

Activity

a) Using worksheets with shadows and objects, children practice matching shadows to the correct object which makes them.

b) Using portable light sources, have the children trace their own hand shadows with a partner. Cut the shadows out and make a class collage.

c) Using flashlights, have children explore how to make different types of shadows. Have them challenge each other to create certain shadows.

Assessment

Again, teacher observation is the best way to assess that children are in fact understanding how objects and lights interact to make shadows.

 ### Right Mode—Extend

Create shadow plays and illustrations.

Objective

To allow the children to use information gathered in a creative expression.

Activity

Have the children select or create their shadow play to perform. Select or create a shadow play to perform in front of the class. Children should plan to illustrate something that they have learned about shadows and use techniques they learned on how to make the shadows they need in their play.

Assessment

Make sure each group has chosen a play and is using skills learned in class instruction to produce shadows for their plays.

Quadrant 4—Creations

 ### Left Mode—Refine

Edit, refine and evaluate.

Objective

To get the children to assess if their shadows are being created in the way they want them to be portrayed in their play.

Activity

Allow time for each child or group to rehearse their play. Make a time to meet with each group and decide how their play is going to work, whether or not they have the right materials, and what changes they need to make before their final performance.

Assessment

Conferences with children or groups.

 ### Right Mode—Integrate

Video tape final performances of shadow plays. Show video to class.

Objective

To allow the children an opportunity to express the new information they have learned about shadows in a creative and fun way.

Activity

Video tape final performances of shadow plays. Show video to class.

Assessment

Student assessment and feedback.

Whales

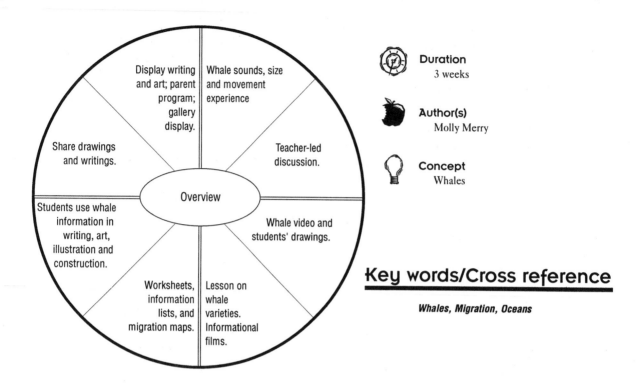

Display writing and art; parent program; gallery display.

Whale sounds, size and movement experience

Share drawings and writings.

Teacher-led discussion.

Overview

Students use whale information in writing, art, illustration and construction.

Whale video and students' drawings.

Worksheets, information lists, and migration maps.

Lesson on whale varieties. Informational films.

 Duration
3 weeks

 Author(s)
Molly Merry

Concept
Whales

Key words/Cross reference

Whales, Migration, Oceans

Overview

 Objective
This unit uses whales as a vehicle for interdisciplinary instruction.

 About the Author
Molly Merry is a classroom teacher in School District Fremont RE 1, Canon City, CO. In over fifteen years teaching experience she has developed particular expertise at integrating fine arts activities into the fabric of her content area instruction. Molly is the 4MAT Implementation Leader for her school district.

Required Resources
Cassette tape of whale voices; 15 foot marker for comparison of size; variety of illustrations of whales; materials for whale bulletin board; art materials for projects.

Bibliography
Lewis, Paul. *Davy's Dream*. Hillsboro, OR 97123, Beyond Words Publishing, Inc.

Watson, Jane. W*hales, Friendly Dolphins and Mighty Giants of the Sea*. Racine, WI 53404, Golden Books, Western Publishing Co., Inc.

The three films in this lesson plan are available from The National Geographic Society, telephone 1-800-368-2728.

Whales

Quadrant 1—Experience

 ### Right Mode—Connect

Whale sounds, size and movement experience.

Objective
To create an experience to connect students to whales through physical concept of size, auditory sounds, and guided imagery. Only in the fourth activity are the children told specifically that they are learning about whales.

Activity
1. Students relax while lying on floor on their backs, breathing up as whales do from blow holes. The teacher has them imagine how it would feel to float like this while they listen to a cassette tape of whale voices. The teacher does not tell them what the sounds are.
2. Students compare their body size to a 15 foot tape on the floor (representing a humpback whale fin).
3. Students compare themselves standing, lying down, stretching to a 100 foot length on the playground. Students guess what things, living and non-living, might be this size. A small car is parked at the end of the 100 feet to represent the tongue of a blue whale.
4. Using information gathered from available resources, the teacher tells whale stories from a whale's point of view, creating a visual, emotional experience for the children. There are numerous excellent children's literature selections available.

Assessment
Participation, involvement, curiosity, active comparing, active listening, and contribution to the group.

 ### Left Mode—Examine

Teacher-led discussion.

Objective
To discuss reactions to sounds and feelings and to participate in discussion of stories.

Activity
1. Teacher leads discussion of whale sounds, listing possible sources for the sounds.
2. Students discuss the size comparisons and react to the experience with the humpback fin and the 100 foot blue whale.

3. Teacher leads discussion of stories, and students who have visited marine aquariums are invited to share their experiences with live whales.

Assessment
Level of participation and willingness to share ideas.

Quadrant 2—Concepts

 ### Right Mode—Image

Whale video and students' drawings.

Objective
To see whale movement, size, and environment.

Activity
Students imagine they are whales as they watch the National Geographic video, "Portrait of a Whale." This video has little talking with great visuals in close-up and slow motion. The teacher leads a discussion focusing on the close-up photography and feelings of size and power. The children are encouraged to wonder how the photographer got so close to the whales, how s/he felt during the filming, and whether or not the photographer was in danger. The children each create a whale picture.

Assessment
Attentiveness to film; quality of illustration.

 ### Left Mode—Define

Lesson on whale varieties. Informational films.

Objective
To introduce new vocabulary and specific information about whales.

Activity
Using photographs and drawings, teacher presents information about whale varieties. Students compare and contrast the following kinds of whales: humpback, blue, right, gray, sperm and orca. Students view National Geographic films "Magnificent Monsters of the Deep" and "Great Whales."

Assessment
Teacher verbally checking for understanding during instruction.

Quadrant 3—Applications

 ## Left Mode—Try

Worksheets, information lists, and migration maps.

Objective
To use information learned about whales to create a whale folder.

Activity
1. Teacher-prepared worksheets.
2. Information lists created from whale lesson classifying each type as to height, weight, migration, distinguishing appearance and behavior, population status, and history with man.
3. Migration maps.

Assessment
Neatness, completeness, organization, ability to follow directions.

Right Mode—Extend

Students use whale information in writing, art, illustration and construction.

Objective
To use whale information in creative writing, art, illustration, and construction.

Activity
1. Illustrate whales to accompany information in folder.
2. Students may choose one written activity: a personal poem; an acrostic poem; a letter to a whale; a letter to their state senator in favor of whale protection.
3. Participate in a class construction of a 25 foot baby blue whale on the hallway bulletin board.
4. Create whale art for display: prints, crayon resist, paper weaving of ocean with sculpted whales; kaleidoscopes.

Assessment
Completion, level of interest, expression of ideas and feelings, application of knowledge.

Quadrant 4—Creations

 ## Left Mode—Refine

Share drawings and writings.

Objective
To evaluate the activities completed in Quadrant Three Right Mode with a focus on praising the inclusion of significant details, not to discourage children about creativity in drawing.

Activity
Critique whale drawings, with an eye for detail. Share writings with a partner, evaluating information and expression of feelings. Label baby blue whale parts and dimensions. Critique art projects for process and representation of whales.

Assessment
Level of participation; attentiveness and sensitivity to partner; application of knowledge.

 ## Right Mode—Integrate

Display writing and art; parent program; gallery display.

Objective
To share what has been learned with other students, parents, and the community at large.

Activity
1. Art and writings are displayed in the hallway.
2. Students present a parent program, reading poems and letters and introducing parents to the blue whale sculpture.
3. Whale art is displayed at the Joan Robey gallery in Denver as part of a show to raise money for the Children's Museum.

Assessment
Student participation and enthusiasm.

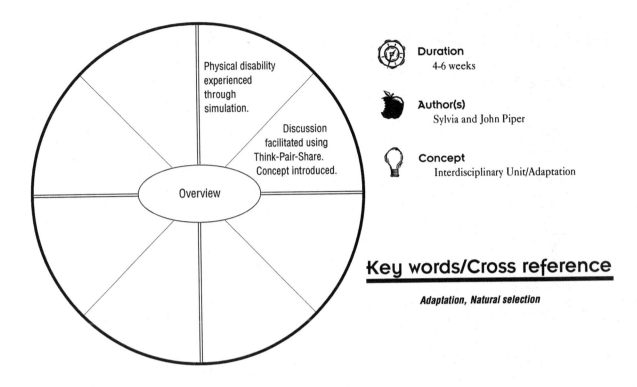

Physical disability experienced through simulation.

Discussion facilitated using Think-Pair-Share. Concept introduced.

Overview

Duration
4-6 weeks

Author(s)
Sylvia and John Piper

Concept
Interdisciplinary Unit/Adaptation

Key words/Cross reference

Adaptation, Natural selection

Overview

Objective
1) Students will learn that adaptations are structural or behavioral responses to the environment. 2) Students will begin to understand how particular adaptations relate to important skills and behaviors, and ultimately to survival.

About the Author
Sylvia Piper is Coordinator of Gifted Education for the Wood County Office of Education, Bowling Green, OH, a position she has held for thirteen years. She has an additional eight years of teaching experience at the elementary and secondary levels. John Piper is Associate Professor of Health Education at Bowling Green State University, Bowling Green, OH. He has over thirty years of teaching, coaching, and administrative experience at the secondary and collegiate levels. John also works as a consultant to educational and business groups throughout the country. Both Sylvia and John are members of the Excel Consultants Group.

Required Resources
1) Materials and equipment necessary for simulating handicapping conditions. 2) Directions for conducting Think-Pair-Share.

Bibliography
Bouchard, Lois. *The Boy Who Wouldn't Talk*. New York: Doubleday, 1969.

English, Jennifer. *My Mommy's Special*. Chicago: Childrens Press, 1985.

Fassler, Joan. *Howie Helps Himself*. Chicago: Albert Whitman & Company, 1975.

Heide, Florence Parry. *Sound of Sunshine, Sound of Rain*. New York: Parents' Magazine Press, 1970.

Hunter, Edith Fisher. *Child of the Silent Night*. Geneva, IL, 1963.

Lasker, Joe. *He's My Brother*. Chicago: A. Whitman & Company, 1974.

Litchfield, Ada B. *A Cane in Her Hand*. Chicago: Albert Whitman & Company, 1977.

Mack, Nancy. *Tracy*. Milwaukee: Raintree Publishers, Ltd., 1976.

MacLachlan, Patricia. *Through Grandpa's Eyes*. New York: Harper & Row, 1979.

Rounds, Glen. *The Blind Colt*. New York: Holiday House, Inc., 1941.

White, Paul. *Janet at School*. New York: Thomas Y. Crowell Company, Inc., 1978.

Wolf, Bernard. *Don't Feel Sorry for Paul*. Philadelphia: J.V. Lippincott Company, 1974.

Quadrant 1—Experience

 ## Right Mode—Connect

Physical disability experienced through simulation.

Objective

1) Students will participate in an experience that will require them to adapt their behavior in order to meet their physical needs. 2) Students will begin to understand that the more appropriate the response behavior, the more successful they will be in adjusting to their handicap.

Activity

Half of the students in the class will be placed in physically handicapping conditions for a predetermined period of time. Examples might include: 1) fingers and thumb of favored hand or both hands taped together, 2) preferred arm placed in a sling, 3) crutches, 4) one shoe built up making one leg shorter than the other, 5) blindfolded, 6) mouth taped shut, 7) ear plugs, 8) wheelchair. Each student is assigned a "buddy" to assist as needed during the activities of the day. Following the experience, students will spend several minutes writing down their feelings about the experience and listing the adjustments they had to make in their behavior. The roles are then reversed; however, be certain a student's handicapping condition is not the same one for which he/she was a buddy earlier and do not match the same buddies together.

Assessment
Participation.

 ## Left Mode—Examine

Discussion facilitated using Think-Pair-Share. Concept introduced.

Objective

1) Students will utilize the cooperative learning strategy, Think-Pair-Share. 2) Students will discuss their feelings and behaviors following the "physical disability" simulation. 3) Students will be introduced to the concept of adaptation.

Activity

Use the cooperative learning strategy Think-Pair-Share to give students an opportunity to discuss their feelings and behaviors as a handicapped person and as one who assisted a handicapped person. Have each pair select one or two major changes or adjustments they had to make which they will share with the entire class. During the sharing portion, the teacher uses a T-chart to categorize these changes or adjustments under "Feelings" or "Behaviors." Through this activity and discussion, the teacher introduces students to the concept of adaptation. Students might be encouraged to read trade books dealing with handicapping conditions to learn more about the feelings and behaviors of these people and how they adapt to their condition.

Assessment
Participation. Quality of discussion. Understanding of concept. Ability to work in pairs.

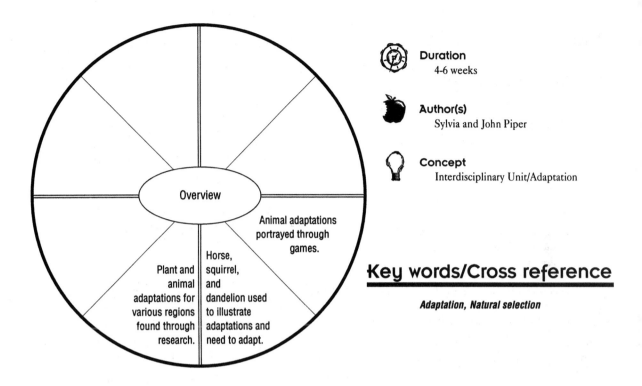

Overview

Animal adaptations portrayed through games.

Horse, squirrel, and dandelion used to illustrate adaptations and need to adapt.

Plant and animal adaptations for various regions found through research.

Duration
4-6 weeks

Author(s)
Sylvia and John Piper

Concept
Interdisciplinary Unit/Adaptation

Key words/Cross reference

Adaptation, Natural selection

Overview

Objective
1) Students will learn that plants and animals exhibit many adaptations. 2) Students will learn how particular physical adaptations relate to important skills and behaviors, and ultimately to survival.

About the Author
Sylvia Piper is Coordinator of Gifted Education for the Wood County Office of Education, Bowling Green, OH, a position she has held for thirteen years. She has an additional eight years of teaching experience at the elementary and secondary levels. John Piper is Associate Professor of Health Education at Bowling Green State University, Bowling Green, OH. He has over thirty years of teaching, coaching, and administrative experience at the secondary and collegiate levels. John also works as a consultant to educational and business groups throughout the country. Both Sylvia and John are members of the Excel Consultants Group.

Required Resources
1) Directions for games — see Abruscato & Harlow resources. 2) Historical background on horses — see Storer Camps resource. 3) A variety of classroom and library resources which will enable students to find adaptations among plants and animals living in various regions of the world. (See bibliography for examples.)

Bibliography
Abruscato, Joe, and Jack Hassard. *The Whole Cosmos Catalog of Science Activities.* Glenview, IL: Good Year Books, 1991.
Ardley, Neil. *The Science Book of Things That Grow.* New York: Harcourt Brace Jovanovich, Publishers, 1991.
Bailey, Jill. *Mimicry and Camouflage.* New York: Facts on File, Inc., 1988.
Braus, Judy (ed.). *Ranger Rick's Naturescope: Discovering Deserts.* Washington, D.C.: National Wildlife Federation, 1989.

Braus, Judy (ed.). *Ranger Rick's Naturescope: Incredible Insects.* Washington, D.C.: National Wildlife Federation, 1989.

Harlow, Rosie, and Gareth Morgan. *175 Amazing Nature Experiments.* New York: Random House, 1991.

Hickman, Pamela M. *Birdwise.* Reading, MA: Addison-Wesley Publishing Company, Inc., 1991.

Hickman, Pamela M. *Bugwise.* Reading, MA: Addison-Wesley Publishing Company, Inc., 1991.

Lingelbach, Jenepher (ed.). *Hands-on Nature: Information and Activities for Exploring the Environment With Children.* Woodstock, VT: Vermont Institute of Natural Science, 1986.

Penny, Malcolm. *The Animal Kingdom: Animal Evolution.* New York: The Bookwright Press, 1987.

Perdue, Peggy K., and Diane A. Vaszily. *City Science.* Glenview, IL: Good Year Books, 1991.

Plant World (The). Chicago: World Book, Inc., 1984.

Russell, Helen Ross. *Ten-Minute Field Trips: A Teacher's Guide to Using The School Grounds for Environmental Studies.* Washington, D.C.: National Science Teachers Association, 1990.

Secrets of Animal Survival. Washington, D.C.: The National Geography Society, 1983.

Sisson, Edith A. *Nature With Children of All Ages.* New York: Prentice Hall Press, 1982.

Storer Camps. *Nature's Classroom: A Program Guide for Camps and Schools.* Martinsville, IN: American Camping Association, 1988.

Tanner, Odgen. *Animal Defenses.* New York: Time-Life Films, Inc., 1978.

Tolman, Marvin N., and James O. Morton. *Life Science Activities For Grades 2–8.* New York: Parker Publishing Company, Inc., 1986.

VanCleave, Janice. *Biology for Every Kid: 101 Easy Experiments that Really Work.* New York: John Wiley & Sons, Inc., 1990.

Whitfield, Philip. *Can the Whales Be Saved?* New York: Viking Kestrel, 1989.

Quadrant 2—Concepts

 ## Right Mode—Image

Animal adaptations portrayed through games.

Objective

1) Students will connect the concept of adaptation with animals. 2) Students will deepen their understanding of adaptation.

Activity

One or both games can be used to illustrate ways in which animals adapt to their environment.

Game 1: Different Beaks. One person becomes a swallow with a thin, pointed beak (paper clip with one end unwound). Another person becomes a sparrow with a thicker beak (clip clothespin). The foods available in a feeder (bowl) are seeds (nuts) and soft creatures (raisins). Allow 20 seconds for the "birds" to use their "beaks" to "feed" and store the food in front of them. Discuss activity. Develop the idea that both birds can find plenty to eat when insects are plentiful (summer), but the swallow must make some kind of adaptation as winter approaches (migration).

Game 2: Predator and Prey. Dye at least 200 toothpicks red and 200 green, or cut red and green pipe cleaners into one-half inch pieces. Randomly distribute equal numbers of each color in a green vegetation area and in a brown dirt area of about the same size. The toothpicks represent insect prey, while students represent insect predators. Give the predators 30 seconds to collect as many prey as possible in the green area. Use a tally card to record the number of green and red prey collected. Repeat this 30-second collection procedure until all the prey are gone. Use this same 30-second collection procedure in the brown dirt area. Discuss the activity. Compare the number of times needed to collect all of the prey in each area. Compare the number of each color collected each time in each area. Develop the idea that some animals are adapted to protecting themselves by resembling their natural surroundings (camouflage). Note: colorblindness would be a handcapping condition in this activity.

Assessment

Participation and enjoyment of activity. Ability to connect the concept of adaptation with animals.

Left Mode—Define

Horse, squirrel, and dandelion used to illustrate adaptations and need to adapt.

Objective

1) Students will learn various adaptations of plants and animals. 2) Students will learn conditions which make it necessary for plants and animals to adapt.

Activity

Students will examine conditions that require certain adaptations if a plant or animal is to survive — climate, habitat, food supply, natural enemies. Study will concentrate on the physical features of the squirrel, horse, and dandelion which contribute to their survival. A variety of media will be used to present the material: film, video, books, illustrations, observation of live examples, etc.

Students discuss the habits and nature of squirrels and are led to understand how squirrels' teeth, coloration, paws, eyes, and tail are adaptations that contribute to their survival.

Teacher provides historical background which acquaints students with the fact that horses have changed over millions of years as a response to their environment and predators. (Discussion on how horses changed may help students understand the concepts of survival of the fittest, natural selection, and evolution.) Students brainstorm ideas which explain physical adaptations of the horse — tall ears that move easily from side to side and back and forth; large, wide eyes set on side of head; large, very sensitive nostrils; long, muscular neck; long tail; hard hoof; and other adaptations students might mention. Teacher helps students clarify ideas and understand how various physical adaptations aid horses in survival.

Students discuss why dandelions are considered a nuisance to most lawn keepers. Have the students relate these negative characteristics to the dandelion's adaptation for survival. Study of the adaptations of dandelions can lead to studies of other plants and their particular adaptations for living in their own type of habitat.

Assessment

Understanding of the content and concept. Ability to connect the concept of adaptation with plants as well as animals.

Quadrant 3—Applications

Left Mode—Try

Plant and animal adaptations for various regions found through research.

Objective

1) Students will reinforce content and concept through directed practice. 2) Students will engage in research. 3) Student will become aware of the importance of documenting information.

Activity

A large bulletin board will be made into a matrix with some or all of the following headings: Polar Regions, Deserts, Rain Forests, Savannas/Grasslands, Woodlands/Forests, Mountains, Oceans/Rivers, and Islands. From a variety of resources available in the classroom or school library, students employ research skills to find examples of adaptations that permit plants and animals to survive in these environments. Students should be encouraged to look for some plants and animals and adaptations that are not well known. Students prepare a notecard for one plant or animal in each of the regions represented. The notecard names the plant or animal and explains the adaptation on the front. The title and author of the resource is placed on the back. (Assignment will vary for different levels of ability.) Students confer with the teacher before placing a notecard in the proper place on the matrix. The class is divided into groups and assigned the task of organizing the information from one of the regions in a meaningful way. Each group shares its organizational pattern and the information about plant and animal adaptations in the region.

Assessment

Quality of work. Understanding of concept and content. Ability to work in groups.

Adaptation 3/5

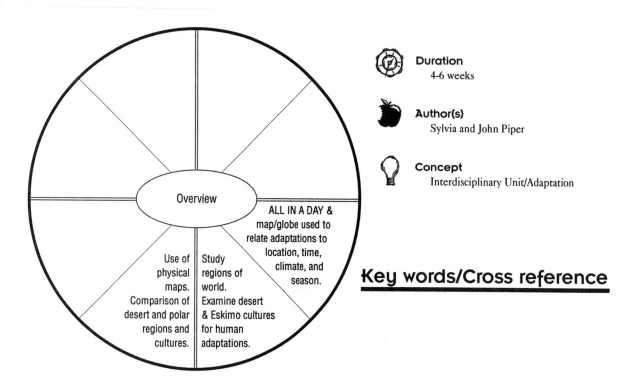

Duration
4-6 weeks

Author(s)
Sylvia and John Piper

Concept
Interdisciplinary Unit/Adaptation

Key words/Cross reference

Overview

Objective

1) Students will understand that humans adapt to their environment. 2) Students will learn that human adaptations for survival help shape cultures. 3) Students will learn that changes in environment often require humans to make new adaptations.

About the Author

Sylvia Piper is Coordinator of Gifted Education for the Wood County Office of Education, Bowling Green, Ohio, a position she has held for thirteen years. She has an additional eight years of teaching experience at the elementary and secondary levels. John Piper is Associate Professor of Health Education at Bowling Green State University, Bowling Green, Ohio. He has over thirty years of teaching, coaching, and administrative experience at the secondary and collegiate levels. John also works as a consultant to educational and business groups throughout the country. Both Sylvia and John are members of the Excel Consultants Group.

Required Resources

1) *All In One Day* by Mitsumasa Anno. 2) *Eskimo Boy: Life In An Inupiaq Eskimo Village* by Russ Kendall. 3) *Sahara: Vanishing Cultures* by Jan Reynolds. (Other titles with similar information may be used in place of *Eskimo Boy* and *Sahara*.)

Bibliography

Anno, Mitsumasa. *All In One Day*. New York: Philomel Books, 1986.
Carratello, John and Patty. *Maps, Charts, Graphs, and Diagrams*. Huntington Beach, CA: Teacher Created Materials, Inc., 1990.
Fredericks, Anthony D. *Social Studies Through Children's Literature: An Integrated Approach*. Englewood, CO: Teacher Ideas Press, 1991.
Hoven-Severson, Leigh. *Connecting Geography and Literature*. Huntington Beach, CA: Teacher Created Materials, 1992.
Hoyt-Goldsmith, Diane. *Arctic Hunter*. New York: Holiday House, 1992.

Jenness, Aylette, and Alice Rivers. *In Two Worlds: A Yup'ik Eskimo Family*. Boston: Houghton Mifflin Company, 1986.

Kendall, Russ. *Eskimo Boy: Life In An inupiaq* Eskimo Village. New York: Scholastic Inc., 1982.

McCarthy, Kevin. *Saudi Arabia: A Desert Kingdom*. Minneapolis: Dillon Press, Inc., 1986.

Reynolds, Jan. *Sahara: Vanishing Cultures*. New York: Harcourt Brace Jovanovich, Publishers, 1991.

Rushdoony, Haig A. *Exploring Our World With MAps: Map Skills for Grades K–6*. Carthage, IL: Fearon Teacher Aids, 1988.

Quadrant 2—Concepts

Right Mode—Image

All In A Day & map/globe used to relate adaptations to location, time, climate, and season.

Objective

1) Students will connect the concept of human adaptation with location on the earth, time zones, climate, and seasons. 2) Students will use map skills to locate countries in different time zones.

Activity

Read *All In One Day* to the students to let them study the illustrations. Flag the countries named in the book on a world map and/or globe. Tell students to use the words of the text and, more importantly, to compare the illustrations to decide what they know or can infer about the countries and the people who live there on this New Year's Day. Create a list of characteristics for each of the eight countries. Lead students to an awareness of how the activities and adaptations of children around the world at the same moment in time are affected by their location on the earth, by time zones, climate, and seasons.

Assessment

Participation and enjoyment of a unique book. Ability to infer information from illustrations. Ability to connect the concept of adaptation with human beings.

Left Mode—Define

Study regions of world. Examine desert & Eskimo cultures for human adaptations.

Objective

1) Students will develop an awareness of regions of the world through the introduction of physical maps.
2) Students will learn about two contrasting regions of the world — desert and polar regions.

Activity

Explain that there are many ways to study our world. One way is to divide the world into regions based on physical features. Brainstorm physical features and land formations of the world. Physical maps (relief, symbols, colored, shaded) and transparencies of maps can be used to teach students how to recognize and locate land formations and regions. Begin with the basics (mountains, plateaus, hills, plains, islands, oceans/rivers) and move to polar regions, deserts, rain forests, savannas/grasslands, woodlands/forests. Ideas to be developed include: 1) Regions vary in size — islands, deserts. 2) Some countries are made up of many different regions — United States, Africa. 3) Some regions are not countries — North Pole, oceans. (Swing to Step 5 to practice map skills before continuing in Step 4.)

Use the book *Sahara: Vanishing Cultures* and its illustrations to study a desert region and its people. Develop an understanding of the culture of the nomadic Tuareg of the desert and the physical characteristics of the desert. Have students point out the adaptions people have made in order to survive in this hot, dry desert region. Study should emphasize major points which will permit students to compare and contrast this region and the life of the Tuareg nomads with other regions and their people.

Use the book *Eskimo Boy: Life In A Inupiaq Eskimo Village* and its illustrations to study a contrasting region of the world and its people. Create an understanding of the culture of the Inupiaq Eskimo and the physical features of the Alaskan polar region. Have students point out adaptions the Eskimos have made in order to survive in the cold polar regions.

Assessment

Understanding of concept and content. Quality of thinking and listening skills. Ability to use maps.

Adaptation 3/5

Quadrant 3—Applications

 ## Left Mode—Try

Use of physical maps. Comparison of desert and polar regions and cultures.

Objective
1) Students will reinforce content and concept through directed practice.
2) Students will compare and contrast information.

Activity
A variety of activities should be used to provide practice using physical and relief maps: 1) Locate various regions on physical maps. 2) Make physical maps using symbols, colors, shading. (Move back to Step 4 before continuing with step 5.) Arrange the students in pairs to compare cultures. Provide a matrix with three headings: Manda/desert; Norman/polar; and students in the pair/local region. List a number of items to be compared down the left side. Examples might include: climate, land features, food, drinking water, transportation, houses, clothing, animals, celebrations, adaptations, feelings. Students may wish to add some items of their own choosing. Each pair completes its matrix and later uses it to make contributions to a class matrix developed to show collectively what facts have been learned.

Lead a discussion using questions designed to require students to use their knowledge as a basis for some complex thinking. Examples: 1) Is the Eskimo culture or Tuareg culture more like your culture? What reasons do you have for your answer? 2) In what ways has Manda's culture and Norman's culture changed since their fathers were young boys? Which culture has changed more? 3) What do you think is happening to cultures which were formed thousands of years ago? How do you feel about this? 4) Are children from different cultures more alike or more different from one another? What reasons do you have for your answer?

Assessment
Quality of work. Understanding of concept and content. Ability to think at complex levels. Ability to work in pairs.

Adaptation 4/5

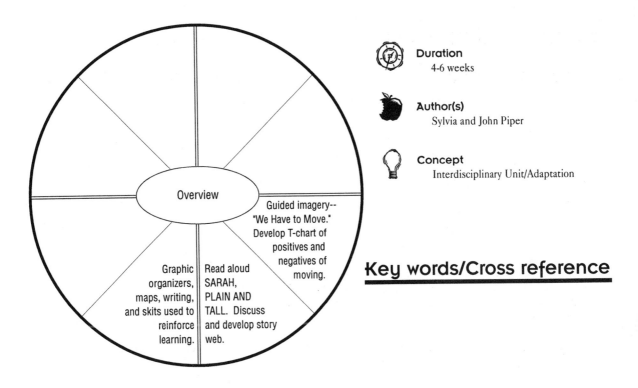

Duration
4-6 weeks

Author(s)
Sylvia and John Piper

Concept
Interdisciplinary Unit/Adaptation

Key words/Cross reference

Center of wheel: Overview

Guided imagery--"We Have to Move." Develop T-chart of positives and negatives of moving.

Read aloud SARAH, PLAIN AND TALL. Discuss and develop story web.

Graphic organizers, maps, writing, and skits used to reinforce learning.

Overview

Objective
1) Students will learn that family members must make adaptations. 2) Students will learn that adaptations made by family members can strengthen the relationships amongst its members.

About the Author
Sylvia Piper is Coordinator of Gifted Education for the Wood County Office of Education, Bowling Green, Ohio, a position she has held for thirteen years. She has an additional eight years of teaching experience at the elementary and secondary levels. John Piper is Associate Professor of Health Education at Bowling Green State University, Bowling Green, Ohio. He has over thirty years of teaching, coaching, and administrative experience at the secondary and collegiate levels. John also works as a consultant to educational and business groups throughout the country. Both Sylvia and John are members of the Excel Consultants Group.

Required Resources
1) *Sarah, Plain and Tall*, by Patricia MacLachlan.
2) Teacher-developed guided imagery, "We Have to Move"—see Bagley resource for ways to develop a guided imagery. 3) Graphic organizers—see Bellanca resource.

Bibliography
Bagley, Michael T., and Karin K. Hess. *200 Ways of Using Imagery in the Classroom.* Monroe, NY: Trillium Press, 1987.
Bellanca, James. *The Cooperative Think Tank Graphic Organizers to Teach Thinking in the Cooperative Classroom.* Palatine, IL: Skylight Publishing, 1990.
Brittenum, Mollie. *Literature Notes/Sarah, Plain and Tall.* Palos Verdes Estates, CA: Frank Schaffer Publications, Inc., 1992.
Cochran, Judith. *Insights to Literature.* Nashville: Incentive Publications, Inc., 1990.
MacLachlan, Patricia. *Sarah, Plain and Tall.* New York: Harper & Row, Publishers, 1985.
Montgomery, Janice, and Candace Taff Carr. *Inside Stories, Book 1: Study Guides for Children's Literature, Grades 3–4.* San Luis Obispo, CA: Dandy Lion Publications, 1988.
Carratello, Patty. *Literature and Critical Thinking, Book 4.* Huntington Beach, CA: Teacher Created Materials, 1988.

Quadrant 2—Concepts

 ## Right Mode—Image

Guided imagery— "We Have to Move." Develop T-chart of positives and negatives of moving.

Objective

1) Students will connect the concept of adaptation with moving to a new community. 2) Students will deepen their understanding of adaptation.

Activity

Students will be taken through a teacher-developed guided imagery in which dad or mom changes jobs and the family has to move to a new community. Focus should be on the adaptation members of the family, especially your students, will have to make. Following the guided imagery, have the students develop a T-chart listing the positive and negative things about moving.

Assessment

Participation. Ability to connect the concept of adaptation with moving to a new community.

Left Mode—Define

Read aloud Sarah, Plain and Tall. *Discuss and develop story web.*

Objective

1) Students will develop their understanding of story structure. 2) Students will use critical thinking skills. 3) Students will employ listening skills. 4) Students will identify and analyze adaptations in the story.

Activity

Students will listen as the teacher reads aloud *Sarah, Plain and Tall.* A teacher-directed discussion using open-ended questions will require students to use critical thinking skills to analyze the story, making connections between the story and the concept of adaptation when appropriate. Development of a group story web will aid students in their understanding of story structure—setting, characters, plot, theme, conflict, and solution.

Assessment

Understanding of concept and content. Quality of thinking and listening skills.

Quadrant 3—Applications

 ## Left Mode—Try

Graphic organizers, maps, writing, and skits used to reinforce learning.

Objective

1) Students will reinforce content and concept through directed-practice.
2) Students will utilize graphic organizers in their practice.

Activity

A variety of activities will provide practice to strengthen students' understanding of the knowledge and skills presented. Examples include: 1) Using a Venn diagram to compare Maggie and Sarah. 2) Mapping Sarah's trip from Maine to one of the prairie states. 3) Making a list of words that could be used to describe the characters of Caleb, Anna, Papa, and Sarah, then creating a matrix to show characteristics they have in common. 4) Selecting two things Sarah did in the story and explaining how each shows that she is not mild-mannered.
5) Identifying examples of personification in the story and creating several original examples. 6) Adapting a story event, such as Jacob teaching Sarah to drive the wagon, into a skit.

Assessment

Quality of practice. Understanding of concept and content.

Adaptation 5/5

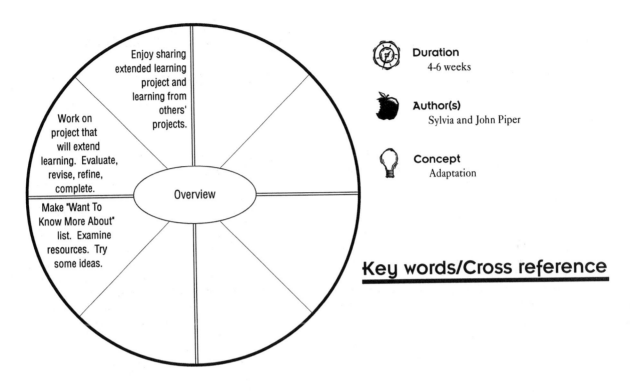

Enjoy sharing
extended learning
project and
learning from
others'
projects.

Work on
project that
will extend
learning. Evaluate,
revise, refine,
complete.

Make "Want To
Know More About"
list. Examine
resources. Try
some ideas.

Overview

Duration
4-6 weeks

Author(s)
Sylvia and John Piper

Concept
Adaptation

Key words/Cross reference

Overview

Objective
1) The students will self-select a project which will extend their learning. 2) The students will complete and share an extended learning project.

About the Author
Sylvia Piper is Coordinator of Gifted Education for the Wood County Office of Education, Bowling Green, Ohio, a position she has held for thirteen years. She has an additional eight years of teaching experience at the elementary and secondary levels. John Piper is Associate Professor of Health Education at Bowling Green State University, Bowling Green, Ohio. He has over thirty years of teaching, coaching, and administrative experience at the secondary and collegiate levels. John also works as a consultant to educational and business groups throughout the country. Both Sylvia and John are members of the Excel Consultants Group.

Required Resources
1) Access to many types of resources, especially good books. 2) A list of ideas for extended learning projects.

Bibliography

Ideas for Extension Activities
Students should have the opportunity to extend their learning in a way that is useful and interesting to them, and commensurate with their ability. They should be encouraged to develop their own ideas for extending their learning; however, students often need an idea as a starting point. This list provides many ideas which may be used as presented, be adapted to meet individual needs and interests, or serve as springboards to developing one's own idea for extension of learning.

Science
1. Select an animal and study its adaptations. Look at characteristics such as teeth, coloration, paws, hands, feet, eyes, and tail. Select a way to share this infor-

mation with the class. Examples of animals that might be studied are: toad, turtle, earthworm, woodpecker, eagle, squirrel, penguin, camel, horse, or human being.

2. Select a bird such as the Arctic tern, swallow, snow goose, or bobolink and research its migration pattern. On a globe or map, track its journey and describe it to the class in an oral report. Explain why birds migrate.

3. Animals other than birds migrate. Research an animal that migrates and select a way to share the story of its migration. Examples of animals that might be studied are: caribou, wolves, whales, salmon, or monarch butterflies.

4. Examine clean bird feathers. Find out how birds' feathers assist with flying. What are some other adaptations birds have for flight? Illustrate your findings and explain them to the class.

5. Research to find out the different ways animals have of adapting to seasonal change. What factors influence animal adaptation to seasons? Place the information in a matrix.

6. Color, or lack of color, plays an important part in nature. Research to find out the answers to questions such as these: Why are some animals brightly colored and others are drab? Why do some animals change color? Is a human being bright or drab? How do human beings change their appearance? Select a unique way to share your findings with the class.

7. Study the beaks of different kinds of birds. Illustrate the different types of beaks and show the type of food usually eaten by a bird with that type of beak. Match each type of beak with a household tool that works in the same way.

8. Much can be told about a bird's way of life from the shape of its feet. Study the different kinds of bird feet and illustrate them. Beside each illustration, give at least one example of a bird with that type of feet and tell how this adaptation is useful to the bird.

9. Only man has been able to create an oral and written language to communicate ideas, but scientists believe that many animals communicate in other ways. Study the way in which at least one type of animal communicates and select a way to share that information. Examples of animals that could be studied are: apes and chimpanzees, bees, ants, or porpoises and whales.

10. Study the ways in which seeds are dispersed. Create a chart showing several ways in which seeds are dispersed and provide an example of a plant that uses that method. Try to find out about the adaptations called pepper shakers and slingshots.

11. Use a shoe box to build a plant maze. (See Tolman & Morton resource.) Plant a bean (that has soaked overnight) in a small pot of soil and place it in the bottom of the maze. Put the lid on the box and stand it in a light, warm place. Keep the bean moist. Describe what happens. How does this relate to adaptation? Explain the experiment and the results to your classmates.

12. Carefully fill half an eggshell with soil and place it in an egg cup. Sprinkle a few marigold seeds over the soil. Keep the eggshell in a warm, light place. Water the soil lightly every day. Let the seeds germinate and grow for about five weeks. Describe what happens. How does this relate to adaptation? Explain the experiment and the results to your classmates.

13. Research the rafflesia, sometimes called the monster flower. What special adaptations allow it to survive in the Malaysian forests? Illustrate the flower and describe its adaptations in an oral or written report.

14. Select a plant and study how it adapts to its environment. Consider environmental factors such as temperature, water supply, levels of light, and food requirements. Select a way to share this information with the class. Examples of plants that might be studied include: cacti, glasswort, bird's nest fern, sundews, Venus's flytrap, edelweiss, or ground willow.

15. Read to find out the difference between the root structures of desert plants and those of woodland plants. Illustrate the difference on a chart and explain why they are so different.

16. Research to discover how the leaves of the plants of the desert and the plants of the tundra have been adapted to survive the dry conditions. Explain this in an oral report. Conduct the experiment on page 34 of Biology for Every Kid to help demonstrate your point.

17. Many plants have adaptations that protect them from plant-eating animals. Read about plants like cacti, hawthorn trees, honey locust trees, rose bushes, stinging nettles, poison ivy, and poison sumac. Prepare a written report to explain how these plants protect themselves.

Social Studies

1. Research the Finnish word for barren land—tundra. Create an example of tundra. (See Hoven-Severson resource.) Share your example with the class. Describe the features of tundra and talk about the plants and animals that have adapted to that type of land.

2. Read about icebergs. Create an iceberg. (See Hoven-Severson resource.) Conduct a survey among your classmates. Have them predict whether your iceberg will sink or float in a tub of water and how much of the iceberg will be below the water. Compare your iceberg to icebergs in the polar regions. How close were the class predictions regarding the amount of ice below the water?

3. Read Nessa's Fish by Nancy Luenn. Work with a partner to adapt the story into a play. Make the necessary props. Perform the play mostly in pantomime. You and your partner will have the speaking parts of Nessa and Grandmother. Ask your teacher or another student to be the narrator. Ask several classmates to pantomime the non-speaking parts.

4. Make a large mural showing the ocean and part of a beach.

An island can be placed in the ocean. Draw or construct animals that would be found in or near the ocean. Place these animals on the mural. Research to be sure your animals are correct in color and structure.

5. Make a pie plate island. (See Hoven-Severson resource.) Include bays, inlets, mountains, trees, rivers. Name your island and make a map of it. Be sure to include its bays, peninsulas, inlets, etc. Design a key for your island map. Write a description of your island or make a travel brochure describing its climate, location, physical features, agriculture, and recreational possibilities.

6. Read *Where the Forest Meets the Sea* by Jeannie Baker and *Rain Forrest* by Helen Cowcher. Be able to explain the importance of the rain forests to the global environment. Prepare and deliver a TV speech that will get people to support saving the rain forests.

7. Read books about mountains including the book *Sierra* by Diane Siebert. Make and illustrate a booklet entitled: Things to Do and See in the Mountains.

8. Research forest animals such as the great horned owl, porcupine, weasel, beaver, mule, deer, rabbit, otter, raccoon, or red fox. As you learn about each animal, complete a chart which has the following headings: name, predator or prey, how it moves, what it eats. Add any other headings you wish.

9. Read *Bringing the Rain to Kapiti Plain* by Verna Aardema. Write a similar story for the American plains using the animals and plants of that area. It may be necessary to read about the American plains before this can be done.

10. Identify some of the animals or plants that have become extinct over the last 100 years. Find out why these animals or plants were not able to survive. Select a way to share this information with your classmates.

11. Imagine that you are a travel agent. Prepare travel plans for a trip to Alaska or Australia. Include information on how you would travel, what you might see and do, and what you will pack. It is now summer where you live.

12. Work with your music teacher or librarian to locate songs from several different countries. Make a song scrapbook of the music you selected. Learn to sing and/or play one or two of them and share with your class.

13. Create a sports book on the sports of several countries or cultures. List the favorite sports of each, then use pictures, drawings, or photographs to illustrate at least one of the sports. Demonstrate a selected sport to your classmates.

14. Create an alphabet book for one of the countries and cultures you have learned about. Include events, landmarks, traditions, customs, animals, plants, etc.

15. "Hello" is a familiar greeting in our country. Do some library research to find the word or words used to greet people in several other countries. Find a creative way to share this information in a mobile.

16. Construct a model of a house like Manda's (desert) or Norman's (Eskimo).

17. Write to an African pen pal through the Afro-Asian Center, P.O. Box 337, Saugerties, NY 12477. (Telephone: 914-246-7828).

18. Read several books about other countries and cultures. As you read the books, mark the location of the country on a world map. Try to read your way around the world. Keep a card file of interesting facts about each country and culture.

19. Read the book *Fly Away Home* by Eve Bunting. Make a list of the adaptations Andrew and his father make to survive in the airport. Under the list, write a paragraph or two telling how you would feel if you had to live like Andrew.

Reading and Language Arts

1. Working individually or in small groups, make a character mobile based on the story *Sarah, Plain and Tall*. Use words, pictures, drawings, and other creative ways to share the information. Draw and explain pictures Sarah would have sent to her brother William.

2. Write a paragraph telling how you would feel if you had to move from the seashore to the prairie farm or from the prairie farm to the seashore.

3. Think about things that might make you want to stay or leave your home. Use a T-chart to list these things under the headings "Stay" and "Leave."

4. Write a newspaper article about Papa and Sarah's wedding.

5. Create a poster to advertise *Sarah, Plain and Tall*. in the school library.

6. Write a poem about the prairie and/or the seashore. Record your poem on an audio tape and share it with the class.

7. Read about the plains and the seashore. Use a Venn diagram to compare and contrast the wildlife and the living conditions in each location.

8. If you could choose the perfect mother for you, what would she be like? Write an advertisement for the newspaper that could help you find her.

9. What would you miss most if you had to leave your home and live in some other place? Use a T-chart to compare your list with the things Sarah missed.

10. Make a reading cube that will inform other people about the book. Put pictures of different events on five sides of the cube and the title and author on the sixth side.

Caleb asked Anna to tell him over and over again about Mama. Write several important things you would tell someone about one of your parents.

11. Sarah had a collection of shells from the seashore. In an oral presentation, describe a collection you have made and share

some of the items. If you do not have a collection, think of something you would like to collect and tell why.

12. Work with a small group to make a mural of the prairie. Begin by making a list of the characteristics mentioned in book and by using reference books to find out more about the plants and animals of the prairie.

13. Read *Sarah, Plain and Tall* yourself. Make up titles for each of the chapters. Think about how each of the major characters in the book—Sarah, Papa, Caleb, and Anna—made adaptations in their lives. Write a paragraph about each character, explaining these adaptations. Compose a song that Sarah or one of the other characters would sing after she decided to stay.

Quadrant 3—Applications

 ## Right Mode—Extend

Make "Want To Know More About" list. Examine resources. Try some ideas.

Objective
1) Students will personalize their learning by selecting things they want to know more about. 2) Students will begin the search process for suitable resources to extend their learning. 3) Students will finalize plans for an extended learning project.

Activity
Under the heading "I Want to Know More About," each student will make a list of things he/she would like to know more about based upon the content, concept, and skills developed in the unit. Students are then given adequate class time to examine resource materials and project ideas before self-selecting an extended learning project. The teacher guides students toward ideas and projects that are commensurate with their ability and assists them as necessary in finding appropriate resources. Students conference with teacher before beginning selected project.

A list of project ideas in each of the three disciplines is included in the "overview" section of this unit. Teachers and/or students can use these ideas as presented, can adapt them to meet individual needs and interests, or use them as springboards to developing one's own extended learning project.

Assessment
Quality and effort put into research and selection of project.

Quadrant 4—Creations

 ## Left Mode—Refine

Work on project that will extend learning. Evaluate, revise, refine, complete.

Objective
1) Students will evaluate, revise, refine, and complete a self-selected project. 2) Students will extend their learning through completion of the project.

Activity
Class time will be provided for students to work on their projects. Students will confer with the teacher as they analyze and evaluate throughout the development of the project.

Assessment
Quality of work habits. Completion of project.

 ## Right Mode—Integrate

Enjoy sharing extended learning project and learning from others' projects.

Objective
1) Students will share what they have learned and created. 2) Students will experience the joy of teaching and learning from one another.

Activity
Each student will share his/her work with classmates and other audiences in a manner appropriate to the type of project completed.

Assessment
Quality and enthusiasm displayed.

The Flag

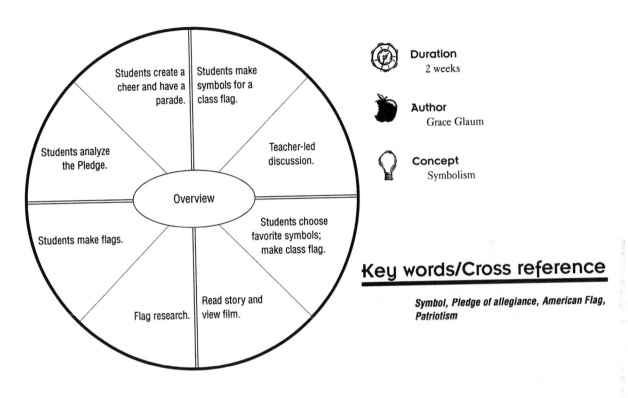

Students create a cheer and have a parade.

Students make symbols for a class flag.

Students analyze the Pledge.

Teacher-led discussion.

Overview

Students make flags.

Students choose favorite symbols; make class flag.

Flag research.

Read story and view film.

Duration
2 weeks

Author
Grace Glaum

Concept
Symbolism

Key words/Cross reference

Symbol, Pledge of allegiance, American Flag, Patriotism

Overview

Objective
Using the American Flag as example, students will learn the concept of symbols and what they stand for.

About the Author
At the time this plan was written, Grace Glaum was a primary teacher in District #163, Park Forest, IL.

Required Resources
Materials for class flags; materials for making early flags

Bibliography
Georgiady, Nicholas and Romano, Louis, *Our Country's Flag*, Follett Publishing Company, Chicago, IL, 1963.
Film:
"Our Country's Flag," 2nd Edition, Coronet Films, 65 East South Water Street, Chicago, IL 60601, 1960, 11 minutes.
This lesson plan was included in the original 4MAT in Action.

The Flag

Quadrant 1—Experience

 ### Right Mode—Connect

Students make symbols for a class flag.

Objective
To build respect for our flag and country.

Activity
Have the children sit in groups. Put the definition of the word "symbol" on the board.

Symbol:

Something used to represent something else, a picture, a color, etc. that stands for something.

Ask students for examples. List can include Smokey the Bear, the red color of Santa's suit, McDonald's Golden Arches.

Then tell them that some symbols are special. What makes them special is that they help us to feel something in our hearts, a kind of special feeling. When that happens, the symbol stands for something much deeper and more important than the symbol itself. When we honor these symbols we show our loyalty, our feelings of caring, for what the symbol means. Conduct a brief discussion along these lines, then ask the children to get together and discuss what symbols they might use to make a class flag.

Assessment
Group participation.

Left Mode—Examine

Teacher-led discussion.

Objective
To show the children how a synthesis of ideas is a rich experience.

Activity
Bring the group back together, put all their ideas on the board and discuss them.

Assessment
The children's enjoyment.

Quadrant 2—Concepts

 ### Right Mode—Image

Students choose favorite symbols; make class flag.

Objective
To have the children make personal choices about the symbols they like best and combine them into a class flag.

Activity
Ask the children to pick the symbols they each like best and make a class flag. Hang them all up in the classroom.

Assessment
The children's enjoyment.

 ### Left Mode—Define

Read story and view film.

Objective
To give the children some facts and information concerning the flag.

Activity
Have the children say the Pledge. Ask them to write a short essay on what the words mean to them. Read the story, *Our Country's Flag*, to them and discuss it briefly. Show the film "Our Country's Flag."

Assessment
A short, written statement by each of the children on what they have learned so far.

The Flag

Quadrant 3—Applications

 ### Left Mode—Try

Flag research.

Objective

To help the children learn how to find out information they need.

Activity

Find out the story of our early flags, flag changes, and how we got our present flag. Have books available in the classroom and have the school librarian assist by having a table of books and resources for the students in the library. Find out what the colors stand for. Show the film again.

Assessment

The method by which the students go about their task. (This is a good time to talk to individual children about how to do independent research.)

 ### Right Mode—Extend

Students make flags.

Objective

Enable students to experience flagmaking.

Activity

Make the early flags, the "Ross" flag, and our present flag. Show the children how to make stars by folding paper.

Assessment

The quality of their work.

Quadrant 4—Creations

 ### Left Mode—Refine

Students analyze the Pledge.

Objective

To have the children discuss and analyze if our flag is a good symbol for our country.

Activity

Have the children analyze the Pledge, phrase by phrase.

Assessment

Their understanding of the phrases.

 ### Right Mode—Integrate

Students create a cheer and have a parade.

Objective

To enjoy a celebration of our flag.

Activity

Make up a cheer for our country and our flag and tell the story of Francis Scott Key and how he wrote "The Star Spangled Banner." End by telling the children our flag is a symbol of all the people who love our country. Have a parade in class with each child carrying the flag s/he has made. Play a recording of Sousa's "The Stars and Stripes Forever."

Assessment

The children's enjoyment.

Note: This unit could be extended by having the children make a flag for planet Earth. They would need to study universal symbols.

Friends

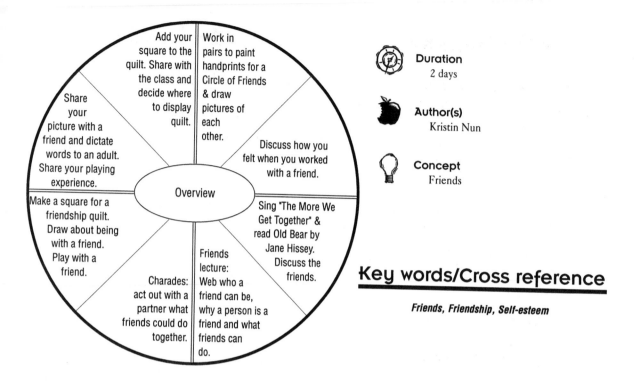

Add your square to the quilt. Share with the class and decide where to display quilt.

Work in pairs to paint handprints for a Circle of Friends & draw pictures of each other.

Share your picture with a friend and dictate words to an adult. Share your playing experience.

Discuss how you felt when you worked with a friend.

Overview

Make a square for a friendship quilt. Draw about being with a friend. Play with a friend.

Sing "The More We Get Together" & read Old Bear by Jane Hissey. Discuss the friends.

Friends lecture: Web who a friend can be, why a person is a friend and what friends can do.

Charades: act out with a partner what friends could do together.

Duration
2 days

Author(s)
Kristin Nun

Concept
Friends

Key words/Cross reference

Friends, Friendship, Self-esteem

Overview

Objective

This is a primary unit to develop the concept of friendship and the qualities of friends.

Required Resources

Art materials: paint, paper, crayons, etc.

Bibliography

Old Bear by Jane Hissey and the big book, *The More We Get Together*, by Tom Glazer from HBJ.

Friends

Quadrant 1—Experience

 ### Right Mode—Connect

Work in pairs to paint hand prints for a Circle of Friends & draw pictures of each other.

Objective
To connect with previous experiences with friends and create an experience to work with a friend.

Activity
Students work in pairs to paint hand prints to make a Circle of Friends. They choose to make pink or gray together by mixing one hand in each color — red & white or black & white. They then draw pictures of each other to share with the class.

Assessment
Level of interest & cooperation shown. Completion of activities.

 ### Left Mode—Examine

Discuss how you felt when you worked with a friend.

Objective
To discuss how it feels to work with your friend.

Activity
Teacher leads discussion on how students felt when they worked with a friend, using drawings to represent these feelings.

Assessment
Level of participation & quality of responses. Student interest & listening skills.

Quadrant 2—Concepts

 ### Right Mode—Image

Sing "The More We Get Together" & read Old Bear by Jane Hissey. Discuss the friends.

Objective
To develop the concept of friendship and qualities of friends by linking their own experiences to those in a book.

Activity
Sing the song, "The More We Get Together," using words/pictures in big book. Read *Old Bear* by Jane Hissey. Teacher leads discussion on friends in story. Use drawings to represent the students' responses about friendship.

Assessment
The interest & listening skills demonstrated, participation in song and discussion and accuracy of responses.

 ### Left Mode—Define

Friends lecture: Web who a friend can be, why a person is a friend and what friends can do.

Objective
To continue to develop the concept of friendship and qualities of a friend.

Activity
Teacher uses a web to let students give input on who a friend can be, why a person is a friend and what friends can do together, adding additional information when needed.

Assessment
Participation in discussion & accuracy of responses. Attentiveness.

Quadrant 3—Applications

 ## Left Mode—Try

Charades: act out with a partner what friends could do together.

Objective
To apply the information received in previous activities and extend their understanding of friendship.

Activity
Students act out with a partner something friends could do together based on drawings teacher gives them or their own ideas.

Assessment
The quality of student ideas & participation.

 ## Right Mode—Extend

Make a square for a friendship quilt. Draw about being with a friend. Play with a friend.

Objective
To provide active, hands-on activities to extend what was learned about friendship.

Activity
Each child makes a square for a friendship quilt by drawing about being with a friend. They play with a friend at center time.

Assessment
Quality of product & participation at center time.

Quadrant 4—Creations

 ## Left Mode—Refine

Share your picture with a friend and dictate words to an adult. Share your playing experience.

Objective
To evaluate work by sharing with others.

Activity
Students share their picture with a friend and dictate words to an adult. They share their playing experiences with the group.

Assessment
Participation and complexity of discussions. Quality of dictation.

 ## Right Mode—Integrate

Add your square to the quilt. Share with the class and decide where to display quilt.

Objective
To share what was learned with others in the class and school.

Activity
Add each square to the quilt and share with the class. Decide as a class where to display quilt.

Assessment
Interest in sharing knowledge with others and quality of ideas.

Learning About Ghana

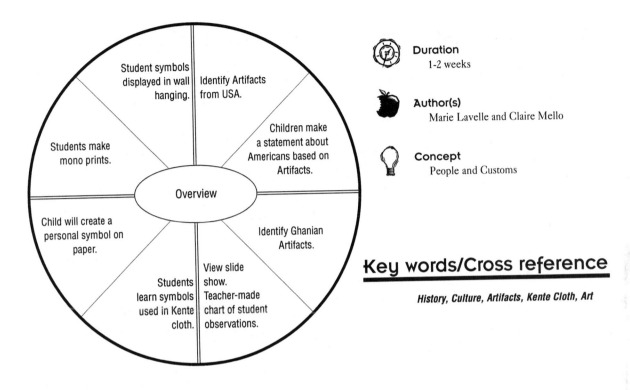

Student symbols displayed in wall hanging.

Identify Artifacts from USA.

Children make a statement about Americans based on Artifacts.

Students make mono prints.

Overview

Child will create a personal symbol on paper.

Identify Ghanian Artifacts.

Students learn symbols used in Kente cloth.

View slide show. Teacher-made chart of student observations.

Duration
1-2 weeks

Author(s)
Marie Lavelle and Claire Mello

Concept
People and Customs

Key words/Cross reference

History, Culture, Artifacts, Kente Cloth, Art

Overview

 Objective
Students will learn how artifacts tell us much about a culture.

 About the Authors
Marie Lavelle and Claire Mello are elementary teachers in Brookline Public Schools, Brookline, MA. They are participants in the Brookline 4MAT Implementation Project led by Nona Bock and Bob Bates.

 Required Resources
Display objects characteristic of American culture; artifacts from Ghana; drawing materials; visual display of Kente cloth symbols; materials for mono prints.

 Bibliography
Ghana Slide Collection from Boston University - African Studies Department, Boston, MA

Learning About Ghana

Quadrant 1—Experience

 ### Right Mode—Connect

Identify Artifacts from USA.

Objective
Have children identify objects from American Culture.

Activity
A large, brown paper bag is filled with familiar objects. Children take turns selecting items from the bag and naming them.

Assessment
The child can name all of the items in the bag.

 ### Left Mode—Examine

Children make a statement about Americans based on artifacts.

Objective
Child will be able to tell about Americans from looking at the object.

Activity
Examples: Mittens - it must be cold.
Seashell - beaches must be part of the environment.
Newspaper - people are literate.
Plastic tape holder - people enjoy music.
Art supplies - people enjoyed crafts.

Assessment
Teacher assessment of what the children deduce about the people from looking at everyday objects.

Quadrant 2—Concepts

 ### Right Mode—Image

Identify Ghanian Artifacts.

Objective
Children identify objects from the Ghanian Culture.

Activity
Display objects from Ghana. Have children tell what they think about Ghanian Culture from the objects. Students create drawings: "A Boy or Girl in Ghana" based on their observations of the Ghanian artifacts.

Assessment
Teacher assessment of the level and type of information generated from looking at the objects.

 ### Left Mode—Define

View slide show. Teacher-made chart of student observations.

Objective
Familiarize children with the country of Ghana, its people and customs through an extensive slide show.

Activity
Children first view slides without comment. The second time, they are asked to make a statement about each slide.

Assessment
Following the slide show, teacher record children's observations.

Learning About Ghana

Quadrant 3—Applications

Left Mode—Try

Students learn symbols used in Kente cloth.

Objective
The children will become familiar with the symbols used in the design of Kente Cloth.

Activity
Present example of Kente Ccloth (real ones are preferable, if available. If not, pictures can be used.) Children choose a favorite symbol and draw it.

Assessment
Children's ability to identify symbols and their meaning.

Right Mode—Extend

Child will create a personal symbol on paper.

Objective
Child will create a personal symbol on paper.

Activity
Child designs a symbol and creates a label for it.

Assessment
Children's ability to express concept through symbol design.

Quadrant 4—Creations

Left Mode—Refine

Students make mono prints.

Objective
Learn process of making a mono print.

Activity
Using Styrofoam and stylus, the child creates a personal design and prints it on cloth.

Assessment
Teacher observation.

Right Mode—Integrate

Student symbols displayed in wall hanging.

Objective
To share mono prints in an all-class wall hanging.

Activity
All prints are arranged in quilt-like fashion to be shared with the whole school.

Assessment
The pleasure the children take in creating and sharing personal symbols with classmates.

Maps

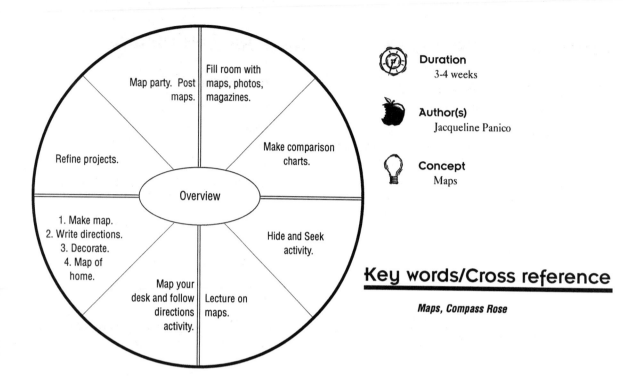

Map party. Post maps.

Fill room with maps, photos, magazines.

Refine projects.

Make comparison charts.

Overview

1. Make map.
2. Write directions.
3. Decorate.
4. Map of home.

Hide and Seek activity.

Map your desk and follow directions activity.

Lecture on maps.

Duration
3-4 weeks

Author(s)
Jacqueline Panico

Concept
Maps

Key words/Cross reference

Maps, Compass Rose

Overview

Objective
The children will understand that maps are images of the real thing, just like photographs.

About the Author
Jacqueline Panico is a teacher at Paterson Public Schools in Paterson, NJ.

Required Resources
Map of Paterson, photos of children, other maps, magazines, a self-made cassette with directions, overhead projector, computer disc - Troll - Maps & Globes.

Bibliography
Social studies book: maps, handouts on map terms, etc.

Maps

Quadrant 1—Experience

 Right Mode—Connect

Fill room with maps, photos, magazines.

Objective
To create an experience for the class which shows that photos and maps are images of the real thing.

Activity
Hang photos of students in the class as well as local landmarks, map of Paterson, posters and magazines in classroom. Have some of the real objects available for the children to touch and see. Let them discuss what they are noticing.

Assessment
Verbalizing thoughts, involvement.

 Left Mode—Examine

Make comparison charts.

Objective
To examine what they noticed in Q1R to themselves.

Activity
Make a comparison chart of images vs. real. Brainstorm feeling words that describe importance of images (group work).

Assessment
Participation in group activity. Cooperation with group.

Quadrant 2—Concepts

 Right Mode—Image

Hide and Seek activity.

Objective
To connect what they have been observing to using maps in their own lives.

Activity
Play hide and seek with some object (candy, pencil, etc.) having to be found by the class. They have to follow directions heard on a cassette you will make in advance set to music.

Assessment
Enthusiasm, participation, problem solving ability, listening skills.

 Left Mode—Define

Lecture on maps.

Objective
To give necessary information about maps.

Activity
Give lecture on maps:
1. need
2. kinds
3. codes/clues
4. how to use
5. colors
6. linear representation
7. compass rose

Use wall maps, social studies book, overhead projector, and computer disk on Maps and Globes (Troll).

Assessment
Participation, verbal responses, thought process.

Quadrant 3—Applications

 ## Left Mode—Try

Map your desk and follow directions activity.

Objective

To reinforce what has been taught.

Activity

1. Make a map of your desk in relation to the rest of the class. 2. Either dictate or have directions on a chart for each child to follow.

Assessment

Ability to draw map. Ability to get to the destination by following directions.

 ## Right Mode—Extend

1. Make map.
2. Write directions.
3. Decorate.
4. Map of home.

Objective

To give the class different options to express themselves and what they know.

Activity

1. Map the 1st and 2nd floors of our school for use in fire drill floor plans. 2. Plan "find the food" directions for our Q4 celebration. 3. Make the decorations with direction words. 4. Draw map of their homes (front of paper = outside, back = inside).

Assessment

Good involvement by each student, working well together in group, information required for project is accurate.

Quadrant 4—Creations

 ## Left Mode—Refine

Refine projects.

Objective

To refine their projects so that they are ready to be shared.

Activity

Teacher moves around the room to each group to assist and keep them on task. Children coach each other and complete the projects.

Assessment

Good coaching skills. Editing is visible.

 ## Right Mode—Integrate

Map party. Post maps.

Objective

To practice and share what they have learned.

Activity

Have a map party. Hang decorations. Play "find the food" so they can eat. Post the floor plan maps around the school and explain to each class.

Assessment

Enjoyment, ability to explain to other classes how a floor plan is used, ability to follow directions and find food.

Native Americans

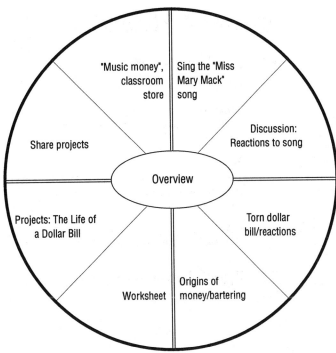

 Duration
8-16 weeks

 Author(s)
Cathy Singagliese

 Concept
Native American communities are influenced by environmental factors.

Key words/Cross reference

Global Communities, Native Americans, Environment, Literature: Annie and the Old One, Gift of the Sacred Dog, Sign of the Beaver

Overview

 Objective
This unit introduces students to the concept that Native American communities are influenced by environmental factors. Students will understand that shelter, food, clothing and tools are determined by the environmental resources and conditions.

 About the Author
Cathy Singagliese is a third grade teacher at Bartle School in Highland Park, NJ. Cathy teaches in a whole language environment and integrates music, art, science, social studies and literature throughout all her 4MAT lesson plans.

 Required Resources
Museum artifacts at county or state museums on an educational loan basis.
Dreamcatcher, Native American flute music on audio cassette.
National Geographic Filmstrips and videos on each region.
Spring Sounds, audio cassette.

 Bibliography
Baylor, Byrd, *The Desert Is Theirs*. Macmillan Publishing Co., 1975.
Baylor, Byrd, *The Way To Start A Day*. Macmillan Publishing Co., 1978.
Cherry, Lynne. *A River Ran Wild*. HBJ, 1992.
de Brebeuf, Jean. The Huron Carol. Dutton Books, 1990.
Goble, Paul. *The Gift of the Sacred Dog*. Macmillan Publishing Co., 1980.
Kjelgaard, Jim. *Snow Dog*. Bantam Skylark, 1980.
Longfellow, Henry Wadsworth. *Hiawatha*. Scholastic Inc., 1983.
Miles, Mishka. *Annie and the Old One*. Little, Brown & Co., 1971.
Prusski, Jeffrey. *Bring Back the Deer*. HBJ, 1988.
Speare, Elizabeth George. *The Sign of the Beaver*. Dell Publishing, 1983.
White Deer of Autumn. Ceremony In The Circle Of Life. Carnival Press, 1983.

Quadrant 1—Experience

 ## Right Mode—Connect

Spend 15 min. outdoors. In teams decide how you could survive 1 week.

Objective
Experience and create a lifestyle that is dependent upon the environment.

Activity
The teacher will take the class on an imaginary trip where they will become stranded for "one week." The entire class will spend 20 minutes in the outdoor courtyard split up into groups of five. Each group must brainstorm ways to survive in this environment using only natural things found in the courtyard for shelter, food, clothing and tools.

Assessment
Students will be able to discuss orally the types of choices they made in the environment.

Left Mode—Examine

Reflect in journal feelings, challenges, successes if really spent 1 week here.

Objective
Reflect upon the experience of depending on the environment to survive.

Activity
The students will write in their journal how it would really feel to live in the courtyard for one week. The students will discuss their feelings about this and include successes and challenges.

Assessment
The students will orally share their journals. Each entry will reflect feeling and examples that relate to realistic examples of shelter, food, etc.

Quadrant 2—Concepts

 ## Right Mode—Image

Guided Imagery of 6 months spent in yard. Indicate changes in environment.

Objective
Develop concept that lifestyle is dependent on environment and may change with the seasons. This change will effect lifestyle in regard to shelter, clothing, food and tools.

Activity
Provide guided imagery with audio cassette of "spring sounds." Students will imagine they had to spend 6 months in the courtyard with their family. They will illustrate a picture describing the changes in shelter, food, clothing and tools.

Assessment
Students will be able to illustrate realistic illustrations noting a change in shelter, food, etc. caused by seasonal differences.

 ## Left Mode—Define

N.A. communities are dependent upon changing environment.

Objective
To understand that Native American communities and lifestyles are influenced and changed by their environment.

Activity
Several activities will develop concept of Native American communities and lifestyles influenced by the environment of the Eastern Woodlands, Plains, Southwest, and Arctic.

Literature: *The Sign of the Beaver, Gift of the Sacred Dog, Annie and the Old One, Snow Dog.*

1. As each novel is read, the students will identify the environment and determine how the environment influenced the shelter, clothing, food and tools of the Native American community. The examples will be written on chart paper and displayed for future additions and reference.

2. National Geographic Filmstrips and videos appropriate for the region and the Native American community are available for whole class instruction or learning centers.

3. The students will paint watercolor murals of each region. In teams, students will carousel to each mural and add a typical shelter, clothing, food or tool

Native Americans

to the Native American community.

Assessment

Students will identify each Native American community in its appropriate region and give three examples in writing of shelter, food, clothing, and tools that are determined by the environment.

Quadrant 3—Applications

 ## Left Mode—Try

Identify shelter, food, clothes, etc. that are dependent on environment.

Objective

Students will be able to identify Woodland, Plains, Southwestern, and Arctic Indians' shelter, food, clothing and tools/weapons from picture book illustrations and give one reason why these are dependent upon the environment.

Activity

Teacher will model identifying shelter, clothing, food and tools/weapons of a regional North American community and model reasoning skills before cooperative activity. Teacher will model with a picture book illustration on an overhead. Students will orally identify examples of shelter, etc., that are dependent upon environment. Students will give reasons why they are dependent, e.g., Deer hides are made for shirts and leggings. Deers live in the environment and are a resource for Native Americans. Weather changes also necessitates thickness of hide and fur.

Students will work in trios analyzing illustrations in picture books depicting Eastern Woodland communities. They will find examples of food, shelter, etc. and write them on color coded poster boards. On back, they will write reasons why these are dependent upon the environment.

Trios will use Send-A-Problem technique and exchange book and cards. Trios will review illustration and card to write additional examples or reasons. Trios will return materials to original group to evaluate.

Students will use Stand And Share technique to orally review all findings. All members reporting "food" will stand. As member reads card, all others will sit if they have no new info to add. Members continue reporting until all examples are discussed.

Cards will be placed in packets with picture books in Learning Center for future activities, e.g. Flash Card Directed Inside-Outside Circle.

Closure: Teacher will summarize objective of lesson and congratulate all students on reasoning and cooperating skills. Students will have an opportunity to use critical thinking skills to illustrate an original picture of a Native American community.

Assessment

Teacher will use informal observation and questioning to check for understanding of concept. Students will illustrate their own picture of Woodland, Plains, Southwest and Arctic communities showing examples of food, shelter, etc. that are realistically appropriate. These will be reviewed and compiled as class book entitled *Native American Communities Depend on Their Environment* for class library.

 ## Right Mode—Extend

Examine Newark Museum N.A. artifacts. Classify by region. Determine use and how it was made.

Objective

Students will examine museum artifacts from the following Native American regions: Woodlands, Plains, Southwest and Arctic. Students will identify and classify artifacts.

Activity

In cooperative teams, students will examine ten museum artifacts mixed randomly among the Native American regions of Woodlands, Plains, Desert and Arctic. The teams will identify the artifact as tool, clothing, shelter, etc. The group will also determine the materials it was made from and its possible use. The team must use all this information to classify the artifacts according to region.

The teams will record their findings on colored index cards and post them on the watercolor murals made in a previous lesson. The entire class will read all the examinations, may re-examine the artifacts, and may re-classify a piece if they choose. The items will be discussed individually and the true region will be exposed.

Assessment

The purpose of this activity is for the students to examine, classify and re-examine their choices based on additional information. Here the students must show a knowledge of each region and have internalized the concept of how environment affects aspects of a community. The knowledge base is being applied to a more complex experience.

Quadrant 4—Creations

Left Mode—Refine

Make a "NEW" tool for a N.A. community in a particular region.

Objective

Students will create a unique tool that reflects the environment of a specific region in a Native American community.

Activity

Students will choose one of the following Native American regions studied: Woodlands, Southwest, Arctic and Plains. In dyads, students will decide what resources are available in the environment and what type of tool could be made from those resources. Students will also decide what tool would be necessary to live in that environment, design a model for that tool and create it with real materials. Teams must be prepared to defend in writing the name of the tool and its proper use.

Assessment

Students will create a tool that accurately reflects the particular resources and needs of a Native American community in a specific region. The students will write an appropriate description of the tool including its name and use.

Right Mode—Integrate

Share tool. Evaluate peers' examples. Create Class N.A. Museum & give guided tours.

Objective

Students will share their unique tool from a Native American region with the entire class and place the tool in the classroom Native American Museum. The Museum will be toured by other classes and opened to the community during multicultural week.

Activity

Students in dyads will orally share their creation. The team will present their tool and follow the guideline questions in the evaluation section. When presentations are completed, all tools will be placed in the classroom Native American Museum. The teams will become tour guides for class visits and for a community walk-through during multicultural week.

Assessment

Teacher and classmates will assess the activity based on the following criteria: 1) Is the tool made from resources found in the environment of the region? 2) Is the tool of practical value? 3) Is the team able to share effectively what they learned about the environment and how it influences the way Native American communities live?

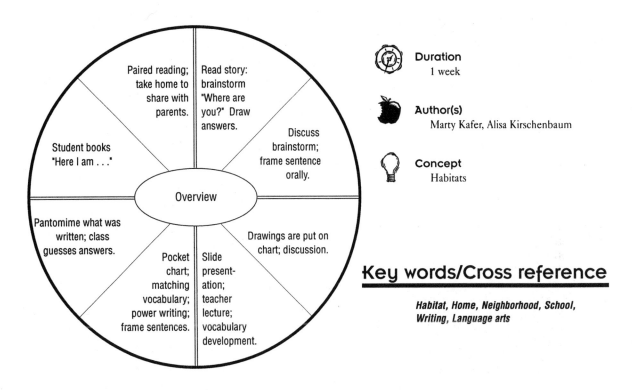

Duration
1 week

Author(s)
Marty Kafer, Alisa Kirschenbaum

Concept
Habitats

Key words/Cross reference

Habitat, Home, Neighborhood, School,
Writing, Language arts

Overview

Authors' Note

INTRODUCTION

Seven major habitats exist in the Bay Area: the Redwood Forest, Oak Forest, Chaparral, Grasslands, Streamside, Baylands, and the Coast. We have chosen to focus on four of these habitats: the Redwood Forest, Oak Forest, Baylands and Coast, as well as the student's immediate environment — the Neighborhood.

We begin with the neighborhood in order to personalize habitats and familiarize the student with his/her surrounding environment. The study begins with the student's immediate surroundings and builds an understanding of what a habitat is. As the student grows to understand his/her environment the curriculum branches out to incorporate other local habitats, their characteristics, plant and animal life.

This unit will assist Primary teachers, Intermediate teachers and teachers at all levels of English Language Acquisition by providing lessons and activities in the science content area. It is our hope you will note changes, suggestions, criticisms and other helpful comments as you teach this unit. We believe this is a work in progress as we continue to teach, modify and revise.

NEIGHBORHOODS

A neighborhood is a habitat. It is a complex habitat because people have altered the shape of the land and even the climate. Plants and animals from other countries have been introduced to neighborhoods, replacing others that had been there for years. The large mammal of the neighborhood is the human being. Humans get nearly all their food from other places. One of the biggest concerns is the waste. In a forest or mountain habitat, the animals get all their food from the area and deposit the waste in the same place. Humans, however, get their food from the supermarket and deposit their waste in the garbage. Unfortunately, the waste is rarely recycled and causes pollution.

The neighborhood habitat affects other habitats around it. Highways and roads are built to transport goods. The pollution from factories and cars travels to neighboring areas. Wood, fuels and other natural resources are being used. Forests are cut and ponds are polluted.

Deer, raccoons, pigeons, dogs, snakes and other animals have adapted to life in neighborhoods. These animals have been able to alter their living styles in order to remain alive. Many of these animals, such as rats, mice and raccoons feast on the plentiful amounts of garbage supplied by humans.

Only certain plants fare well in neighborhoods. Eucalyptus trees brought from Australia have grown successfully in California. Grasses and weeds grow in any place that soil is exposed. Crab grass, milkweed, and Russian thistle also grow readily. Plants that thrive in the neighborhood habitat have one thing in common: they are able to survive and reproduce successfully under difficult conditions.

Neighborhoods are constantly changing. As buildings continue to grow, the animal and plant populations continue to change. There are always areas to go to see "wild places." Parks, vacant lots, cemeteries and backyards continue to be a place where one can find insects, plants and animals.

Objective
Students will show their understanding of a neighborhood as a habitat.

About the Authors
Marty Kafer and Alisa Kirschenbaum are Elementary Curriculum Specialists with the Cupertino U.S.D., Cupertino, CA. They are members of the 4MAT implementation project led by Suzanne Sanders.

Required Resources
Slides of the neighborhood; poster board classification chart, chart paper, slide projector, tape.

Bibliography
Herberman, Ethan. *The City Kid's Field Guide.* Simon and Schuster Books Inc., New York. 1989.

Pringle, Laurence. *City and Suburb: Exploring an Ecosystem.* MacMillan Publishing Co., Inc., New York. 1975.

Ross, Don and Sue Levytsky. *Where In The World Is Walter?* Longmeadow Press. Stanford, CT. 1989.

Quadrant 1—Experience

Right Mode—Connect
Read story: brainstorm "Where are you?" Draw answers.

Objective
After hearing the story, *Where In The World Is Walter?*, students will be able to name different places in the neighborhood.

Activity
Teacher reads story, *"Where In The World Is Walter?"* aloud to class. Class brainstorms the question, "Where are you?" (school, room, desk, etc.). On a 4" x 6" piece of paper, students draw their answers to the question.

Assessment
Students' drawings will show an understanding of what is in a neighborhood habitat by including at least two details of their neighborhood (chair and desk; house and tree; slide and swing).

Left Mode—Examine
Discuss brainstorm; frame sentence orally.

Objective
Students will participate in a discussion and demonstrate understanding of the frame sentences: "Here I am. I am in _____."

Activity
Teacher will encourage discussion and oral responses from the students by pointing to different answers of the brainstorm. Students respond to the prompt by answering as completely as possible, "Here I am. I am in my classroom." Students with limited or no English proficiency will be able to point to the correct picture card for their answer. Children with more language facility will create more complex descriptions, pictures, etc.

Assessment
Students are attentive and demonstrate their understanding of the frame sentence.

Quadrant 2—Concepts

 ### Right Mode—Image

Drawings are put on chart; discussion.

Objective

Students will show an understanding that there are several places (i.e., home, class, etc.) which make up their habitat — the neighborhood.

Activity

Create a poster board classification chart listing the places which make up their habitat (neighborhood). Have each student place their 4" x 6" drawing from the activity in quadrant 1R under the correct heading. Discuss placement of pictures on chart.

Assessment

Students will correctly place their drawing on the chart.

 ### Left Mode—Define

Slide presentation; teacher lecture; vocabulary development.

Objective

After viewing a slide presentation, students will share at least one thing about the school and neighborhood.

Activity

Teacher will present slides of typical things found around the school and neighborhood. Discussion and vocabulary will be introduced and expanded upon. After slides, students will be put into mixed ability language pairs and share one thing they remembered. Students will use sentences if possible or may point to visuals around the classroom.

Assessment

Students' ability to share one thing they saw during the slide show. Teacher observation of dialogue and student participation.

Quadrant 3—Applications

 ### Left Mode—Try

Pocket chart; matching vocabulary; power writing; frame sentences.

Objective

By participating in an activity, students will express knowledge of neighborhood and school vocabulary.

Activity

Depending on language proficiency, students will take part in one of the following activities:

1. Pocket chart exercises – Pass out picture cards of school and neighborhood objects. Who has the "desk"? Student brings "desk" picture up to pocket chart.
2. Frame Sentences – Students recite, "I have the desk. The desk is in the classroom."
3. Matching picture to word – Using the pocket chart or making a matching game (concentration), students will match the picture to the word.
4. Power writing – Students will write about the following: "Name two places that you like to play." Example answer: I like to play in two places. I like to play at school. I like to play in my backyard.

Assessment

Accurate completion of pocket chart, frame sentences or power writing.

 ### Right Mode—Extend

Pantomime what was written; class guesses answers.

Objective

Using previous language experiences from 3L, students will retell by pantomime specific places of the neighborhood habitat.

Activity

Using the individual power writings (from 3L) students will pantomime the places they wrote about. Students who did other exercises will choose a place and do a pantomime. Other students in the class will guess where the pantomime is.

Assessment

Class will correctly identify location of pantomime based on student performances.

Quadrant 4—Creations

Left Mode—Refine

Student books "Here I am . . ."

Objective

Using three drawings, students will complete a book about the neighborhood as a habitat.

Activity

Students will choose three different school and/or neighborhood locations and illustrate them. Students will write independently or through dictation the locations represented. An idea for the book is, "Here I am. I am _____" by Room 6. Example: "Here I am. I am sitting in my chair . . . sleeping in my bed . . . etc.

One paper (12" x 18") could be folded into thirds for each student to draw the three pictures.

Assessment

Students complete book showing three different locations.

Right Mode—Integrate

Paired reading; take home to share with parents.

Objective

Using their book, students will retell what they have written.

Activity

Students will share their completed page of the book with a partner. Next students will share what their partner has written to the class – example: "The three places Maria wrote about were her bedroom, the playground, and the principal's office."

Assessment

Teacher observation of pair share. Students' ability to express the ideas of their partner.

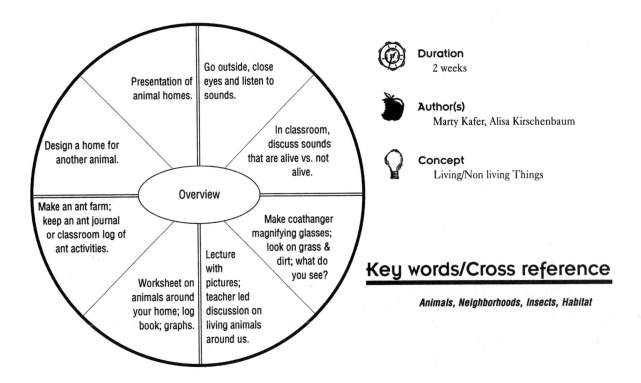

 Duration
2 weeks

 Author(s)
Marty Kafer, Alisa Kirschenbaum

Concept
Living/Non living Things

Key words/Cross reference

Animals, Neighborhoods, Insects, Habitat

Overview

 Objective
To engage students in observations of the animal, insect and bird worlds within their neighborhood habitat.

About the Authors
Marty Kafer and Alisa Kirschenbaum are Elementary Curriculum Specialists with the Cupertino U.S.D., Cupertino, CA. They are members of the 4MAT implementation project led by Suzanne Sanders.

Required Resources
Coat hangers, magnifying glasses, ant farm materials, homework #1.

Quadrant 1—Experience

 Right Mode—Connect

Go outside, close eyes and listen to sounds.

Objective
Students will experience their surrounding environment auditorially and visually.

Activity
In the classroom, discuss the procedure that will take place outside. Go outside and find a private space that is not next to another person. For five minutes, students will close their eyes and just listen to the sounds of the schoolyard. Some students may wish to use their "deer ears" by cupping their hands around the back of the ear. Repeat this experience using the visual and auditory senses. Could you see animals you could not hear? Did you hear things you could not see? Which was easier? Harder? Did you want to use your eyes when you were supposed to be listening only?

Assessment
Students' willingness to participate and involvement in the exercise.

 Left Mode—Examine

In classroom, discuss sounds that are alive vs. not alive.

Objective
Remembering that animals are living things, students will determine the differences between sounds that are alive vs. sounds that are not alive.

Activity
Come back into the classroom and brainstorm all the sounds that were heard outside. Show pictures and/or discuss concepts of alive and not alive. In groups or with partners, take five minutes to talk about the sounds that were heard. Make a chart listing the sounds that were alive in one column and the sounds that were not alive in another column. Each group will report its findings to rest of the class.

(To challenge older students, discuss the needs of living things, i.e., food, water, air, etc.)

Assessment
Participation of students and their ability to rename at least one sound from outside.

Quadrant 2—Concepts

 Right Mode—Image

Make coat hanger magnifying glasses; look at grass & dirt; what do you see?

Objective
Students will discover that within a habitat, there are mini-habitats that sometimes go unnoticed.

Activity
Have a wire coat hanger for each student. Bend the wire into a circle. This represents a magnifying glass. Show students a real magnifying glass. Go outside to a grassy area. In partners or individually, have students observe what is inside the boundaries of their coat hanger magnifying glass. After a few minutes, have students choose another area to observe. Make sure students look at two different types of micro-environments (i.e., dirt, grass, mud, concrete, etc.). Have students draw what they saw in their magnifying glass.

Assessment
Students' drawings will reflect two different mini-habitats.

 Left Mode—Define

Lecture with pictures; teacher-lead discussion on living animals around us.

Objective
To introduce and reinforce the concept that animals need a home.

Activity
Teacher lectures using pictures and realia (if possible). Discuss homes and the need for shelter. Why do these animals live in neighborhoods? How have they survived throughout the years? Why have some animals become rare in neighborhoods? Engage students in a discussion of characteristics of common birds, insects and animals commonly seen around the neighborhood.
(Older students might explore, compare and contrast the needs for food and shelter.)

Assessment
Teacher verbally checks for understanding during the lecture.

Quadrant 3—Applications

Left Mode—Try

Worksheet on animals around your home; log book; graphs.

Objective

Using information learned about common birds, insects and animals, students will conduct home observations of the animal life around their neighborhood.

Activity

Students will keep a record of various life forms encountered at home. Using a teacher-created worksheet, students will sketch and record animals around their home. After students complete this assignment, students will graph the various numbers of animals encountered. Have students discuss which animals were commonly seen and which were not. Did they see more animals during the day (diurnal) or at night (nocturnal)? How did the animals react when the students approached them? Why do animals react this way? What kinds of survival skills do animals have and need?

Assessment

The completion and correctness of the worksheet will reflect detailed observations of neighborhood animal life.

Right Mode—Extend

Make an ant farm; keep an ant journal or classroom log of ant activities.

Objective

Home and shelter will further be defined as students participate in the building of a habitat for ants.

Activity

Find an ant nest in the soil. Dig deeply to get both the ants and the soil and put into a jar. Place the bottom of the jar in a flat pan of water. This will prevent the ants from escaping. Place black construction paper around the outside of the jar and tape into place. The ants will then tunnel close to the sides of the jar. Do not put the ants in direct sunlight and keep the jar at room temperature. When observing the ants, take the black paper off the jar, you may wish to use magnifying glasses. Replace after observation. When feeding the ants, feed them crumbs, bits of apple, honey or sugar. You can place the food on a small piece of cotton and place it in the jar. Make sure the ants have water either by placing it directly on the soil (use an eye dropper) or on a small sponge. (Other animal habitats may be substituted for this activity. Some suggestions are snail homes or earthworms.)

Why do the ants need to make their home underground? How do ants work together to build their home? What other types of animals could live in this type of home? Could people live under the ground?

Have students keep a daily journal or log about the ants' activities. Be sure to have students include illustrations, comments and questions in their ant log.

Assessment

Quality of the log content detailing the ant farm and the ants' activities.

Quadrant 4—Creations

 ## Left Mode—Refine

Design a home for another animal.

Objective
Using the information acquired about habitat and homes, students will design and create a home for another type of animal.

Activity
Using a variety of media, students will create an imaginary home for an animal. Students may also wish to invent a "city critter." Questions to think about may be: "What kind of animal lives under the lunch tables? Your desk? The chalkboard? What kind of food does this animal eat? Does this animal sleep during the day or night? What kinds of things are necessary for this animal to live? Is there anything that threatens this animal? How will the design of this home protect and help with the survival of the animal?

Assessment
Students will create a home with a practical design to sustain animal life.

 ## Right Mode—Integrate

Presentation of animal homes.

Objective
Students demonstrate their knowledge of a habitat by presenting their completed animal home.

Activity
Students will present their creations to the class. Have students point to and explain why they chose to add particulars (i.e., plants, rivers, etc.) to their habitat. Audience may wish to ask questions or make comments about the presentations.

Assessment
Students will explain how and why they made their animal habitat in a presentation to the class.

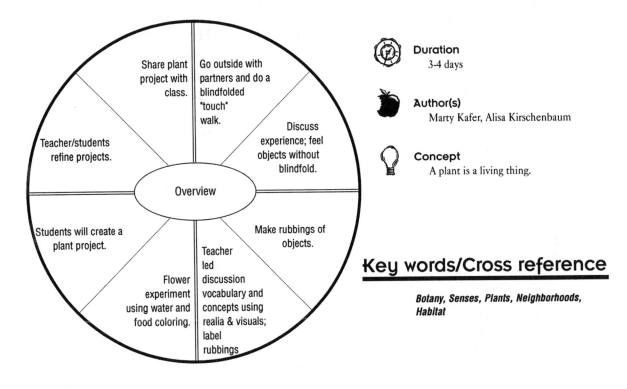

Share plant project with class.

Go outside with partners and do a blindfolded "touch" walk.

Discuss experience; feel objects without blindfold.

Teacher/students refine projects.

Overview

Make rubbings of objects.

Students will create a plant project.

Teacher led discussion vocabulary and concepts using realia & visuals; label rubbings

Flower experiment using water and food coloring.

Duration
3-4 days

Author(s)
Marty Kafer, Alisa Kirschenbaum

Concept
A plant is a living thing.

Key words/Cross reference

Botany, Senses, Plants, Neighborhoods, Habitat

Overview

 Objective
Students will experience plants as a part of their neighborhood habitat.

 About the Authors
Marty Kafer and Alisa Kirschenbaum are Elementary Curriculum Specialists with the Cupertino U.S.D., Cupertino, CA. They are members of the 4MAT implementation project led by Suzanne Sanders.

 Required Resources
Blindfolds, visuals of plants, plant realia (twigs, leaves, flower, etc.), food coloring, celery, carnations, "pop-up" book directions.

 Bibliography
Wilkes, Angela. *My First Nature Book*. Alfred A. Knopf, New York, 1990.

Quadrant 1—Experience

 ### Right Mode—Connect

Go outside with partners and do a blindfolded "touch" walk.

Objective

Students will experience nature through tactile, auditorilly, and olfactory senses.

Activity

Students choose partners. One person is blindfolded. The other person takes his/her partner on a "touch" walk outside experiencing as many different natural things as possible. Before going outside, review appropriate behavior and expectations. Students should try and lead their partner to trees, plants, weeds, rocks, etc. After five minutes, switch roles.

Have students create a visual of the experience on poster paper.

Assessment

The visual will reflect student's involvement in the "touch" walk experience.

 ### Left Mode—Examine

Discuss experience; feel objects without blindfold.

Objective

Through discussion of the touch walk, students will express and extend their knowledge of the experience.

Activity

Using the Listen, Think, Pair, Share strategy, have students answer the following question, 'What did you hear? touch? smell?" Have students answer each part of the question separately, each time using the Listen, Think, Pair, Share strategy.

Have students return to the schoolyard to experience the same objects without the blindfold. What is different? Which way did you prefer?

Assessment

Quality of students' discussion reflects what they have learned.

Quadrant 2—Concepts

 ### Right Mode—Image

Make rubbings of objects.

Objective

Students will have a closer look at plants through the use of texture.

Activity

Collect plant samples. Using the side of a crayon, have students make rubbings of various types of plants and parts of plants.

Assessment

The quality and size of the rubbing collection.

 ### Left Mode—Define

Teacher-lead discussion of vocabulary and concepts using realia & visuals; label rubbings.

Objective

To give background knowledge on plants and seeds.

Activity

Teacher-lead lecture on vocabulary and functions of plants—roots, tree parts, common flowers, seeds, plants, bush, twig, etc. Use visuals and realia. Help students label their rubbings. Compare and contrast students' rubbings.

Assessment

Teacher checks for understanding throughout lesson.

Quadrant 3—Applications

 ## Left Mode—Try

Flower experiment using water and food coloring.

Objective
Students will understand the function of roots and will use observations from food coloring experiment to complete a graph.

Activity
Get a glass of water and put in two to three drops of blue food coloring. Put a stalk of celery or a white carnation in the glass. Have students make predictions of what will happen. Write the predictions on a chart. Students will graph the number of days/hours it took for the flower/celery to change colors. Students will make a visual representation of the time it took for the flower/celery to change colors. Compare the results. Have students reflect upon roots and their relationship to this experiment.

Given a flower, students will carefully dissect the different parts. Students will then mount the parts of the flower on a piece of paper and label.

Assessment
Using students' predictions, check for understanding about the function of roots.

 ## Right Mode—Extend

Students will create a plant project.

Objective
Using what they have learned about plants, students will choose one of the following projects.

Activity
1) Collect leaf examples from around the neighborhood. Mount and label where they came from. 2) Make a poster by drawing plants around the neighborhood. 3) Using a manila folder, create a pop-up scene of plants in the neighborhood. Write a story about the plants. Mount the story on the folder (see example at the end of this unit).

Assessment
Completed projects demonstrate knowledge of plants.

Quadrant 4—Creations

 ## Left Mode—Refine

Teacher/students refine projects.

Objective
Students will have an opportunity to complete and refine their projects.

Activity
The teacher will review each student's progress on his/her project and will make suggestions for enhancing the work already completed.

Assessment
Student's ability to refine and complete the project.

 ## Right Mode—Integrate

Share plant project with class.

Objective
To allow students to share completed projects.

Activity
Students will present their plant displays.

Assessment
Quality of presentations.

Neighborhoods (4 of 4)

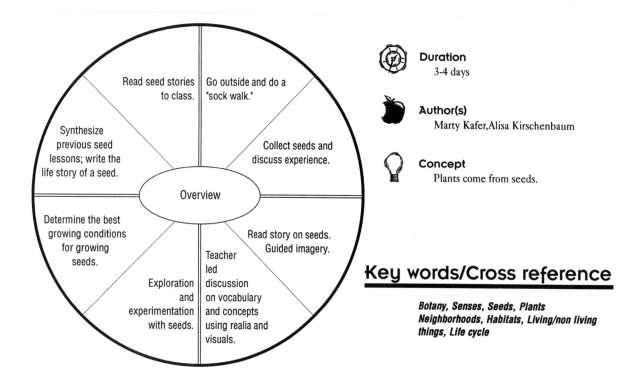

Duration
3-4 days

Author(s)
Marty Kafer, Alisa Kirschenbaum

Concept
Plants come from seeds.

Key words/Cross reference

*Botany, Senses, Seeds, Plants
Neighborhoods, Habitats, Living/non living
things, Life cycle*

Overview

Objective
This unit will introduce students to common seeds
and plants around their neighborhoods.

About the Authors
Marty Kafer and Alisa Kirschenbaum are
Elementary Curriculum Specialists with the
Cupertino U.S.D., Cupertino, CA. They are mem-
bers of the 4MAT implementation project led by
Suzanne Sanders.

Bibliography
Berger, Melvin. *All About Seeds.* Scholastic Inc., New
York, 1992.
Jordan, Helene J. *How A Seed Grows.* Thomas Y.
Crowell Co., New York, 1960.
My First Nature Book. Alfred A. Knopf, New York,
1990.
For older students:
DeVito, Alfred and Gerald H. Krockover. *Creative
Sciencing.* Little, Brown & Co., Boston, 1980.

Quadrant 1—Experience

 ### Right Mode—Connect

Go outside and do a "sock walk."

Objective

Students will be introduced to how seeds are dispersed.

Activity

Brainstorm the neighborhood animals (dog, cat, raccoon, opossum, mouse, etc.). Each student chooses an animal s/he would like to be. Give each student a large sock (or two if there are enough). The sock represents the animal's fur. Students will put socks over their shoes. Tell students to think about what might happen as they walk around the playground field. Go outside and take a five minute walk.

Assessment

Students will actively and appropriately engage in walking around the playground.

 ### Left Mode—Examine

Collect seeds and discuss experience.

Objective

Students will develop an understanding of how seeds are dispersed.

Activity

Carefully take off the socks and bring back into the classroom. Students will take off the seeds collected from their socks and put them onto a piece of paper. Discuss experience. How is a sock like the fur of an animal? How does this help plants? Are there other ways that seeds can be moved?

Assessment

By discussing the experience, students will show an understanding of the dispersal of seeds.

Quadrant 2—Concepts

 ### Right Mode—Image

Read story on seeds. Guided imagery.

Objective

To further knowledege and understanding of seeds through literature.

Activity

Teacher reads students a story about seeds. Teacher conducts a guided imagery while students imagine they are seeds in the cycle of dispersal.

Assessment

Students' active listening and engagement in the story. Involvement in the imagery experience.

 ### Left Mode—Define

Teacher-lead discussion on vocabulary and concepts using realia and visuals.

Objective

To give background knowledge about seeds and their importance to plants.

Activity

Teacher-lead lecture on vocabulary and functions of seeds. How do seeds become a plant? What do seeds need to grow? What kinds of seeds are there? (apple, peach, etc.).

Assessment

Teacher checks for understanding throughout lesson.

Quadrant 3—Applications

 ## Left Mode—Try

Exploration and experimentation with seeds.

Objective

By exploring and experimentation, students will further their understanding about the similarities and differences of seeds.

Activity

1) Using the seeds collected from the sock walk, students will sort seeds. This can be done individually, with partners, or in cooperative groups.
2) Look at seeds through a magnifying glass. Compare shape, size, color and texture. Discuss how these characteristics relate to the movement of seeds (Older students might write about this). How might other types of seeds (fruit seeds, heavier seeds, etc.) be dispersed?
3) Plant some of the seeds collected.
4) Grow lima beans. Give each student a clear plastic cup, a paper towel, and three lima beans. Put the paper towel inside the cup. Pour enough into the cup to get the towel damp. Place the lima beans between the paper towel and the side of the cup so that the bean can be observed. Keep the paper towel damp (but not wet to discourage mold).

Assessment

Students will express at least two characteristics about seeds and how this affects their dispersal. Example: Because the seed is flat and light, the wind can move it.

 ## Right Mode—Extend

Determine the best growing conditions for growing seeds.

Objective

Through experimentation and observation, students will determine the best growing conditions for their plant.

Activity

Using the lima bean, sprouts from 3L or other seeds (such as mung, pumpkin, corn, grass, elm, maple, marigold, radish, or scarlet runner bean) plant in a variety of growing conditions—sun vs. no sun, water vs. no water, light vs. dark, hot vs. cold, etc. Keep a log of what happens to the seeds. Illustrate the log and write down questions, observations, predictions, etc.

Assessment

Quality of the content in the log.

Quadrant 4—Creations

 ## Left Mode—Refine

Synthesize previous seed lessons; write the life story of a seed.

Objective

Students will show their understanding of seed concepts through a language arts project.

Activity

Review and synthesize the previous lessons about seeds. Remember to incorporate the part animals play in seed dispersal, other ways seeds are dispersed, characteristics of seeds, how seeds grow, the needs of seeds, etc. Younger students will create a storyboard of the life of a seed, including seed dispersal, seed needs and growth. Older students will incorporate the seed concepts into a written story or play.

Assessment

Projects will reflect student's understanding of the stages of a seed.

 ## Right Mode—Integrate

Read seed stories to class.

Objective

To allow students to share completed projects.

Activity

Students will read stories, act out plays, or show storyboards.

Assessment

Quality of presentations.

Watery Ways

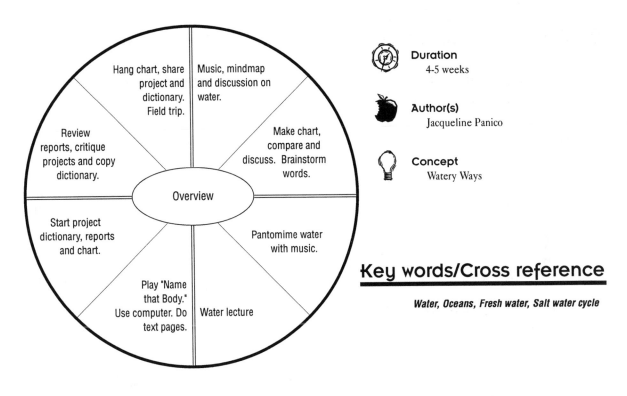

Hang chart, share project and dictionary. Field trip.

Music, mindmap and discussion on water.

Review reports, critique projects and copy dictionary.

Make chart, compare and discuss. Brainstorm words.

Overview

Start project dictionary, reports and chart.

Pantomime water with music.

Play "Name that Body." Use computer. Do text pages.

Water lecture

 Duration
4-5 weeks

Author(s)
Jacqueline Panico

Concept
Watery Ways

Key words/Cross reference

Water, Oceans, Fresh water, Salt water cycle

Overview

 Objective
Children will learn the names of the different bodies of water, how they were formed, how to measure the water, where they are on maps, and how they are used.

 About the Author
Jacqueline Panico is a teacher at Paterson Public Schools in Paterson, NJ.

 Required Resources
Troll software: *Maps and Globes.*
Silver Burdett/Ginn reading series, *Castles of Sand and On The Horizon.*
Cassettes with ocean rain and stream sounds.
Field trip to the Great Falls.
Math series; chapter on measurement.

Bibliography
Silver Burdett/Ginn Reading Series
Silver Burdett/Ginn Math Series
Troll Software

Watery Ways

Quadrant 1—Experience

Right Mode—Connect

Music, mindmap and discussion on water.

Objective

To create an experience for the class that creates feelings and mental pictures.

Activity

Play rain and ocean music. Do a stream-of-consciousness mindmap of feelings. Talk about the sounds and what they are. Do we need water? Where does it come from and what are its uses?

Assessment

Facial expressions, participation and responses.

Left Mode—Examine

Make chart, compare and discuss. Brainstorm words.

Objective

To examine the feelings and name the bodies of water heard.

Activity

Groups will chart feeling words for rain, then ocean. Compare the charts. Discuss in groups, why they think I played rain first, then ocean. Brainstorm body of water words.

Assessment

Interaction with classmates, responses of students.

Quadrant 2—Concepts

Right Mode—Image

Pantomime water with music.

Objective

To make a connection between the feelings, words, and sounds the class has heard, and the concept.

Activity

Pantomime: Rain becomes puddles = brooks = streams = lakes = rivers = oceans, while playing the Q1 soundtracks.

Assessment

Participation and enthusiasm.

Left Mode—Define

Water lecture.

Objective

To develop the concept of Watery Ways.

Activity

Lecture class on: 1) Bodies of water, 2) Fresh/salt water, 3) Location of bodies of water on maps of U.S.A. and Paterson, 4) Read stories from reading series related to water, 5) Measure water, 6) Discuss uses of H2O.

Assessment

Participation, accuracy of measurement, ability to locate waterways on maps, story summaries.

Watery Ways

Quadrant 3—Applications

Left Mode—Try

Play "Name that Body." Use computer. Do text pages.

Objective
To reinforce the concept that has been discussed.

Activity
Use Troll software - *Maps and Globes* to check knowledge. Play "Name That Body." Do workbook pages from the reading and math series.

Assessment
Responses to computer work, workbook pages and game participation.

Right Mode—Extend

Start project dictionary, reports and chart.

Objective
To allow the children to practice what they've learned by giving them an option about how they do it.

Activity
1) Using sand and water, demonstrate watery changes from rain to puddles, etc. 2) Make Dictionary of Watery Terms with pictures and definitions. 3) Write report on Paterson's waterways - the fun and industry in past and present related to the water. 4) Make chart on measurement of map bodies of water in standard and metric. Label.

Assessment
Concentration and involvement in projects.

Quadrant 4—Creations

Left Mode—Refine

Review reports, critique projects and copy dictionary.

Objective
To oversee the progression of the projects and encourage problem solving and peer coaching.

Activity
Teacher and students will critique projects. Review reports to see if you can help keep on target. Make copies of dictionary to be passed out at a later date.

Assessment
Children improving coaching skills and willing to edit their work.

Right Mode—Integrate

Hang chart, share project and dictionary. Field trip.

Objective
To allow children to share what they have learned about the concept.

Activity
Hang chart in the hall. Share the sand and water project with the first grades. Pass out the copies of the dictionary. Take a field trip to the Great Falls.

Assessment
Excitement about sharing their project and pride in the work they have done.

Creative Housing

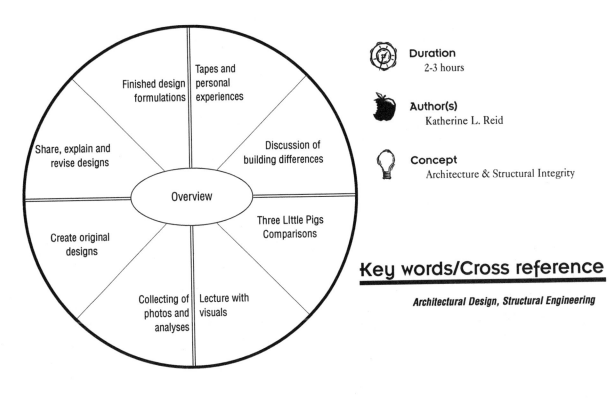

Duration
2-3 hours

Author(s)
Katherine L. Reid

Concept
Architecture & Structural Integrity

Key words/Cross reference

Architectural Design, Structural Engineering

Overview

Objective
Students will learn how houses are designed to meet the needs of its occupants and to provide safety for its occupants.

About the Author
Katherine L. Reid is an Instructional Specialist in the Pasadena Independent School District, Pasadena, TX. She is a participant in the Pasadena 4MAT Implementation Project and is a certified 4MAT System presenter.

Required Resources
Cassette recording of a thunderstorm; architect guest lecturer; photos of interesting or unusual homes and accompanying observation check-list (teacher-prepared); paper and markers for student projects.

Bibliography
Song: "*The Three Little Pigs*," by LL Cool J.
Scieszka, Jon. *The True Story of The Three Little Pigs*, Viking, New York, New York, 1989.
Ross, Elizabeth. *The Three Little Pigs*, Western Publishing Co., Inc., New York, 1973.

Creative Housing

Quadrant 1—Experience

Right Mode—Connect

Tapes and personal experiences.

Objective

To relate a student's personal experience in a stormy situation to a particular building in which the student felt secure.

Activity

1. Play a tape on which there are sounds of a thunderstorm. 2. Have students listen and recall being in a story. 3. Have students share where they were and how it felt to be in a secure building during a storm. 4. Students should recall the details of the building, such as of what materials it was built. 5. Have students draw a picture of their experience.

Assessment

The effectiveness with which students can use their personal experiences to recall aspects of a strong and secure structure.

Left Mode—Examine

Discussion of building differences.

Objective

To have students recognize differences in houses and buildings and to recognize aspects of safe and secure buildings.

Activity

1. In a large group discussion, have students discuss different buildings (school, church, home) and their differences: size, materials, design, function. 2. Students should list differences in buildings. 3. Students should discuss what makes a building safe and secure. Students should remember the building they were in during a storm in which they felt secure. 4. Students should list the characteristics of a strong, secure structure.

Assessment

The degree to which students can recognize differences in houses and buildings, and will identify characteristics of strong buildings.

Quadrant 2—Concepts

Right Mode—Image

Three Little Pigs Comparisons.

Objective

To use a familiar story, "The Three Little Pigs," to relate the concepts of housing and the consequences of poor housing design.

Activity

1. Play the song, "The Three Little Pigs," by LL Cool J. 2. Have students recall and act out the events of the story. 3. Have students reflect on what happened to the pigs' houses when the wolf huffed and puffed. 4. In small groups, have students discuss the pigs' houses as to how and why one was stronger than the others. Discuss the differences in the houses, materials they were made of, size, etc. 5. Have students compare their own house or apartment to the pigs' houses.

Assessment

The extent with which students recall the story of "The Three Little Pigs" and discuss why the pigs' houses were not secure.

Left Mode—Define

Lecture with visuals.

Objective

To share information concerning the role of architects in designing safe and secure structures.

Activity

1. The teacher or a visiting architect will show photos of actual houses and structures, which are discussed as to the information below: 2 a, b, c.
2. Information on the following will be shared with students:
a. Architects plan structures for clients based on their needs and desires: size, style, purpose.
b. Structures are created for personal safety: strong foundations and building materials.
c. Architects work with other designers to make their buildings beautiful: interior, landscape, fabrics, etc.

Assessment

How well students will recognize differences in houses and relate the role of an architect to the need for different types of houses.

Quadrant 3—Applications

 ## Left Mode—Try

Collecting of photos and analyses

Objective
To check for student understanding of basic principles of architectural design.

Activity
1. Students will collect at least three photos of interesting and unusual homes. 2. Students will critique each design based on a check list of items considered by an architect: pleasing to look at, strong, looks like it would serve the function for which it was intended. 3. Students will share their findings with other students.

Assessment
Each student completes a check list evaluation form for each of three photos of homes. Assesses for completeness of check lists.

 ## Right Mode—Extend

Create original designs

Objective
To use the knowledge of architectural design in designing a strong and functional house for The Three Little Pigs.

Activity
1. Discuss which needs of pigs might influence an architect's designs.
2. Discuss what a pig might want in a house.
3. Working individually, each student will use felt markers and white paper to design a unique house for "The Three Little Pigs."

Assessment
Each student completes a house design that meets the needs of "The Three Little Pigs." Students will be assessed on the quality of their designs.

Quadrant 4—Creations

 ## Left Mode—Refine

Share, explain and revise designs

Objective
To evaluate the house designs created for "The Three Little Pigs."

Activity
1. Students will share their completed designs with other students in the class.
2. In small groups, students will explain to the other students why the designs were created as they were.
3. Individually, students will evaluate their own designs as to ways these designs could have been improved.
4. Collectively, students will discuss how their designs could have been improved. Assess based on quality of discussions.

Assessment
All students share their pig house designs with other students and make some decisions as to ways these designs could have been improved.

 ## Right Mode—Integrate

Finished design formulations.

Objective
To formulate ideas for the creation of a sketch of a house in which the student would like to live.

Activity
1. Students will discuss their needs and wishes concerning a house design.
2. Students will sketch their ideas for their dream house onto paper.
3. Those students wishing to develop a three-dimensional model of their house may do so.

Assessment
Students complete a sketch of a house in which they would like to live. Assess based on quality of sketches.

English Alphabet

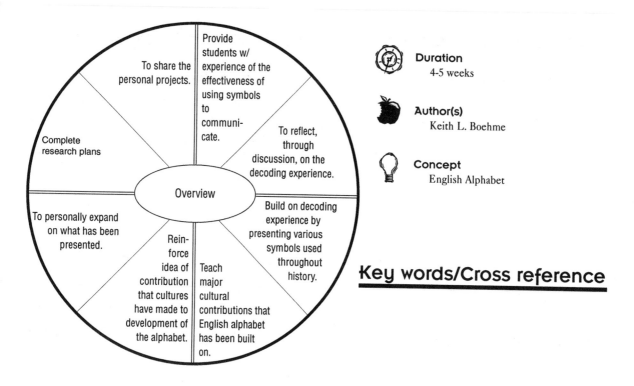

Duration
4-5 weeks

Author(s)
Keith L. Boehme

Concept
English Alphabet

Key words/Cross reference

Overview

Objective
To teach the major cultural contributions that the English alphabet has been built upon.

About the Author
Keith has taught in Cincinnati, Ohio for the last 12 years in a Montessori Program. Prior to that, Keith was involved in a project which called for the creation of a Montessori environment for severely brain damaged children.

Required Resources
8" x 11" cards, pictographs of Sumerian Cunieform, Egyptian Heiroglyphics, Semetic writing, the Phoenician Alphabet, the Roman Tablet, an illuminated tablet written in English.

English Alphabet

Quadrant 1—Experience

 ### Right Mode—Connect

Provide students w/ experience of the effectiveness of using symbols to communicate.

Objective

To provide students with an experience of the effectiveness of using symbols to communicate.

Activity

The class is divided into small teams. Each team decodes the message and performs what the message asks.

Assessment

Active involvement of each member in the group in deciphering the secret code and performing what the message asks one to do.

 ### Left Mode—Examine

To reflect, through discussion, on the decoding experience.

Objective

To reflect, through discussion, on the decoding experience.

Activity

Discussion on the decoding activity. Points in the discussion should include a) symbols used to convey information (reflecting directly on the activity), b) the advantage of having symbols to record events of the past (note role of the story teller), c) ask "What would the world be like today without written symbols. Would computers be possible?"

Assessment

Contribution/enthusiasm of students in the discussion.

Quadrant 2—Concepts

 ### Right Mode—Image

Build on decoding experience by presenting various symbols used throughout history.

Objective

To build on the decoding experience by presenting various symbols used throughout history.

Activity

The following symbols, representing major contributions to the English alphabet, are placed on large (8x11) cards: pictographs, Sumerian Cunieform, Egyptian Hieroglyphics, Semetic writing, the Phoenician alphabet, the Greek alphabet, the Roman alphabet and an illuminated tablet, written in English. Eight students are invited from the class and asked to arrange themselves in order (while the class watches) according to which they feel came first in humanities history. Class discussion follows in the arrangement and reordering is done.

The following labels are placed on the board: Prehistoric, Sumerian, Egyptian, Phoenician, Semetic, Greek, Roman, English. Students are asked which symbol systems represent the listed cultures. Open-ended discussion follows.

Other possible activities:

Present the mystery of the Rosseta Stone. Show the video on communication through whistling.

Assessment

Involvement in the discussion/activities.

 ### Left Mode—Define

Teach major cultural contributions that English alphabet has been built on.

Objective

To teach the major cultural contributions that the English alphabet has been built on. To look at the future of writing.

Activity

Present, orally, timeline cards which highlight significant events in the development of the English alphabet. Each card consists of a picture of the culture on one side and the story on the reverse. Students read a small essay entitled "The Future of Writing." In small teams, the students answer questions which are designed to reflect on the essay.

Many other subjects can be introduced (spiraling). Health: the skeletal system of the hand. Cultural: human evolution and the development of writing. Writing: calligraphy.

Note: I am looking for good video suggestions.

Assessment

Students begin making suggestions of possible personal research projects based on interest from each presentation. Each suggestion is recorded to stimulate others.

Quadrant 3—Applications

 ## Left Mode—Try

Reinforce idea of contribution that cultures have made to development of the alphabet.

Objective

To reinforce the idea of the contribution that many cultures have made to the development of the alphabet.

Activity

1. Students create their own timeline, in book form. Each culture should have a picture, a summary of the contribution, and an example of the symbol that culture used.
2. Research the development of one letter from the alphabet as well as present uses.

Assessment

Quality of the students' pictures/summaries of each culture. Presentation of reports/ability to answer questions.

 ## Right Mode—Extend

To personally expand on what has been presented.

Objective

To personally expand on what has been presented.

Activity

Using the personal research project list, each student will select a topic he/she would like to further research.

Assessment

Quality/enthusiasm of exploring/investigating their project selection.

English Alphabet

Quadrant 4—Creations

 ### Left Mode—Refine

Complete research plans.

Objective
To personally expand on what has been presented.

Activity
Each student (or small team) completes a research project plan. This form includes project topic, how it will be researched, materials needed, how it will be displayed/presented and any community trips planned. The project (or its summary) should be placed in the book.

Assessment
Quality of the project plan form. Students completing the project as designed.

 ### Right Mode—Integrate

To share the personal projects.

Objective
To share the personal projects.

Activity
Each student presents their project. The students take notes on the presentation and add these notes to the book.

Assessment
Quality of the project, display and presentation. Note: When all projects have been presented, a reflective question will be asked. This will require the student to review his/her book. The question should tap into the heart of the concept and serve as a stepping stone to further integration/lessons, etc.

Beethoven as Rebel

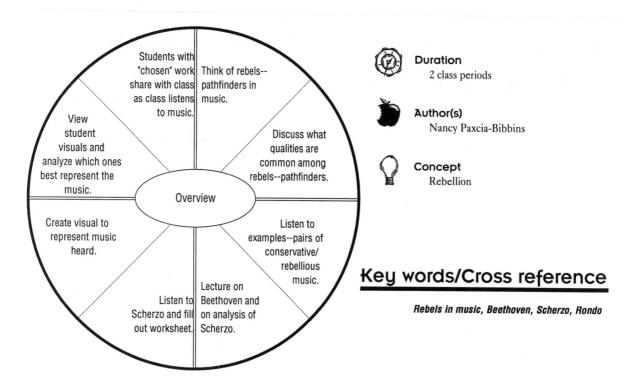

Students with "chosen" work share with class as class listens to music.

Think of rebels-- pathfinders in music.

Discuss what qualities are common among rebels--pathfinders.

View student visuals and analyze which ones best represent the music.

Overview

Create visual to represent music heard.

Listen to examples--pairs of conservative/ rebellious music.

Listen to Scherzo and fill out worksheet.

Lecture on Beethoven and on analysis of Scherzo.

Duration
2 class periods

Author(s)
Nancy Paxcia-Bibbins

Concept
Rebellion

Key words/Cross reference

Rebels in music, Beethoven, Scherzo, Rondo

Overview

Objective
This lesson is designed to introduce Beethoven as a pathfinder in music and to increase understanding of his music through the study of the form (rondo) of this selection.

About the Author
Since 1986, Nancy Paxcia-Bibbins has been the music teacher at Indian Creek Elementary School, Indianapolis, Indiana (with the exception of a year and a half when she was on sabbatical to pursue a doctoral degree at Ball State University). Prior to Indian Creek, she taught middle school choral music for ten years, and before that, high school choral music for five years. Nancy has also taught music education courses at Ball State University, Muncie, Indiana and Marian College, Indianapolis, Indiana.

Required Resources
Recording of Beethoven's Symphony #7, recording of Mozart's Serenade, K. 375; Menuetto (or another "conservative" example); tape of musical examples of "pairs"—musical conservative/musical rebel; worksheet; unlined paper, pencil, and colored markers.

Bibliography
The Bowmar Orchestral Library: *Concert Matinee, no. 63.* Melville, N.Y.: Belwin Mills Publ. Co., 1965.

Beethoven as Rebel

Quadrant 1—Experience

 ### Right Mode—Connect

Think of rebels—pathfinders in music.

Objective

To stimulate students' thinking about pathfinders—
"rebels"—in music.

Activity

Ask students to think of some musical rebels, e.g., Elvis
Presley (combination of black and white music, movement). Other rock star rebels?

Assessment

Involvement of students in discussion.

 ### Left Mode—Examine

Discuss what qualities are common among rebels—pathfinders.

Objective

To have students analyze qualities of a rebel in music.

Activity

Analyze what a rebel is. What makes them rebels?
Doing things differently, against norms, etc.?

Assessment

Involvement of students in discussion.

Quadrant 2—Concepts

 ### Right Mode—Image

Listen to examples—pairs of conservative/rebellious music.

Objective

To encourage students to recognize qualities of music
that are different from the norm and to hear that the
"rebellious" becomes the "conservative."

Activity

1) Play examples of musical "pairs"—determine which
sounds "conventional" and which sounds "rebellious."
(Use examples of jazz, rock, popular music to which students can identify.) 2) Have students raise hand after listening to each pair. Ask: Which one sounds rebellious,
the first one or the second one? 3) Play some "pairs" in
which the "rebellious" of one pair becomes the "conservative" of the other pair, e.g., Elvis as "rebel," then
Beatles as "rebel." (Play tape: Conventional/Rebellious
music) 4) Play "typical third movement" (Mozart:
Serenade, K. 375, Menuetto, Masters of Classical Music,
Vol. I) and then, listen to Beethoven Scherzo from
Symphony #7. 5) Which one sounds more rebellious?

Assessment

The number of appropriate responses shown by students' raising hands.

 ### Left Mode—Define

Lecture on Beethoven and on analysis of Scherzo.

Objective

To inform students of Beethoven's revolutionary ten-
dencies as well as his conformity to classic standards
and to listen to the Scherzo, showing how musical elements are used in his work.

Activity

1) Tell the class that Beethoven was a rebel—musically,
in lots of ways—chords, way of developing melodies. 2)
Tell the class that one of the critics said that Beethoven
must have been drunk when he wrote his symphony,
and that he was "ripe for the mad house." 3) Tell class:
scherzo—playful or lighthearted—different from the
usual "dignified minuet." 4) Show themes and play. 5)
Tell class how listening for elements of music can help
to identify themes. Pass out chart. a) Discuss chart—
tempo, tone color, etc. Define terms together.

Assessment

Attentiveness of students to lecture.

Beethoven as Rebel

Quadrant 3—Applications

 ### Left Mode—Try

Listen to Scherzo and fill out worksheet.

Objective
To have students practice recognizing the elements heard in Scherzo.

Activity
1) Have students fill out worksheet: Listen to music.

DAY TWO - Scherzo

(Provide unlined paper. Have students bring markers or crayons.) (Have tape ready for 4R activity.)

2) Pass back worksheets. Go over responses together.

Assessment
Answers to worksheets.

DAY TWO - Return worksheet. Ask class who remembers what rondo form is.

 ### Right Mode—Extend

Create visual to represent music heard.

Objective
To have students create their own visual representation of the themes heard in the Scherzo.

Activity
1) Teacher demonstrates some charting of themes—show repetition, contrast with use of different color markers and abstract representation of melodies. 2) Class charts themes as music proceeds (will exchange maps).

Assessment
Involvement of students and creativity in charts students produce.

Quadrant 4—Creations

 ### Left Mode—Refine

View student visuals and analyze which ones best represent the music.

Objective
To have students analyze their charts to determine whether they represent the music and lead students to "discover" rondo form.

Activity
Teacher draws diagram: A B A B A. Tell them it is a type of rondo form. (Tell class that there are other rondo designs, but A comes back). Any of your maps represent this?

Assessment
Students' analysis of their own work.

 ### Right Mode—Integrate

Students with "chosen" work share with class as class listens to music.

Objective
To share examples of what students have learned about the music.

Activity
Ask for volunteers to share charts with the class—tape on board. Students point and listen.

Assessment
Quality of examples and response of students to fellow classmates' work.

Beethoven Style

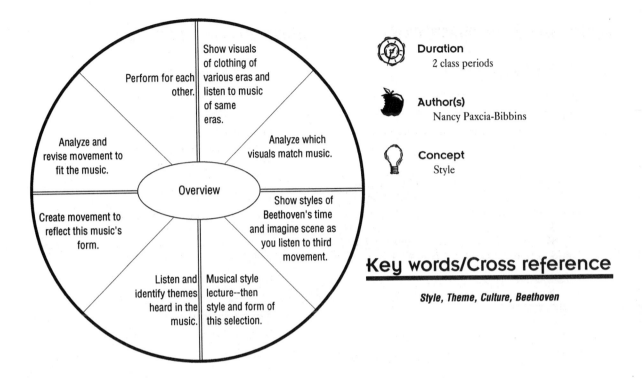

Show visuals of clothing of various eras and listen to music of same eras.

Perform for each other.

Analyze and revise movement to fit the music.

Overview

Analyze which visuals match music.

Create movement to reflect this music's form.

Show styles of Beethoven's time and imagine scene as you listen to third movement.

Listen and identify themes heard in the music.

Musical style lecture--then style and form of this selection.

Duration
2 class periods

Author(s)
Nancy Paxcia-Bibbins

Concept
Style

Key words/Cross reference

Style, Theme, Culture, Beethoven

Overview

Objective
This lesson familiarizes students with elements of musical style (especially, Classic period) and reinforces study of A-B-A form.

About the Author
Since 1986, Nancy Paxcia-Bibbins has been a music teacher at Indian Creek Elementary School, Indianapolis, Indiana (with the exception of a year and a half when she was on sabbatical to pursue a doctoral degree at Ball State University). Prior to Indian Creek, she taught middle school choral music for ten years, and before that, high school choral music for five years. Nancy has also taught music education courses at Ball State University, Muncie, Indiana and Marian College, Indianapolis, Indiana.

Required Resources
Recording of Beethoven's Symphony #1; visual of clothing styles in different eras (e.g., charleston era, big band era, rock and roll, etc., also, styles of Classic period); taped examples of same styles.

Bibliography
Beethoven, Jane, Jennifer, Davidson, Catherine Nadon-Gabrion, Carmino Ravosa, Phyllis Weikart, and Darrell Bledsoe. *World of Music, Book 5: Record 6.* Morristown: Silver Burdett & Ginn, 1988.

Beethoven Style

Quadrant 1—Experience

Right Mode—Connect

Show visuals of clothing of various eras and listen to music of same eras.

Objective

To connect students' interests in style with visual and aural images.

Activity

1) Show students visual of styles in different eras (Charleston era, big band of the forties, sixties—early and late, seventies). 2) Play music of same eras. (Tape) 3) Play rock—Beethoven's Fifth (Walter Murphy version).

Assessment

Student attention and involvement to activity.

Left Mode—Examine

Analyze which visuals match music.

Objective

To analyze visual and aural images.

Activity

1) Compare styles of clothes and music. Ask students to match the music with the styles. PLAY EXAMPLES ONE AT A TIME. 2) Ask about Beethoven's Fifth. Who recognizes it? What's the problem with matching styles? (older music, but modern rhythmic accompaniment). 3) Play Beethoven's Symphony. #1, 3rd movement—small section.

Assessment

Quality and quantity of student responses.

Quadrant 2—Concepts

Right Mode—Image

Show styles of Beethoven's time and imagine scene as you listen to third movement.

Objective

To relate styles of twentieth century to style of late eighteenth century.

Activity

1) Play Beethoven Symphony #1—Third Movement. Show pictures of people/clothes of that period. Have class imagine the scene of people and places of this time as they listen to the music. 2) Ask students to share their "images."

Assessment

Quality and quantity of student responses.

Left Mode—Define

Musical style lecture—then style and form of this selection.

Objective

To present information on music style of the Classic period and concepts about Beethoven and the Symphony #1—Third Movement.

Activity

1) Discuss style in music. The Classic Period—formality, regularity. Compare with the 20th century—more variety in forms, harmony, etc. (Reminder of Beethoven as rebel—but within framework of the times he lived in.) His music still reflects his time.
2) Read about Beethoven. Discuss years—born five years before Paul Revere's ride—"British are coming."
3) Show themes. Look at score. a) Play themes for class as they watch score. b) Class listens as teacher shows class how themes appear within the piece. Teacher writes numbers on the chalkboard relating to themes shown in the book as the class listens and watches. (Theme 1-Theme 2) (1-2) (1-2) 1 (3-3) (1-2) (1-2)
4) Tell class—like previous listening lesson, this is not traditional 3rd movement (slower, dignified), but it is A B A (ternary form).
5) Draw diagram of the overall form: A B A.

Assessment

Attention of students to presentation.
Review themes. Play themes.

Quadrant 3—Applications

Left Mode—Try

Listen and identify themes heard in the music.

Objective

To practice recognizing and identifying themes of the movement.

Activity

1) Play 45 seconds of record. Listen for tempo and dynamics. 2) Listen to themes. What instruments play themes? (a. strings, b. strings, c. woodwinds, repeated, strings, scalewise).

Assessment

Verbal responses to questions.

Right Mode—Extend

Create movement to reflect this music's form.

Objective

To add creative response to the music heard.

Activity

1) Review terms: locomotor (change in location) and nonlocomotor (movement in place) movement. Class names some examples (e.g., walking as locomotor, swaying as nonlocomotor). 2) Ask for volunteers to serve as model for movement activity. Listen to music first to imagine movement to fit with music. 3) Then class creates movement activity to demonstrate A B A form. Combine locomotor and nonlocomotor movements. Have class decide how movements can relate to the movement of the themes (e.g., Theme 1—going forward? Theme 3—in place?, etc.).

Assessment

Involvement and contributions of the class.

Quadrant 4—Creations

Left Mode—Refine

Analyze and revise movement to fit the music.

Objective

To have students evaluate their movement activity for appropriateness to the music heard.

Activity

1) Have class analyze whether the movements they have created fit the music that they hear. 2) Teacher asks leading questions: What about the mood? Tempo? Feeling? Melodic movement? Do they fit the style of the music? Students revise, if necessary.

Assessment

Quality and involvement of students in the task.

Right Mode—Integrate

Perform for each other.

Objective

To share with each other a physical response to the music heard.

Activity

1) Volunteer group performs while the music is played. 2) Class divides into groups and all perform. (Step B can be eliminated if student behavior or limitations on time warrant its exclusion.)

Assessment

Attention and involvement of students.

Bernstein Celebration

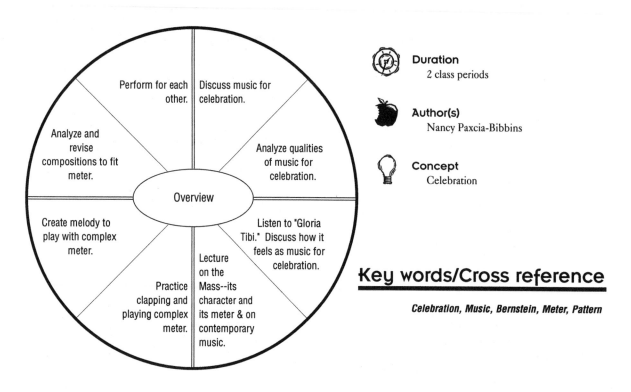

Overview

- Perform for each other.
- Discuss music for celebration.
- Analyze and revise compositions to fit meter.
- Analyze qualities of music for celebration.
- Create melody to play with complex meter.
- Listen to "Gloria Tibi." Discuss how it feels as music for celebration.
- Practice clapping and playing complex meter.
- Lecture on the Mass--its character and its meter & on contemporary music.

Duration
2 class periods

Author(s)
Nancy Paxcia-Bibbins

Concept
Celebration

Key words/Cross reference

Celebration, Music, Bernstein, Meter, Pattern

Overview

Objective
This lesson introduces Bernstein's Mass with emphasis on contemporary music and complex meter (5/8).

About the Author
Since 1986, Nancy Paxcia-Bibbins has been a music teacher at Indian Creek Elementary School, Indianapolis, Indiana (with the exception of a year and a half when she was on sabbatical to pursue a doctoral degree at Ball State University). Prior to Indian Creek, she taught middle school choral music for ten years, and before that, high school choral music for five years. Nancy has also taught music education courses at Ball State University, Muncie, Indiana and Marian College, Indianapolis, Indiana.

Required Resources
Recording of Bernstein's Mass; non-pitched instruments (two for each group of three, if possible); paper and pencil.

Bibliography
Beethoven, Jane, Jennifer, Davidson, Catherine Nadon-Gabrion, Carmino Ravosa, Phyllis Weikart, and Darrell Bledsoe. *World of Music, Book 5: Record 8.* Morristown: Silver Burdett & Ginn, 1988.

Quadrant 1—Experience

 ### Right Mode—Connect

Discuss music for celebration.

Objective
To stimulate students to think of music as a mode of celebration.

Activity
1) Teacher facilitates a discussion, beginning with: "Let's make today a day of celebration. What shall we celebrate? How will we celebrate? Food? Clothes? Activities?" 2) Encourage students to use their imagination to make this a day of celebration. 3) Ask students: What about music?

Assessment
Involvement of students in discussion.

 ### Left Mode—Examine

Analyze qualities of music for celebration.

Objective
To lead students to analyze the qualities of music used for celebration.

Activity
Ask students to compare the kind of music that might be used for different kinds of celebrations. Ask how they would describe music for a celebration? (fast, slow, major, minor, etc.?)

Assessment
Quality of student responses.

Quadrant 2—Concepts

 ### Right Mode—Image

Listen to "Gloria Tibi." Discuss how it feels as music for celebration.

Objective
To stimulate feelingful response to Bernstein's Gloria.

Activity
1) Tell students that they will listen to music written for a celebration (Bernstein, Gloria). 2) Listen. Ask students, "How does it make you feel? What do you like best—least—about this music as music for a celebration?"

Assessment
Quality of student responses.

 ### Left Mode—Define

Lecture on the Mass—its character and its meter & on contemporary music.

Objective
To present the facts about Bernstein's Mass, and to introduce concepts about complex meter.

Activity
1) Tell them that the music they heard was written for the celebration of the opening of J.F.K. Center—using Mass. 2) Tell the class about the creation of Mass—Mass created in 1971—combination of many musical styles—"modern man's crisis of faith"—performance art of the 70's. Describe the combination of "popular" and "classical" traditions—an example of the performance art of the 70's. Contrast the contemporary style with the previous lesson—Beethoven. Discuss differences between Classic style (formality, balance, regularity) and the Bernstein example. 3) Read about Bernstein in text. 4) Facts—Bernstein died, Oct. 1990. 5) Read "unusual meter." 6) Remind students of previous lessons: duple, triple meter—or music that moves in 2 or 3. 7) Tell class: meter in 5—complex meter is a combination of 2 & 3 together.

Assessment
Attention of students to lecture.

Bernstein Celebration

Quadrant 3—Applications

 ### Left Mode—Try

Practice clapping and playing complex meter.

Objective
To have students practice recognizing and performing complex meter and relate concept to Gloria Tibi.

Activity
1) Meter: —ask the class how the music is divided? (3 & 2). 2) Show 3 & 2 with words, gloria tibi 2 & 3 with words, Mary Jefferson. 3) Practice 3 & 2 pattern with clap on strong beats, tap on weaker ones. 4) Listen to music and practice the 3 & 2 pattern with the music.

Assessment
Involvement of students in activity.

Right Mode—Extend

Create melody to play with complex meter.

Objective
To encourage students to create their own musical experiences using complex meter.

Activity
1) Divide students into groups of three—have students create four measures of pattern in meter of five using body percussion and non-pitched instruments—contrast on accented, unaccented beats (using 2 & 3, or 3 & 2). 2) Give students one minute to decide which "job" they will perform. (Tell them that the teacher will assign the jobs if they haven't decided among themselves within that time frame.) Jobs: a) Play accented beat. b) Play unaccented beat(s). c) Add a melody with recorder using G pentatonic to go with meter. d) Tell students to prepare their creations for class performance.

Assessment
Involvement and ideas of students.

Quadrant 4—Creations

Left Mode—Refine

Analyze and revise compositions to fit meter.

Objective
To have students evaluate their works.

Activity
1) Have class write down analysis of what works, what doesn't. 2) Teacher-checks groups for concepts fitting to meter. 3) Collect papers of analysis.

Assessment
Quality of papers and discussion of the students.

Right Mode—Integrate

Perform for each other.

Objective
To share concepts learned by the groups.

Activity
Half of class performs for other half. Reverse.

Assessment
Quality of presentations and attention of fellow students.

Handel

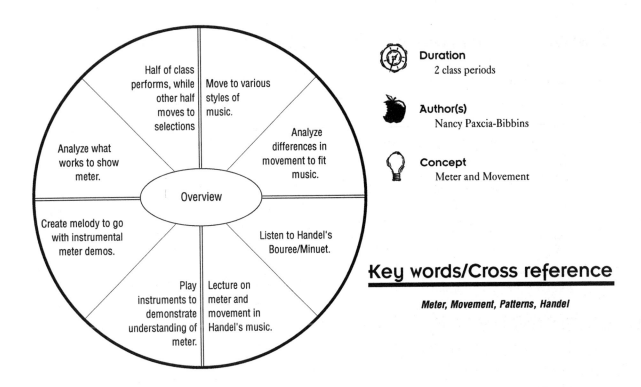

Overview

- Half of class performs, while other half moves to selections
- Move to various styles of music.
- Analyze differences in movement to fit music.
- Analyze what works to show meter.
- Create melody to go with instrumental meter demos.
- Listen to Handel's Bouree/Minuet.
- Play instruments to demonstrate understanding of meter.
- Lecture on meter and movement in Handel's music.

Duration
2 class periods

Author(s)
Nancy Paxcia-Bibbins

Concept
Meter and Movement

Key words/Cross reference

Meter, Movement, Patterns, Handel

Overview

Objective
This lesson relates meter and movement in two sections of Handel's Royal Fireworks music.

About the Author
Since 1986, Nancy Paxcia-Bibbins has been a music teacher at Indian Creek Elementary School, Indianapolis, Indiana (with the exception of a year and a half when she was on sabbatical to pursue a doctoral degree at Ball State University). Prior to Indian Creek, she taught middle school choral music for ten years, and before that, high school choral music for five years. Nancy also taught music education courses at Ball State University, Muncie, Indiana and Marian College, Indianapolis, Indiana.

Required Resources
Recording of Royal Fireworks music of Handel; pencil and paper; tape of musical examples with which to move: e.g., march, rock, waltz, jazz; non-pitched instruments and glockenspiels or other melody instruments with removable bars (one per class member, if possible).

Bibliography
Beethoven, Jane, Jennifer, Davidson, Catherine Nadon-Gabrion, Carmino Ravosa, Phyllis Weikart, and Darrell Bledsoe. *World of Music, Book 4: Record 3.* Morristown: Silver Burdett & Ginn, 1988.

Handel

Quadrant 1—Experience

 Right Mode—Connect

Move to various styles of music.

Objective

To relate various types of movement as affected by music students hear.

Activity

Play examples of music with which students are told to move (tape with examples of march, waltz, rock, slow jazz, electronic music).

Assessment

Observation of student responses.

 Left Mode—Examine

Analyze differences in movement to fit music.

Objective

To help students understand that there is a relationship between movement and music.

Activity

Analyze and discuss movement in the music heard. What does music do to you in terms of your body? Encourage student analysis.

Assessment

Quality of discussion and class reaction to activity.

Quadrant 2—Concepts

 Right Mode—Image

Listen to Handel's Bouree/Minuet.

Objective

To relate music to physical response of Handel's Royal Fireworks music - Bouree and Minuet.

Activity

Have students listen to Bouree and Minuet separately and imagine physical response of the 17th century. Share their "images."

Assessment

Quality of discussion.

 Left Mode—Define

Lecture on meter and movement in Handel's music.

Objective

To introduce students to the bouree and minuet as dance forms (movement) in the 17th century, and to extend their understanding of the musical selection and the composer.

Activity

1) Tell students about the music and the composer. Handel was commissioned to write Royal Fireworks Music. It uses dance forms - bouree and minuet. . 2) Use music text to read "About the Music." Discuss other music of Handel - especially popular, The Messiah. 3) Teach terms: bouree = folk dance, and minuet = court dance.

Review or teach the concept of Meter, and music "swings" - in 2 or 3 - duple or triple meter. Show the class how meter signatures indicate meter. Write examples of 2/4, 2/8, 3/4, and 3/8 on the board.

Assessment

Attention and behavior of the class.

Handel

Quadrant 3—Applications

 Left Mode—Try

Play instruments to demonstrate understanding of meter.

Objective
To practice listening to music with an understanding of meter.

Activity
1) Show class patterns to clap and tap as they listen to the music. (Use a hand-clap for the down-beat and a finger tap on palm for up beat.) 2) Ask class to decide which section is in 2 which in 3 as they listen to the Bouree and the Minuet. 3) After listening, ask class to raise their hands when asked: "Who thinks the Bouree was in two? in three? "Who thinks the Minuet was in two? in three?

Assessment
Correct response of the students.
Day Two

Objective
To recognize meter signatures and to play instruments to demonstrate meter. (Review and extension of Day One lesson.)

Activity
1) Look at p. 189. Ask: What are the signs in the music to tell you how the music "swings," i.e., what is the meter? 2) Divide into threes. Each group given non-pitched instruments. Play instrumental accompaniment to show meter of bouree or minuet (half of class assigned bouree, other half, assigned minuet). Show contrast in meter and strong beat, light beat, contrast. 3) Play music while students play instruments to Bouree or Minuet. (Listen to section not chosen to play.)

Assessment
Response of students to questions and instrument-playing of students.

 Right Mode—Extend

Create melody to go with instrumental meter demos.

Objective
To provide students an opportunity to add creations of their own.

Activity
Pass out one glockenspiel or other melody instrument for each group. Have students create their own melodies in C Pentatonic to fit with meter.

Assessment
Involvement of students and attention to assignment.

Quadrant 4—Creations

 Left Mode—Refine

Analyze what works to show meter.

Objective
To provide the students with the opportunity to evaluate what they have created.

Activity
Teacher checks each group - is the downbeat, upbeat differentiation appropriate to music? Is the melody appropriate to the meter accompaniment? Have students evaluate what they are creating. Write down what they think works, what needs to be improved, what questions they would like to ask when teacher comes to their pair. (Papers to be turned in to teacher.)

Assessment
Quality of questions and papers

 Right Mode—Integrate

Half of class performs, while other half moves to selections.

Objective
To relate meter, movement, and music.

Activity
Half of class perform to music, while other half of class moves to music. Reverse.

Assessment
Quality of the response of the students.

Haydn Form

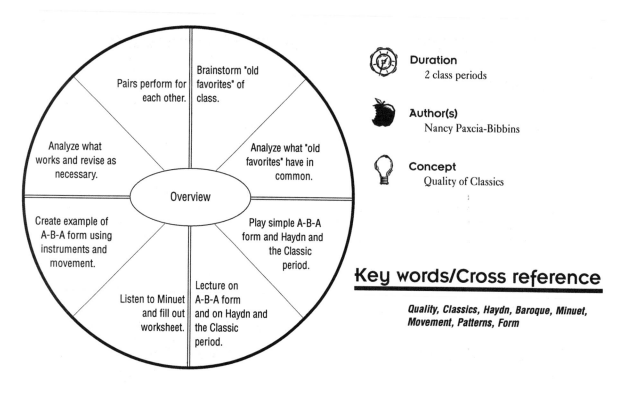

Duration
2 class periods

Author(s)
Nancy Paxcia-Bibbins

Concept
Quality of Classics

The circle diagram contains the following segments around "Overview":

- Brainstorm "old favorites" of class.
- Analyze what "old favorites" have in common.
- Play simple A-B-A form and Haydn and the Classic period.
- Lecture on A-B-A form and on Haydn and the Classic period.
- Listen to Minuet and fill out worksheet.
- Create example of A-B-A form using instruments and movement.
- Analyze what works and revise as necessary.
- Pairs perform for each other.

Key words/Cross reference

Quality, Classics, Haydn, Baroque, Minuet, Movement, Patterns, Form

Overview

Objective
This lesson is designed to promote understanding of the music of Haydn and to study A-B-A form.

About the Author
Since 1986, Nancy Paxcia-Bibbins has been a music teacher at Indian Creek Elementary School, Indianapolis, Indiana (with the exception of a year and a half when she was on sabbatical to pursue a doctoral degree at Ball State University). Prior to Indian Creek, she taught middle school choral music for ten years, and before that, high school choral music for five years. Nancy has also taught music education courses at Ball State University, Muncie, Indiana and Marian College, Indianapolis, Indiana.

Required Resources
Recording of Haydn's Symphony #94; song sheets of simple A-B-A examples, e.g., "Twinkle, Twinkle, Little Star," "Shoo-fly"; worksheet; pencil and paper; non-pitched instruments (one per class member, if possible).

Bibliography
The Bowmar Orchestral Library: Concert Matinee, no. 63. Melville, N.Y.: Belwin Mills Publ. Co., 1965.

Haydn Form

Quadrant 1—Experience

Right Mode—Connect

Brainstorm "old favorites" of class.

Objective
To relate ternary form to concepts with which students can identify.

Activity
1) Have students make a list of different foods they have enjoyed trying. Different sports - different songs - different clothes. 2) Write down the "old favorites" that you keep going back to. When you fix lunch, what would you fix? When you relax at home, what would you wear? When you get dressed up, what would you wear?

Assessment
Involvement of the students.

Left Mode—Examine

Analyze what "old favorites" have in common.

Objective
To encourage analysis of qualities of "old favorites."

Activity
1) Draw a "mind map" of qualities of "old familiars." (Write down each "old familiar" and first words that come to mind about each one.) Example:

mellow	bread
good	cheese
crackers	taste

2) Look at "mind maps" and analyze any similarities in different "old favorites."

Assessment
Quality of student responses.

Quadrant 2—Concepts

Right Mode—Image

Play simple A-B-A form and Haydn and the Classic period.

Objective
To relate "old favorites" to music and ternary form - back to the familiar.

Activity
1) Ask students to listen to the following music and determine if there is any connection between the previous discussion and what they hear. a) Sing Shoo-Fly (A-B-A), b) Listen to example of instrumental A-B-A. (Play Twinkle, Twinkle, Little Star). c) Listen to Haydn's Minuet from Symphony #94.

Assessment
Student answers. Do they pick up on "going back?"

Left Mode—Define

Lecture on A-B-A form and on Haydn and the Classic period.

Objective
To present information on Haydn's Minuet and to present information about the Classic and Baroque Periods.

Activity
1) Explain musical organization . . . form A-B-A - going back to A section in music - "old familiar" principle. 2) (Reminder of minuet in Handel's Royal Fireworks.) In Haydn's time, a minuet was usually used as third section, called a movement, of a symphony and was usually A B A (ternary form). 3) Explain that in the Classic Period there were four sections - movements - to a symphony. To our ears, each section may sound like a separate piece of music, but that they were all part of the overall design of the symphony. Tell them that was also part of the Classic Period's predictability - the "old familiar" - they could count on the symphony as having four movements. 4) Discuss differences in eras: Baroque (Handel) - irregularity, unpredictability - "flowery" - decorative. Classic (Mozart) - formal balance, predictability (use of A B A, typical) melodies more "clear-cut" - simpler to determine. 5) Play themes I and II. Show themes on overhead. Explain scalewise, skipwise movement. 6) Read information about Haydn (hand-out).

Assessment
Student attention and involvement in listening to presentation.

Haydn Form

Quadrant 3—Applications

 ### Left Mode—Try

Listen to Minuet and fill out worksheet.

Objective
To focus student listening on concepts presented.

Activity
Listen to music. Fill out worksheet.

Day Two
Minuet
Return worksheet. Ask students who remembers composer and period of last lesson's listening.

Assessment
Answers on worksheet and verbal responses.

 ### Right Mode—Extend

Create example of A-B-A form using instruments and movement.

Objective
Students add their creativity to the music to which they are listening.

Activity
1) Have students divide into pairs. Each pair given two non-pitched instruments. Decide on activities to reflect form of music. (A B A) 2) Create two non-locomotor movements, and use two instruments to demonstrate A B A. (Can use one for each section, or combine in different way for each section.) 3) Play music as students "try-out" their creations

Assessment
Students' attention to assignment and ability to work well with partner.

Quadrant 4—Creations

 ### Left Mode—Refine

Analyze what works and revise as necessary.

Objective
To have students evaluate what they are hearing and how it fits with their "creations."

Activity
Teacher goes to pairs, to see if they have concept. Students take one minute to write down their analysis of whether movements are fitting to music, other problems they might have. Pass in papers.

Assessment
Check papers and questions of students.

 ### Right Mode—Integrate

Pairs perform for each other.

Objective
To share what students have learned.

Activity
Share with class. Half of pairs perform, while other half watches. Then reverse.

Assessment
Quality of presentations.

Mozart Romance

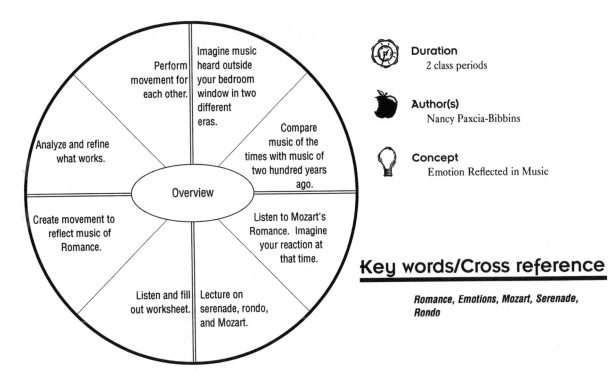

Duration
2 class periods

Author(s)
Nancy Paxcia-Bibbins

Concept
Emotion Reflected in Music

Key words/Cross reference

Romance, Emotions, Mozart, Serenade, Rondo

Overview

Objective
This lesson investigates the qualities and form (rondo) of Mozart's Romance.

About the Author
Since 1986, Nancy Paxcia-Bibbins has been a music teacher at Indian Creek Elementary School, Indianapolis, Indiana (with the exception of a year and a half when she was on sabbatical to pursue a doctoral degree at Ball State University). Prior to Indian Creek, she taught middle school choral music for ten years, and before that, high school choral music for five years. Nancy has also taught music education courses at Ball State University, Muncie, Indiana and Marian College, Indianapolis, Indiana.

Required Resources
Recording of Mozart's Eine Kleine Nacht Musick; worksheet; pencil and paper; cards designed to represent a variety of locomotor and nonlocomotor movements.

Bibliography
Beethoven, Jane, Jennifer, Davidson, Catherine Nadon-Gabrion, Carmino Ravosa, Phyllis Weikart, and Darrell Bledsoe. *World of Music, Book 4: Record 5.* Morristown: Silver Burdett & Ginn, 1988.

Mozart Romance

Quadrant 1—Experience

 ### Right Mode—Connect

Imagine music heard outside your bedroom window in two different eras.

Objective
To involve the students in imagining music heard in contemporary times and in the 18th century.

Activity
Ask the class: How many have a bedroom window? 1) Have class shut their eyes. Tell them: a) Imagine you're in the bedroom and you hear romantic music just outside the window. b) Imagine what it sounds like. 2) Imagine same thing—only this time, a long time ago: 1787.

Assessment
Observation of student responses.

 ### Left Mode—Examine

Compare music of the times with music of two hundred years ago.

Objective
To help students to recognize differences in music of two eras.

Activity
Students analyze and compare music of those two occasions. Share their observation.

Assessment
Quality of student responses.

Quadrant 2—Concepts

 ### Right Mode—Image

Listen to Mozart's Romance. Imagine your reaction at that time.

Objective
To relate Mozart's Romance to preceding discussion.

Activity
Tell students: Listen to music actually heard in the evening. 1) Imagine you are a palace guest in 1787. 2) Write your reactions—not as current times—but how you might have felt in 1787. Collect papers. Share discussion of ideas.

Assessment
Quality of papers and discussion.

 ### Left Mode—Define

Lecture on serenade, rondo, and Mozart.

Objective
To tell students about the music, its background, and how it is put together and about the composer.

Activity
Teach the facts. 1) Text reading about the serenade and about Mozart. 2) Discuss how music is put together. a) Uses three themes—(play for class). b) show letters for themes. c) Tell the class about the form: A B A C A (Rondo form)

Assessment
Attention of students.

Mozart Romance

Quadrant 3—Applications

Left Mode—Try

Listen and fill out worksheet.

Objective

To practice understanding of musical concepts as students listen.

Activity

1) Students listen to music. 2) Worksheet—fill in as they listen. 3) Collect.

Assessment

Worksheet answers and attentiveness of the students to listening.

Day Two

Return worksheet. Ask class who remembers what rondo form is.

Right Mode—Extend

Create movement to reflect music of Romance.

Objective

To add understanding and an original dimension to the music.

Activity

1) Ask class to create movement activity to reflect the Romance. 2) Divide into groups of four or five. Students decide which role assigned to each student. a) Movement director (locomotor and nonlocomotor directors, if 5 in group), b) Shape director, c) Recorder, d) Noise monitor (cooperative learning model). 3) Students pick cards for locomotor, nonlocomotor, and shape for group. 4) Play and show letters as class listens quietly, while they are imagining what movements would fit the music. 5) Class creates movement.

Assessment

Involvement and seriousness of the students.

Quadrant 4—Creations

Left Mode—Refine

Analyze and refine what works.

Objective

To have students evaluate and understand the qualities of the music and form of Romance.

Activity

1) Teacher checks with groups—appropriate movement for music? 2) Have students analyze if their "creations" do represent a rondo. Have them write down their analysis of what they have created. Be prepared to ask questions. Are the movements appropriate to the character of the music? Discuss with teacher and groups, how they can improve their work. Collect papers.

Assessment

Discussion and written analyses.

Right Mode—Integrate

Perform movement for each other.

Objective

To share student creations with the class.

Activity

Student Performances!—play music with groups performing movement for each other.

Assessment

Quality of presentations and response of fellow students.

Music/Pitch

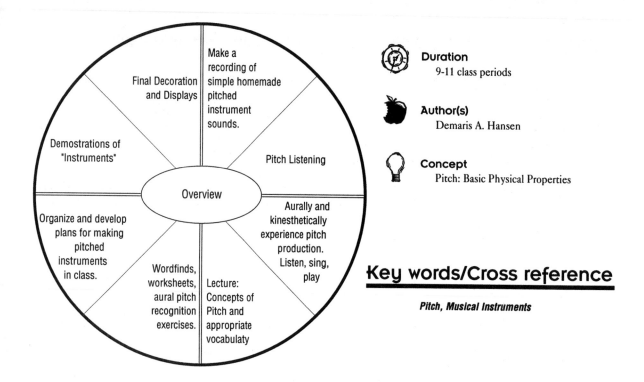

Duration
9-11 class periods

Author(s)
Demaris A. Hansen

Concept
Pitch: Basic Physical Properties

Key words/Cross reference

Pitch, Musical Instruments

Overview

Objective

The purpose of this unit is to introduce students to the basic physical properties of pitch production.

About the Author

Dr. Demaris Hansen is Education Program Consultant, Fine Arts Specialist, Kansas State Board of Education, Topeka. She is a certified 4MAT System Trainer.

Required Resources

Cassette player/recorder and tape for creating class pitched sounds; recordings demonstrating variety of pitched music; oscilloscope, rubber bands, piano, guitar, or cello strings; activities for guided practice; varietal materials for student projects

Music/Pitch

Quadrant 1—Experience

Right Mode—Connect

Make a recording of simple homemade pitched instrument sounds.

Objective

To introduce pitch quality by creating a class-produced recording.

Activity

Encourage students to bring from home one object that can produce a pitch (e.g. a bottle that can be blown into or struck, a whistle, or a bell). Students can also choose various pitched instruments available in the music class. Make a tape recording of the pitch or pitches of each "instrument."

Assessment

The ability to cooperate and participate in the activity.

Left Mode—Examine

Pitch Listening

Objective

To analyze the relationship of pitch to the size of the pitch-making instrument.

Activity

Play back the recording. Ask the children to listen for the pitches which are high and low. Ask the following questions: Which instruments produced high sounds? Which produced low sounds? What differences exist between high-pitched and low-pitched instruments? Did the amount of water in the glass or bottle make a difference in pitch when it was blown or struck? Can the pitch of the instrument be altered by changing its size or the amount of fluid it holds?

Assessment

The quality of responses to questions.

Quadrant 2—Concepts

Right Mode—Image

Aurally and kinesthetically experience pitch production. Listen, sing, play.

Objective

To aurally and kinesthetically experience pitch production.

Activity

1) Listen to twentieth century compositions by Henry Cowell, Anton Webern, John Cage, Peter Maxwell Davies, etc.) which demonstrate a wide variety of pitched sounds.
2) Play an improvised piece on a keyboard which has only one or two pitches to demonstrate how pitch variations are needed to create interest in music.
3) Sing a favorite song with the class. Then, change keys and sing it in a key which is obviously too high or too low for children so they can physically experience pitches which are beyond their physical capabilities.

Assessment

On-task listening and participation in activities.

Left Mode—Define

Lecture: Concepts of Pitch and appropriate vocabulary

Objective

To introduce vocabulary pertinent to the concept of pitch.

Activity

1) Through lecture/demonstration, illustrate the components of pitch which are appropriate for the grade level(s) chosen to learn pitch. Include some or all of the following vocabulary to describe and demonstrate: vibration (oscillation), oscilloscope, frequency, volume, fundamental, harmonics, overtone series, A440 (standard tuning), wave forms, timbre, etc. Use large rubber bands, piano strings, guitar or cello strings to demonstrate vibration and string density and length. A pebble dropped into a bowl of water is also a good visual representation of sound moving the air.
2) Show a drawing of the human ear and discuss how vibrations in the air trigger the hearing mechanisms in the brain.
3) Explain why there is a universal standard tuning pitch.
4) Discuss why some people have low or high voices (in relationship to vocal cord length and density).
5) Use an oscilloscope to show actual wave forms.

Assessment

A quiz over terminology.

Music/Pitch

Quadrant 3—Applications

Left Mode—Try

Word finds, worksheets, aural pitch recognition exercises.

Objective
To solidify terms and concepts associated with pitch.

Activity
Complete word finds, puzzles, mystery games. Complete activities offered in classroom music texts or science books. Review student's ability to recognize high, low, and same pitches.

Assessment
Quality of written work and participation in games.

Right Mode—Extend

Organize and develop plans for making pitched instruments in class.

Objective
To organize and develop plans for making pitched instruments in class. To encourage cooperation and participation from all students.

Activity
Students will divide into small groups and choose to design either a blown, struck, plucked, or bowed instrument to make in class (e.g. monochord, pan pipe, xylophone, dulcimer). Teachers can find the necessary construction materials through shop classes or donations from community lumber and construction companies. Parent volunteers can also assist with the construction phase. Students should take turns assembling the instrument.

Assessment
Students will be given points on their ability to stay on-task and cooperate with one another.

Quadrant 4—Creations

Left Mode—Refine

Demonstrations of "Instruments"

Objective
To evaluate instrument construction and playability. To evaluate the student's understanding of the general scientific principles of how pitches are made on their instrument.

Activity
1) Each group will demonstrate its instrument's design and playability and explain the scientific principles of its sound.
2) Students will be asked to compare their instruments with "real" instruments and discuss the ways in which theirs are different.
3) They will be encouraged to investigate how pitch ranges could be expanded and ways to better construct their instruments.
4) More advanced classes can further examine the phenomenon of harmonics.
5) Have students write or find a piece of music that could be played and recorded using the instrument they have constructed.
6) Try combining the instruments in the same piece and record.

Assessment
The quality of participation and discussion.

Right Mode—Integrate

Final Decoration and Displays

Objective
To display instruments in the music room, library, or school display case and share with the students' families and teachers.

Activity
1) Students will be allowed to decorate, put on final touches, or expand pitch ranges on their instrument.
2) They will write a letter to their family describing their work and what they learned and invite them to visit the school to see it.
3) Play recordings made in class for opening announcements at school.
4) Save instruments at school to use in conjunction with unit on melodic contour which follows the pitch unit.

Assessment
Quality of completed projects.

Mysteries

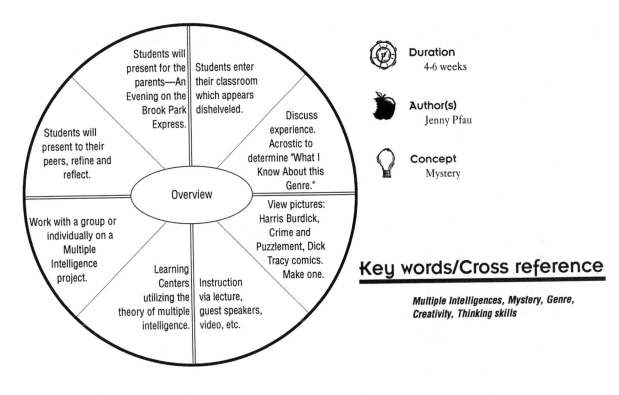

Duration
4-6 weeks

Author(s)
Jenny Pfau

Concept
Mystery

Overview (center)

Students enter their classroom which appears dishelveled.

Discuss experience. Acrostic to determine "What I Know About this Genre."

View pictures: Harris Burdick, Crime and Puzzlement, Dick Tracy comics. Make one.

Instruction via lecture, guest speakers, video, etc.

Learning Centers utilizing the theory of multiple intelligence.

Work with a group or individually on a Multiple Intelligence project.

Students will present to their peers, refine and reflect.

Students will present for the parents—An Evening on the Brook Park Express.

Key words/Cross reference

Multiple Intelligences, Mystery, Genre,
Creativity, Thinking skills

Overview

Objective
Students will learn about the genre of mysteries utilizing the theory of Multiple Intelligences. Students will develop a clearer understanding of the theory of Multiple Intelligences through practical application.

About the Author
Jenny Pfau is employed at Brook Park Elementary School – The Talent Development Academy in Lawrence Township Schools in Indianapolis, Indiana. She teaches fifth grade students in the Academically Talented Program.

Bibliography

Campbell, Linda (1992) *Teaching and Learning Through Multiple Intelligences;* New Horizons For Learning.

Chapman, Carolyn (1993) *If The Shoe Fits . . .;* IRI/Skylight Publishing, Inc.

Flack, Jerry (1990) *Mystery and Detection: Thinking and Problem Solving with the Sleuths;* Teacher Ideas Press.

Miller, Marvin (1990) *You Be the Jury;* Scholastic, Inc.

Sarnoff, Jane (1975) *The Code and Cipher Book;* Reynold Ruffins/Berne Convention.

Shushan, Ronnie (1984) *Big Book of Games;* Workman Publishing.

Sobol, Donald (1967) *Two-Minute Mysteries;* Scholastic, Inc.

Treat, Lawrence (1982) *Crime and Puzzlement;* David R. GodineVan Allsburg, Chris (1984) The *Mysterious Harris Burdick;* Houghton MifflinClue – A board game *How To Host A Teenage Mystery* – Board Game – (1993) Decipher, Inc.

Sleuth – A Simulation Interact, Inc. Learning Through Discovery.

Mysteries

Quadrant 1—Experience

 Right Mode—Connect

Students enter their classroom which appears disheveled.

Objective

To stimulate interest in the genre of mysteries.

Activity

Students will enter their classroom following a break or lunch period only to find the classroom in complete disarray. Chairs and desks should be overturned, items should be out of place, etc.

Assessment

Students' active involvement and curiosity.

 Left Mode—Examine

Discuss experience. Acrostic to determine "What I Know About this Genre."

Objective

To encourage student reflection on the classroom disaster experience. To make the connection to the fact that this experience is a mystery. To utilize an acrostic poem as the means to find out what the class already knows about this genre.

Activity

The teacher facilitates a verbal discussion of the "classroom mystery" discovery. She/he leads to the point that the class is trying to solve a mystery. During the discussion the teacher creates an acrostic of the word MYSTERY on the chalkboard or overhead and gleans from the class information they already know about mystery which she/he can then fill into the acrostic as this discussion occurs.

Assessment

Level of participation in class discussion and willingness to share ideas.

Quadrant 2—Concepts

 Right Mode—Image

View pictures: Harris Burdick, Crime and Puzzlement, Dick Tracy comics. Make one.

Objective

To integrate the concept of mystery into various works of art/pictures or cartoons.

Activity

Students will be shown a variety of pictures: Harris Burdick, Crime and Puzzlement, and Dick Tracy cartoons. The teacher should allow several students to share with the class the mystery they feel is occurring in this picture/cartoon. The class will then be asked to create their own mysterious picture or cartoon. Use the school binding machine to create your own classroom book of mysterious pictures/cartoons!

Assessment

Students' ability to transfer mystery ideas into the visual form.

 Left Mode—Define

Instruction via lecture, guest speakers, video, etc.

Objective

To teach elements of a mystery.

Activity

The teacher will present information on this genre utilizing a multi-model approach. Students will begin keeping a "Mystery and Detection" log to record their new learning. Guest speakers could include: homicide detectives, arson investigators, a finger print analyst, drug investigators, mystery writers, research biologists/chemists, employees of a missing persons bureau, etc.

Assessment

Level of student interest, quality of questions and comments during discussion, quality of log entries.

Mysteries

Quadrant 3—Applications

Left Mode—Try

Learning Centers utilizing the theory of Multiple Intelligence.

Objective

To reinforce and review the elements of mysteries.
To review the theory of multiple intelligences.

Activity

The teacher will create numerous learning centers with a mystery theme. As the students work through the center he/she needs to identify which of the seven multiple intelligences was utilized as they completed the center.

Center ideas:

Bodily/Kinesthetic:

- The boardgame – CLUE.
- Act out a well-known fairy tale which involves a crime – people in the group should guess which fairy tale is being acted out and what crime has been committed.
- What's Been Changed? – Students will form pairs facing one another; they are to carefully study one another. Signal players to turn away from their partner. Each partner should change 3 things about his/her appearance. Signal players to face one another again and detect what 3 things have been changed. Students will learn the importance of becoming a critical observer.

Visual/Spatial:

- View Encyclopedia Brown, Agatha Christie or Sherlock Holmes videos. Have the students stop the video before the crime is solved and record their prediction in their own Mystery and Detection Crime Book.
- Include several photo mysteries from the Book of Games which the students can solve.
- Utilize one of a number of computer programs available. Example – *Snooper Troops* sold by Tom Snyder Productions.
- Perform the experiment Mystery Powders, description of this hands-on science activity can be found in *Mystery and Detection* by Jerry Flack.
- Set out several ink pads with information about the different types of finger prints, allow students to make their own "fingerprint card."
- Place the book *Magic Eye A New Way of Looking At The World* or other book which cultivates the visual/spatial intelligence.

Verbal/Linguistic:

- Set up a listening center which contains Sherlock Holmes/Agatha Christie or other audio tapes which tell mysteries.
- Supply several You Be The Jury books by Marvin Miller for the students to peruse.
- Create a law school primer about crimes committed in fairy tales.
- Provide several Two Minute Mystery books by Donald Sobol.
- Secure audio tapes of old melodramas which the students can listen to and solve.

Logical/Mathematical:

- Utilize the Interact Simulation – "Sleuth."
- How to Host a Teenage Mystery – the board game.
- Mystery puzzles which must be completed in order to solve the crime.
- Include the book *Code and Cipher* or similar material which utilizes logic to solve the mystery presented.
- Computer programs which involve logic and/or math.

Musical/Rhythmic:

- Ask students to compose musical theme music for their favorite mystery stories.
- Have the students create sound effects to accompany a mystery melodrama.

Intrapersonal/Interpersonal:

These intelligences should be represented in all the centers. Depending on how you as the teacher set them up – the centers can be done either individually or in a group.

Assessment

Participation and involvement in the centers. Ability to discern which intelligence is utilized.

Right Mode—Extend

Work with a group or individually on a Multiple Intelligence project.

Objective

To extend what has been learned.

Activity

Students will create an activity to complete given the Multiple Intelligences Menu of Ideas. (See attached Menu for this activity.)

Assessment

Participation and on-task behavior of students.

Quadrant 4—Creations

 ## Left Mode—Refine

Students will present to their peers, refine and reflect.

Objective
To share their presentation with peers. To have students look critically at their work and the work of their peers. To have students discern the multiple intelligence(s) of their project. To reflect upon this project.

Activity
Students will present their project. During the introduction of their project to the class, students need to identify which multiple intelligence(s) was utilized in their project. Verbal feedback from the peers should occur once the project has been completed. Students will then need to complete a page which allows for reflection of their project.

Assessment
Ability to critique their peers' project. Ability to discern which multiple intelligence(s) are utilized in the project. Depth of student reflection of this project.

 ## Right Mode—Integrate

Students will present for the parents—An Evening on the Brook Park Express.

Objective
To share projects with parents, to celebrate their own/each others work.

Activity
Students will host for the parents – An Evening on the Brook Park Express.

Assessment
Quality of completed projects, presentations, participations, and enjoyment of learning.

Biography

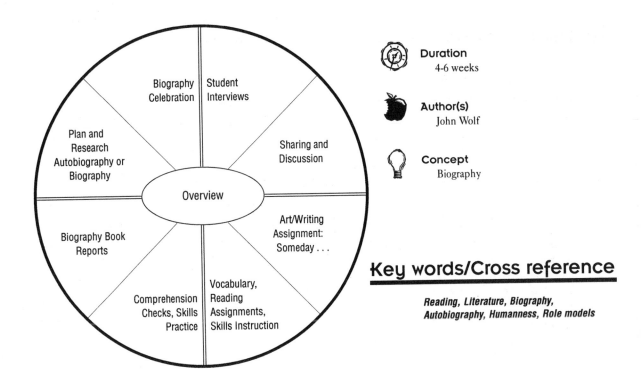

Biography Celebration

Student Interviews

Plan and Research Autobiography or Biography

Sharing and Discussion

Overview

Biography Book Reports

Art/Writing Assignment: Someday . . .

Comprehension Checks, Skills Practice

Vocabulary, Reading Assignments, Skills Instruction

Duration
4-6 weeks

Author(s)
John Wolf

Concept
Biography

Key words/Cross reference

Reading, Literature, Biography, Autobiography, Humanness, Role models

Overview

Objective
Biography is an important form of literature. It allows us to peer into the lives of significant human beings, seeing their greatness and their flaws. It deepens our understanding of the influences of time and place on a person's life. By reading biography, we form role models and process what it is to be human. We begin to see that it is important to have a vision of our own future, to be confident of our own gifts, and to work hard to reach our goals.

About the Author
John Wolf is a fourth grade classroom teacher and a 4MAT trainer in the NorthEast ISD in San Antonio, Texas.

Biography

Quadrant 1—Experience

 Right Mode—Connect

Student Interviews

Objective

For students to share their life experiences and personal likes with each other.

Activity

Each student will conduct an interview with a class-mate. The interviews will be concerned with major life events and other personal information. First the class brainstorms possible questions together (questions might be about their birth, family, pets, travels, injuries, sports, special lessons or talents, the best and worst things that have happened to them, favorite music, what they want to be when they grow up). The teacher may want to model an interview with a student. After the students have chosen partners, ask them to decide who will interview first. Give them ten to fifteen min-utes to ask questions and take notes. Then the students reverse roles.

Assessment

The information acquired in the interviews.

 Left Mode—Examine

Sharing and Discussion

Objective

To share information gathered and reflect on the simi-larities and differences among the students' lives and likes.

Activity

Independently, each student checks five or six things to share about his or her partner with the whole group. The pairs take turns introducing each other and pre-senting their information. At the conclusion, the teacher leads a discussion that reflects on the similarities and differences in each other's lives and likes.

Assessment

The information shared and the quality of discussion.

Quadrant 2—Concepts

 Right Mode—Image

Art/Writing Assignment: Someday . . .

Objective

For the student to express a personal vision in writing and images.

Activity

Each student brainstorms five things that s/he especially likes, followed by a list of five things that s/he especially dislikes. Then each student thinks of two things they would like to do someday. The students choose one of these to put in a sentence that starts, "Someday . . . " The sentence can be revised and edit-ed. The final copy is written on an unlined sheet of white paper, with the student drawing a full page illus-tration of the sentence.

Assessment

Thoughtfulness of choice, quality of product.

 Left Mode—Define

Vocabulary, Reading Assignments, Skills Instruction

Objective

To read with comprehension and insight, to introduce these specific skills: sequence, details, summarization, drawing conclusions, main idea, and character's feelings.

Activity

Use available textbook selections, literature units, film-strips, encyclopedia entries, periodical articles, movies, and guest speakers to introduce students to biographies. I like to incorporate mini-wheels on various topics, such as famous disabled people (Helen Keller, Beethoven), overcoming prejudice (Jackie Robinson, Rosa Parks, Martin Luther King, Jr.), unappreciated artists (van Gogh, Emily Dickinson, Mozart), and historical figures.

Assessment

Verbal feedback from students.

Biography

Quadrant 3—Applications

 ### Left Mode—Try

Comprehension Checks, Skills Practice.

Objective

To check for understanding of vocabulary, comprehension, and skills.

Activity

Use standard textbook and teacher-made worksheets to evaluate student knowledge and progress. Journal writings can give insights into the student's responses to the lives and times of the people studied. Pattern poems and metaphors can be effective in checking what a student has learned about a person.

Assessment

Performance on worksheets, journal writings.

5 Right Mode—Extend

Biography Book Reports.

Objective

To read and report on a biography book.

Activity

The student reads, completes a written report, and gives an oral presentation on a biography book. Students are allowed to choose their manner of presentation from: dressing up in character, making a poster, making a game, preparing a handout, or discussing related items from a "biography bag."

Assessment

Quality of written report and oral presentation.

Quadrant 4—Creations

 ### Left Mode—Refine

Plan and Research Autobiography or Biography.

Objective

To plan, revise, and edit a final project in which the student extends his/her learning about biography by becoming a biographer.

Activity

The student must plan, research, and write an autobiography or a biography of a relative, friend, or neighbor. Several interviews will be necessary to adequately obtain information. In the first interview the student should obtain information about the subject's birth, family, moves, schools, and other major life events. In the second interview the student should ask for anecdotal stories from various times during the subject's life, so that the personality of the subject will come alive in the writing. The third interview should be with secondary sources to obtain more anecdotal stories. Journal entries and teacher checks should occur at consistent intervals to gauge the progress of the student's work. The teacher could also provide a checklist to the student, so that the student can self-evaluate his or her work.

Assessment

Progress on project, self-evaluation checklists.

 ### Right Mode—Integrate

Biography Celebration.

Objective

Share biographies and celebrate the learning.

Activity

Prepare a "Biography Celebration." Decorate the room with the names of all people studied during the unit (as a class and individually), streamers, balloons, and a banner. Invite parents and administrators. Each student shares his or her favorite part of their own biography. Play a game that it is a spin-off of Jeopardy that I call "Who Am I?" Divide the class into small teams and give the class a clue about a famous person's life that they have studied. Assign each question points and on a "Daily Double" allow each team to risk as many of their points as they want to. "Publish" the biographies in a class book to be placed in the library. End the celebration with refreshments.

Assessment

The success of the celebration experience.

Construction

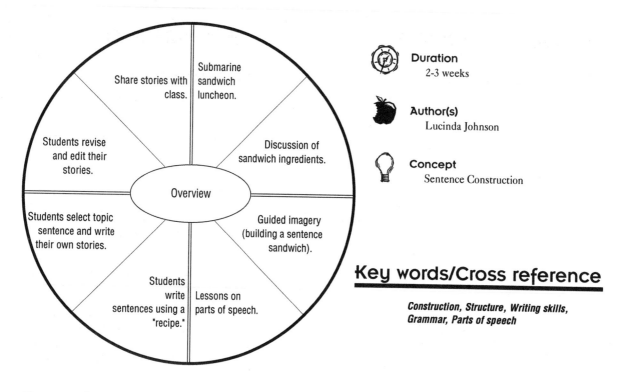

Share stories with class.

Submarine sandwich luncheon.

Students revise and edit their stories.

Discussion of sandwich ingredients.

Overview

Students select topic sentence and write their own stories.

Guided imagery (building a sentence sandwich).

Students write sentences using a "recipe."

Lessons on parts of speech.

Duration
2-3 weeks

Author(s)
Lucinda Johnson

Concept
Sentence Construction

Key words/Cross reference

Construction, Structure, Writing skills, Grammar, Parts of speech

Overview

Objective
Students will begin and end sentences correctly. Students will recognize the main parts of a sentence and recognize the lesser parts that make a sentence more descriptive. Students will identify subject, predicate, and parts of speech in a sentence. Students will write complete sentences.

About the Author
Lucinda Johnson has over 15 years of teaching experience, six of them teaching fourth grade. She has also taught Chapter 1 reading, 6th grade, elementary art and physical education. She is a teacher at Weston Elementary School, Otsego Local Schools, OH.

Required Resources
Q1: Meat, bread, sandwich toppings, other food items, plates and utensils for making and eating lunch in room.

Q2: Text, resource books, Schoolhouse Rock Grammar video.

Q3: Worksheets, test, construction paper, teacher made "recipe" (topic) cards.

Q4: Construction paper, markers.

Construction

Quadrant 1—Experience

 ### Right Mode—Connect

Submarine sandwich luncheon.

Objective

Students will "build" a submarine sandwich recognizing the importance of some ingredients over others.

Activity

Students bring in food items and paper products for submarine sandwiches. (Plan to eat lunch in the room.) Encourage students to build their sandwich using their favorite meats and as many condiments as they like.

Assessment

Involvement in activity.

 ### Left Mode—Examine

Discussion of sandwich ingredients.

Objective

Students will discuss the relative importance of the sandwich ingredients.

Activity

Discuss the items chosen for sandwiches. Which items were most essential and which added flavor and taste? Are there several ways to make a good sandwich? Note that bread and meat was a part of almost everyone's sandwich and without these ingredients it would not be a submarine sandwich. The other items could have been left out, but made the sandwich taste better.

Assessment

Participation in discussion.

Quadrant 2—Concepts

 ### Right Mode—Image

Guided imagery (building a sentence sandwich).

Objective

Students will imagine sandwich parts as the parts of a sentence.

Activity

Guided imagery. (Sentence Builders) Students close their eyes and imagine themselves in the kitchen creating a sentence sandwich. The bottom half of the bun is the period. This is always found at the bottom (or end) of the sentence. The top of the bun is the capital letter, always found at the beginning of our sentence. Lift the top of the bun off of the bottom to make our sentence. Begin your sandwich with mustard, catsup or mayonnaise. You choose. Take whichever one you chose and write the word "the" on the inside of the top bun. Next we will choose two slices of meat. The first slice is "class." "Class is the meat or subject of the sentence. The second slice is "ate" or the predicate. Your sentence is now complete if you want to stop here: "The class ate." This conveys a complete thought, but let's add more to this sentence to improve it. Choose your favorite item to add to the sandwich (tomato, onion, lettuce). What did the class eat? . . . Sandwiches. Add this to the bottom of the sentence. It now says: The class ate sandwiches. Can we add more items to make it even more descriptive? What kind of sandwiches did the class eat? . . . Submarine. Add this to the sentence. "The class ate submarine sandwiches." Choose another item to tell what kind of sandwiches the class ate . . . Delicious. How did the class eat? . . . Slowly. "The class ate delicious submarine sandwiches slowly." You could continue to add items if you wanted more on the sandwich. You can make it as plain or as full as you'd like.

Assessment

Participation in activity.

 ### Left Mode—Define

Lessons on parts of speech.

Objective

Students will identify the main ingredients of a good sentence and the lesser ingredients that make a sentence more descriptive.

Activity

Use textbook activities, transparencies, and the video, *"Schoolhouse Rock Grammar"* to teach basic parts of speech and sentence structure.

Assessment

Participation in discussions and attention to presentations.

Quadrant 3—Applications

 ## Left Mode—Try

Students write sentences using a "recipe."

Objective

Students will practice writing correct sentences, identifying simple subjects and simple predicates, and creating more descriptive sentences.

Activity

Pairs of students draw a "recipe" (topic) card from a deck of teacher made cards. Each card names a topic and lists several "ingredients" (questions) students are to consider when writing their sentence. They choose various colors of construction paper and markers to build a sentence in the shape of a submarine sandwich. Each part of the sandwich has a word in the sentence written on it. The top bun has the first word and is capitalized, and the bottom bun will have an ending punctuation mark (. or !). Use worksheets, quizzes, and creative writing activities to reinforce learning.

Assessment

Completion and competency on worksheets and quizzes.

 ## Right Mode—Extend

Students select topic sentence and write their own stories.

Objective

Students will write a creative story using complete sentences.

Activity

Students select one of the sandwich sentences displayed in the room as a story starter. Students apply their knowledge of sentence structure while writing their stories.

Assessment

Completion of task.

Quadrant 4—Creations

 ## Left Mode—Refine

Students revise and edit their stories.

Objective

Students will refine their stories.

Activity

Students edit, rewrite, and make a final copy of their story.

Assessment

Completion and accuracy of project.

 ## Right Mode—Integrate

Share stories with class.

Objective

Students will share project with the class.

Activity

Students read their stories to the class as class listens for correct sentence structure.

Assessment

Assessment of project.

Descriptive Writing

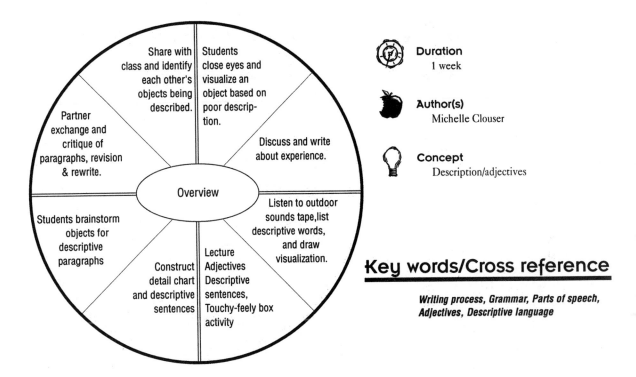

Overview

- Share with class and identify each other's objects being described.
- Students close eyes and visualize an object based on poor description.
- Partner exchange and critique of paragraphs, revision & rewrite.
- Discuss and write about experience.
- Students brainstorm objects for descriptive paragraphs
- Listen to outdoor sounds tape, list descriptive words, and draw visualization.
- Construct detail chart and descriptive sentences
- Lecture Adjectives Descriptive sentences, Touchy-feely box activity

Duration
1 week

Author(s)
Michelle Clouser

Concept
Description/adjectives

Key words/Cross reference

Writing process, Grammar, Parts of speech, Adjectives, Descriptive language

Overview

Objective

The students will successfully construct a Descriptive Paragraph.

About the Author

Michelle Clouser, 3rd Grade Teacher, Marion Community Schools, Marion, IN. Michelle received her 4MAT training in the Marion 4MAT Project, led by Carol Benefiel Secttor.

Required Resources

Cassette tape of outdoor sounds.

Descriptive Writing

Quadrant 1—Experience

 ### Right Mode—Connect

Students close eyes and visualize an object based on poor description.

Objective
To peak the students' interest and curiosity.

Activity
The students will be instructed to close their eyes as the teacher describes an object, but does so leaving out key descriptive words.

Assessment
Were the students confused as to what the object was or looked like? Did they ask for more information?

 ### Left Mode—Examine

Discuss and write about experience.

Objective
The students will recognize, discuss and list areas of the description and its deficiencies and make additions to the description.

Activity
Discuss the previous description and what made it hard to get a mental picture of the object. Also, construct new verbal descriptions and descriptive words.

Assessment
Were the students able to identify what the deficiencies were? Were the students able to list words that would make the description more accurate?

Quadrant 2—Concepts

 ### Right Mode—Image

Listen to outdoor sounds tape, list descriptive words, and draw visualization.

Objective
The student will describe in their own words and pictures their perception of a sound that is on tape.

Activity
The students will listen to an "outside sound" on a tape and get a mental picture in their mind of the setting. They will write down adjectives to describe the sounds and draw a picture of what they "saw." They will compare this with their partner.

Assessment
Were the students able to come up with a description and picture based on the tape?

 ### Left Mode—Define

Lecture
Adjectives
Descriptive sentences,
Touchy-feely box activity

Objective
The students will be able to list descriptive words, write descriptive sentences and create a detail chart.

Activity
Lecture and discussion. Review adjectives, writing descriptive sentences and creating a detail chart based on using five senses. Review discussion of paragraph structure.

Assessment
Were the students able to create a correct detail chart and descriptive sentences?

Descriptive Writing

Quadrant 3—Applications

 ### Left Mode—Try

Construct detail chart and descriptive sentences.

Objective

The students will construct a detail chart and write a descriptive paragraph of a given object. The teacher supplies this object.

Activity

The students will first construct a detail chart of a given specific object and then write a descriptive paragraph following the correct paragraph procedures based on the specific object and detail chart.

Assessment

Were the students able to create an accurate and sensible descriptive paragraph based on the object?

 ### Right Mode—Extend

Students brainstorm objects for descriptive paragraphs

Objective

The students will create a descriptive paragraph based on an object of their own choosing that specifically interests them.

Activity

The students will brainstorm objects that are unique or relative to them and create a detail chart and a descriptive paragraph. They also will be responsible for telling why they chose this specific object.

Assessment

Were the students able to correctly construct a descriptive paragraph using appropriate descriptive words, correct paragraph and sentence structure?

Quadrant 4—Creations

 ### Left Mode—Refine

Partner exchange and critique of paragraphs, revision & rewrite.

Objective

The students will assist each other with improving their paragraphs.

Activity

The students will first review their own paragraphs for mistakes and then will participate in a partner exchange. The students will critique each other and suggest areas of improvement and point out strengths of the description. Time will be given for revision and rewrite. (How well could the classmate identify the described object based on the description?)

Assessment

Were the students able to assist each other politely while making improvements in their paragraphs?

 ### Right Mode—Integrate

Share with class and identify each other's objects being described.

Objective

The students will share paragraphs with the class and try to identify the objects being described.

Activity

Each student will share their paragraph with the class and after the class has identified the object, tell why he/she chose this particular object. They may also bring their object in if possible.

Assessment

Did the students enjoy participating in this sharing time and successfully identify the objects described? (A comment card will be given to each child for them to voice their opinion of this activity.)

Fact vs. Opinion

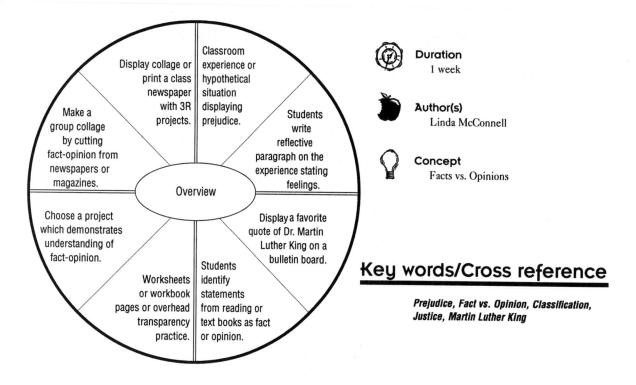

Make a group collage by cutting fact-opinion from newspapers or magazines.

Display collage or print a class newspaper with 3R projects.

Classroom experience or hypothetical situation displaying prejudice.

Students write reflective paragraph on the experience stating feelings.

Choose a project which demonstrates understanding of fact-opinion.

Overview

Display a favorite quote of Dr. Martin Luther King on a bulletin board.

Worksheets or workbook pages or overhead transparency practice.

Students identify statements from reading or text books as fact or opinion.

Duration
1 week

Author(s)
Linda McConnell

Concept
Facts vs. Opinions

Key words/Cross reference

Prejudice, Fact vs. Opinion, Classification, Justice, Martin Luther King

Overview

Objective
Students will learn to discriminate between fact and opinion statements using the life and work of Dr. Martin Luther King as the content of the unit.

About the Author
Linda McConnell is a 4th grade teacher in Grand Island, NE. She has 20 years classroom experience in grades 1, 3, 4 and 5.

Required Resources
Books, tapes, videos about Dr. Martin Luther King, Jr.

Bibliography
Martin Luther King by Rae Bains. Troll Associates.
Martin Luther King: The Peaceful Warrior by Ed Clayton. Prentice-Hall, Inc.

Fact vs. Opinion

Quadrant 1—Experience

 Right Mode—Connect

Classroom experience or hypothetical situation displaying prejudice.

Objective
Initiate a problem solving situation which allows for personal student involvement and responses. Capture student attention.

Activity
Classroom experience where students with red squares on the bottom of their chairs have to "wait" on a partner by heading their papers during the day, handing their papers in, sharpening their pencils, etc.

Assessment
Reaction of the students to being unfairly selected for "work."

 Left Mode—Examine

Students write reflective paragraph on the experience stating feelings.

Objective
Guide student to reflection and analysis of the experience. Establish a positive attitude toward the diversity of different people's experience.

Activity
Analyze the experience by making a class T table: I had to . . . I felt . . . Write a reflective paragraph about the experience. (Example: I had to "tie my partners shoe." This becomes the fact part of the activity. I felt "taken advantage of." This becomes the opinion part.)

Assessment
Quality of contribution to the task and quality of the T charts.

Quadrant 2—Concepts

 Right Mode—Image

Display a favorite quote of Dr. Martin Luther King on a bulletin board.

Objective
Take students to a broader reality. Present concept into another experience, in this case, an art experience and written sentences.

Activity
The students listen to a video or book about Dr. Martin Luther King, Jr. Excerpts from his speeches are particularly valuable. Students may research materials themselves. Students choose a favorite quote and print it on a bulletin board character. (On back) students write five sentences telling true "happenings" from Dr. King's life.

Assessment
Art project (opinion part). Five sentences (fact part).

 Left Mode—Define

Students identify statements from reading or text books as fact or opinion.

Objective
Discriminate between fact and opinion statements. Draw attention to important, discrete details.

Activity
Read fact or opinion statements or show an overhead and have students label fact or opinion. Write the words of the sentence which indicate student choice. (Key words: "I believe," "I think," etc.)

Assessment
Individual or group "notes" or activity sheet.

Fact vs. Opinion

Quadrant 3—Applications

 ### Left Mode—Try

Worksheets or workbook pages or overhead transparency practice.

Objective
Hands-on activities for practice and mastery.

Activity
Worksheet or workbook exercises for fact vs. opinion.

Assessment
Worksheets.

Right Mode—Extend

Choose a project which demonstrates understanding of fact-opinion.

Objective
Encourage and provide multiple options so students can plan a unique "proof" of their learning.

Activity
Choose one of the following:
1) Write and illustrate a cartoon containing a fact and an opinion.
2) Write a commercial with three facts and three opinions about your product and "deliver" it to classmates.
3) Find fact and opinion statements in easy fiction books.
4) Write fact and opinion books about your classmates, school or yourself.
5) Interview a school staff member and color code their responses as fact or opinion.

Assessment
Cartoon, commercial, written paper, booklet, or interview.

Quadrant 4—Creations

Left Mode—Refine

Make a group collage by cutting fact-opinion from newspapers or magazines.

Objective
Require students to organize their learning in some personal, meaningful way.

Activity
Produce an activity in Quadrant 3R and publish it in a class newspaper. Divide into cooperative groups and make collages or murals of fact and opinion statements from book, newspapers, movies, etc.

Assessment
Mural or collage.

Right Mode—Integrate

Display collage or print a class newspaper with 3R projects.

Objective
Celebrate the sharing of learning.

Activity
Share projects, newspaper, collages by putting them in the hall, reading to other classes, taking home to parents.

Assessment
Completed projects displayed.

Folk Stories

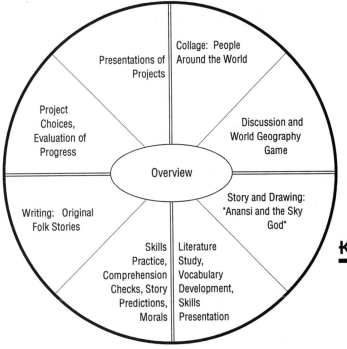

Presentations of Projects

Collage: People Around the World

Project Choices, Evaluation of Progress

Discussion and World Geography Game

Overview

Writing: Original Folk Stories

Story and Drawing: "Anansi and the Sky God"

Skills Practice, Comprehension Checks, Story Predictions, Morals

Literature Study, Vocabulary Development, Skills Presentation

Duration
4-6 weeks

Author(s)
John Wolf

Concept
Folk Stories Around the World

Key words/Cross reference

Folk stories, Folk tales, Literature, Storytelling, Geography, Culture, Fables, Patterns

Overview

Objective

For thousands of years and in all cultures around the world, folk stories have been used to entertain and instruct children. Besides being a vehicle to pass on cultural traditions, beliefs, and myths, they provide valuable moral instruction. Folk stories from many traditions are easily available to the students and teacher, are delightful to study and discuss, and can be presented in a variety of interesting and meaningful ways.

About the Author

John Wolf is a fourth grade classroom teacher and 4MAT trainer in North East ISD in San Antonio, Texas.

Required Resources

Poster board, magazines to cut, world maps.

Bibliography

Here are some of my favorite folk tales published as children's picture books:

Haley, Gail E. *A Story, A Story.* New York: Atheneum, 1970.

Dayrell, Elphinstone. *Why the Sun and the Moon Live in the Sky.* Baston: Houghton Miflin, 1968.

Aardema, Verna. *Why Mosquitoes Buzz in People's Ears.* New York: The Dail Press, 1975.

Steptoe, John. *Mufaro's Beautiful Daughters.* New York: Scholastic, Inc., 1987.

Paterson, Katherine. *The Tale of the Mandarin Ducks.* New York: Scholastic, Inc.

Williams, Jay. *Everyone Knows What a Dragon Looks Like.* New York: Four Winds Press, 1976.

McDermott, Gerald. *Arrow to the Sun.* New York: Penguin Books, 1974.

Goble, Paul. *The Gift of the Sacred Dog.* New York: Macmillan, 1980.

Goble, Paul. *Buffalo Woman.* New York: Macmillan, 1984.

Goble, Paul. *The Girl Who Loved Wild Horses.* New York: Macmillan, 1978.

DePaola, Tomie. *The Legend of the Bluebonnet.* New York: G. P. Putnam's Sons, 1983.

DePaola, Tomie. *The Legend of the Scarlet Paintbrush.* New York: G.P. Putnam's Sons,

Baker, Olaf. *Where the Buffaloes Begin.* New York: Puffin, 1981.

San Souci, Robert. *The Legend of Scarface.* New York: Doubleday, 1971.

Folk Stories

Quadrant 1—Experience

 Right Mode—Connect

Collage: People Around the World

Objective

To provide the students with an experience that opens them up to the extraordinary diversity among people throughout the world.

Activity

The students make a collage of images of people from around the world. In the collage they may want to try to show differences and similarities among people by their positioning of the images they collect. Grouping: small (3-5), heterogeneous

Materials:

posterboard, scissors, glue, magazines

Personal Note:

I have the luxury of having some cast-aside National Geographic magazines, but news and travel magazines also have fine images for this activity. I allow the students to overlap or separate the images. Time: 45 minutes to an hour.

Assessment

Informally evaluate students on their participation, involvement, and enthusiasm while making the collage. The teacher can have informal talks with the groups while monitoring their progress. Leading questions might include: What have you discovered so far? Why did you choose that image? Have you thought about how you are going to place the images on the posterboard?

Left Mode—Examine

Discussion and World Geography Game
Activity 1: Discussion

Objective

To analyze differences and similarities among people around the world.

Activity

In the same small collage groups, have students list 5 major differences among people that they noticed from doing the collage activity. Have one person from each group share with the larger group. Then have the students brainstorm 5 similarities among all people. These should be broad. Share with the larger group.

Personal Note:

Cooperative learning strategies are helpful in this type of activity.

Assessment

Quality of ideas suggested in the brainstorming activity, participation, new insights.

Activity 2:

World Geography Game

Objective

To check the students' knowledge of the countries of the world, and to prepare the students to know where some of their folk stories are from.

Activity

Provide each small group with a world map. Call out a country and the students
search for and locate the country. The student within the group that locates the country first "wins" that round.

Assessment

Ability to locate the major countries of the world.

Folk Stories

Quadrant 2—Concepts

 ### Right Mode—Image

Story and Drawing: "Anansi and the Sky God."

Objective

To move the student into understanding that the telling of folk stories is a tradition shared by people all over the world.

Activity

The African folk tale, *A Story*, retold and illustrated by Gail E. Haley, is the tale of how stories came to the people and animals of the earth. The Sky God keeps all the stories in a golden box and Anansi, the spider man, asks how he might purchase them. The Sky God is amused and gives him three impossible tasks to complete. Anansi uses trickery to complete the tasks and gain the chest of stories. After reading or telling the story to the students, ask them to draw a scene from the story. The teacher can start a bulletin board that students can add to with each folk tale that the teacher reads aloud and that they read independently. The Sky God's golden box of stories can be the focal point of the bulletin board and story summaries or story diagrams can be coming from the box.

Assessment

Student enjoyment, involvement in making the image, and discussion about the story for story elements, characterization, plot twists, and moral.

 ## Left Mode—Define

Literature Study, Vocabulary Development, Skills Presentation

Objective

To enjoy quality literature, to increase comprehension and vocabulary, and to introduce or improve in these specific skills: detail finding , sequence, outcome predictions, main idea, summarization, and story elements.

Activity

Teach folk stories through basal stories, literature units, storytelling, reading books aloud, a book center of folk stories, and filmstrips. Stories can be grouped by origins or themes: African folk tales, Native American folk tales, Asian folk tales, Fairy tales, Tall tales, Cinderella stories, trickster stories. Social Studies can be integrated through cultural and historical studies that coincide with the themes. Give direct instruction in any of these skills areas that have not already been introduced: finding details, sequence, predicting outcomes, main idea, summarization, and story elements.

Assessment

Informal verbal checks and student interest.

Quadrant 3—Applications

Left Mode—Try

Skills Practice, Comprehension Checks, Story Predictions, Morals

Objective

To practice skills, check for comprehension, and evaluate for understanding of vocabulary.

Activity

Use a variety of evaluative techniques, including comprehension questions, vocabulary work, and skills practice sheets. Predict outcomes: Stop reading or telling a story before the final solution and have small groups discuss how the story might end. Share the best ideas with the whole class. Then finish reading the story. Main Idea: Have each student write the moral of the story. Share in small groups, then as a whole group. Summarization: At the end of a story, read an example of a good summary for that story. After a subsequent story write a summary as a class. After yet another story, have the students write a summary in a small group. Finally have the students individually write summaries. Story Elements: Story mapping.

Assessment

Objective evaluations of worksheets, quality of story predictions, morals, summarizations, and story elements.

Right Mode—Extend

Writing: Original Folk Stories

Objective

To write original folk stories in different literary styles.

Activity

As a response to studying different types of folk stories, have the students write original stories based on the patterns they have discovered in their study. For example, after reading several fables, have the students write an original fable. The same could be done after studying repetitive folk tales, tall tales, and legends.

Assessment

The ability of the student to show imagination and creativity within the patterns of the types of folk stories studied.

Quadrant 4—Creations

Left Mode—Refine

Project Choices, Evaluation of Progress.

Objective

To plan and begin implementing a project.

Activity

The students may work individually or in small groups to prepare and present a folk tale project. Project ideas include: presenting a folk tale as a play or puppet show, storytelling, reading folk tales to younger students, writing an original folk tale, or reading and doing a book report on a collection of folk tales.

Assessment

Choice of projects, ability to objectively analyze progress on project.

Right Mode—Integrate

Presentations of Projects

Objective

To share projects with classmates and others.

Activity

Present plays, puppet shows, storytelling, readings, and/or book reports. Videotaping the performances and inviting parents and other students can make this an even greater learning experience.

Assessment

The quality of presentation and preparation, and the joy of sharing it with others.

Friendship

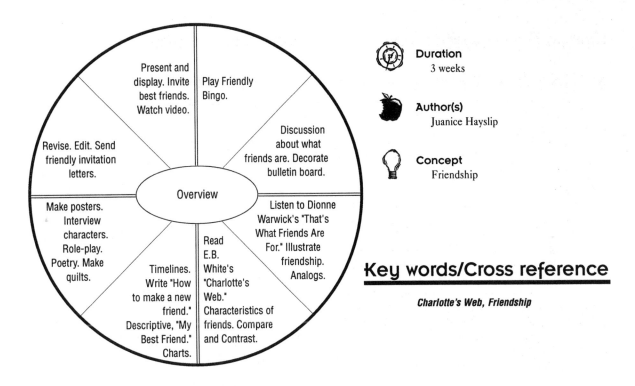

Overview

- Present and display. Invite best friends. Watch video.
- Play Friendly Bingo.
- Discussion about what friends are. Decorate bulletin board.
- Revise. Edit. Send friendly invitation letters.
- Make posters. Interview characters. Role-play. Poetry. Make quilts.
- Timelines. Write "How to make a new friend." Descriptive, "My Best Friend." Charts.
- Read E.B. White's "Charlotte's Web." Characteristics of friends. Compare and Contrast.
- Listen to Dionne Warwick's "That's What Friends Are For." Illustrate friendship. Analogs.

 Duration
3 weeks

Author(s)
Juanice Hayslip

Concept
Friendship

Key words/Cross reference

Charlotte's Web, Friendship

Overview

 Objective
Using the theme of friendship and literature, the students will understand more about characters and their feelings.

 About the Author
Juanice Hayslip is a fourth grade classroom teacher in Irving, TX. She is a certified 4MAT trainer.

 Required Resources
Posterboard, assorted art supplies, yarn, tempera paint, recording of *"That's What Friends Are For."* Thematic Unit *"Friends"* from Teacher Created Materials and from *"Dionne Warwick Friends."* Arista Recording. Copies of E.B. White's *"Charlotte's Web."*

Bibliography
White, E.B. *"Charlotte's Web."* Dell, 1952. For additional reading: Patterson, Katherine. *"Bridge to Terabithia."* Harper, 1977.

Quadrant 1—Experience

Right Mode—Connect

Play Friendly Bingo.

Objective

To create an experience that allows the students to learn more about one another and possibly establish new friendships based on interests and likes.

Activity

Students play friendly bingo by going around and finding someone whose favorite is the same as theirs. They get a bingo when they have filled in four spaces in a row across, down or diagonally. Make a 16 grid Bingo card with a variety of favorites (food, TV shows, color, holiday, book, movie, soft drink, fast food, rock group, sport, animal, month, ice cream, game, season, hero, snack).

Assessment

Students' engagement and enjoyment.

Left Mode—Examine

Discussion about what friends are. Decorate bulletin board.

Objective

To provide students with the opportunity to discuss what friendship means to them.

Activity

Guide students in reflecting on their feelings as they played "Friendship Bingo." Students brainstorm on ways to be a friend and use ideas to construct a word web on the bulletin board.

A FRIEND IS

Assessment

Contribution and quality of personal statements.

Quadrant 2—Concepts

Right Mode—Image

Listen to Dionne Warwick's "That's What Friends Are For." Illustrate friendship. Analogs.

Objective

Students will create an analog of friendship.

Activity

While listening to Dionne Warwick's, *"That's What Friends Are For,"* the students will create drawings that represent acts of friendship.

Assessment

Quality of individual drawings.

Left Mode—Define

Read E.B. White's "Charlotte's Web." Characteristics of friends. Compare and Contrast.

Objective

To read and study E.B. White's *"Charlotte's Web"* and learn about friendship through the characters.

Activity

Chapters will be assigned to groups. Classroom instruction will focus on characterizations while analyzing the book for theme. Students will use prediction strategies as they begin a chapter. Chapter specific activities will include comparison, using a Venn diagram, sequence of events, writing dialogue and descriptions. Integration of science will be used as the students study the habits and characteristics of a spider. In math, a graph will show the results of the Friendship Bingo.

Assessment

How the small groups contribute to large group discussion will demonstrate understanding of literature.

Quadrant 3—Applications

Left Mode—Try

Timelines. Write "How to make a new friend" Descriptive, "My Best Friend" Charts.

Objective

To check students' comprehension of literature.

Activity

The students will use the vocabulary in several writing activities. Compare and contrast friendships in story. Make a pictorial timeline of how friendship grew in the story. Write how to make a new friend with someone that is different than you. Descriptive writing, "My Best Friend." Teacher made questionnaires.

Assessment

Quality of students' activities. Grades of questions and vocabulary worksheets. Involvement and performance in other activities.

Right Mode—Extend

Make posters. Interview characters. Role-play. Poetry. Make quilts.

Objective

To creatively apply what has been learned.

Activity

Make posters to promote friendship. Interview characters from *"Charlotte's Web."* Role-play any of the situations in the story using props and scenery of barn setting. Make a friendship quilt. Write descriptive poems of characters. Student will choose one of these projects.

Assessment

Quality of effort put into project.

Quadrant 4—Creations

Left Mode—Refine

Revise. Edit. Send friendly invitation letters.

Objective

Show importance of refining and editing projects: write friendly letters.

Activity

Practice and rehearse. In small groups, the students will critique each others' projects in a friendly way. Teacher will coach them to refine where needed. Also, in small groups, the student will write letters to friends and in other classes telling them about *"Charlotte's Web"* and inviting them to the celebration.

Assessment

Ability to work cooperatively in small groups while giving and receiving criticism. Completion of letters.

Right Mode—Integrate

Present and display. Invite best friends. Watch video.

Objective

To share with others what they have learned about friendship by performing and displaying projects. Go out and make a new friend!

Activity

Posters and Friendship quilt will be displayed. Students will present a scene from "Charlotte's Web" and conduct character interviews about the value of friends. The descriptive poems will be read to our guests. "Spider" cake and "yummy spiders" are the refreshments. Show video. Decorate the room with connected paper dolls representing the students.

Assessment

Quality of completed projects, presentation, participation and enjoyment of learning.

Responsibility for Homework

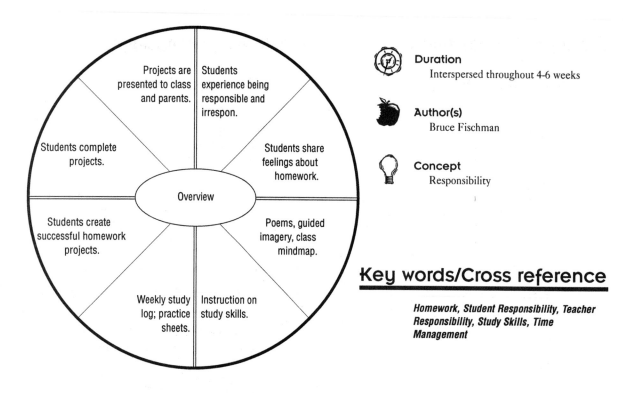

Projects are presented to class and parents.

Students experience being responsible and irrespon.

Students complete projects.

Students share feelings about homework.

Overview

Students create successful homework projects.

Poems, guided imagery, class mindmap.

Weekly study log; practice sheets.

Instruction on study skills.

Duration
Interspersed throughout 4-6 weeks

Author(s)
Bruce Fischman

Concept
Responsibility

Key words/Cross reference

Homework, Student Responsibility, Teacher Responsibility, Study Skills, Time Management

Overview

Objective
Students will understand the purpose of independent learning and successful strategies they may apply to be more responsible learners.

About the Author
Dr. Bruce Fischman teaches fourth grade at Hereford Elementary School, Upper Perkiomen School District, East Greenville, PA. He has been involved in education for over twenty years as a classroom teacher, reading supervisor and reading specialist, and staff development director for writing. He is a certified 4MAT System trainer for his school district.

Required Resources
Two plants to demonstrate responsible care; teacher-prepared guided imagery on "Experiences of Successful and Unsuccessful Homework"

Bibliography:
Canter, Lee. *Homework Without Tears for Teachers Grades 1-3*. Santa Monica, CA: Lee Canter & Associates, Inc., 1988.
Silverstein, Shel. *A Light in the Attic*. New York: Harper and Row Publishers, 1981.

Author's Notes
This unit was positively received by both students and their parents. The Before/After skits in Step Six were performed as Paper Bag Dramatics. For this activity, the students collected items which could be used in skit demonstrations. At the class party in Step Eight, parents were invited to participate in the activity: each small group draws an item from the paper bag. The group then has ten minutes to prepare its skit, and two to five minutes for performance. The students and the audience really enjoyed the improvisations.

Responsibility for Homework

Quadrant 1—Experience

 Right Mode—Connect

Students experience being responsible and irresponsible.

Objective

To create an experience for students to understand why homework is necessary.

Activity

Teacher starts the year with two plants on his/her desk. One will receive responsible care for a week, and one will not. At the end of the week, the teacher will involve the students in a discussion on the noticeable differences between the two plants. Questions such as "How is our life of learning like a plant? What makes our learning grow? What hinders our learning?" will be asked of the students. The discussion should also include other areas where students must be responsible, such as caring for pets and younger siblings, performing family chores, etc.

Assessment

Degree of student involvement in discussion.

 Left Mode—Examine

Students share feelings about homework.

Objective

To analyze student feelings about previous activity. To introduce the purpose of homework.

Activity

Discussion of personal responsibilities will lead into a discussion of homework. The teacher focuses on the purpose of homework and the opportunity for practice geared to individual needs. Feelings about completing homework and student experiences regarding practice should be shared. The teacher should share feelings that most of the time homework helps learning, but some kinds of homework hinder it. The teacher will make a commitment to be responsible about assigning helpful homework.

Assessment

Contribution to the group discussion.

Quadrant 2—Concepts

 Right Mode—Image

Poems, guided imagery, class mindmap.

Objective

To connect students to the meaning of homework in the year to come.

Activity

Teacher shares poems about homework from *A Light in the Attic*, by Shel Silverstein. Students participate in guided imagery, in which they visualize themselves completing a homework assignment and not completing an assignment. Teacher and students create a class mind map with "HOMEWORK" in the center and "Advantages," "Disadvantages," "Feelings," "Purpose" forming the spokes of the web. Students brainstorm additions.

Assessment

Quality of involvement and contributions.

 Left Mode—Define

Instruction on study skills.

Objective

To teach the specifics of study skills.

Activity

Teacher introduces and discusses different study ideas and methods to help students focus on their own: organization; time management; ways to study both difficult and easy material; study breaks; schedules; routine; materials; assignment books, and their responsibilities. The teacher also describes his/her responsibilities to plan helpful homework varied to meet individual student needs.

Assessment

Quality of participation, especially student questions and responses to teacher questions.

Quadrant 3—Applications

 ## Left Mode—Try

Weekly study log; practice sheets.

Objective
To reinforce understanding of individual home study habits.

Activity
Students will keep a weekly Study Log noting "Before/After" homework routine, schedules, processes, organization. Teacher incorporates Lee Canter's Homework Without Tears practice sheets.

Assessment
Quality of student journals and practice sheets.

Right Mode—Extend

Students create successful homework projects.

Objective
Students will apply what they have learned.

Activity
Students will work in groups to show others (peers, family, friends) ideas for completing homework. Possible cooperative group activities are Before/After Skit; Posters; Class Manual on Homework Hints; Animated Flip Books; Letter to Parents.

Assessment
Quality of effort put into project.

Quadrant 4—Creations

 ## Left Mode—Refine

Students complete projects.

Objective
To extend what has been learned.

Activity
Students work in response groups and share their written thinking plans for their homework projects. Each group will write comments on another group's plan, adding comments in different colors, until each group has commented on all other plans. Each group then completes its own project.

Assessment
Ability to work with peers and refine and improve one's work. Ability to honor the work of others.

Right Mode—Integrate

Projects are presented to class and parents.

Objective
To complete and share projects. To enjoy each other's work.

Activity
Group homework projects are shared with classmates. Parents are invited to an "I AM RESPONSIBLE" party where certificates of responsibility will be awarded to students and to the teacher.

Assessment
Quality of completed projects, presentation, participation, and enjoyment of the learning.

Similes

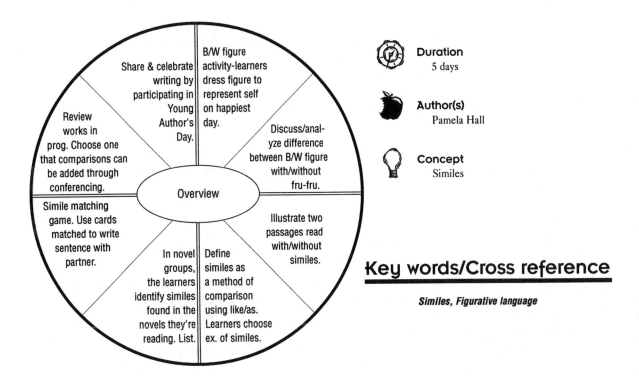

Overview

- B/W figure activity-learners dress figure to represent self on happiest day.
- Discuss/analyze difference between B/W figure with/without fru-fru.
- Illustrate two passages read with/without similes.
- Define similes as a method of comparison using like/as. Learners choose ex. of similes.
- In novel groups, the learners identify similes found in the novels they're reading. List.
- Simile matching game. Use cards matched to write sentence with partner.
- Review works in prog. Choose one that comparisons can be added through conferencing.
- Share & celebrate writing by participating in Young Author's Day.

Duration
5 days

Author(s)
Pamela Hall

Concept
Similes

Key words/Cross reference

Similes, Figurative language

Overview

Objective
The learner will communicate well if he/she understands and uses figurative language in his/her writing.

About the Author
Pamela Hall is a teacher at Woodland Elementary in Graham, TX. She is a certified 4MAT trainer for her district.

Required Resources
File on similes. Student's writing/novels.

Bibliography
Scholastic reading/writing literature.

Similes

Quadrant 1—Experience

Right Mode—Connect

B/W figure activity-learners dress figure to represent self on happiest day.

Objective

Create an experience for learners to connect what they know about communicating happiness.

Activity

After brainstorming happy events and how we look and feel when we're happy, learners will dress a black/white stick figure to represent happiness. (Students will use fru-fru decorations such as feathers, glitter, balloons, doilies, etc.)

Assessment

Participation and enjoyment of brainstorming and activity.

Left Mode—Examine

Discuss/analyze difference between B/W figure with/without fru-fru.

Objective

The learners will analyze the difference between figure with/without fru-fru.

Activity

The learners will discuss plain figure using words to describe it. Then, learners will discuss fru-fru dressed figure using words and phrases with "like" or "as" in them. Learners will be challenged to explain why they choose the comparisons they did.

Assessment

The learners participation in discussion and ability to express what they felt like.

Quadrant 2—Concepts

Right Mode—Image

Illustrate two passages read with/without similes.

Objective

The learners will express through illustrations, images seen in their minds from passages read to them.

Activity

After listening to passage A being read (no figurative language included), the learner will illustrate image seen in mind's eye. Learner will repeat activity with passage B (figurative language included). Upon completion of two illustrations, learner will compare through discussion.

Assessment

Display illustrations. Clear contrast should be seen between illustrations.

Left Mode—Define

Define similes as a method of comparison using like/as. Learners choose ex. of similes.

Objective

Learner will differentiate between example/non-examples using similes.

Activity

Teacher will define similes as a method of comparison using like or as. Learners will understand similes as a form of figurative language used to better communicate with others.

Assessment

Learners will use thumbs up/down to indicate similes/no similes in sentences read.

Similes

Quadrant 3—Applications

 ### Left Mode—Try

In novel groups, the learners identify similes found in the novels they're reading. List.

Objective
Learners will identify examples of similes in the novels being read.

Activity
In their novel groups, the learners will identify similes in the novels and list them on chart paper.

Assessment
Learners will work cooperatively within their groups.

 ### Right Mode—Extend

Simile matching game. Use cards matched to write sentence with partner.

Objective
Learners will match objects being compared.

Activity
Learners will take turns reading card given (word on card represents first object). Learner with matching card will respond verbally. The two learners will then use the comparison on the cards in a sentence using like or as.

Assessment
Sentences written using similes.

Quadrant 4—Creations

 ### Left Mode—Refine

Review works in prog. Choose one that comparisons can be added through conferencing.

Objective
Learners will embellish works in progress with similes.

Activity
Learners will review works in progress and choose a piece to which comparisons (similes) could be added. Learners will continue writing progress with peer conferences/revision. The learner will complete piece.

Assessment
Peer conference/revision.

 ### Right Mode—Integrate

Share & celebrate writing by participating in Young Author's Day.

Objective
Learners will share their writing.

Activity
Learners will participate in Young Author's Day. Visitors, including family, friends, teachers, classmates, and people from the community will come to school and listen to authors read their published pieces.

Assessment
Quality of published work and enjoyment of sharing it.

Division

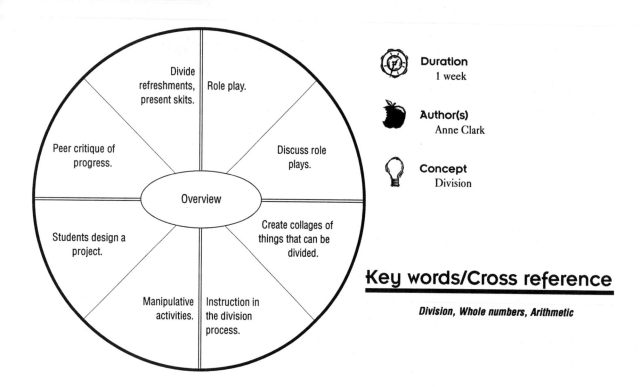

Duration
1 week

Author(s)
Anne Clark

Concept
Division

Key words/Cross reference

Division, Whole numbers, Arithmetic

Overview

Objective

To deepen the concept of division by engaging students in real applications of the process.

About the Author

Anne Clark is an instructional specialist in the K-5 gifted/talented program in the North East Independent School District in San Antonio, Texas. She is a certified 4MAT Trainer.

Required Resources

Basic manipulative materials.

Division

Quadrant 1—Experience

 ### Right Mode—Connect

Role play.

Objective
To engage students in the understanding that groups of objects are divided often in everyday life. To create a reason for students to learn division.

Activity
Students are handed cards with everyday scenarios in which students will brainstorm and then role play situations that require division. Suggestions: cutting a pizza or birthday cake into equal portions, splitting up a task between partners, etc.

Assessment
Student involvement in the role play.

 ### Left Mode—Examine

Discuss role plays.

Objective
To analyze the ways in which students solved the problem by successfully sharing or dividing groups of objects or people.

Activity
Discuss role plays. List other situations.

Assessment
Student participation.

Quadrant 2—Concepts

 ### Right Mode—Image

Create collages of things that can be divided.

Objective
To engage students in hands-on construction incorporating a variety of division situations.

Activity
Create collages of pictures and real things that can be divided.

Assessment
Quality of student collages.

 ### Left Mode—Define

Instruction in the division process.

Objective
To teach the vocabulary and concept of division and make the process understandable to the students.

Activity
Instruction in division. Define terms. Activities involving food items and manipulatives will be utilized to teach the process. The students work together through a demonstration of how a sharing task with equal increments can be done in a one step at a time and how the task can be done more efficiently in one process.

Assessment
Observation of participation and success with manipulative activities.

Quadrant 3—Applications

 ## Left Mode—Try

Manipulative activities.

Objective

To allow students to practice concepts and reinforce understanding of division.

Activity

Work with Cuisinaire rods and other manipulative activities to test ideas. Problem situations involving moving of real objects. Use worksheets, flash cards, fact bingo, games, text pages, records, make own flash cards, etc.

Assessment

Scoring of independent work.

 ## Right Mode—Extend

Students design a project.

Objective

To allow students to apply what they have learned by creating a project.

Activity

Students design a project that will explain division, such as a new math game, puzzle, collection of news articles, video tape and/or pictures of real life situations showing use of division, etc.

Assessment

Completion of project design.

Quadrant 4—Creations

 ## Left Mode—Refine

Peer critique of progress.

Objective

To enable students to establish a criteria for evaluation and to cooperatively analyze projects.

Activity

Switch projects to test directions, rules, appropriateness, accuracy, etc. Peer critique of projects in small groups.

Assessment

Quality of student engagement and ability to work together. Quality of projects and their relevance to furthering understanding of division.

 ## Right Mode—Integrate

Divide refreshments/present skits.

Objective

To delight in what was learned and share in the successfulness of the learning by utilizing the process of division.

Activity

A class party is held with costs for each group determined by the process of division and figuring unit prices of necessary groceries as determined from weekly newspaper grocery store ads. Divide refreshments. Present division skits and projects to large groups.

Assessment

Quality of student projects and observation of students' enjoyment.

Fractions

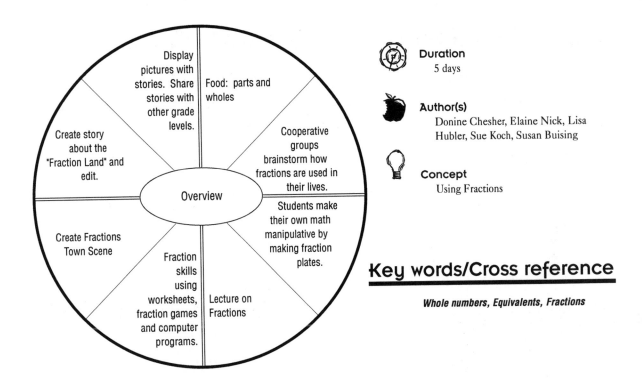

Overview

- Display pictures with stories. Share stories with other grade levels.
- Food: parts and wholes
- Create story about the "Fraction Land" and edit.
- Cooperative groups brainstorm how fractions are used in their lives.
- Create Fractions Town Scene
- Students make their own math manipulative by making fraction plates.
- Fraction skills using worksheets, fraction games and computer programs.
- Lecture on Fractions

Duration
5 days

Author(s)
Donine Chesher, Elaine Nick, Lisa Hubler, Sue Koch, Susan Buising

Concept
Using Fractions

Key words/Cross reference

Whole numbers, Equivalents, Fractions

Overview

Objective
The students will be able to identify add and subtract fractions.

About the Authors
Donine Chesher, Sue Koch, Lisa Hubler, Susan Buising, and Elaine Nick are teachers at Gracemor Elementary School, North Kansas City, MO.

Required Resources
Snack foods that can be divided from wholes to parts: saltines, Hershey bars, graham crackers, etc.; paper plates, rulers, markers, scissors for "Fraction Plates;" worksheets, computer games for guided practice; art materials for "Fraction Town" class mural.

Fractions

Quadrant 1—Experience

Right Mode—Connect

Food: parts and wholes

Objective
Introduce the concept of fractions.

Activity
Bring in miscellaneous food (cookies, Hershey Chocolate bar, saltines, graham crackers) and allow students to recognize equal parts that make up a whole.

Assessment
Observation of student attention.

Left Mode—Examine

Cooperative groups brainstorm how fractions are used in their lives.

Objective
To allow students to discuss fractions in their lives.

Activity
Cooperative groups brainstorm how fractions are used in their lives.

Assessment
Student participation.

Quadrant 2—Concepts

Right Mode—Image

Students make their own math manipulative by making fraction plates.

Objective
Create their own fraction manipulatives.

Activity
Make fraction plates:
"Fractions Made Easy With Fraction Plates"
Each student makes his own fraction plate pieces. Each student will need a clock face, pencil/pen, ruler, scissors, and seven paper plates. Colored paper plates are pretty to use, but white ones will work fine and are cheaper. The center point of the clock face is lined up with the center point of the paper plate. The students use the numbers on the clock as a guide to know where to divide each paper plate into the proper sections. Each of the marked points should be lined up with the center point of the paper plate and then using a ruler, a line is drawn from the center to that point. The students write the name of each fractional part on the paper plate as it is cut apart.

Fraction Name	Clock Numbers to Mark
Whole	None
Halves	12 and 6
Thirds	12, 4, and 8
Fourths	12, 3, 6, and 9
Sixths	12, 2, 4, 6, 8, and 10
Eighths	Mark 12, 3, 6 and 9

and then mark half-way between each of these points

Twelfths	12, 1, 2, 3, 4, 5, 6, 7, 8, 9, 10 and 11

Students use the fraction plates as manipulatives as they learn to add and subtract fractions and as they learn about equivalent fractions.

Assessment
Quality of fraction plates.

Left Mode—Define

Lecture on Fractions

Objective
Teach fractions of a region, addition and subtraction of fractions, equivalent fractions.

Activity
Use fraction plates to teach concepts.

Assessment
Observation of participation and success with fraction concepts.

Fractions

Quadrant 3—Applications

 ### Left Mode—Try

Fraction skills using worksheets, fraction games and computer programs.

Objective
Practice fraction skills.

Activity
Worksheets, fraction games and computer programs.

Assessment
Scoring of independent work.

 ### Right Mode—Extend

Create Fractions Town Scene

Objective
Reinforce mastery of fractions.

Activity
Cooperative groups create a "Fraction Town" scene (land of Fourths, Thirds, etc.).

"Fraction Town:"
A class discussion is held on the different areas you might find in a city or town (ex. courthouse square, shopping area, apartments, etc.). Students are then placed into cooperative groups of three to four and they choose an area to illustrate on the class mural. Each student in the group chooses a fraction of their choice to represent in the illustration. Before each group begins to draw their section, they determine what items can be drawn in their scene and how it can be divided equally into the fraction they have chosen. Example: If a student chooses 1/2, he must draw objects in the scene which can easily be divided in 1/2. The student can then color 1/2 of the object one color. The students might also choose to have only 1/2 of a section of a building showing in their section of the city. The student must be able to divide the majority of their scene into their fraction, and color the fraction part of each object.

Assessment
Completion of fraction scene.

Quadrant 4—Creations

 ### Left Mode—Refine

Create story about the "Fraction Land" and edit.

Objective
Organize and synthesize fraction knowledge into written word.

Activity
Create story about the fraction land and edit.
In their cooperative groups, the students create a story about their section of the Fraction Land that describes what is in their picture and what might be happening in their town. In cooperative groups, the stories and edited are prepared for display.

Assessment
Completion of fraction story.

 ### Right Mode—Integrate

Display pictures with stories. Share stories with other grade levels.

Objective
Students share in their success.

Activity
Display picture with story. Share story with younger grade. The stories are displayed with the class mural. Students share the stories with other grade levels.

Assessment
Observation of students' enjoyment.

Intro to Geometric Shapes

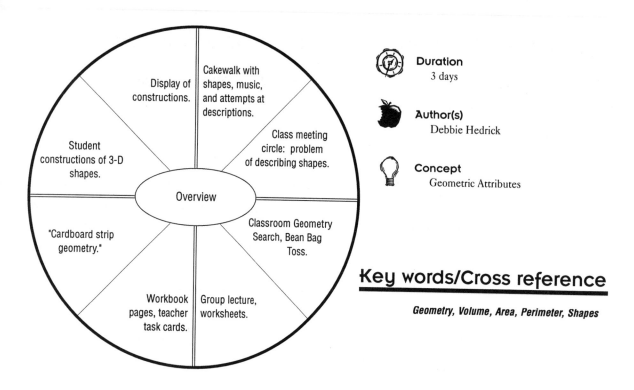

Duration
3 days

Author(s)
Debbie Hedrick

Concept
Geometric Attributes

Key words/Cross reference

Geometry, Volume, Area, Perimeter, Shapes

Overview

Objective
To introduce students to the concept of the attributes of geometric shapes in the structure of the world around them.

About the Author
At the time this plan was written, Debbie Hedrick was an elementary teacher for Madison Local Schools, Mansfield, OH.

Required Resources
Large color-coded shapes and music for "shape walk" activity; Geometry Search Worksheet and prepared boxes and beanbags for toss; attribute blocks; teacher-prepared task cards for guided practice

Bibliography:
Overholt, Dr. J.L., *Dr. Jim's Elementary Math Prescriptions,* Santa Monica, CA: Goodyear Publishing Co., Inc., 1978.

Sternberg, B.J. Clan Set 60 (Attribute Logic Blocks). Hayward, CA: Activity Resources Co., Inc., 1974.

Intro to Geometric Shapes

Quadrant 1—Experience

 ### Right Mode—Connect

Cakewalk with shapes, music, and attempts at descriptions.

Objective

To match shapes and attributes of geometric figures.

Activity

Take class outside to blacktop. Bring one cardboard shape for each child (color coded) and masking tape. Tape the shapes to the blacktop. (Put them on the surface in a square, cakewalk fashion.) Bring wheel or shape cards, and a cassette tape recorder with a music tape. Spin the wheel as children walk around the square to music. When it stops, the children standing on that shape and color must describe an attribute of that figure.

Assessment

Observe variety and knowledge or proper adjectives when describing shapes.

 ### Left Mode—Examine

Class meeting circle: problem of describing shapes.

Objective

To have the children realize the need for proper terms to describe geometric shapes.

Activity

Class meeting circle: Discuss the problem of describing shapes without correct vocabulary. Where do we find this information, what kind of books, etc.?

Assessment

Observe participation in class discussion.

Quadrant 2—Concepts

 ### Right Mode—Image

Classroom Geometry Search, Bean Bag Toss.

Objective

To connect basic geometric knowledge to everyday objects/shapes.

Activity

Classroom Geometry Search: Pass out worksheet with shapes drawn. Students write in everything they see in the room that is the corresponding shape. Bean Bag Toss. Students divide into small groups. Toss geometric shapes into the correct slot of a box. They score another point if they can name the shape and tell something about it.

Assessment

Number of correct responses in both activities.

 ### Left Mode—Define

Group lecture, worksheets.

Objective

To become knowledgeable concerning geometric attributes and vocabualry describing those attributes.

Activity

Whole group lecture using attribute blocks. Go through each shape and attributes. Discuss similarities and differences in shapes. With some groups, teacher could introduce volume, area, and perimeter.

Assessment

Worksheets on geometric attributes.

Quadrant 3—Applications

 ### Left Mode—Try

Workbook pages, teacher task cards.

Objective
Worksheets on geometric attributes.

Activity
Teacher task cards on volume, area, and perimeter.

Assessment
85% accuracy on workbook pages and task cards.

Right Mode—Extend

"Cardboard strip geometry."

Objective
To construct the frameworks for 2 and 3 dimensional geometric figures.

Activity
"Cardboard Strip Geometry" from Dr. Jim's Math Activities Book. Using cardboard strips and brads to connect them, construct geometric figures. First, use one-dimensional figures, they try to build some 3-D figures. Consider what constructions are stable and unstable.

Assessment
Observation of student participation and uniqueness of shapes.

Quadrant 4—Creations

Left Mode—Refine

Student constructions of 3-D shapes.

Objective
To show application of geometric knowledge

Activity
Using teacher-made task cards, showing the outline of several geometric figures, students work in pairs to try to replicate the drawing on the task card. Then, the students must add one detail of their own (make a 3-D construction or alter shape, etc.).

Assessment
Evaluate each pair's construction. Is it formed from the task card? Has it been changed?

Right Mode—Integrate

Display of constructions.

Objective
To discover applied use in the everyday world for geometric frameworks.

Activity
In "Science fair fashion," pairs of students display their constructions around the classroom. Each pair must provide an index card, describing method of construction and architectural structures where this shape might be found.

Assessment
Informal student question and answer period during displays.

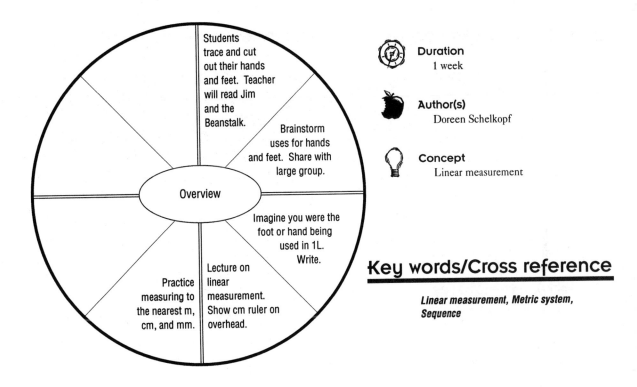

Duration
1 week

Author(s)
Doreen Schelkopf

Concept
Linear measurement

Students trace and cut out their hands and feet. Teacher will read Jim and the Beanstalk.

Brainstorm uses for hands and feet. Share with large group.

Overview

Imagine you were the foot or hand being used in 1L. Write.

Lecture on linear measurement. Show cm ruler on overhead.

Practice measuring to the nearest m, cm, and mm.

Key words/Cross reference

Linear measurement, Metric system, Sequence

Overview

Objective
Students will learn three basic forms of measurement: Linear, Liquid, Weight.

About the Author
Doreen Schelkopf teaches intermediate grades in Geneva, NE. She received her 4MAT training in the Doane College, NE, Master's degree program taught by Sue Burch and Sue Rasmussen.

Required Resources
Pencils, drawing paper, writing paper, tape, cm ruler (clear), overhead, 5 jars (various sizes), liquid, liquid measuring containers, clay, large containers of tubs, balance scales, and gram weights.

Bibliography
AIMS-1982-Floaters and Sinkers, *"Clay Boats"*
AIMS-1986-Math + Science, A Solution, *"Mini Metric Olympics"*
Jim and the Beanstalk by Raymond Briggs

Quadrant 1—Experience

Right Mode—Connect

Students trace and cut out their hands and feet. Teacher will read Jim and the Beanstalk.

Objective
To develop an interest in linear measurement (length of objects).

Activity
Students will trace and cut out their hands and feet. Also, teacher will read Jim and the Beanstalk.

Assessment
Observation of students.

Left Mode—Examine

Brainstorm uses for hands and feet. Share with large group.

Objective
To brainstorm ideas for the uses of hands and feet. To discuss reasons for Jim's measuring in the book.

Activity
Brainstorm in small groups what the hands and feet could be used for. Be prepared to share with the large group. Compare sizes of feet and hands and hang them in order of size. Discuss why Jim needed to measure the giant's face for glasses, mouth for dentures, etc.

Assessment
Observation of discussion and student participation.

Quadrant 2—Concepts

Right Mode—Image

Imagine you were the foot or hand being used in 1L. Write.

Objective
To put students in the place of their hand or foot. To imagine themselves as something else.

Activity
Imagine you were the foot or hand being used for something mentioned in 1L, write about or draw your reaction.

Assessment
Completion of picture or written piece.

Left Mode—Define

Lecture on linear measurement. Show cm ruler on overhead.

Objective
To determine which measurement is more appropriate (e.g. length of pencil—cm. is best choice).

Activity
Lecture on linear measurement. Show cm ruler on overhead. Teach differences between meter, centimeter, and millimeter.

Assessment
Check for understanding.

Quadrant 3—Applications

 ### Left Mode—Try

Practice measuring to the nearest m, cm, and mm.

Objective
To reinforce concepts taught.

Activity
Practice measuring distances to the nearest mm, cm and m. They will complete worksheets after measuring different objects.

Assessment
Accuracy of measurements.

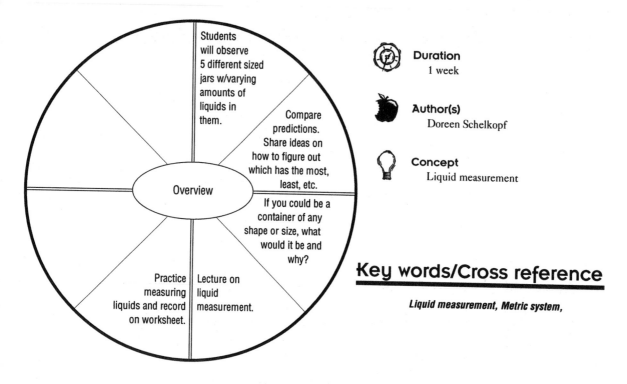

Students will observe 5 different sized jars w/varying amounts of liquids in them.

Compare predictions. Share ideas on how to figure out which has the most, least, etc.

Overview

If you could be a container of any shape or size, what would it be and why?

Practice measuring liquids and record on worksheet.

Lecture on liquid measurement.

Duration
1 week

Author(s)
Doreen Schelkopf

Concept
Liquid measurement

Key words/Cross reference

Liquid measurement, Metric system,

Overview

Objective
Students will learn basic forms of measurement: Linear, Liquid, Weight.

About the Author
Doreen Schelkopf teaches intermediate grades in Geneva, NE. She received her 4MAT training in the Doane College, NE, Master's degree program taught by Sue Burch and Sue Rasmussen.

Required Resources
Pencils, drawing paper, writing paper, tape, cm ruler (clear), overhead, 5 jars (various sizes), liquid, liquid measuring containers, clay, large containers of tubs, balance scales, and gram weights.

Bibliography
AIMS-1982-Floaters and Sinkers, *"Clay Boats"*
AIMS-1986-Math + Science, A Solution, *"Mini Metric Olympics"*
Jim and the Beanstalk by Raymond Briggs

Quadrant 1—Experience

 ### Right Mode—Connect

Students will observe 5 different sized jars w/varying amounts of liquids in them.

Objective

To develop an interest in the measurement of liquids.

Activity

Students will observe five different sized jars with varying amount of liquids in them. They will predict how the five jars can be ordered from the least to the greatest amount of liquid.

Assessment

Observation of students and the completion of their predictions.

 ### Left Mode—Examine

Compare predictions. Share ideas on how to figure out which has the most, least, etc.

Objective

To compare predictions and devise a way to figure out their order.

Activity

Compare predictions. Share ideas on how to figure out which has the most, least, and so on.

Assessment

Discussion of various plans.

Quadrant 2—Concepts

 ### Right Mode—Image

If you could be a container of any shape or size, what would it be and why?

Objective

To imagine oneself as a container. To foster creative thinking related to liquids and various containers.

Activity

If you could be a container of any shape or size, what would it be and why? What liquid would you like to hold? Share your choice with a partner and write about your choice.

Assessment

Completion of description.

 ### Left Mode—Define

Lecture on liquid measurement.

Objective

To determine which measurement is more appropriate (ml, l).

Activity

Lecture on liquid measurement. Show different containers used to measure milliliters and liters.

Assessment

Check for understanding.

Quadrant 3—Applications

 Left Mode—Try

Practice measuring liquids and record on worksheet.

Objective
To reinforce concepts taught.

Activity
Practice measuring liquids and record on worksheet.
Measure and put liquids from 1R in order.

Assessment
Accuracy of measurements.

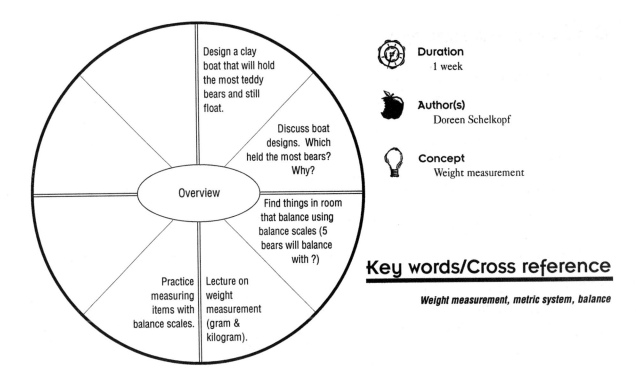

Design a clay boat that will hold the most teddy bears and still float.

Discuss boat designs. Which held the most bears? Why?

Overview

Find things in room that balance using balance scales (5 bears will balance with ?)

Lecture on weight measurement (gram & kilogram).

Practice measuring items with balance scales.

 Duration
1 week

 Author(s)
Doreen Schelkopf

Concept
Weight measurement

Key words/Cross reference

Weight measurement, metric system, balance

Overview

 Objective
Students will learn basic forms of measurement: Linear, Liquid, Weight.

 About the Author
Doreen Schelkopf teaches intermediate grades in Geneva, NE. She received her 4MAT training in the Doane College, NE, Master's degree program taught by Sue Burch and Sue Rasmussen.

Required Resources
Pencils, drawing paper, writing paper, tape, cm ruler (clear), overhead, 5 jars (various sizes), liquid, liquid measuring containers, clay, large containers of tubs, balance scales, and gram weights.

Bibliography
AIMS-1982-Floaters and Sinkers, "Clay Boats"
AIMS-1986-Math + Science, A Solution, "Mini Metric Olympics"
Jim and the Beanstalk by Raymond Briggs

Quadrant 1—Experience

 ### Right Mode—Connect

Design a clay boat that will hold the most teddy bears and still float.

Objective

To actively involve students in an enjoyable experience that requires predicting and creative design with clay.

Activity

To design a clay boat that will hold the most teddy bears and still float in the container. Make a prediction on how many bears your boat will hold before trying it out.

Assessment

Observation of students experimenting.

 ### Left Mode—Examine

Discuss boat designs. Which held the most bears? Why?

Objective

To analyze boat designs.

Activity

Discuss boat designs. Which held the most bears? Why?

Assessment

Observing the level of participation in the discussion.

Quadrant 2—Concepts

 ### Right Mode—Image

Find things in room that balance using balance scales (5 bears will balance with ?)

Objective

To get ready to use balance scales to measure in grams.

Activity

Using the teddy bears from Quadrant One, find things in the room that balance using balance scales (5 bears will balance with ?)

Assessment

Observation of students using the balance scales.

 ### Left Mode—Define

Lecture on weight measurement (gram & kilogram).

Objective

To determine which measurement is more appropriate.

Activity

Lecture on weight measurement (gram and kilogram).

Assessment

Check for understanding.

Quadrant 3—Applications

 ### Left Mode—Try

Practice measuring items with balance scales.

Objective
To reinforce concepts taught.

Activity
Practice measuring items with balance scales. How much did your bears weigh in 1R that would float in the boat?

Assessment
Accuracy of measurements.

Measurement (4 of 4)

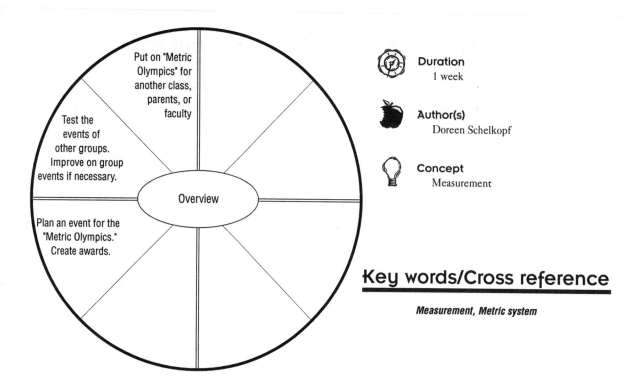

Put on "Metric Olympics" for another class, parents, or faculty

Test the events of other groups. Improve on group events if necessary.

Plan an event for the "Metric Olympics." Create awards.

Overview

Duration
1 week

Author(s)
Doreen Schelkopf

Concept
Measurement

Key words/Cross reference

Measurement, Metric system

Overview

Objective
Students will learn basic forms of measurement: Linear, Liquid, Weight.

About the Author
Doreen Schelkopf teaches intermediate grades in Geneva, NE. She received her 4MAT training in the Doane College, NE, Master's degree program taught by Sue Burch and Sue Rasmussen.

Required Resources
Pencils, drawing paper, writing paper, tape, cm ruler (clear), overhead, 5 jars (various sizes), liquid, liquid measuring containers, clay, large containers of tubs, balance scales, and gram weights.

Bibliography
AIMS-1982-Floaters and Sinkers, *"Clay Boats"*
AIMS-1986-Math + Science, A Solution, *"Mini Metric Olympics"*
Jim and the Beanstalk by Raymond Briggs

Quadrant 3—Applications

 ## Right Mode—Extend

Plan an event for the "Metric Olympics." Create awards.

Objective
To expand learning by planning an Olympic event in groups and to know when to use various measuring devices.

Activity
In groups of four, they will be responsible for: 1) Planning an event for the Metric Olympics using weight, linear, or liquid measurement. 2) Making a records chart to keep track of the scores for the competitors. 3) Creating awards to be presented to the winners. 4) Making a chart explaining the event, what the rules are, and demonstrating the event.

Assessment
Completion of group's project.

Quadrant 4—Creations

 ## Left Mode—Refine

Test the events of other groups. Improve on group events if necessary.

Objective
To try out events and make sure they are workable.

Activity
Test the events of other groups. Improve on group events if necessary.

Assessment
Observation of groups experimenting.

 ## Right Mode—Integrate

Put on "Metric Olympics" for another class, parents, or faculty

Objective
To host "Metric Olympics."

Activity
Put on "Metric Olympics" with another class, parents, or faculty participating.

Assessment
Student and competitor delight in participating in the "Olympics."

Money

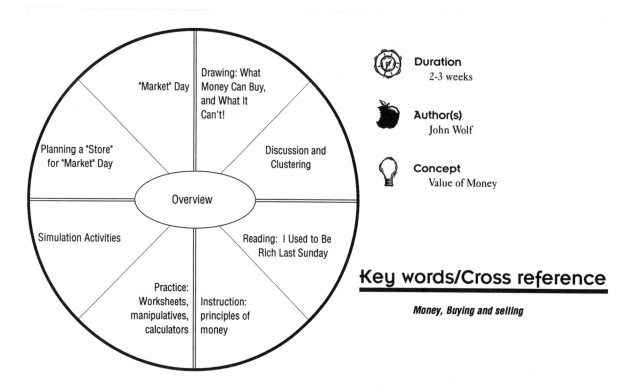

"Market" Day

Drawing: What Money Can Buy, and What It Can't!

Planning a "Store" for "Market" Day

Discussion and Clustering

Overview

Simulation Activities

Reading: I Used to Be Rich Last Sunday

Practice: Worksheets, manipulatives, calculators

Instruction: principles of money

Duration
2-3 weeks

Author(s)
John Wolf

Concept
Value of Money

Key words/Cross reference

Money, Buying and selling

Overview

Objective
Students will learn the value of money and how it is used.

About the Author
John Wolf is a fourth grade classroom teacher and a certified 4MAT trainer for the North East ISD in San Antonio, Texas.

Bibliography
Viorst, Judith: I Used to Be Rich Last Sunday.

Quadrant 1—Experience

Right Mode—Connect

Drawing: What Money Can Buy, and What It Can't!

Objective
To have students think about the role money plays in their lives and their dreams

Activity
Draw small pictures or symbols for what you would do with a million dollars if you won it in a contest or lottery.

Assessment
Thoughtfulness and completeness of the student's responses.

Left Mode—Examine

Discussion and Clustering

Objective
To share and discuss thoughts stimulated by previous activity, to deepen their insights, and to check for current knowledge.

Activity
In small cluster groups, have the students share and explain their drawings to each other. Then have the students list the ideas that were most commonly shared and several of the most original ideas. These are shared with the whole group. Then the teacher can lead the class in brainstorming things that money can't buy. Discuss how these things are different. Finally, have the students individually cluster what they already know about money.

Assessment
The ability of the group to analyze their responses to the drawing activity for commonality and originality, the thoughtfulness of their discussion, and the individual clusters about what they already know.

Quadrant 2—Concepts

Right Mode—Image

Reading: I Used to Be Rich Last Sunday

Objective
To lead the student from personal experience towards the need to know how to use money.

Activity
Read aloud Judith Viorst's delightful children's book, I Used to Be Rich Last Sunday. Ask the students to try to help Alexander keep track of his money on their own paper. Personal Note: I do not help or check my students with their tabulations, as I do not want there to be any right or wrong answer at this point. It is the experience that matters. It also gives me an informal way to see how well the student can work with money.

Assessment
Student response to the book.

Left Mode—Define

Instruction: principles of money

Objective
To teach specific concepts and skills related to money.

Activity
Use a variety of instructional methods to teach the concepts at the appropriate level for your students. The use of manipulatives (whether they be paper, plastic, or the real thing) should be considered a must.

Assessment
Informal verbal checking and "teacher loops" (quickly reviewing the concepts taught in the sequence they were taught in).

Quadrant 3—Applications

Left Mode—Try

Practice: Worksheets, manipulatives, calculators

Objective

To objectively evaluate the student's understanding of the concepts and skills.

Activity

Give guided and independent practice using manipulatives, textbook pages, worksheets, and calculator activities.

Assessment

evaluation of worksheets.

Right Mode—Extend

Simulation Activities

Objective

To extend the student's learning and relate the concepts to life situations.

Activity

Here are three simulation activities I improvise on and the students enjoy because it relates to real life situations.

Fast Food Restaurant Simulation

As a whole class, name and devise a priced menu for an imaginary new fast food restaurant. Choose one student and give them $10 of pretend money. Another student will work the "cash register". The first student "orders" from the menu and the second student must total the order (use a calculator to figure the tax if your students are capable of that skill) and make change. Then ask everyone to get a partner and repeat the activity, with or without the manipulatives.

Checkbook Simulation

Materials: 4 pretend checks for each student, at least one die per three students.

The student will roll the die each round to determine his/her monthly income, house payment, car payment, utility bills, and grocery bill. After each bill, the student will write a check and balance his/her "checkbook." Calculators can be used to check the work. I try to stimulate their fantasies by describing the house or car they will be getting. Here is a chart that you can use or modify to get you started.

If you roll a . . .	1 or 2	3 or 4	5 or 6
your profession . . .	teacher	engineer	lawyer
monthly take-home . .	$1,300	$1,800	$2,500
house payment . . .	$800	$1,100	$600
car payment . . .	$350	$120	$230
utilities . . .	$180	$230	$140
groceries . . .	$175	$215	$265

Stock market Simulation

Materials: dice and calculators, the following worksheet

Follow the worksheet to give your students a stimulating experience in "playing" the stock market.

Money

Quadrant 4—Creations

 ### Left Mode—Refine

Planning a "Store" for "Market" Day

Objective

To take the student to personal usefulness in developing an imaginary business.

Activity

Each student is to develop an "imaginary" store on a piece of paper. Each store should have 4 to 6 items for sale. No item should cost more than $3. It is to be attractively named and easily read. This is preparation for the culminating activity.

Assessment

Imagination and originality.

 ### Right Mode—Integrate

"Market" Day

Objective

To use their knowledge of money.

Activity

Students set up their imaginary stores and buy and sell from each other using paper money. I organize the activity by having them buy and sell from their cooperative group first. Then one half of the class closes their stores while they buy from the other half. They then sit and let the others do some shopping. Each time a "sale" is made, the customer writes his/her name on a purchase sheet and the shop owner writes down the amount of the purchase. The last part of the activity is to total up the amount of sales and see who made the most "money."

Assessment

Ability of the student to buy, make change, and total the sales using imaginary money.

Personal Note: Integrated into a unit on economics, the students could be responsible for planning, making, advertising, and selling real items for a profit (or loss).

Patterns

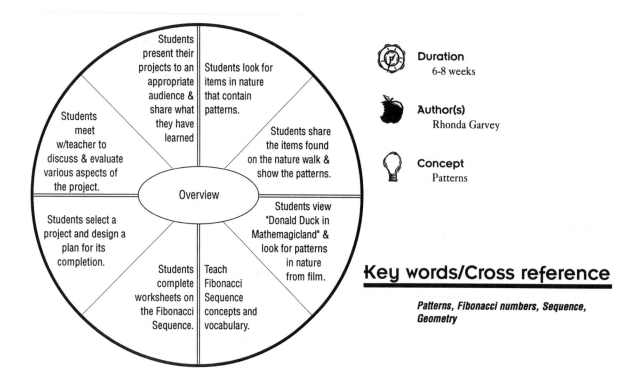

Students present their projects to an appropriate audience & share what they have learned

Students look for items in nature that contain patterns.

Students meet w/teacher to discuss & evaluate various aspects of the project.

Students share the items found on the nature walk & show the patterns.

Overview

Students select a project and design a plan for its completion.

Students view "Donald Duck in Mathemagicland" & look for patterns in nature from film.

Students complete worksheets on the Fibonacci Sequence.

Teach Fibonacci Sequence concepts and vocabulary.

Duration
6-8 weeks

Author(s)
Rhonda Garvey

Concept
Patterns

Key words/Cross reference

Patterns, Fibonacci numbers, Sequence, Geometry

Overview

Objective
Students will become more interested in math and practice meaningful computational skills. Students will develop higher level thinking skills. Students will integrate history, design, geometrical constructions, botany, zoology, astronomy, and philosophy with math as the focus. Students will enhance cooperative learning skills.

About the Author
Rhonda Garvey developed and implemented an elementary and middle school gifted education program at Napoleon City Schools, as well as developed and implemented the G.E.A.R.S. (Gifted Education Advancing Rossford Students) Program, at Rossford Exempted Village Schools. She teaches gifted classes (grades four through six) and coordinates the G.E.A.R.S. Program in Rossford.

Required Resources
Q1: Grocery sacks (one per student), paper and pencils, magnifying glasses (one for each two students).

Q2: Film: "Donald Duck in Mathemagicland," movie projector, movie screen, chalkboard and chalk, teacher resource (see bibliography).

Q3: Student worksheets (see bibliography), scissors, crayons, colored pens, pine cones pre-soaked to close them up (one pine cone for each group), calculators (one per group), a real sunflower (if possible), metric rulers (with mm), paper, paper cup (one per group), compass, protractor, glue, construction paper, and envelopes.

Q4: Materials and resources needed for students to complete individual projects.

Bibliography
Beard, Col. R.S. *Patterns in Space*. Palo Alto, California: Creative Publications, 1973.
Brousseau, Brother Alfred. *"Fibonacci Quarterly."* St. Mary's College, California.
Buzan, Tony. *Use Both Sides of Your Brain*. New York: Dutton, 1983.
"D-STIX" kit from Creative Publications.
Doczi, Georgi. *The Power of Limits*. Boulder: Colorado. 1981.
"Donald Duck in Mathemagicland": film by Walt Disney.
Garland, Trudi. *The Fascinating Fibonaccis*. Palo Alto,

Patterns

California: Dale Seymour Publications, 1987.

Ghyka, Matila. *The Geometry of Art and Life.* New York: Dover, 1977.

Huntly, H.E., *The Divine Proportion.* New York: Dover, 1970.

McKenna, Alexis. *Doodling Your Way to Better Recall.* Tucson, Arizona: Zephyr Press, 1979.

Purce, Jill. *The Mystic Spiral.* New York: Avon, 1974.

Seymour, Dale. *Creative Constructions.* Palo Alto, California: Creative Publications, 1980.

*Wahl, Mark. *A Mathematical Mystery Tour: Higher-Thinking Math Tasks.* Tucson, Arizona: Zephyr Press, 1988.

*Wahl, Mark. *"Mystery Tour Guide."* Tucson, Arizona: Zephyr Press, 1988.

*Resources for teacher information and student worksheets.

Quadrant 1—Experience

Right Mode—Connect

Students look for items in nature that contain patterns.

Objective

Students will enhance observation skills as they search for patterns in nature.

Activity

Students need a grocery sack, paper and a pencil. The teacher takes the group on a nature walk. Students look for items in nature that contain patterns. When students observe an item with a pattern that can be taken with them (example: a leaf), it should be placed in their sack. If the item cannot be taken (example: a tree), they are to sketch the item and make notes of the patterns observed.

Assessment

Quality of student involvement.

Left Mode—Examine

Students share the items found on the nature walk & show the patterns.

Objective

Students' curiosity about patterns will be aroused as they reflect upon the patterns observed in nature.

Activity

Students share the items found on the nature walk and show the patterns exhibited. Magnifying glasses may be needed to examine patterns in the smaller specimens. Students discuss why they think nature uses patterns.

Assessment

Quality and depth of student sharing and discussion.

Quadrant 2—Concepts

Right Mode—Image

Students view "Donald Duck in Mathemagicland" & look for patterns in nature from film.

Objective

Students will make a connection between mathematics and the patterns found in nature.

Activity

Students view "Donald Duck in Mathemagicland" and look for patterns in nature shown in the film. Students discuss the patterns observed and responses are written on the chalkboard.

Assessment

Attentiveness of students and quality of discussion.

Left Mode—Define

Teach Fibonacci Sequence concepts and vocabulary.

Objective

Students will learn the concepts and vocabulary of the Fibonacci Sequence and The Golden Rule.

Note: From this point, the unit is divided into two main topics (Fibonacci Sequence and The Golden Rule). There are four Fibonacci activities and six Golden Rule activities. You may wish to teach the material (step 4), and have the students reinforce the learning (step 5) for one activity at a time. All of the activities under a topic should be completed before beginning step 6 for that topic. Students may need to review the three following concepts in decimal use if they are to experience success in the third Fibonacci activity:

- Meaning of the decimal part of a number, i.e., that it is part of a whole and that the places represent tenths, hundredths, and thousandths of a whole.

- Conversion of any fraction to a decimal by dividing with the calculator.

- Measurement of items with a centimeter ruler to the nearest millimeter and naming the result as a decimal number of centimeters. (This review can be found in any good math text.)

Activity

Teach the following Fibonacci Sequence* concepts and vocabulary:

- Helices, helix, sequence, Fibonacci Sequence, infinite, finite (correlates with "The Pinecone Numbers" worksheets).

- Clockwise and counterclockwise curves (correlates with "Coloring Sunflower Spirals" worksheets).
- "Babies," "youngsters," and "adults" in rabbit life cycles; "ideal" versus "real" answers in science (correlates with "Leonardo's Rabbits" worksheets).
- Hexagon, parthenogenesis (correlates with "The Number Secret of the Bees" worksheets).

Teach the following Golden Rule* concepts and vocabulary:

- Ratio, relative and absolute comparisons (correlates with "Introducing Ratios" worksheets).
- The Golden Ratio, "Classic" Greek, profile of characteristics, trend, sample, random (correlates with "The Greeks and Their Golden Ratio" worksheets).
- "Perfect" human face (correlates with "Golden Faces" worksheets).
- Golden Rectangle, arcs, spiral (correlates with "The Golden Rectangle" worksheets).
- Calculus, limit (correlates with "The Fibonacci Numbers Strike Again" worksheets).
- Commutative (correlates with "The Fibonaccis, The Golden Ratio, and Some Calculator Tips" worksheets).

* See resources listed in bibliography for teaching the above concepts.

Assessment

Subjective measure of student understanding.

Quadrant 3—Applications

Left Mode—Try

Students complete worksheets on the Fibonacci Sequence.

Objective

Students will enhance higher level thinking skills while reinforcing the concepts.

Activity

Students complete the following worksheets** on the Fibonacci Sequence: The Pinecone Numbers, Coloring Sunflower Spirals, Leonardo's Rabbits, Number Secrets of the Bees. (These correlate with the concepts and vocabulary taught in step four.)

Students complete the following worksheets** on The Golden Rule: Introducing Ratios, The Greeks and Their Golden Ratio, Golden Faces, The Golden Rectangle, A Golden Rectangle Puzzle (optional), The Fibonacci Numbers Strike Again, The Fibonaccis, The Golden Rule and Some Calculator Tips. (These correlate with the concepts and vocabulary taught in step four.)

** See resource listed in the bibliography for student worksheets.

Assessment

Quality of student activities and worksheets.

Right Mode—Extend

Students select a project and design a plan for its completion.

Objective

Students will personalize their learning through a choice of learning activities.

Activity

Students select one of the following projects and design a plan for its completion (correlate with the Fibonacci Sequence):

- Research and report on the life of Fibonacci.
- Make and demonstrate an abacus.
- Research how the Moslem's invented their number system. Include a diagram of the number system.
- Complete a detailed, colored drawing or design using spirals or helices.
- Research the spiral and its meaning in ancient art, philosophy, and architecture.
- Research and diagram or build the DNA double helix molecule.

Patterns

- Research and report on infinity.
- Research and report on Einstein and his theory of relativity.
- Research and construct a model of the Leaning Tower of Pisa.
- Research and report on the town of Pisa, Italy.
- Create a detailed, colored drawing of fantasy flowers that shows Fibonacci numbers operating on them in different ways.
- Make a display of climates and soils that encourage growth of different species of sunflowers and daisies. Use a flower field guide as a resource.
- Count the clockwise and counterclockwise spirals and petals of different species of daisies. Record and diagram your findings.
- Find at least three different pine cone species. Paint the scales of each helix a different color. Try to paint four cones of the same species to show the four Fibonacci Numbers for that sequence. Create a display of your work.
- Check the hexagons on a pineapple for number sequences. Chart or diagram your results for a display.
- Draw and color at least five different species of Fibonacci flowers. Take notes on their Fibonacci Sequences and numbers. Use the notes and drawings to create a display.
- Report why ancient Greeks and Egyptians considered "7" a number of "completion."
- Report on the dawning of the modern scientific age with the discovery of Uranus in 1781, by William Herschel.
- Visit a beekeeper and secure a honeycomb to be used in connection with a report on the life of bees.
- Research and report on the "Sieve of Eratosthenes."

Students will select one of the following projects and design a plan for its completion (correlates with the Golden Ratio):

- Measure and diagram the ratios of your family's bodies.
- Find at least ten pictures of animals for a booklet. Measure each for the Golden Ratio. Report your findings.
- Measure and diagram at least five real statues for the Golden Ratio.
- Design and build a "Golden Ratio Robot."
- Draw and color five strange faces for a booklet full of Golden Ratios.
- Draw, color and redesign a Greek face and statue so

they have no Golden Ratios.
- Create a new ratio, name it, and write about how you discovered it. Draw a diagram showing how it would be used.
- Find faces of at least five different nationalities in magazines. Measure to see which have more or fewer Golden Ratios. Diagram your results.
- Diagram animal species that have spiral or helical horns, tusks, teeth, etc. Include animal parts that would grow in the spiral curve it continued: rhino horn, wolf fang, beaver tooth, fingernail.
- Compare and contrast (include diagrams) spirals of five different shells.
- Make a bulletin board exhibit of spirals in nature. Use pictures or tracings that are colored. Make the exhibit in spiral form.
- Using a ruler and calculator, check at least ten common rectangular objects, both big (door, playground, school wall) and small (light switch, page) to determine if they are Golden Rectangles. Document findings, both negative and positive).
- Report on the United Nations building, its architect, when it was built, how it was built, its floor plan, etc. Was it designed to be a Golden Rectangle?
- Research and report on "calculus," a kind of closer-and-closer study approach to a number. What is a "limit"?

Assessment

Quality of student plans.

Quadrant 4—Creations

Left Mode—Refine

Students meet w/teacher to discuss & evaluate various aspects of the project.

Objective
Students will develop their creativity and higher level thinking skills as they refine and complete their projects.

Activity
Students meet with teacher periodically to discuss and evaluate various aspects of the project such as resources, objectives, final project form, sharing method, and completion date. Necessary changes and refinements are made.

Assessment
Ability to carry out plan and make necessary changes.

Right Mode—Integrate

Students present their projects to an appropriate audience & share what they have learned

Objective
Students will share what they have learned.

Activity
Students present their projects to an appropriate audience and share what they have learned.

Assessment
Quality of project and presentation.

Place Value

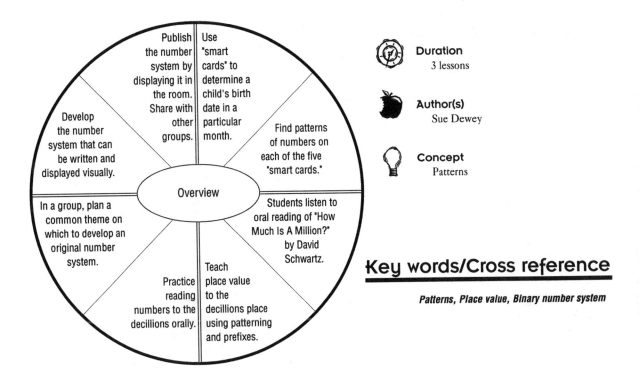

Overview

- Use "smart cards" to determine a child's birth date in a particular month.
- Find patterns of numbers on each of the five "smart cards."
- Students listen to oral reading of "How Much Is A Million?" by David Schwartz.
- Teach place value to the decillions place using patterning and prefixes.
- Practice reading numbers to the decillions orally.
- In a group, plan a common theme on which to develop an original number system.
- Develop the number system that can be written and displayed visually.
- Publish the number system by displaying it in the room. Share with other groups.

Duration
3 lessons

Author(s)
Sue Dewey

Concept
Patterns

Key words/Cross reference

Patterns, Place value, Binary number system

Overview

Objective
To explore the patterns in our number system and to be able to read numbers to the decillion place.

About the Author
Sue Dewey has worked for many years with the 4MAT model and cooperative learning strategies. She currently teaches fifth grade at Thomas Jefferson Elementary School in Kenmore, NY.

Required Resources
Smart cards and explanation.

Bibliography
The book or big book *"How Much Is A Million?"* by David Schwartz.

Quadrant 1—Experience

Right Mode—Connect

Use "smart cards" to determine a child's birth date in a particular month.

Objective

To engage the student in a personal experience.

Activity

Create "smart cards" based on the binary number system. Ask individual students if his birth date is on the smart card shown. Using the mathematical formula, (magically) determine the birth date.

Assessment

Enthusiasm of student participation.

Left Mode—Examine

Find patterns of numbers on each of the five "smart cards."

Objective

To have the student analyze the five smart cards for patterns.

Activity

Display each smart card. Have the students study them and try to find patterns on each. Discuss each pattern for consistency.

Assessment

Participation of students and number of correct patterns found.

Quadrant 2—Concepts

Right Mode—Image

Students listen to oral reading of "How Much Is A Million?" by David Schwartz.

Objective

To have students imagine how much a million is. To have students make the connection between patterns and our number system.

Activity

Read the book *"How Much Is A Million?"* by David Schwartz. Discuss various examples of numbers to the thousands place, the ten thousands place, the hundred thousands place and the millions place.

Assessment

Interest in the book and participation in the discussion.

Left Mode—Define

Teach place value to the decillions place using patterning and prefixes.

Objective

To teach the prefixes in our number system and show how our system is patterned.

Activity

Place three dashes on the board, i.e., _ _ _. Tell the students all positive whole numbers in our number system are arranged in a pattern and have them practice reading a number to the hundreds place. Show them, by using commas for family names, that they can read larger numbers following the same pattern they used to read numbers to the hundreds place. After naming the thousands and the millions families, lead them to discover the following prefixes used to name families. These are: billion, trillion, quadrillion, quintillion, hexillion, septillion, octillion, nonillion and decillion. Place commas with these family names written on them between a series of dashes.

Assessment

After removing this from the board, the students should be able to successfully rearrange the prefixes in order. This activity can be done as a whole class or individually on paper.

Place Value

Quadrant 3—Applications

 Left Mode—Try

Practice reading numbers to the decillions orally.

Objective
To review and practice reading numbers to the decillion place.

Activity
Have students replace the numbers you wrote on the board with numbers of their choice. Give turns reading the new numbers. This can be done many times.

Assessment
Correctness of their response.

 Right Mode—Extend

In a group, plan a common theme on which to develop an original number system.

Objective
To work together cooperatively, to explore objects that relate to each other and to visualize what a different number system might look like. The students should also discover that it is very difficult to change the three places in each family to greater or fewer places.

Activity
Students work together to develop a theme, or a group of objects that somehow relate to each other. An example might be colors. Each word, i.e., blueillion, redillion, magentaillion would be displayed on a different colored shape of paper. These will be the new family names for their newly created number system.

Assessment
Participation in the group and an agreed upon theme.

Quadrant 4—Creations

 Left Mode—Refine

Develop the number system that can be written and displayed visually.

Objective
To develop an original number system that follows patterns learned.

Activity
The students will decide on family names based on the theme they chose. They will write a list of their new family names and will construct a visual to be displayed between family groups.

Assessment
Quality of the finished product.

 Right Mode—Integrate

Publish the number system by displaying it in the room. Share with other groups.

Objective
To share and reflect. What if our number system changed? How would that affect your life?

Activity
Have students display their number system. They will also explain how it works.

Assessment
Quality of understanding through the explanations and the enjoyment of each participant.

Watermelon 1/3

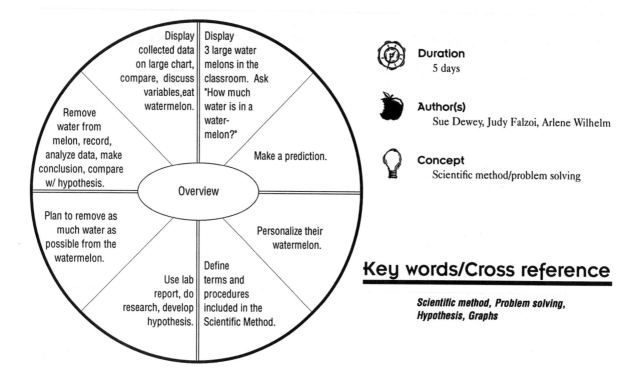

Duration
5 days

Author(s)
Sue Dewey, Judy Falzoi, Arlene Wilhelm

Concept
Scientific method/problem solving

Key words/Cross reference

Scientific method, Problem solving, Hypothesis, Graphs

The circle diagram contains the following text, clockwise from top right:

- Display 3 large water melons in the classroom. Ask "How much water is in a water-melon?"
- Make a prediction.
- Personalize their watermelon.
- Define terms and procedures included in the Scientific Method.
- Use lab report, do research, develop hypothesis.
- Plan to remove as much water as possible from the watermelon.
- Remove water from melon, record, analyze data, make conclusion, compare w/ hypothesis.
- Display collected data on large chart, compare, discuss variables, eat watermelon.

Center: Overview

Overview

Objective
Use of Scientific Method in an interdisciplinary thematic unit.

About the Authors
Sue Dewey, Judy Falzoi and Arlene Wilhelm teach fifth grade together at Jefferson Elementary School in Kenmore-Tonawanda, NY. Each brings a willingness to explore creative ways of integrating science into the whole language curriculum.

Required Resources
3 large watermelons

Quadrant 1—Experience

Right Mode—Connect

Display 3 large watermelons in the classroom. Ask "How much water is in a watermelon?"

Objective
To enter into an experience.

Activity
Students' attention will be captured by displaying the watermelons and by using a group problem-solving activity before using the Scientific Method. The teacher will ask the question, "How much water is in a watermelon?" Discussion will occur and all reasonable ideas as well as questions will be accepted.

Assessment
Teacher will observe number of ideas generated and engagement of all students in group discussion.

Left Mode—Examine

Make a prediction.

Objective
To reflect on the experience and make a prediction.

Activity
The students will share what they already know about the parts of a watermelon and how much they predict will be water. Each group's predictions will be recorded on chart paper and displayed.

Assessment
The ability of each student to make a reasonable prediction.

Quadrant 2—Concepts

Right Mode—Image

Personalize their watermelon.

Objective
Use of another medium to connect personal knowledge to the concept.

Activity
Students will personalize watermelons. Their group's watermelon will become a person – complete with a personality, biography and other human characteristics. They will know their watermelon inside and out. Within each cooperative group, some will be illustrators while others will be biographers. Through discussion, before writing and illustrating, members will create a common picture in their minds of the watermelon's appearance, place of work or play, likes and dislikes, etc. Biographers will communicate with illustrators. Information will be shared. They will edit and revise together. Illustrations will be displayed and biographies read aloud to entire class. Classmates will listen to the biography and then identify the illustration that fits the description.

Assessment
Quality of production.

Left Mode—Define

Define terms and procedures included in the Scientific Method.

Objective
To define each of the six steps of the Scientific Method.

Activity
Each of the six steps will be written on a colorful strip of paper: Purpose, Research, Hypothesis, Experiment, Analysis, Conclusion. In random order, the following questions will be also written on strips of manila paper: What do I want to know?, What do I already know about this?, What do I think the answer is?, How can I find out the answer?, What have I observed?, What have I discovered? Each group will match these questions with a step. The teacher will give information about each part of the Scientific Method explaining that this is an organized way of discovering facts. The groups will then reevaluate their answer and see if they are correct. The teacher will randomly call on students to move the questions to a location under one of the six steps allowing the entire class to evaluate if it is correct. This completed activity will become part of a bulletin board display.

Assessment
Verbal checking of correct responses.

Quadrant 3—Applications

Left Mode—Try

Use lab report, do research, develop hypothesis.

Objective
To use the Scientific Method.

Activity
Students will use a lab report to begin answering the question, "How much water is in a watermelon?" Their hypothesis must be reasonable and based upon researched facts. (Measurement terms have already been taught in a previous lesson using this theme.) They will record the purpose of the experiment, record researched facts using content reading (already taught in a previous lesson using this theme), and personal experience. Using the collective knowledge of the group, they will each record their own hypothesis.

Assessment
Information recorded correctly on the first three steps of the lab report.

Right Mode—Extend

Plan to remove as much water as possible from the watermelon.

Objective
Plan an experiment.

Activity
In cooperative groups, the students will plan a procedure for removing the water from the watermelon. They will also decide what tools will be needed to do this and assign members of the group to bring these in. This will be recorded under step four on their lab report – Experiment.

Assessment
Teacher evaluation of written response.

Quadrant 4—Creations

Left Mode—Refine

Remove water from melon, record, analyze data, make conclusion, compare w/ hypothesis.

Objective
Conduct hands-on experiment.

Activity
In cooperative groups, students will measure circumference and length of their watermelon. They will weigh the watermelon in pounds and kilograms. Then, they will use their procedure for extracting water from the watermelon. It will be measured and data recorded under step five (Analysis) on their lab report. A written conclusion will be recorded.

Assessment
Ability of students to complete the experiment and complete steps five and six on their lab report.

Right Mode—Integrate

Display collected data on large chart, compare, discuss variables, eat watermelon.

Objective
Share data and conclusion with other students.

Activity
On a large wall display, students will record how much water they extracted from their watermelon. Comparisons will be made and variables discussed. Groups will evaluate themselves. The use of each step of the Scientific Method will be discussed. Original predictions will be shared and compared. Watermelon ice cream and/or pie will be enjoyed by all.

Assessment
Teacher will observe the quality of the final product and enjoyment of the celebration.

Watermelon 2/3

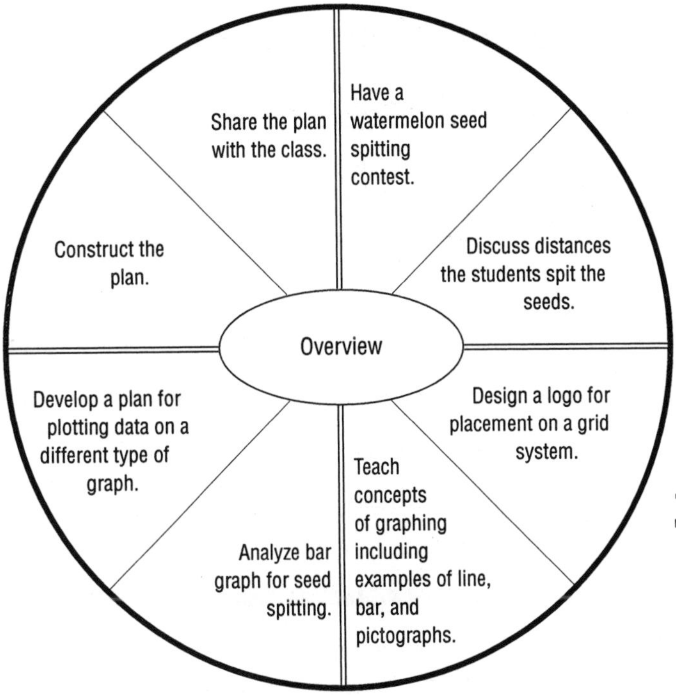
Have a watermelon seed spitting contest.
Discuss distances the students spit the seeds.
Design a logo for placement on a grid system.
Teach concepts of graphing including examples of line, bar, and pictographs.
Analyze bar graph for seed spitting.
Develop a plan for plotting data on a different type of graph.
Construct the plan.
Share the plan with the class.
Overview

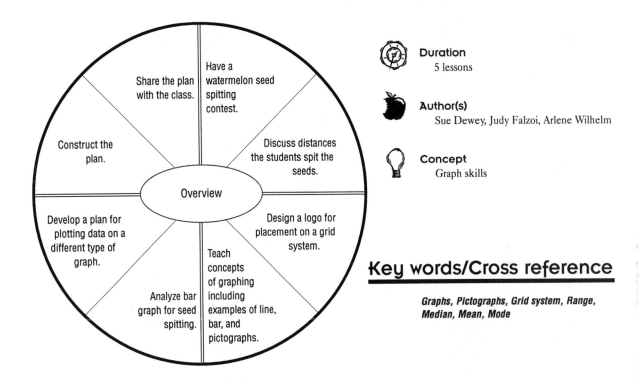

Duration
5 lessons

Author(s)
Sue Dewey, Judy Falzoi, Arlene Wilhelm

Concept
Graph skills

Key words/Cross reference

Graphs, Pictographs, Grid system, Range, Median, Mean, Mode

Overview

Objective
Integration of math skills into an interdisciplinary thematic unit.

About the Author
Sue Dewey, Judy Falzoi and Arlene Wilhelm teach fifth grade together at Jefferson Elementary School in Kenmore-Tonawanda, NY. Each brings her special talent to the team.

Required Resources
Watermelon seeds, rulers.

Quadrant 1—Experience

Right Mode—Connect

Have a watermelon seed spitting contest.

Objective
To become actively engaged in an experience.

Activity
Using the watermelon seeds retrieved from the previous lesson, the students will have a contest to see how far they can each spit a seed. The students will each be given a 12 inch ruler. They will place these end to end and stand next to their ruler. They will be given a number in order from 1 to 25 to correspond to how many feet they are away from the starting line. They will be a part of a human linear measurement tool. As the seed lands, the student nearest to it calls out the number of feet it traveled.

Assessment
Active participation and enjoyment of students.

Left Mode—Examine

Discuss distances the students spit the seeds.

Objective
To reflect on the experience and see the relationship of individual data to that of the whole group.

Activity
Student will share their personal data with the class. They will then organize it by distance, shortest to longest. Accuracy of measurement will also be discussed at this point.

Assessment
Participation of the students in their reflections and in the correctness of the organized data.

Quadrant 2—Concepts

Right Mode—Image

Design a logo for placement on a grid system.

Objective
To enable the student to make the connection between collecting data and analyzing it.

Activity
Students will develop a logo for their watermelon seed. They will illustrate these or a square Post-it note. They will then place their logo on a grid that has been displayed on the wall in the hall. When completed, this will be a graph visualizing the collected data.

Assessment
Quality of student product.

Left Mode—Define

Teach concepts of graphing including examples of line, bar, and pictographs.

Objective
To define terms used in graphing.

Activity
Lesson 1 – Use the overhead projector to duplicate the bar graph that had been developed in the hall. Explain the horizontal and vertical axes, labels of each axis, title and what each logo stands for.
Lesson 2 – Show different types of graphs: bar, line and pictographs and discuss differences and similarities using a three circle Venn Diagram.
Lesson 3 – Explain the difference between range, mean, median and mode.

Assessment
Written vocabulary match.

Watermelon 2/3

Quadrant 3—Applications

 ### Left Mode—Try

Analyze bar graph for seed spitting.

Objective

To manipulate data for understanding of graphing vocabulary.

Activity

Using the data collected from the bar graph "Seed Spitting Contest," have the students find the range, mean, median and mode for the distance that seeds were spit.

Assessment

Accuracy of answers.

 ### Right Mode—Extend

Develop a plan for plotting data on a different type of graph.

Objective

The student will develop a plan to produce several types of graphs.

Activity

Given data on the growth of watermelon vines and pumpkin vines over a period of time, the student will plan two graphs. They will choose from the following types: pictograph, bar graph, double bar graph, line graph, and double line graph. They will gather materials and information needed to produce this graph.

Assessment

Student engagement during this planning time.

Quadrant 4—Creations

 ### Left Mode—Refine

Construct the plan.

Objective

To produce a quality product based on new learnings.

Activity

Construct the graphs that were planned.

Assessment

Ability of the students to complete the project and to analyze their work as to correctness, neatness and effectiveness.

 ### Right Mode—Integrate

Share the plan with the class.

Objective

To have students share their graphs with the class.

Activity

Have students display their individual graphs around the large "Seed Spitting Contest" graph that is displayed in the hall. Invite another class to hear a presentation about the seed spitting contest and the graphing that was then done.

Assessment

Student ability to report on what they had done and enjoyment of the students.

Watermelon 3/3

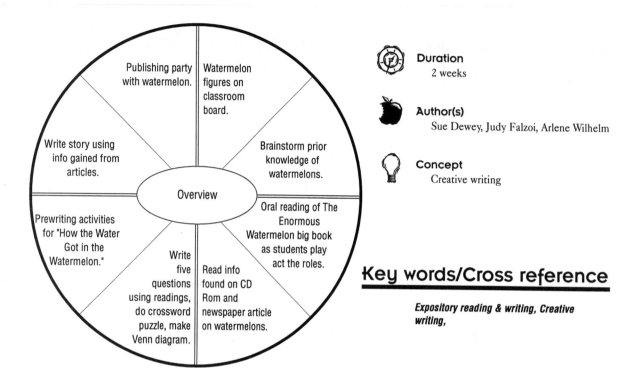

Publishing party with watermelon.

Watermelon figures on classroom board.

Write story using info gained from articles.

Brainstorm prior knowledge of watermelons.

Overview

Prewriting activities for "How the Water Got in the Watermelon."

Oral reading of The Enormous Watermelon big book as students play act the roles.

Write five questions using readings, do crossword puzzle, make Venn diagram.

Read info found on CD Rom and newspaper article on watermelons.

Duration
2 weeks

Author(s)
Sue Dewey, Judy Falzoi, Arlene Wilhelm

Concept
Creative writing

Key words/Cross reference

Expository reading & writing, Creative writing,

Overview

Objective
Use of language arts in a multidisciplinary thematic unit.

About the Author
Sue Dewey, Judy Falzoi and Arlene Wilhelm teach fifth grade together at Jefferson Elementary School in Kenmore-Tonawanda, NY. Creativity and an eagerness to develop interdisciplinary thematic units based on conceptual teaching are common threads in their work.

Bibliography
The Enormous Watermelon retold by Brenda Parkes and Judith Smith (Rigby Press, 1986), Grollier's CD Rom, Compton's CD Rom, The Mini Page newspaper article © 1994 by Universal Press Syndicate.

Watermelon 3/3

Quadrant 1—Experience

 ### Right Mode—Connect

Watermelon figures on classroom board.

Objective

To create an experience for students to begin recalling facts about watermelons.

Activity

On classroom board, place three construction paper watermelons designed to represent the three states which produce the most watermelons — California, Florida, Texas. Students must determine the states these figures represent and how they reached those conclusions.

Assessment

Identification of the three states.

 ### Left Mode—Examine

Brainstorm prior knowledge of watermelons.

Objective

To work cooperatively to recall prior knowledge concerning watermelons.

Activity

On watermelon-shaped paper, pairs brainstorm facts they have heard, seen, read or learned pertaining to watermelons. The facts will be shared, discussed and reviewed with the whole class and then displayed on the classroom bulletin board.

Assessment

Pairs will have a minimum of 8 facts written on their watermelon slices.

Quadrant 2—Concepts

 ### Right Mode—Image

Oral reading of The Enormous Watermelon *big book as students play act the roles.*

Objective

To experience the concept of watermelons through literature and the senses.

Activity

Shared reading activity of big book The Enormous Watermelon. Orally read the book to the whole class. Re-read the book with individuals acting out the roles of the characters in the story and other students reading the passages. Act this out several times, changing student roles.

Assessment

Creative responses to role-playing and the expression and enthusiasm of the narrators.

 ### Left Mode—Define

Read info found on CD Rom and newspaper article on watermelons.

Objective

To develop the skills needed to effectively read and comprehend expository text.

Activity

Lesson 1: Students will be encouraged to recall the type of literature or medium through which they learned the facts discussed in the previous lesson. After discussing and defining fictional and non-fictional literature, the teacher lists, on large chart paper, these differences.

Lesson 2: Before reading the selection, students are given vocabulary words they will encounter within the text. Students place each of the words in one of the following columns, "Know It Well," "Heard of It," "Say What?". The placement of the words is discussed and the students are encouraged to discover the meanings through the context of the reading. The class reads the article from Compton's Encyclopedia, discussing vocabulary words and facts found within the reading. After reading, definitions of vocabulary words are discussed and any new comments concerning fictional and non-fictional reading are added to the chart.

Assessment

Quality of definitions of vocabulary words and responses received for chart.

Quadrant 3—Applications

Left Mode—Try

Write five questions using readings, do crossword puzzle, make Venn diagram.

Objective
To us knowledge gained to analyze types of expository writing.

Activity
Lesson 1: Pairs of students write questions using the facts found in reading. Students are encouraged to use "why" and "how" questions and are discouraged using strictly "what" questions. Partners exchange papers with another set of partners and determine the answers to the questions. Students evaluate each other's answers. Whole class completes large classroom cross-work puzzle reflective of the information found in the article.

Lesson 2: Students read newspaper article, The Mini Page, concerning watermelons. Students make Venn diagram comparing encyclopedia article to newspaper article. Discuss differences between the two types of expository text.

Assessment
Quality of questions and answers and responses on Venn diagram.

Right Mode—Extend

Prewriting activities for "How the Water Got in the Watermelon."

Objective
Pre-writing activities for expository text.

Activity
Using a story web, individual students plan to write a newspaper article detailing how the water got into the watermelon. Students will need to plan who, what, where, and why. In small conference groups, students share their pre-writing ideas and accept suggestions and comments from others. After the web is completed, students will transfer the information into outline form.

Assessment
Quality of webs and outlines and responses to each other's work.

Quadrant 4—Creations

Left Mode—Refine

Write story using info gained from articles.

Objective
To create an expository text and then evaluate and refine it.

Activity
Students begin writing the expository text. As the work is completed, they proofread, revise and edit their work. Working with a partner, they then proofread and edit each other's work. They then begin the final draft.

Assessment
Quality of work and responses to one another's work.

Right Mode—Integrate

Publishing party with watermelon.

Objective
To celebrate knowledge gained.

Activity
A publishing party will be conducted during which students may share their stories and enjoy watermelon.

Assessment
Quality of final product.

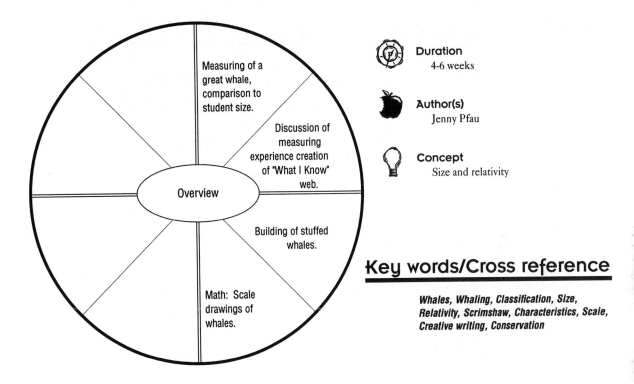

Duration
4-6 weeks

Author(s)
Jenny Pfau

Concept
Size and relativity

Key words/Cross reference

Whales, Whaling, Classification, Size, Relativity, Scrimshaw, Characteristics, Scale, Creative writing, Conservation

Overview

Objective

This unit consists of 4 "spiraled" 4MAT cycles. It uses the content surrounding whales and whaling to integrate math, language arts, social studies, science, and visual arts activities.

About the Author

Jenny Pfau is currently employed with Lawrence Township Schools, Indianapolis, IN, where she works as a 5th grade teacher in a full-time, self-contained classroom with gifted students.

Bibliography

Bank Street College Of Education. *The Voyage of the Mimi, The Book*, Videos, and *Overview Guide*. Scotts Valley, CA: WINGS for learning, 1989.

Buffington, Kath; Fleming, Maria; Kovacs, Deborah; Steuer, Karen; Ward, Nathalie. Whales. Scholastic Professional Books, Scholastic, Inc., 1992.

Greenleaf, Elisabeth Bristol. *Ballads and Sea Songs*. Cambridge, Massachusetts by Harvard University Press, 1933.

Houston, James. *Ice Swords: An Undersea Adventure*. NY: Atheneum, 1985.

Linsley, Leslie. *Scrimshaw*. NY: Hawthorn/Dutton, 1976.

Melville, Herman. *Moby Dick*. Retold by Bernice Selden, Troll Associates, 1988.

Payne, Roger. *"Humpbacks: Their Mysterious Songs."* National Geographic Society, January, 1979.

Payne, Roger. *"The Songs of the Whale."* National Geographic Society, 1972.

Taylor, Theodore. *The Hostage*. NY: Delacorte, 1988.

Weir, Robert. *Whaling on the Atlantic Grounds, Journal of the Clara Bell 1855-1858*. Education Department, Mystic Seaport Museum, 1986.

Williams, Harold. *One Whaling Family*. Boston: Houghton Mifflin, 1964.

Quadrant 1—Experience

Right Mode—Connect

Measuring of a great whale, comparison to student size.

Objective

To provide the students with an awareness of the size of five great whales in comparison to their own body size.

Activity

Students, working in small groups, are asked to go outside to a grassy area and measure out the length of the whale which they have been assigned. Each group will mark this length with yarn. Whales students will measure include:

Blue whale—91 ft.	Humpback whale—45 ft.
Fin whale— 80 ft.	Sperm whale—55 ft.
Right whale—50 ft.	

The groups are then asked to estimate the number of class members it would take, lying head to foot, to equal the length of "their" whale.

Assessment

Involvement of the students in the experience and their contribution to it.

Left Mode—Examine

Discussion of measuring experience creation of "What I Know" web.

Objective

To discuss the measuring experience, and to focus the thinking of students on the topic of whales!

Activity

Bring the group together and ask them to reflect on the size comparison experience. Students are encouraged to share information which they already know on the topic of whales. The teacher can record this information by creating a web.

Assessment

Student contribution to the group discussion and quality of web which is created.

Quadrant 2—Concepts

Right Mode—Image

Building of stuffed whales.

Objective

Students will work in groups to make stuffed paper whale models for the classroom.

Activity

Materials: Rolls of heavy paper, packing tape, poster paints, large safety pins, heavy strong, old newspapers (shredded), large paper clips.

Directions: First, decide what scale you will use for your whales. Lay out enough heavy paper to make the body of your whale twice. (Remember your whale will be two-sided.) Cut out two bodies, two flukes, and four flippers. Sew the two sides together with string and a large needle leaving the tail area open so you can stuff shredded or crumpled newspaper inside. Stuff the whale until you are satisfied with the shape. Sew the tail closed. Sew together the two flippers and the flukes. Sew or tape the stuffed flippers into position. Cut a slot in the tail section, about six inches long. Slip the flukes into the slot and tape them into position. Paint your whale. Using the large needle again, thread nylon line inside the seam line near the head, and tie into place. Sew other end near tail, adjust length and knot into place. Slip a large paper clip onto the line. Use it as a hook to attach your whale to a hook on the ceiling. Look up and smile!

Assessment

Quality and authenticity of stuffed whale.

Left Mode—Define

Math: Scale drawings of whales.

Objective
To teach specific information in an interdisciplinary fashion around the topic of whales. The content disciplines with their specific objectives include:

Math – Students will be able to use the concept of scale drawings in order to create "scaled" whales on graph paper.

Activity
The teacher presents information using lecture, videos, films, music, visuals, discussion, technology, field trips, guest speakers and learning stations as well as allowing time for individual inquiry from the text set of material which has been placed in the classroom.

Assessment
Level of student interest and quality of products completed. Tests, essays and/or journal responses might also be used.

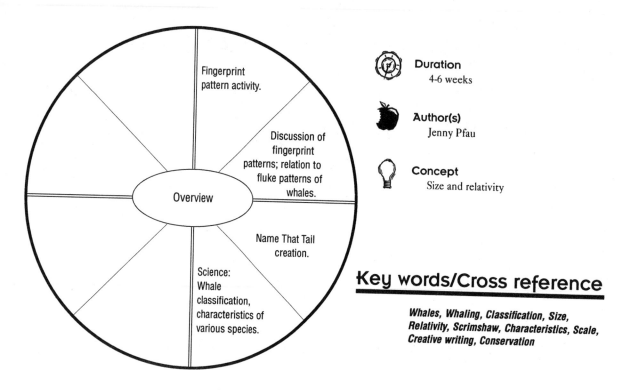

Overview

Fingerprint pattern activity.

Discussion of fingerprint patterns; relation to fluke patterns of whales.

Name That Tail creation.

Science: Whale classification, characteristics of various species.

Duration
4-6 weeks

Author(s)
Jenny Pfau

Concept
Size and relativity

Key words/Cross reference

Whales, Whaling, Classification, Size, Relativity, Scrimshaw, Characteristics, Scale, Creative writing, Conservation

Overview

Objective

This unit consists of 4 "spiraled" 4MAT cycles. It uses the content surrounding whales and whaling to integrate math, language arts, social studies, science, and visual arts activities.

About the Author

Jenny Pfau is currently employed with Lawrence Township Schools, Indianapolis, IN, where she works as a 5th grade teacher in a full-time, self-contained classroom with gifted students.

Bibliography

Bank Street College Of Education. *The Voyage of the Mimi, The Book*, Videos, and *Overview Guide*. Scotts Valley, CA: WINGS for learning, 1989.

Buffington, Kath; Fleming, Maria; Kovacs, Deborah; Steuer, Karen; Ward, Nathalie. Whales. Scholastic Professional Books, Scholastic, Inc., 1992.

Greenleaf, Elisabeth Bristol. *Ballads and Sea Songs*. Cambridge, Massachusetts by Harvard University Press, 1933.

Houston, James. *Ice Swords: An Undersea Adventure*. NY: Atheneum, 1985.

Linsley, Leslie. *Scrimshaw*. NY: Hawthorn/Dutton, 1976.

Melville, Herman. *Moby Dick*. Retold by Bernice Selden, Troll Associates, 1988.

Payne, Roger. *"Humpbacks: Their Mysterious Songs."* National Geographic Society, January, 1979.

Payne, Roger. *"The Songs of the Whale."* National Geographic Society, 1972.

Taylor, Theodore. *The Hostage*. NY: Delacorte, 1988.

Weir, Robert. *Whaling on the Atlantic Grounds, Journal of the Clara Bell 1855-1858*. Education Department, Mystic Seaport Museum, 1986.

Williams, Harold. *One Whaling Family*. Boston: Houghton Mifflin, 1964.

Quadrant 1—Experience

 ### Right Mode—Connect

Fingerprint pattern activity.

Objective
Students will recognize that living things can be identified by their unique structure and characteristics.

Activity
Students will analyze and match their fingerprint patterns.
Materials: Ink pad, index cards cut in half, two small collection boxes, bulletin board area.
Procedure:

1) Give each student two index cards and have them use the ink pad to make a copy of the same fingerprint on each card.

2) Students place one of their fingerprint cards in one box, one in another.

3) Choosing at random, mount the fingerprints from one box on the bulletin board and allow each student to examine the fingerprints carefully.

4) Have each student choose a fingerprint from the remaining box.

5) One by one, have the students try to match the fingerprint they have chosen with one of the mounted prints.

Assessment
Participation in activity.

 ## Left Mode—Examine

Discussion of fingerprint patterns; relation to fluke patterns of whales.

Objective
Students will discuss the matching experience and focus their thinking on the fact that the uniqueness of fingerprint patterns used for human identification is the same key fluke patterns provided for whale identification.

Activity
Bring the group together and ask the students to reflect on how they arrived at their choices for matching of fingerprints. Discuss the pattern-recognition techniques used by students in this activity. Lead into a discussion about how researchers use these same techniques for telling one whale from another. When reseachers want to tell one whale from another, they try to look at the whale's fluke or tail. The underside of the humpback's flukes has a black and white pattern that is different on each individual — a kind of natural "name tag" or "fingerprint."

Assessment
Student contribution to group discussion.

Quadrant 2—Concepts

 Right Mode—Image

Name That Tail creation.

Objective

Students will role-play researchers by using a whale-naming, cooperative activity – Name That Tail!

Activity

Play Name That Tail game! Divide the class into groups of 5 or 6. Show each group of students examples of whale flukes, discuss how scientists could have arrived at the name given to each whale because of the fluke pattern they observed. Give each student in the group two index cards and ask them to sketch a fluke on one card and create a possible name on the other card. Once everyone in the group is finished, shuffle the fluke cards together. Lay out the name cards so that each member of the group can see the names. Have students take turns drawing from the fluke card stack and trying to match the fluke with the name given by the "scientist" from their group.

Assessment

Ability of students to create flukes, participation in group game.

 Left Mode—Define

Science: Whale classification, characteristics of various species.

Objective

To teach specific information in an interdisciplinary fashion around the topic of whales. The content disciplines with their specific objectives include:

Science — Students will be able to explain the major classification of whales as well as be able to describe the unique characteristics and behaviors of several species of whales.

Activity

The teacher presents information using lecture, videos, films, music, visuals, discussion, technology, field trips, guest speakers and learning stations as well as allowing time for individual inquiry from the text set of material which has been placed in the classroom.

Assessment

Level of student interest and quality of products completed. Tests, essays and/or journal responses might also be used.

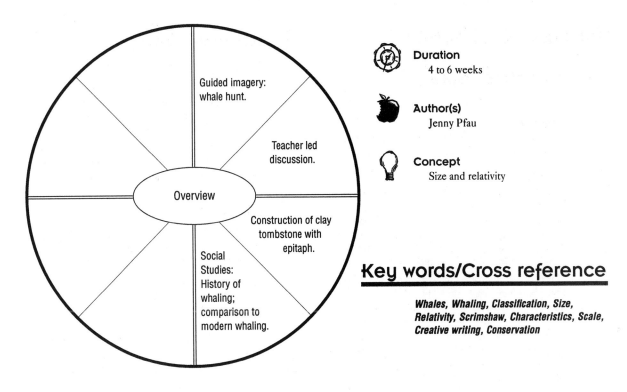

Guided imagery: whale hunt.

Teacher led discussion.

Overview

Construction of clay tombstone with epitaph.

Social Studies: History of whaling; comparison to modern whaling.

Duration
4 to 6 weeks

Author(s)
Jenny Pfau

Concept
Size and relativity

Key words/Cross reference

Whales, Whaling, Classification, Size, Relativity, Scrimshaw, Characteristics, Scale, Creative writing, Conservation

Overview

Objective

This unit consists of 4 "spiraled" 4MAT cycles. It uses the content surrounding whales and whaling to integrate math, language arts, social studies, science, and visual arts activities.

About the Author

Jenny Pfau is currently employed with Lawrence Township Schools, Indianapolis, IN, where she works as a 5th grade teacher in a full-time, self-contained classroom with gifted students.

Bibliography

Bank Street College Of Education. *The Voyage of the Mimi, The Book, Videos,* and *Overview Guide.* Scotts Valley, CA: WINGS for learning, 1989.

Buffington, Kath; Fleming, Maria; Kovacs, Deborah; Steuer, Karen; Ward, Nathalie. Whales. Scholastic Professional Books, Scholastic, Inc., 1992.

Greenleaf, Elisabeth Bristol. *Ballads and Sea Songs.* Cambridge, Massachusetts by Harvard University Press, 1933.

Houston, James. *Ice Swords: An Undersea Adventure.* NY: Atheneum, 1985.

Linsley, Leslie. *Scrimshaw.* NY: Hawthorn/Dutton, 1976.

Melville, Herman. *Moby Dick.* Retold by Bernice Selden, Troll Associates, 1988.

Payne, Roger. *"Humpbacks: Their Mysterious Songs."* National Geographic Society, January, 1979.

Payne, Roger. *"The Songs of the Whale."* National Geographic Society, 1972.

Taylor, Theodore. *The Hostage.* NY: Delacorte, 1988.

Weir, Robert. *Whaling on the Atlantic Grounds, Journal of the Clara Bell 1855-1858.* Education Department, Mystic Seaport Museum, 1986.

Williams, Harold. *One Whaling Family.* Boston: Houghton Mifflin, 1964.

Quadrant 1—Experience

 ## Right Mode—Connect

Guided imagery: whale hunt.

Objective
To create an experience enabling children to imagine what it is like for the hunted whale.

Activity
Teacher will involve students in a guided imagery focusing on the idea that whales do not have a chance escaping from whalemen who are hunting for them. Students should close their eyes and pretend to be the hunted whale during the imagery. Guided Imagery: The six-man New England whaleboat quietly approached the unsuspecting sperm whale from behind. As the boat drew nearer, the harpoonist hurled his long lance that was attached to a rope coiled in the tub line. As the lance struck its mark, the wounded whale leaped out of the sea, frightened and in pain. Like a crazed monster, the whale thrashed the waves with its mighty flukes, then disappeared into the watery depths, taking the towline with it. For a few moments, an eerie calmness hung in the air. Suddenly the stricken beast surfaced, then shot forward like a speeding bullet, dragging the boat behind it in a Nantucket Sleigh Ride, the whale had no escape, he was caught!

Assessment
The enjoyment and engagement of the children.

 ## Left Mode—Examine

Teacher led discussion.

Objective
To discuss reactions to the guided imagery experience.

Activity
Teacher-led discussion of the children's reactions to how it felt to be a whale who was being hunted.

Assessment
Student contribution to the group and individual responses.

Quadrant 2—Concepts

 ## Right Mode—Image

Construction of clay tombstone with epitaph.

Objective
Students will create an original epitaph for a whale that died as a result of being hunted.

Activity
Students will create an epitaph for a whale that died as a result of being hunted by a steam-powered catcher boat or the harpoon gun — two inventions that made it impossible for whales to escape the men who hunted them. They will engrave their inscription onto a small clay tombstone model. The teacher can turn a sandbox into a whale cemetery by standing these monuments upright in the sand.

Assessment
Quality of carved epitaph.

 ## Left Mode—Define

Social Studies: History of whaling; comparison to modern whaling.

Objective
To teach specific information in an interdisciplinary fashion around the topic of whales. The content disciplines with their specific objectives include:
Social Studies — Students will be able to recount a brief history and description of whaling, comparing modern practices with those of the 19th century whalers.

Activity
The teacher presents information using lecture, videos, films, music, visuals, discussion, technology, field trips, guest speakers and learning stations as well as allowing time for individual inquiry from the text set of material which has been placed in the classroom.

Assessment
Level of student interest and quality of products completed. Tests, essays and/or journal responses might also be used.

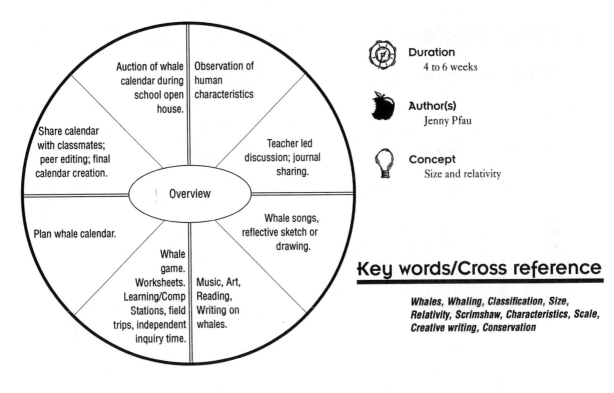

Author(s)
Jenny Pfau

Concept
Size and relativity

Key words/Cross reference

Whales, Whaling, Classification, Size, Relativity, Scrimshaw, Characteristics, Scale, Creative writing, Conservation

Overview

Objective

This unit consists of 4 "spiraled" 4MAT cycles. It uses the content surrounding whales and whaling to integrate math, language arts, social studies, science, and visual arts activities.

About the Author

Jenny Pfau is currently employed with Lawrence Township Schools, Indianapolis, IN, where she works as a 5th grade teacher in a full-time, self-contained classroom with gifted students.

Bibliography

Bank Street College Of Education. *The Voyage of the Mimi, The Book*, Videos, and *Overview Guide*. Scotts Valley, CA: WINGS for learning, 1989.

Buffington, Kath; Fleming, Maria; Kovacs, Deborah; Steuer, Karen; Ward, Nathalie. Whales. Scholastic Professional Books, Scholastic, Inc., 1992.

Greenleaf, Elisabeth Bristol. *Ballads and Sea Songs*. Cambridge, Massachusetts by Harvard University Press, 1933.

Houston, James. *Ice Swords: An Undersea Adventure*. NY: Atheneum, 1985.

Linsley, Leslie. *Scrimshaw*. NY: Hawthorn/Dutton, 1976.

Melville, Herman. *Moby Dick*. Retold by Bernice Selden, Troll Associates, 1988.

Payne, Roger. "*Humpbacks: Their Mysterious Songs.*" National Geographic Society, January, 1979.

Payne, Roger. "*The Songs of the Whale.*" National Geographic Society, 1972.

Taylor, Theodore. *The Hostage*. NY: Delacorte, 1988.

Weir, Robert. *Whaling on the Atlantic Grounds, Journal of the Clara Bell 1855-1858*. Education Department, Mystic Seaport Museum, 1986.

Williams, Harold. *One Whaling Family*. Boston: Houghton Mifflin, 1964.

Quadrant 1—Experience

Right Mode—Connect

Observation of human characteristics

Objective

To sensitize students to communicative behavior by observing and recording ways humans communicate.

Activity

Begin by asking these questions as you speak, "What am I doing right now?" "How am I communicating with you?" Watch me, what do you observe? "Are there other ways for me to communicate with you?" Have students take five minutes to talk with two or more of their classmates around their desks. They can talk about some favorite TV shows or books. Tell them to observe what their classmates do as they talk in order to communicate. What might they be saying with hands, body movements, or in order to communicate differently from another? Ask students to keep a simple journal for the next day. They should make careful observations about how they and their friends, family, or community members communicate with each other. Explain that students will have an opportunity to share their observations the next day.

Assessment

Participation in activity and discussion

Left Mode—Examine

Teacher led discussion; journal sharing.

Objective

Students will share some of their findings from their observations of human communication. Students will recognize that animals also create ways in which to communicate.

Activity

Ask for sharing of the journals which were kept. Ask the students if they saw any patterns in the way people communicated. Also ask them what people did to communicate different feelings such as anger, happiness, humor, etc. Lead the discussion from human communication to animal communication. Ask the students to share the way their pets communicate with them. Conclude with a discussion of whales and how they communicate.

Assessment

Student contribution to group discussion, quality of journal observations.

Quadrant 2—Concepts

Right Mode—Image

Whale songs, reflective sketch or drawing.

Objective

Students will recognize the "composition" and communicative qualities of humpback whales' songs.

Activity

Play for the class the recording of humpback whales' songs. Students are asked to sketch or create drawings with crayons while they listen to these songs. Their drawings should reflect what they think the whale is trying to communicate by singing their song.

Assessment

Students' participation in the activity and quality of their crayon drawings or sketches.

Left Mode—Define

Music, Art, Reading, Writing on whales.

Objective

To teach specific information in an interdisciplinary fashion around the topic of whales. The content disciplines with their specific objectives include:

Music — Students will develop an understanding of the history of sea chanties and respond to numerous sea chanties. Students will gain an in-depth knowledge of the sounds of the humpback whale by looking at research conducted by Katie and Roger Payne.

Art — Students will learn information about the history of the art of scrimshaw as well as what subjects were frequently chosen to use when completing this craft. Students will create a piece of scrimshaw utilizing the same techniques as 19th century whalers.

Reading — Students will read a book which has whales as its focus. Examples include: The Voyage of The Mimi: The Book, The Hostage, Moby Dick, Ice Swords: An Undersea Adventure, or One Whaling Family.

Creative Writing — Students will learn about various types of poetry including: acrostic, haiku, narrative, limerick, cinquain and diamonte. Students will then create a poetry book entitled: Cetacean Creations utilizing the various poetry types which they have learned. The central theme of each poem will be cetacean (whales).

Activity

The teacher presents information using lecture, videos, films, music, visuals, discussion, technology, field trips, guest speakers and learning stations as well as allowing time for individual inquiry from the text set of material which has been placed in the classroom.

Assessment

Level of student interest and quality of products completed. Tests, essays and/or journal responses might also be used.

Quadrant 3—Applications

Left Mode—Try

Whale game. Worksheets. Learning/Comp Stations, field trips, independent inquiry time.

Objective

To reinforce students' understandings of concepts presented in the various content areas.

Activity

The Whale Game — see bibliography, worksheets, learning stations, Audubon computer packet, making of a piece of scrimshaw, and independent inquiry time.

Assessment

Student participation and interest.

Right Mode—Extend

Plan whale calendar.

Objective

Students will plan the creation of a Whale Calendar.

Activity

Students will reflect upon their learning experiences in the various content areas and plan the creation of a whale calendar. This calendar should incorporate each segment of the interdisciplinary unit.

Assessment

On task behavior of students, quality of synthesized information into calendar pages.

Quadrant 4—Creations

Left Mode—Refine

Share calendar with classmates; peer editing; final calendar creation.

Objective

To auction the Whale Calendar during the school open house. To celebrate each other's work.

Activity

The teacher will hold a class auction, selling the Whale Calendar Creations during Open House at school.

Assessment

Participation and enjoyment of learning. Final product completed.

Right Mode—Integrate

Auction of whale calendar during school open house.

Objective

To have students share with their classmates their calendar creation so that peer editing can occur. To have students look critically at their own work and the work of their classmates. Finally, to create their finished product — the whale calendar.

Activity

Students will share their calendar with their classmates and ask for peer editing. The students will then reflect upon the suggestions made by their peers and work to create their finished calendar.

Assessment

Quality of student contribution to their classmates. Ability to critique work for substance and originality.

Line and Design

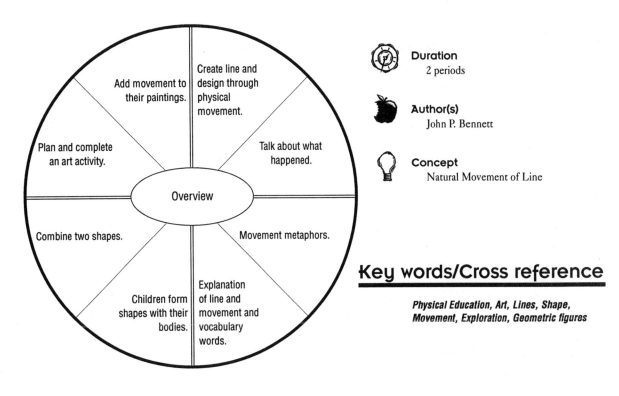

Overview

- Create line and design through physical movement.
- Add movement to their paintings.
- Plan and complete an art activity.
- Combine two shapes.
- Children form shapes with their bodies.
- Explanation of line and movement and vocabulary words.
- Movement metaphors.
- Talk about what happened.

Duration
2 periods

Author(s)
John P. Bennett

Concept
Natural Movement of Line

Key words/Cross reference

Physical Education, Art, Lines, Shape, Movement, Exploration, Geometric figures

Overview

Objective
To teach students the concept of line through kinesthetic movement.

About the Author
At the time this plan was written, John P. Bennett, Ed.D., was teaching in the Physical Education Department of Northern Illinois University, DeKalb, IL. He has done extensive work on the enhancement of cognitive development through body (kinetic) movement.

Required Resources
Construction paper and markers.

Author's Notes
The physical component of development is as important as intellectual and emotional development. It enhances or jeopardizes growth. The role of movement in one's ability to get along in society cannot be underestimated. How one moves is influenced by what one perceives. We perceive through all our sensory mechanisms (sight, hearing, touch, smell, taste, feel). Children must be given the opportunity to explore and experiment with movement using all of their sensory mechanisms in a stimulating environment. Environments must be structured to appeal to as many different learning styles as is feasible. We need a variety of techniques in order to make the most of our students' abilities.

Our goal as teachers should be to develop the whole brains of our students. They arrive in school with a strong right brain orientation and we force them to switch almost totally to left brain processing. It is time we put the whole brain and the whole body to use. Physical expression, when it is allowed to be original with the individual, is a powerful means of engaging the whole brains of our students. The 4MAT System is designed to facilitate whole brain development.

Quadrant 1—Experience

 ## Right Mode—Connect

Create line and design through physical movement.

Objective
To create line and design through physical experience.

Activity
(Need magic markers and construction paper.) One child is asked to walk across the room in a straight line. The other children are asked to draw a representation of the line they saw. Another is asked to walk across the room in a jagged line. Again the children draw what they see. Repeat with a variety of lines. Then ask the children to draw a nervous line, a galloping line, a sliding line, a pushing line, and a windy line.

Assessment
Student engagement and enjoyment.

 ## Left Mode—Examine

Talk about what happened.

Objective
To enhance the children's ability to examine experience.

Activity
Discussion of what happened. Was it hard to draw the lines you saw when Tom and Mary moved across the room? What is a line?

Assessment
Student contribution to the group discussion.

Quadrant 2—Concepts

 ## Right Mode—Image

Movement metaphors.

Objective
To add to the student's understanding of the concept of line and movement.

Activity
Ask the children to do the following with their bodies:

- Can you show how a snowflake would move in a soft, gentle snow? Now show me a hard, blowing snow!
- Can you show how a marshmallow would melt in a cup of hot chocolate?
- In groups of four, can you show me how a plant would sprout and grow in springtime?
- Can you show how a drop of rain falls from the sky and hits the ground in a light rain? In a heavy rain? Can you walk this shape? Do it another way.
- Can you show me how a cricket would move if s/he had the hiccups?
- Show me how a ping pong ball bounces.
- Show me how a ship would sail on a calm day. How would it sail on a stormy day? Can you do a movement sequence to this pattern?

Assessment
Student participation and ability to follow directions.

Line and Design

 ## Left Mode—Define

Explanation of line and movement and vocabulary words.

Objective
To develop the concept of movement in line.

Activity
Teacher explains: Lines and movements create shapes. When lines are put together they create shapes. Lines can create things we recognize that are found all around us.

Vocabulary:

creative
imagine
design
line
nervous
jagged
sliding
pushing
windy

Assessment
Teacher verbal check for understanding.

Quadrant 3—Applications

 ## Left Mode—Try

Children form shapes with their bodies.

Objective
To give practice in creating shapes from lines.

Activity
Have some of the children form rectangles, then circles, then triangles, then squares with their bodies. Have the other children draw the shapes they see. Exchange places: doers and drawers.

Assessment
Students ability to model and draw the shapes presented to them.

 ## Right Mode—Extend

Combine two shapes.

Objective
To combine lines and shapes and emphasize contrasts.

Activity
Have the children combine two shapes to make something new. Tell them the new shape must look "heavy." Repeat the exercise, except this time the new shape must look "light and fluffy." Repeat the exercise, except this time the new shape must look "sharp and jagged." Repeat one more time, except this time the new shape must look "smooth."

Assessment
Quality of student representations.

Line and Design

Quadrant 4—Creations

Left Mode—Refine

Plan and complete an art activity.

Objective

To plan and complete an art activity. To form shapes from lines.

Activity

Ask the children to select several colors of paper. Then ask them to cut lines of different types and widths. Have them arrange their lines on a large piece of paper and paste them on. Remind them that the arrangements of their lines will create shapes on their papers.

Assessment

Student and teacher reaction to creations.

Right Mode—Integrate

Add movement to their paintings.

Objective

To add movement to shape. To translate movement on a two-dimensional surface to their own bodies.

Activity

Now have the children paint people or lines on their papers. People who are moving through, under, over, or into the shapes they have already created. Pick some of the simpler ones when the children have finished and ask them to interpret through movement the content of the pictures.

Assessment

The enjoyment of the children. Free them from worrying about the product. Let them enjoy the process and product will improve. Promote exploration, expansion, excelling.

Birds/Adaptation

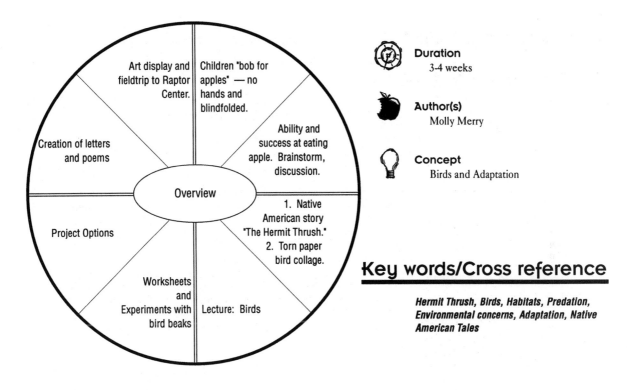

Art display and fieldtrip to Raptor Center.

Children "bob for apples" — no hands and blindfolded.

Creation of letters and poems

Ability and success at eating apple. Brainstorm, discussion.

Overview

1. Native American story "The Hermit Thrush." 2. Torn paper bird collage.

Project Options

Worksheets and Experiments with bird beaks

Lecture: Birds

Duration
3-4 weeks

Author(s)
Molly Merry

Concept
Birds and Adaptation

Key words/Cross reference

Hermit Thrush, Birds, Habitats, Predation, Environmental concerns, Adaptation, Native American Tales

Overview

Objective
Birds will be the vehicle to teach the concept of adaptation. Throughout the study, while introducing species, habitat, predation, and population status, the underlying concept is adaptation.

About the Author
Molly Merry is a classroom teacher in School District Fremont RE 1, Canon City, CO. In her over twenty year teaching experience she has developed particular expertise at integrating fine arts activities into the fabric of her content area instruction. Molly is the 4MAT Implementation Leader for her school district.

Required Resources
Apples and tub of water for bobbing activity; materials for bird collages; any "Field Guide to Birds", Audubon, or National Geographic "Ranger Rick" magazines; our State Division of Wildlife has good films on birds of prey and water birds; materials for Quadrant Three experiments and art activities.

Bibliography
National Wildlife Federation, *Naturescope: Birds.*
Casey, Peter. *Birds of North America.* Exeter Books.

Quadrant 1—Experience

Right Mode—Connect

Children "bob for apples" — no hands and blindfolded.

Objective

To connect students to the concept of Adaptation as it applies to humans.

Activity

Engage students in traditional "bobbing for apples" using a large tub filled with water and apples.

Assessment

Student engagement and enjoyment of the activity.

Left Mode—Examine

Ability and success at eating apple. Brainstorm, discussion.

Objective

To discuss and analyze the apple bobbing activity.

Activity

Teacher led discussion on the process of bobbing for apples. This discussion could be patterned in a mindmap. What makes it so difficult for people to stick their heads under water? What would have to happen in terms of our human characteristics to make this activity easy for us? Introduce idea of "Adaptation." What kinds of activities are we well-adapted to, and what kinds are we not? Transition discussion to other living things, including birds.

Assessment

Student contributions to group discussion

Quadrant 2—Concepts

Right Mode—Image

1. Native American story "The Hermit Thrush."
2. Torn paper bird collage.

Objective

To portray concept of bird adaptation through art. To deepen understanding of adaptation through story.

Activity

1. Students listen to an oral story, *"The Hermit Thrush,"* a Native American tale about the beauty and shyness of the Hermit Thrush. 2. Students will create a "bird" of their design using torn paper, arranged in a collage. Teacher leads class in mindmapping "bird adaptation" or "what makes a bird a bird."

Assessment

Student attentiveness during the story, student participation in art activity and willingness to volunteer ideas during mindmapping.

"The Hermit Thrush:" Once, long, long ago, the Great Spirit called all the birds of the Earth to a gathering. You see, at that time, though birds could fly, they could not yet sing. The Great Spirit felt the silence deeply, and chose the birds as the animal he wanted to bless with song.

When the birds were all assembled, the Great Spirit shivered at the beauty and variety. There was a plumage of all the colors of the rainbow, birds that walked close to the ground, and others with legs so long they almost towered to the sky. There were birds that frolicked like acrobats, and others that ran as fast as the wind. The Great Spirit knew he had chosen a wondrous group to give the gift of song.

Now, the problem was that all the birds wanted to know who would receive the most beautiful song. Of course the Great Spirit had planned for this question. So he told the birds of Earth how he would choose each song. At dawn the next day, at the same moment, all the birds were to rise into the air to fly as high and long as they could. As each bird tired and returned to Earth, he would give them their song. The bird that flew the longest and highest would receive the most beautiful song. Well, standing at the edge of the crowd, listening to this, was a little, plain looking bird. This was the Thrush, and he became very sad because he knew he had no chance of receiving the most beautiful song. The Thrush had short wings and was not a powerful flier. But the Thrush was a clever bird, and through the night he devised a plan.

The next morning, just before dawn, the Thrush managed to work his way toward the Golden Eagle. At the moment just before dawn, the tiny Thrush jumped into the tail feathers of the Eagle. Eagle was so excited he didn't notice Thrush at all. Then, right at dawn, all the birds lifted into the air, almost darkening the sky again, there were so many of them. Eagle, effortlessly flew upward, passing many birds in the first few seconds. But Eagle knew he wanted to win the most beautiful song, so he saved his strength. He flew to the highest point he could to watch the other birds, and there he stayed, soaring in the currents of the wind. As Eagle watched, the sky thinned as one by one the birds tired and flew back to Earth. Even when most of the birds were down, Eagle remained up high, wanting to make sure no one could beat him. All this time Thrush remained hidden in the tail feathers of Eagle. Before long, Eagle began to tire, yet he remained in the sky until all the birds were back on the Earth, and all were watching him. When he knew he was assured a victorious landing, he began to descend. At that moment, the little Thrush leaped from the tail feathers and flew frantically upward. The Eagle, seeing this, tried desperately to follow, but all his strength was gone. The Eagle could only float to Earth in defeat. The Thrush, seeing he had won, followed Eagle. But when Thrush landed, he rushed to hide in the bushes, fearing Eagle's anger. The Great Spirit gave the most beautiful song ever heard to the Thrush. And today, if you are ever out in the forest and you hear the most beautiful sound you have ever heard, one that sends shivers down your spine, don't try to find the singer. It will be the Thrush who today is known as the Hermit Thrush because he is still hiding from Eagle, and sings his song from his solitary hiding place.

Left Mode—Define

Lecture: Birds.

Objective
To teach information relating to adaptation.

Activity
1. Teach bird characteristics, types of feathers, migration reproduction, evolution, communication. 2. Teach bird families: shore birds, forest birds, birds of prey, water birds, song birds. 3. Teach habitat and adaptation: camouflage, beaks, feet, legs, flight, and migration. 4. Teach man's impact through hunting, pollution, pesticides, and loss of habitat.

Assessment
Attentiveness, quality of questions, motivation for self-learning.

Quadrant 3—Applications

Left Mode—Try

Worksheets and Experiments with bird beaks.

Objective
To demonstrate learning.

Activity
1. Students keep folders of bird drawings with lists of characteristics; Worksheets; Students participate in experiment with tweezers, toothpicks, and a strainer to simulate feeding methods in a "pond" of water, bird seed, raisins, sliced apples. Students will also crack peanuts with a pliers.

Assessment
Participation, quality and correctness of work, completion of assignments.

Right Mode—Extend

Project Options.

Objective
To demonstrate knowledge through creativity.

Activity
1. Students make kaleidoscope art using bird shapes.
2. Student groups make large murals of birds and bird habitat
3. Students write poems of address.
4. Students participate in a school bake sale to raise money for a local raptor rehabilitation center.
5. Students make a big book of bird habitats or families.

Assessment
Participation, quality of work, completion of work, accuracy, enthusiasm.

Quadrant 4—Creations

 ## Left Mode—Refine

Creation of letters and poems.

Objective
To demonstrate concern for the future using new learning.

Activity
1. Students write letters to Senators and Representatives asking for legislation to protect habitat by controlling pollution and the use of pesticides. 2. Students read big book and poems to younger students.

Assessment
Quality of work, willingness, expression of ideas.

 ## Right Mode—Integrate

Art display and field trip to Raptor Center.

Objective
To experience birds of prey, and celebrate understandings.

Activity
1. Display art. 2. Field trip to local raptor center to see birds of prey, discover why the birds are needing rehabilitation, and to give money collected in bake sale.

Assessment
Level of empathy, enthusiasm, quality of questions, sense of accomplishment.

Oceans

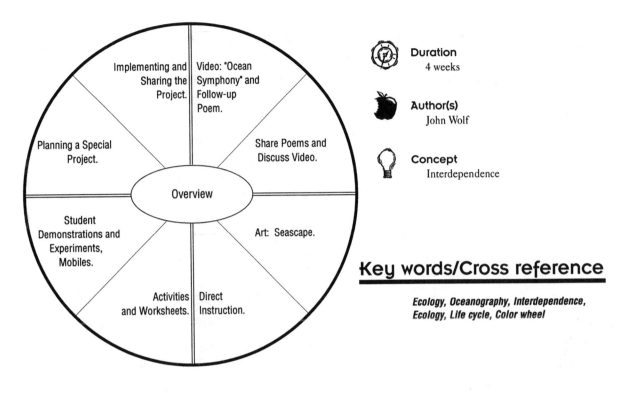

Implementing and Sharing the Project.

Video: "Ocean Symphony" and Follow-up Poem.

Planning a Special Project.

Share Poems and Discuss Video.

Overview

Student Demonstrations and Experiments, Mobiles.

Art: Seascape.

Activities and Worksheets.

Direct Instruction.

Duration
4 weeks

Author(s)
John Wolf

Concept
Interdependence

Key words/Cross reference

Ecology, Oceanography, Interdependence, Ecology, Life cycle, Color wheel

Overview

Objective
The oceans are important to the health of our planet and provide valuable resources to mankind. Through this unit, students will understand the physical, biological, and ecological importance of the oceans.

About the Author
John Wolf is a fourth grade teacher and a certified 4MAT trainer for the North East ISD in San Antonio, Texas.

Required Resources
Construction paper, scissors, glue, Naturescope edition on Oceans, video, textbook, worksheets.

Bibliography
Ocean Symphony. MCA Home Video, 1987. Directed and produced by Al Giddings.
Flipper. MGM/UA, 1963. Directed by James Clark.
Little Mermaid. Walt Disney Studios, 1989.
Naturescope: "Oceans" available from National Wildlife Federation, 1400 Sixteenth Street, N.W., Washington, D. C. 20077-9964

Quadrant 1—Experience

 ## Right Mode—Connect

Video: "Ocean Symphony" and Follow-up Poem.

Objective
To provide images of the ocean and its inhabitants as if the student was experiencing the ocean directly.

Activity
View the outstanding documentary film, *Ocean Symphony*, a visual feast of ocean images that includes sections on coral reefs, kelp forests, whales, the great white shark, and seals. It is a nonverbal film with ethereal musical accompaniment. Show it in its entirety or select individual sections to view. Immediately following the video, ask the students to compose a free poem about the ocean and its effect on our lives in response to the images and feelings they experienced while watching the video. Personal Note: I found this film at Blockbuster Videos and chose to show only portions of it due to its length. There are other ocean videos available, though this one was far superior in quality to any others I watched. I also showed the Disney song, *"Under the Sea,"* from the *Little Mermaid* before the film and it captured the students' attention. If *Ocean Symphony* is not available to you, the beginning of the movie, *Flipper,* has some underwater sequences that you might consider.

Assessment
Attention to and enthusiasm generated by the video and the expressiveness of the poems.

 ## Left Mode—Examine

Share Poems and Discuss Video.

Objective
To reflect on the images and feelings experienced during the video presentation, to share the poems.

Activity
Allow the students to voluntarily share their poems with the class. Display the poems in the room. Lead a discussion about the images they remember from the video, life experiences they have had at the ocean, and a comparison of the two. Find out what the students already know about the ocean.

Assessment
The quality of the discussion, the appreciation of each other's poetry.

Quadrant 2—Concepts

 ## Right Mode—Image

Art: Seascape.

Objective
To create a visual image of life under the sea.

Activity
The students will make a seascape out of cut construction paper, using the concepts of complimentary and contrasting colors, focal point, and the use of line to show underwater movement. Each student should choose a shade of blue or green construction paper (18" X 24") for the background color. Black would also be acceptable. Show the students a color wheel and teach or review the concept of complementary and contrasting colors. The students will choose complementary colors for the ocean floor, the coral, and living things that are to blend into the environment. Contrasting colors are to be chosen for the living things that are to attract the eye. Provide the students with pictures of ocean creatures from which to draw. The focal animal should be larger and strategically placed. The students first cut and place a strip of paper along the bottom of the background to create the effect of an ocean floor. The coral is then cut and placed. After the focal animal is drawn and cut out, the students draw curving, symmetrical lines at least an inch apart all along the animal. Each section should be numbered on the back, cut apart, and then separated slightly on the paper so that a thin strip of the background paper is seen between each section. Smaller animals and sea anemones are also drawn, cut, and placed. I only allow the students to glue at the end of the class and when they are completely finished.

Assessment
The creativity, flexibility, and originality of thought displayed in the seascape.

Oceans

 ## Left Mode—Define

Direct Instruction.

Objective
To teach physical, biological, and ecological information about the oceans to the students.

Activity
Choose a variety of teaching techniques to teach the major concepts associated with the study of the ocean. I use the *Naturescope* edition on the ocean as my guide and it is organized in this manner: The Physical Ocean (geography, saltwater, water movement), Life in the Ocean (the three zones, food chains/webs, endangered species), Along the Coast (tides, beaches, reefs, kelp forests), and Man and the Ocean (exploration, resources, ecology). Lectures, films, textbook reading, optical data, filmstrips, and the reading of periodical articles would be appropriate. Integration across the curriculum could easily by achieved.

Assessment
Student feedback to verbal monitoring.

Quadrant 3—Applications

 ## Left Mode—Try

Activities and Worksheets.

Objective
To check the student's understanding of the concepts presented.

Activity
The student completes worksheets, section reviews, and activities pertaining to concepts taught. There are numerous outstanding activities that are included in the *Naturescope* issue referred to earlier and in the bibliography. One example is the activity to follow up the lesson on the three zones of life in the ocean. The students make a "viewfinder" that allows them to "see" the life in each zone as they "descend" into the ocean by pulling a paper strip with pictures of ocean creatures through their viewfinder.

Assessment
Student performance on worksheets and activities.

 ## Right Mode—Extend

Student Demonstrations and Experiments, Mobiles.

Objective
To extend the learning with "hands-on" activities that can be manipulated and altered by the student.

Activity
A variety of activities are provided in the *Naturescope* that allow for more active experimentation and thinking. I have my students make a large mobile of a sea animal, using bulletin board paper, construction paper, and newspaper stuffing. They double the bulletin board paper (color of their choice), draw the animal about the size of their desk, cut it out, label the inner side to avoid later confusion, and decorate it with construction paper. Then they glue the edges together around most of the animal, but leave an opening for stuffing the insides with newspaper (or the scraps of bulletin board paper). Finish gluing the figure together and hang.

Assessment
Participation in activities, products made, and conclusions drawn from experiments.

Quadrant 4—Creations

Left Mode—Refine

Planning a Special Project.

Objective

For each student to plan a project that will allow either for further investigation or for action devoted to teaching others about the ocean or helping preserve the ocean.

Activity

Students plan an ocean project individually or in small groups. Possibilities include: an ecological project pertaining to the ocean, an informative bulletin board, research on environmental groups like Greenpeace and the Cousteau Society, reports, posters, or plays. The projects should be meaningful and progress on the projects should be regularly recorded in a journal.

Assessment

Choice of project, progress as measured in the journal entries and in conferences.

Right Mode—Integrate

Implementing and Sharing the Project.

Objective

To share with others what has been learned or accomplished through the special projects.

Activity

As the students projects come to a close, have them share with their class what they have learned or accomplished.

Assessment

The meaningfulness of the project to the student and the audience, and the quality of presentation.

Plant Classification

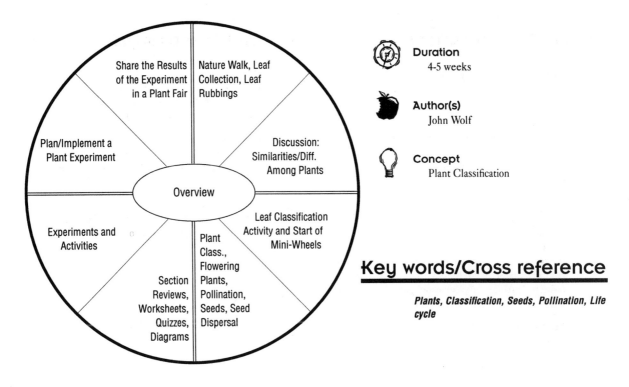

Duration
4-5 weeks

Author(s)
John Wolf

Concept
Plant Classification

Key words/Cross reference

Plants, Classification, Seeds, Pollination, Life cycle

Overview

Objective

The students will learn that botanists classify plants by how they reproduce. They will learn many details about the life cycle of flowering plants, and will use the scientific skills of classification, observation, and identification in hands-on activities. They will extend their learning through planning and conducting a science experiment on plants.

About the Author

John Wolf is a fourth grade classroom teacher and a certified 4MAT trainer for the North East ISD in San Antonio, Texas.

Required Resources

Leaves, six kinds of bean seeds, paper towels, ziplock bags, flowers, gladiolas, various vegetable or flower seeds.

Bibliography

AIMS Materials: *"Maple Seed Mix-Up," "Flower Power"*
  available from AIMS Education Foundation
  P.O. Box 8120, Fresno, CA 93747

Naturescope
  available from National Wildlife Foundation
  1400 Sixteenth Street, N.W.
  Washington, D. C 20077-9964

Hands-On Nature
  VINS, P. O. Box 86
  Woodstock, VT 05091

Plant Classification

Quadrant 1—Experience

 ### Right Mode—Connect

Nature Walk, Leaf Collection, Leaf Rubbings.

Objective
To observe plants closely and directly.

Activity
Take the students on a "nature" hike around the school grounds to observe plants and collect leaves. Challenge the children to find the largest plant, the smallest plant, and the plant with the largest leaf. Carefully collect one leaf per group from a variety of plants, being careful not to harm the parent plant. This collection will be used in the 2R piece, so you may want to place each collection in separate plastic bags. Return to the classroom and make leaf rubbings by placing the leaf (underside up) under a piece of white paper. Then color on the paper over the leaf to make the rubbing.

Assessment
The attention given to observing plants, the respect given to the plants in collecting leaves, the enjoyment of making leaf rubbings.

 ### Left Mode—Examine

Discussion: Similarities/Diff. Among Plants

Objective
To discuss what the children discovered, to analyze the importance of plants to man, to check for prior knowledge on the subject.

Activity
In the classroom, discuss the various kinds of plants observed on the "nature" hike. Question the students about the importance of plants to mankind and how new plants are started.

Assessment
The quality of the discussion.

Quadrant 2—Concepts

 ### Right Mode—Image

Leaf Classification Activity and Start of Mini-Wheels.

Objective
The students will use the scientific skill of classifying.

Activity
Pass out the leaf collections from the 1R activity to small groups of four or five. The students should group, or classify, the leaves in any way that they want to. As each group finishes, have them explain their classification system to you. Then put the leaves together in one pile again and challenge the students to classify them in a different way. They might group them by size, shape, color, feel, and even smell. As a class, discuss the various ways they classified the leaves.

My textbook is divided into five sections, so I do a mini-wheel for each these topics: plant classification, reproduction of flowering plants, pollination, seeds, and seed dispersal. These mini-wheels go through this sequence for each of the sections: 2R - 2L - 3L - 3R . Here are the right-mode openers for each section:

Plant Classification:
This activity follows the scientific method. The teacher needs to mix six kinds of beans (various sizes). The question is: How many of each kind of seed do you think will be in 1/8 cup of this mixture? Allow the students to see what an 1/8 cup looks like and let them write down their predictions for each kind of bean. Give each student 1/8 cup of the mixture and ask the student to sort, or classify, the different kinds of beans. The student counts how many of each bean she received, records her results, and puts the predictions and results into bar graph form. Finally, each student must draw at least two conclusions from the experiment.

Each student will try to germinate one of each of the six types of seeds. Use scotch tape to hold the seeds onto a paper towel (school-quality works best), dampen the paper towel and place in a zip lock bag. Label the bag with the child's name. You can make this an additional experiment by using one or both of these questions: Which seed will germinate first? Which seed will have grown the most in a week? Use measuring skills to determine the answer to the last question.

Flowering Plants:
The students observe flowers brought in by the teacher and look through wildflower identification books and

flower seed catalogs.

Pollination:
View a nonverbal film about pollination.

Seeds:
Observe a variety of flower and vegetable seeds. Plant pinto beans in paper cups.

Seed Dispersal:
Play "Maple Seed Mix-up" from the AIMS Science Materials.

Assessment
Classification and observation skills displayed by the student.

 ## Left Mode—Define

Plant Class., Flowering Plants, Pollination, Seeds, Seed Dispersal.

Objective
To give the students information in a sequential and logical manner.

Activity
The teacher uses lectures, textbook readings, optical data, children's picture books, filmstrips, and guest speakers to cover the material chosen. The students take notes and outline the textbook section.

Assessment
Informal verbal feedback, quality of notes and outlines.

Quadrant 3—Applications

 ## Left Mode—Try

Section Reviews, Worksheets, Quizzes, Diagrams.

Objective
For the student to respond to the teaching to show mastery of content.

Activity
The students can show their understanding of the content through diagrams, worksheets, use of vocabulary, worksheets, and textbook section reviews.

Assessment
Objective evaluation of daily work.

 ## Right Mode—Extend

Experiments and Activities

Objective
To extend the student's learning, to provide manipulative experiences.

Activities
Here are five separate activities for the 3R portions of the mini-wheels. References are explained further in the bibliography of this unit plan.
Plant Classification:
AIMS Science Activity
"Unique U." This activity teaches the children how to make an identification tree for keying out the members of their class.
Flowering Plants:
AIMS Science Activity
"Flower Power." This activity allows the student the opportunity to find, count, and draw the parts of a gladiola flower.
Pollination:
Perform the "Pollination Puppet Show" from *Hands-On Nature.*
Seeds:
Dissect a soaked lima bean to find the embryo.
Seed Dispersal:
Take a nature hike to look for seeds and discuss the adaptations that help the seeds disperse.

Assessment
Student performance on the activities.

Quadrant 4—Creations

Left Mode—Refine

Plan/Implement a Plant Experiment.

Objective
To plan an experiment on plants.

Activity
Each student will plan and execute a science experiment on plants that extends his or her learning in a personal and meaningful way. Allow students to work in diads or triads if they wish. The teacher will make available science experiment books for the students to browse for ideas. The teacher can conference with the student(s) to evaluate progress. The final product must include a visual (science fair style, if you wish) and a presentation.

Assessment
Choice of project, evaluation of progress.

Right Mode—Integrate

Share the Results of the Experiment in a Plant Fair.

Objective
To share the results of the experiment with others.

Activity
The students can make a class "Plant Science Fair" and invite others to observe their products and hear their presentations. Prizes can be awarded.

Assessment
Quality of the visual product and presentation.

Wolves

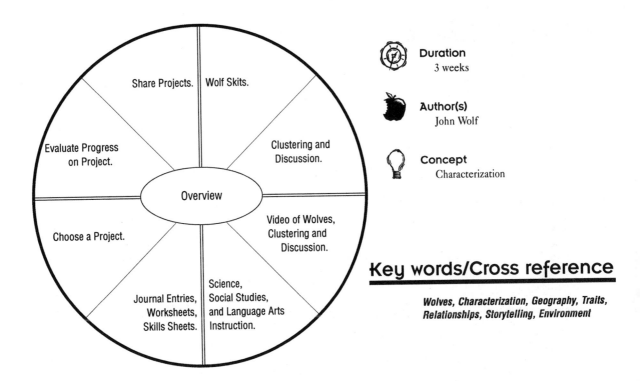

Duration
3 weeks

Author(s)
John Wolf

Concept
Characterization

Key words/Cross reference

Wolves, Characterization, Geography, Traits,
Relationships, Storytelling, Environment

Overview

Objective
Wolves have been deeply misunderstood by man and
actually play an important role in the balance of nature.
As of this writing, wolves are very controversial because
of plans to reintroduce them in Yellowstone National
Park, the current proposal to kill off 400 wolves in
Alaska, and the attempts to save the highly endangered
red wolf and Mexican wolf. The objective of this unit
is to understand the ecology of the wolf and to examine the relationship of the wolf with mankind.

About the Author
John Wolf is a fourth grade classroom teacher and a
certified 4MAT trainer for the North East ISD in
San Antonio, Texas.

Required Resources
A video showing wolves in their natural environment.

Bibliography
Never Cry Wolf. Walt Disney Studios, 1983. (available
at most video rental places)

White Wolf. National Geographic Videos.
Wolf Haven International, 3111 Offut Lake Road,
Tenino, Washington 98589
George, Jean Craighead. *Julie of the Wolves.* New
York: Harper and Row, 1972.
Robinson, Sandra Chisholm. *The Wonder of Wolves.*
Boulder, Colorado: Roberts Rinehart, Inc., 1989.
Moore, Jo Ellen, Evans, Joy, and Tryon, Leslie. *A
Unit About Wolves.* Monterey, California:
The Evan-Moor Corp., 1989.
Savage, Candace. *Wolves.* San Francisco: Sierra Club
Books, 1988.
Mowat, Farley. *Never Cry Wolf.* New York: Bantam
Books, Inc., 1963.
Goble. Paul. *Dream Wolf.* New York: Bradbury Press,
1990.
Zoo Books: WolvesWexo, John Bonnett
Wildlife Education, Ltd.
3590 Kettner Blvd.
San Diego, CA 92101

Quadrant 1—Experience

 ## Right Mode—Connect

Wolf Skits.

Objective

To explore the students' attitudes about and perceptions of wolves.

Activity

Small groups of students plan, prepare, and rehearse a short skit that has a wolf as a central character. The skit may be a fairy tale, a well-known story, a fable, or an original story. The class can brainstorm stories with wolf characters in them to help them get started.

Stories might include: Little Red Riding Hood, The Three Little Pigs, The True Story of the Three Little Pigs, The Boy Who Cried Wolf, and Peter and the Wolf. The students improvise and prepare their skits.

Assessment

Task orientation of the students, participation in the group project.

 ## Left Mode—Examine

Clustering and Discussion.

Objective

To analyze the characteristics people commonly associate with wolves.

Activity

The teacher writes the word "Wolf" on chart paper or the chalkboard and the students brainstorm words that describe how wolves were portrayed in their skits and in common literature. The teacher leads an analysis and discussion of the words the students have attributed to wolves. This list is saved for a comparison with a later list.

Assessment

The generation of words in the clustering, the thought processes in reflecting on the associations attributed to wolves.

Quadrant 2—Concepts

 ## Right Mode—Image

Video of Wolves, Clustering and Discussion.

Objective

To see wolves as they really are in their natural habitat, to compare what we observe in the video with the common perceptions of wolves.

Activity

View a video or film that shows wolves in their natural environment. I have used portions of the popular film, *Never Cry Wolf,* but be careful not to show the part with nudity. I turn off the sound and put background music on. After viewing the video, recluster the word "Wolf" on another piece of chart paper or next to the first cluster on the chalkboard. Examine both clusters and discuss why there is such a difference between the two.

Assessment

The impact on the students in changing and expanding their understanding of wolves.

Wolves

Left Mode—Define

Science, Social Studies, and Language Arts Instruction.

Objective

To teach content to the students in an effective and interesting manner.

Activity

Have the students generate a list of all the things that they would like to learn about wolves. Group the questions and post them on chart paper in a center about wolves. As the students find their answers, they write the information on the chart paper.

This unit can be used as a Science unit or an integrated thematic unit. These topics can be explored in the different subject areas if used as a thematic unit: Science-physical and behavioral traits of wolves, predator/prey relationships, food chains/food webs in a community, endangered species/species survival; Social Studies-geography of wolves, map reading, resource conflicts with wolves, cultural study of Native people and wolves, Arctic studies; Language Arts-literature unit on *Julie of the Wolves*, fairy tales, fables, Native American wolf stories *(Dream Wolf)*, persuasive writing (Should wolves be reintroduced to Yellowstone National Park?), poetry; Math-word problems using wolf facts; Art-drawing wolves, habitat/community creations using cut construction paper and environmental objects (grass, seeds, etc.)

Personal Note:

I start this part of the unit by having the students list what they want to learn about wolves. Then we begin by studying an encyclopedia entry on the wolf. The students read the article in small groups and then I lead a guided reading lesson over the material. There are many fine books and teacher units available on wolves. I have listed what I have found in the bibliography section of the overview at the beginning of this unit.

Assessment

The effectiveness and the continuity of the teacher's presentation of information, the ability of the student to locate information from various sources.

Quadrant 3—Applications

Left Mode—Try

Journal Entries, Worksheets, Skills Sheets.

Objective

To reinforce content taught, to check for understanding.

Activity

The students complete worksheets and take quizzes over the content presented in the previous step. Vocabulary development, comprehension in the literature unit, persuasive writing, map reading skills, math problem-solving, and science concepts are all checked at this time.

Assessment

Objective evaluation of performance on daily work.

Right Mode—Extend

Choose a Project.

Objective

To continue the student's learning by beginning projects on wolves.

Activity

The students work individually or in small groups to plan and begin implementing a personally meaningful project either on wolves or on a topic that is related to our unit of study. Ideas include: 1) make an informative/interactive bulletin board to be displayed in a visible and accessible area of the school or in a business in the community, 2) create a puppet show or presentation to perform for other classes in the school that educated the public about wolves and the controversies surrounding them, 3) raise money through recycling and other environmental projects in order to "adopt" a wolf from Wolf Haven International (3111 Offut Lake Road, Tenino, Washington 98589, 1-800-GIV-WOLF), 4) Organize a petition to the National Park Service and to elected officials in Washington to express views on the reintroduction of wolves to Yellowstone National Park and Black Gap Wildlife Refuge (adjacent to Big Bend National Park).

Assessment

The significance of the project proposal and student involvement in implementing the plan.

Quadrant 4—Creations

 ## Left Mode—Refine

Evaluate Progress on Project.

Objective
To evaluate progress on projects.

Activity
Have each student write in a journal to evaluate progress on the project and to inform you of any problems that are being encountered. Journal prompts can include: What have you done on your project so far? What difficulties are you encountering? What are the strengths and weaknesses of your project at this time? How could you improve your project? Do you feel you are far enough along on your project to meet the deadline?

Assessment
The ability of the student to articulate the strengths and weaknesses of the project and to state what must be done to improve and complete the project.

 ## Right Mode—Integrate

Share Projects.

Objective
To share what the students have learned with others.

Activity
Groups and individuals share their presentations with classmates, other classes in the school, parents, and administrators. The bulletin board is prominently displayed for others to see and interact with. If a wolf is "adopted" from Wolf Haven, you will receive an informative packet with a picture and biography of your wolf, a quarterly newsletter, and some small giveaways.

Assessment
The success of the projects in terms of personal involvement and action or the ability to effectively communicate to an audience what they have learned.

Waste Management

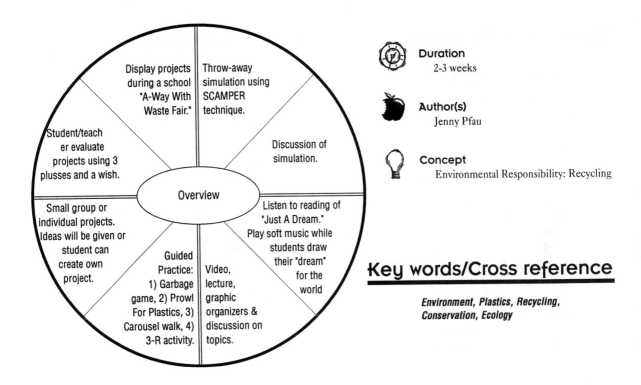

Display projects during a school "A-Way With Waste Fair."

Throw-away simulation using SCAMPER technique.

Student/teacher evaluate projects using 3 plusses and a wish.

Discussion of simulation.

Overview

Small group or individual projects. Ideas will be given or student can create own project.

Guided Practice: 1) Garbage game, 2) Prowl For Plastics, 3) Carousel walk, 4) 3-R activity.

Video, lecture, graphic organizers & discussion on topics.

Listen to reading of "Just A Dream." Play soft music while students draw their "dream" for the world

Duration
2-3 weeks

Author(s)
Jenny Pfau

Concept
Environmental Responsibility: Recycling

Key words/Cross reference

Environment, Plastics, Recycling, Conservation, Ecology

Overview

Objective
This unit will introduce the learner to the municipal solid waste stream and encourage them to participate in managing solid waste.

About the Author
Jenny Pfau is a teacher in Lawrence Township Schools in Indianapolis, IN, where she works in a full-time, self-contained 5th grade classroom with gifted students.

Required Resources
Just A Dream.

Bibliography

Eberle, Robert F. (1971) *'SCAMPER: Games For Imagination Development."* Buffalo, NY DOK Publishers.
Lennon, Gail. (1992) *"Waste Not Want Not"* Challenge Magazine, Good Apple Publications.
Partners With The Earth. (1992) Heritage Education Foundation, Inc. Indianapolis, IN.
Showers, Paul. (1974) *Where Does The Garbage Go?* Thomas Y. Crowell Company.
The Education Center Inc. (1991) *"On The Prowl For Plastics."* Mailbox Magazine, Oct./Nov.
Van Allsburg, Chris. (1990) *Just A Dream.* Houghton Mifflin Company.

Waste Management

Quadrant 1—Experience

✳ Right Mode—Connect

Throw-away simulation using SCAMPER technique.

Objective

To provide an awareness of the need for recycling in our society. To review strategies for creative problem solving.

Activity

Students are asked to collect one or two items of garbage from home or school. The students will work in groups to experience a throw-away simulation. Begin by dividing the class into groups of 3-4 students and ask each student to share with their group one throw-away item they have collected. Next, ask the group to generate all the possible alternate uses for the item which has been presented using the SCAMPER technique in their brainstorming:

S - Substitute this article for something else.
C - Combine it with other item(s).
A - Adapt or alter the item in some way.
M - Modify, minify, or magnify the article.
P - Put the article to other uses.
E - Elaborate and add details.
R - Rearrange or reverse the article.

Assessment

Students' involvement and contribution to the experience.

✳ Left Mode—Examine

Discussion of simulation.

Objective

To heighten students' awareness that they, too, can do something to reduce garbage in our society.

Activity

Discuss the simulation experience with the class. As the class generates ideas of what to do with the garbage which is thrown away, try to make them aware of their role in this reduction process. List these ideas on chart paper as they are generated.

Assessment

Student contribution to the group discussion and quality of list generated.

Quadrant 2—Concepts

✳ Right Mode—Image

Listen to reading of "Just A Dream." Play soft music while students draw their "dream" for the world.

Objective

Use of another medium to formulate the concept of how our actions do make a difference with the problem of municipal solid waste.

Activity

Students listen while the teacher reads *Just A Dream*. Once the book has been read, discuss the concepts presented. After the discussion, play soft background music while the students draw their "dream" for the world in which they live.

Assessment

Quality of discussion and "dream" drawings.

✳ Left Mode—Define

Video, lecture, graphic organizers & discussion on topics.

Objective

To teach specific information about the classification of waste, plastic wastes, packaging waste and ways to manage the waste problem.

Activity

The teacher presents information using lecture, videos, graphic organizers, and discussion. The teacher reads to the class the book, *Where Does The Garbage Go?*

Assessment

Level of student interest and the quality of questions and comments.

Waste Management

Quadrant 3—Applications

 ### Left Mode—Try

*Guided Practice: 1) Garbage game 2) Prowl For Plastics
3) Carousel walk 4) 3-R activity.*

Objective

To reinforce students' understandings of concepts
related to waste and waste management.

Activity

Garbage Game: Divide the class into small groups. Give
each group 10-15 index cards on which you have placed
pictures of a variety of municipal solid waste. Ask each
group to classify the index cards into the classification
categories which they learned about during the instruction given during Quadrant Two, Left Mode—
Classifying Municipal Solid Waste.

Prowl For Plastics: Give each student a Prowl For
Plastics sheet. Ask them to go home and "prowl" in
their pantry for plastics. They should list the products
on their sheet on which they found the appropriate
plastics code. Share items found in class.

Carousel Walk: On large chart paper, place a picture of an
item which has been over-packaged. Below the picture,
write these questions: 1) What function does the packaging serve? 2) Is the packaging necessary or unneces-
sary? 3) Design a new package for this item that uses
less packaging. (Make five or six of the above described
chart papers, each with a different item, and place the
chart papers around the classroom.) Divide the class
into small groups. Station each group at one piece of the
chart paper. Allow time for each group to respond to the
questions. After sufficient time, play "carousel" type
music, this is the signal for each group to rotate clockwise to the next piece of chart paper. Continue this procedure until all groups return to their seats. The teacher
may then walk around the room reviewing with the
class the ideas which were generated by each group.

3-R (Reduce, Reuse or Recycle) Activity: Arrange the class
into small teams. Provide each team with an envelope
containing individual statement strips which illustrate
the act of reducing, reusing or recycling as well as some
blank strips. Explain that they should work as a group
to classify the statement strips based on the 3-R philosophy of reduce, reuse, or recycle. Once the students
have classified the statements into three categories,
advise students they are to generate two new statement
strips for each of the three categories. Their ideas are to
be written on the blank statement strips from the envelope. In a whole group discussion, have each group read
their additional ideas.

Assessment

Group participation and interest.

 ### Right Mode—Extend

*Small group or individual projects. Ideas will be given or stu-
dent can create own project.*

Objective

To extend what has been learned.

Activity

Students will decide upon a project to be done alone or
with a group which will extend their learning. Project
ideas will be given or the student(s) may create their
own project.

SUGGESTIONS:

1. Develop a questionnaire to determine attitudes of
   neighbors, family, and friends toward solid waste
   management and recycling. Conduct a survey using
   your questionnaire. Present your findings to the
   class.
2. Make recycled paper.
3. Form an environmental club at school to encourage
   recycling.
4. Visit and interview a local paper, aluminum or glass
   recycling business in our community. Share your discoveries with the class.
5. Survey local fast food restaurants to determine how
   many of them recycle the packaging they use.
   Present your findings.
6. Interview an employee of a garden center to find out
   more about composting. Make a report on why people should compost and how it is done.
7. Interview a local community leader to discover what
   the city is doing about the solid waste problem.
   Video or record your interview and make a presentation to your class.
8. Gather trash at home or at school and make something artistic.
9. Create your own project.

Assessment

On-task behavior of students.

Waste Management

Quadrant 4—Creations

Left Mode—Refine

Student/teacher evaluates projects using 3 pluses and a wish.

Objective

To have students look critically and constructively at their own work and the work of their classmates.

Activity

3 Plusses and a Wish—ask each student to share their project with the class. The student presenter(s), other class members and teacher, will orally or in written form, evaluate the project using three positive statements and one wish concerning the project.

Assessment

Quality of student group contribution. Ability to critique work for substance and originality.

Right Mode—Integrate

Display projects during a school "A-Way With Waste Fair."

Objective

To share projects with the entire school in an "A-Way With Waste Fair." To celebrate each other's work.

Activity

Students will display their projects during an "A-Way With Waste Fair" which they have organized for their school.

Assessment

Presentations, participation, and enjoyment of learning.

Ancient Egypt

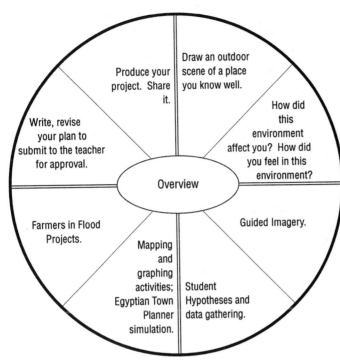

Produce your project. Share it.

Draw an outdoor scene of a place you know well.

Write, revise your plan to submit to the teacher for approval.

How did this environment affect you? How did you feel in this environment?

Overview

Farmers in Flood Projects.

Guided Imagery.

Mapping and graphing activities; Egyptian Town Planner simulation.

Student Hypotheses and data gathering.

Duration
2 weeks

Author(s)
Nona Bock and Lynn Dowall

Concept
Enivronment and the Ancient Egyptians

Key words/Cross reference

Creation and history of cities, Land Forms, Climate, Irrigation systems, Ancient Egypt, Nile River, Environment

Overview

Objective
Students will learn that as our environment affects our lives so did the environment affect the lives of the ancient Egyptians.

About the Author
Nona Bock is a 6th grade teacher and staff developer at Pierce School, Brookline, Massachusetts. She has been involved in education for over twenty-one years. In addition to her teaching experience in several Massachusetts school districts, she has also taught in Ecuador. She is a member of the Excel Consultants Group.

Lynn Dowall is a teacher in Brookline Public Schools. She has been a participant in the Brookline 4MAT Implementation Project led by Nona Bock and Bob Bates.

Required Resources
Drawing paper, pens, pencils, markers, crayons; maps, atlas, film or video on "Ancient Egypt," materials for student projects.

Authors' Note
This plan represents one cycle from an integrated two-month long unit which is comprised of several connected 4MAT wheels.

Ancient Egypt

Quadrant 1—Experience

Right Mode—Connect

Draw an outdoor scene of a place you know well.

Objective

The purpose of this step is for the students to have a personal experience and connect on a personal level. (It's not for teaching information.) Materials: Drawing paper, markers, pens, pencils, crayons.

Activity

Draw an outdoor scene of a place you remember well.

Assessment

Quality of work.

Left Mode—Examine

How did this environment affect you? How did you feel in this environment?

Objective

The purpose now is for students to reflect on a personal experience.

Activity

Tell how the environment (climate, land forms) you drew affected you. [Encourage the students to talk about shelter, food, clothing, feelings.]

Assessment

Quality of student participation.

Quadrant 2—Concepts

Right Mode—Image

Guided Imagery.

Objective

The purpose of this step is to help students picture the concept. Materials: Script for guided imagery (included).

Activity

When students are relaxed and have their eyes closed, the teacher leads them in a guided imagery that describes the environment of the Nile Valley, including land forms, climate, flooding, and irrigation.

Assessment

Quality of student participation and follow-up discussion.

Script of Guided Imagery For the Teacher: This is to be read slowly, with pauses between sentences.

We are going to use a guided imagery to explore the environment of Ancient Egypt. Close your eyes. Relax. Get comfortable. Put everything else out of your mind. Just listen.

Imagine that you are in a very warm place, very warm. You can feel the hot wind against your cheek. You squint in the bright light of the glaring sun and brush the fine dust from your forehead. You look up at the sky, a huge sky that stretches from one horizon across the heavens to the other. There is no haze or mist; there is no fog, there are no clouds. There will be no rain. There rarely is.

Look out into the distance until you can see the line where the sky meets the desert. Far, far away. All the land looks like a desert. The harsh dry landscape is made up of sand and rocks and cliffs and is painted in tans and beiges and shadowy browns.

Turning around, you see a thin green strip of plants and grasses and swamps and then a vast river, a broad highway of a river. Beyond the river and bordering it is another lush strip of vegetation and beyond that, once again, desert.

Soon the river will rise, as it does each year, and the annual flooding of the Nile River will begin. The muddy water will cover the green fields on either side of the river for weeks, even months. "Reservoirs" have been dug to collect the water from field to field. The flood will leave behind dark rich soil, fertile soil in which all kinds of crops will grow.

This is the end of our guided imagery.

Ancient Egypt

When you have completed your mind picture, slowly return to the classroom. Open your eyes. Collect your thoughts and get ready to share your visions and feelings.

Left Mode—Define

Student Hypotheses and data gathering.

Objective

The purpose of this step is to provide the information that supports the concept.

Activity

Students will hypothesize and gather information about land forms, climate, waterways, flooding and irrigation and their significance. Teacher lectures on the above, and students read assigned text chapters. Use maps, atlases, and an appropriate film or video on "Ancient Egypt."

Assessment

Thoroughness of information gathered.

Quadrant 3—Applications

Left Mode—Try

Mapping and graphing activities; Egyptian Town Planner simulation.

Objective

The purpose of this step is to allow students to practice what is being taught.

Activity

Mapping activities, graphing (climate, rainfall), simulation of Egyptian village planning, and other practice activities you would normally use. A number of these activities can be assigned for homework.

Assessment

Quality of maps, graphs, group activities, and quizzes. Note: Learning and practice activities in segments 2L and 3L are usually interwoven.

Right Mode—Extend

Farmers in Flood Projects.

Objective

The purpose of this step is to integrate what is learned with a personal expression of the learning.

Activity

Students plan a project depicting what an Egyptian farmer's life would have been like if the Nile River did not flood. Students should also select a format in which to present their work, such as a scrapbook, model, mural, or play.

You may want to do this project using a comparison of Egypt when the Nile overflowed and Egypt without the flooding of the Nile. Another possible format for this presentation could be an album with pictures of a village that show this comparison.

(We planned this activity for small groups. The teacher may need to guide students by asking open-ended questions to encourage them to include specifics such as type of irrigation system, location of housing and buildings, allocation of labor and time.)

Assessment

Quality of thought put into the project.

Quadrant 4—Creations

Left Mode—Refine

Write, revise your plan to submit to the teacher for approval.

Objective

The purpose of this step is for students to analyze their plan, striving for excellence.

Activity

The student groups need to write and revise their project plan. This should include specifics. It is then submitted to the teacher to be critiqued. Revision continues until the plan is approved.

Assessment

Ability to critique work and revise for substance and originality.

Right Mode—Integrate

Produce your project. Share it.

Objective

The purpose of this lesson is for the students to produce and share their work.

Activity

Students make their product to share with the class. Presentations.

Assessment

Quality of content in completed projects, presentation and participation.

Boundaries NJ Counties

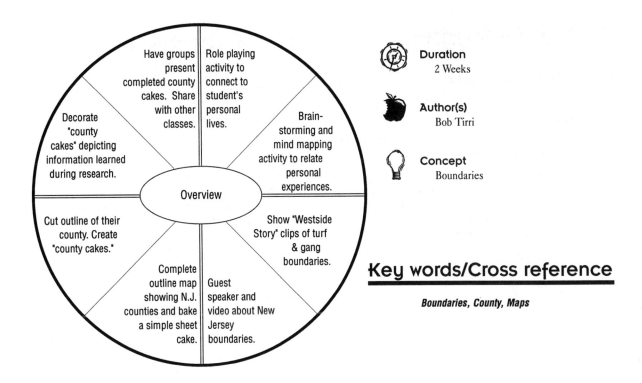

Have groups present completed county cakes. Share with other classes.

Role playing activity to connect to student's personal lives.

Brain-storming and mind mapping activity to relate personal experiences.

Decorate "county cakes" depicting information learned during research.

Overview

Cut outline of their county. Create "county cakes."

Show "Westside Story" clips of turf & gang boundaries.

Complete outline map showing N.J. counties and bake a simple sheet cake.

Guest speaker and video about New Jersey boundaries.

Duration
2 Weeks

Author(s)
Bob Tirri

Concept
Boundaries

Key words/Cross reference

Boundaries, County, Maps

Overview

Objective
Fifth grade students will gain a knowledge of New Jersey counties through participation in the creation of a New Jersey cake map.

About the Author
Bob Tirri is Principal of School 21 in Paterson, New Jersey. He has eighteen years experience teaching 5th through 8th grade. He is a certified 4MAT Trainer.

Required Resources
Video of *West Side Story;* city, county and state maps (political and outline); materials for baking 21 cakes; contact with AAA representative; video on New Jersey geography; collaborative sessions with school librarian.

Bibliography
Ellis, Herbert Lee and Irwin, Leonard B., *New Jersey, The Garden State.*
Oxford Book Company, New York. 1962.
Fay, Elaine and Stansfield, Charles, New Jersey *Yesterday and Today.*
Silver, Burdett & Ginn Inc. Morristown, New Jersey. 1987.
Paterson Chamber of Commerce. *Get-A-Life in Paterson, New Jersey.* 1992.
Rand McNally Children's Atlas of the United States. Rand McNally, Chicago. 1989.

Quadrant 1—Experience

Right Mode—Connect

Role playing activity to connect to students' personal lives.

Objective

To connect the concept of boundaries to the students' personal experiences.

Activity

Role playing. After students become settled, have one student move to another student's desk and begin going through it. The second student should react in an aggressive way. The role playing should be scripted to demonstrate a reaction by someone having their personal "boundary" violated by another.

Assessment

Student reaction to the role playing. Discussion.

Left Mode—Examine

Brainstorming and mind mapping activity to relate personal experiences.

Objective

To share reactions to the role playing in 1R.

Activity

Brainstorm about the role playing activity. Mind map the responses. Categorize responses concerning their feelings and the causes of the reactions of the role players. Draw out the concept of boundary and invaded turf through the brainstorming activity. Relate to personal experiences.

Assessment

Student reactions and responses.

Quadrant 2—Concepts

Right Mode—Image

Show "West Side Story" clips of turf & gang boundaries.

Objective

To broaden students thoughts to larger boundaries.

Activity

Show clips from the musical *"West Side Story"* which depict gang ownership of turf and examine the boundaries involved. Expand to the idea of man-made versus natural boundaries.

Assessment

Student responses and participation in discussion.

Left Mode—Define

Guest speaker and video about New Jersey boundaries.

Objective

To introduce the county boundaries of New Jersey.

Activity

Expand the concept of boundaries by moving from neighborhood boundaries (school district boundaries, etc.) through city and county boundaries. When accomplished, invite a guest speaker in from AAA to discuss New Jersey boundary divisions through the presentation of a video about New Jersey. Distribute map from AAA which shows the state's county boundaries.

Assessment

Evaluation sheets of presentation.

Quadrant 3—Applications

Left Mode—Try

Complete outline map showing N.J. counties and bake a simple sheet cake.

Objective

To have students reinforce knowledge obtained in quadrant two.

Activity

Have students label and color code counties of New Jersey on a blank outline map of the state. Discussion of scale will occur while reviewing students' completed maps. Home Economics teacher will develop and present a lesson on how to bake a simple square sheet cake. Cake will be baked during visit to Home Economics room. Create collaborative groups, assign each group a county with the task of researching the county to find information requested on a teacher-prepared fact sheet.

Assessment

Complete maps, cakes, fact sheets.

Right Mode—Extend

Cut outline of their county. Create "county cakes."

Objective

To have students collaboratively prepare outline maps.

Activity

Outline and cut a manila outline of their county. Collaborative groups will use an appropriate portion of the sheet cake and their manila outline to create a "county cake."

Assessment

Accuracy of manila county outlines and the created county cake.

Quadrant 4—Creations

Left Mode—Refine

Decorate "county cakes" depicting information learned during research.

Objective

To apply information to student-created project.

Activity

The cake will be decorated with icing and food coloring to highlight natural and manmade features within the county.

Assessment

Completed county cakes and quality of details depicting county characteristics.

Right Mode—Integrate

Have groups present completed county cakes. Share with other classes.

Objective

To bring closure to the unit and have students share their knowledge with others.

Activity

Piece together the various county cakes to form a large cake map of New Jersey. Have students share information about their counties as they present their cakes. Invite other classes in to view the completed state cake. Invite parents in to see state cake and hear presentations. Students and parents may "internalize" learning by eating their county.

Assessment

Presentation of cakes and interaction with guests.

Celebrating Freedom

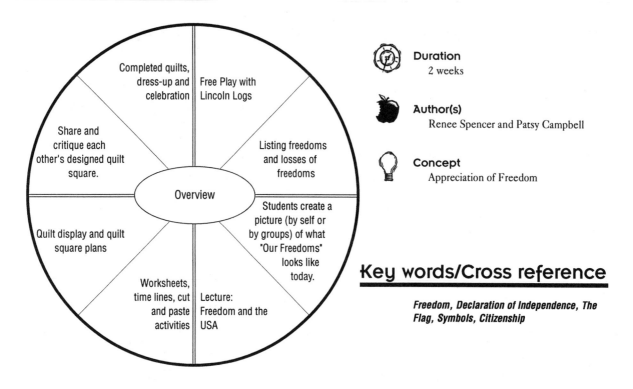

Completed quilts, dress-up and celebration

Free Play with Lincoln Logs

Share and critique each other's designed quilt square.

Listing freedoms and losses of freedoms

Overview

Quilt display and quilt square plans

Students create a picture (by self or by groups) of what "Our Freedoms" looks like today.

Worksheets, time lines, cut and paste activities

Lecture: Freedom and the USA

Duration
2 weeks

Author(s)
Renee Spencer and Patsy Campbell

Concept
Appreciation of Freedom

Key words/Cross reference

Freedom, Declaration of Independence, The Flag, Symbols, Citizenship

Overview

Objective
The students will develop an awareness and appreciation for freedoms we share because of our citizenship.

About the Authors
Renee Spencer is a teacher at Westside Elementary School, and Patsy Campbell teaches at Broadmoor Elementary School, Lafayette Parish School Board, Lafayette, LA. They are participants in the Lafayette 4MAT Implementation Project led by Patricia Ann Sonnier.

Required Resources
Lincoln Logs; art materials for student drawings; filmstrip or other A/V on early colonies and Declaration of Independence; sample quilts for classroom display; materials for students' quilt squares.

Quadrant 1—Experience

Right Mode—Connect

Free Play with Lincoln Logs.

Objective
To connect the students to the experience of loss of freedom.

Activity
1) All children engage in free play with Lincoln logs. After 2-3 minutes, six children (randomly selected) are told to go to their desk with no reason given, all others allowed to play five more minutes with logs.
2) Children discuss feelings about playing, having to leave the group or being allowed to stay.
Vote on and chart which group would want to be a part of, the one told to leave the group or the one allowed to play.

Assessment
Discussion and group chart.

Left Mode—Examine

Listing freedoms and losses of freedoms.

Objective
To guide students in sharing times and places they've attained and lost freedoms.

Activity
Have them list personal freedoms and discuss how they got those freedoms and maybe how they were lost or could have been lost. Teacher-led discussion of students' own personal experiences with gaining and losing freedoms.

Assessment
Involvement of students in discussion and ability to put thoughts on paper.

Quadrant 2—Concepts

Right Mode—Image

Students create a picture (by self or by groups) of what "Our Freedoms" looks like today.

Objective
To link personal experiences with a broader concept of freedom.

Activity
Students will create a picture (by self or in a group) of what "Our Freedoms" look like to them today.

Assessment
Participation of students.

Left Mode—Define

Lecture: Freedom and the USA.

Objective
To develop an appreciation for our country's and our own freedoms.

Activity
1) Read a story about country's early beginnings and view filmstrip on original colonies and Declaration of Independence. Lead into discussion about freedoms enjoyed by all now. How did we get them?
2) Reciting of the Pledge of Allegiance and breaking it down into its smaller components.
3) Instruction on Freedoms: ones that we have, how did we get them, how do we keep them. (Topics covered: The Flag, President's Day, Symbols, Nation's Beginning.)

Assessment
Participation.

Quadrant 3—Applications

Left Mode—Try

Worksheets, time lines, cut and paste activities.

Objective
Check for understanding of Concept of Freedom.

Activity
1) Worksheets. 2) Development of a Time Line with given facts. 3) Drawing and coloring of a flag.

Assessment
Accuracy of Time Line and information on worksheets and color sheet.

Right Mode—Extend

Quilt display and quilt square plans.

Objective
To see application of thoughts on freedom.

Activity
Display early quilts in classroom. Each student plans and designs a quilt square for part of a class quilt depicting the concept of Freedom.

Assessment
Discussion of quilts and the children's involvement and enjoyment in making of square.

Quadrant 4—Creations

Left Mode—Refine

Share and critique each other's designed quilt square.

Objective
Evaluate 3R activity with intent of praising effort to include concept of freedom in design and not to discourage creativity.

Activity
Share design with class and critique.

Assessment
Level or participation, application of knowledge, sensitivity to others.

Right Mode—Integrate

Completed quilts, dress-up and celebration.

Objective
To share what they have learned with others.

Activity
1) Declare it Red, White and Blue Day.
2) Hang the completed class quilt in a high-traffic area for all to see (library, cafeteria, office, grade-level wing).
3) Celebrate the hanging of the quilt with cherry pie and the Star-Spangled Banner playing in the background.

Assessment
Participation in dressing up, eating pie and hanging quilt. Looking for lots of smiles and swelled chests!

Culture & Environment

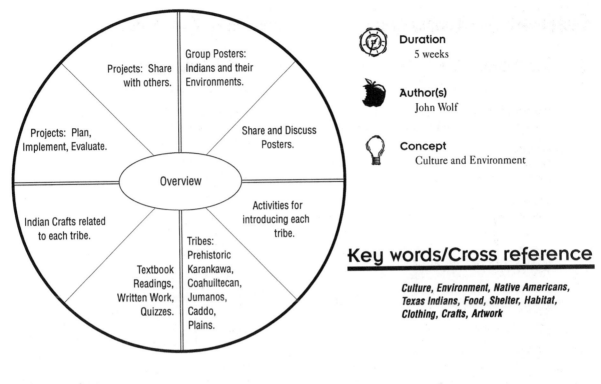

Duration
5 weeks

Author(s)
John Wolf

Concept
Culture and Environment

Key words/Cross reference

Culture, Environment, Native Americans,
Texas Indians, Food, Shelter, Habitat,
Clothing, Crafts, Artwork

Overview

Objective
The fourth grade curriculum in Texas includes studies of the Native American Indian groups that lived
in Texas. These cultures were profoundly affected
by the physical environment and natural resources
available to them. An understanding of the relationship of the Indians to their surroundings is essential
to understanding the Indians themselves.

About the Author
John Wolf is a fourth grade classroom teacher and
certified 4MAT trainer for the North East ISD in
San Antonio, Texas.

Required Resources
Posterboard, assorted art supplies, clay, yarn, beads,
feathers, tempera paint, corn husks, paper plates.

Bibliography
Dances With Wolves. Orion films, 1990. Directed by
Kevin Costner.
Warren, Betsy. *Indians Who Lived In Texas.* Dallas:
Hendrick-Long Publishing Co., 1970.

Newcomb, W. W. *The Indians of Texas.* Austin:
University of Texas Press, 1961.
Winrey, Dorman H., et. al. *Indian Tribes of Texas.* Waco,
Texas: Texian Press, 1971.
Fields, F. T. *Texas Sketchbook.* Humble Oil and Refining Co.
Shafer, Harry J. *Ancient Texans.* Austin: Texas Monthly
Press, 1986.
McDermott, Gerald. *Arrow to the Sun.* New York:
Penguin Books, 1974.
Goble, Paul. *The Gift of the Sacred Dog.* New York:
Macmillan, 1980.
Goble, Paul. *Buffalo Woman.* New York: Macmillan, 1984.
Goble, Paul. *The Girl Who Loved Wild Horses.* New York:
Macmillan, 1978.
DePaola, Tomie. *The Legend of the Bluebonnet.* New York:
G. P. Putnam's Sons, 1983.
DePaola, Tomie. *The Legend of the Scarlet Paintbrush.*
New York: G.P. Putnam's Sons,
Storm, Hyemeyohsts. *Seven Arrows.* New York:
Ballantine, 1972.
Warren, Betsy. *Inside a Tepee.* Austin: RanchGate Books,
1989.

Quadrant 1—Experience

 ## Right Mode—Connect

Group Posters: Indians and their Environments.

Objective

To challenge the student to think about the connection between the availability and type of resources in an environment and the way it would affect how a Native American culture would express itself.

Activity

Divide the class into five cooperative groups with 4 or 5 students in each group. Assign a leader for each group and have the leaders draw from five slips of paper with these environments written on them: coastal, desert, forest, mountains, plains. On a poster board, using markers, colors, construction paper, wooden sticks, feathers, and whatever else you have available in your art supplies, each group is to show the shelter, clothing, food, and tools of an Indian group that might live in that environment.

Assessment

Participation in the activity, thought processes used in deciding what to include in the product.

 ## Left Mode—Examine

Share and discuss posters.

Objective

The students will share, discuss, and justify what they included in their products.

Activity

Each group presents their poster to the class, explaining what they have included and why they believe an Indian group in that environment would express itself in that manner. The other students can ask questions of the presenting group and the teacher moderates the discussion.

Assessment

Quality of the thoughts in justifying or challenging what is included in the products.

Quadrant 2—Concepts

 ## Right Mode—Image

Activities for introducing each tribe.

Objective

To provide the students with stimulating experiences that lead them into an understanding of the Indian tribes they will be studying.

Personal Note: Study each tribe in a mini-wheel that follows this sequence: 2R - 2L - 3L - 3R. Then repeat the cycle with the next tribe. The following activities are the 2R pieces to these mini-wheels

Activities

Prehistoric Indians:

Simulate an archaeological experience through the use of fantasy. Pretend you have packed your car and you are driving southwest of San Antonio, Texas to some cave shelters along the lower Pecos River. As you carefully dig for archeological evidence, pretend to find items such as: animal teeth, pottery shards, charred wood, flint points, etc.

Karankawa Indians:

Tell the story of Cabeza de Vaca and his rescue by the Karankawa Indians. A good source of information for this is the book, *Texas Sketchbook* (see the bibliography).

Coahuiltecan Indians:

Simulate a rabbit hunt on the playground using the cooperative "surround" technique. Choose three students to be "rabbits" and five students to be the "hunters." The rest of the class forms a horseshoe around the rabbits. The "hunters" are waiting to ambush the "rabbits" in the open end of the horseshoe. The "tribe" pretends to beat the bushes and begins to close in on the "rabbits." The "rabbits" run to the open end of the horseshoe and are "hunted" by being tagged. Make sure everyone knows their roles before you begin.

Jumanos Indians:

Show pictures of Anasazi Indian ruins, pueblos, pottery, and sand painting. Read aloud the children's book, *Arrow to the Sun.*

Caddo Indians:

Show the pictures on pages 6-14 in the book, *Indians Who Lived In Texas* .

Plains Indians:

Show short, appropriate sections of the popular movie, *Dances With Wolves.* I like to show the scenes when the soldier is coming into the Indian village for the first time and when the tribe is moving to hunt the buffalo. Read aloud the children's book, *Gift of the Sacred Dogs*, by Paul Goble. I like to read aloud books by Paul Goble each day that we study the Plains Indians.

Assessment

Student participation, student interest generated by the activities.

Left Mode—Define

Tribes: Prehistoric, Karankawa, Coahuiltecan, Jumanos, Caddo, Plains.

Objective

The student will learn about the major Texas Indian tribes, where they lived, and how their environment shaped their culture.

Activity

The teacher uses lectures, readings, and note-taking to convey the information needed by the students. Students should note the geographical region of the tribe and understand how the resources of that area contributed to the expression of that culture. Food, shelter, clothing, way of life, and size of tribe should all be stressed.

Assessment

Informal verbal feedback.

Quadrant 3—Applications

Left Mode—Try

Textbook Readings, Written Work, Quizzes.

Objective

The student will show mastery of material on written work.

Activity

The students reread independently the text that was studied as a class and answer questions relating to the tribe. Verbal checks and short quizzes can also be used.

Assessment

Objective evaluation of written work.

Right Mode—Extend

Indian Crafts related to each tribe.

Objective

To recreate Indian skills in craft activities related to each tribe.

Activity

Follow the activity below immediately after learning about that individual tribe. Then return to the 2R piece and begin studying the next tribe.

Lower Pecos River Indians:
Recreate cave pictographs with a crayon resist and tempera paint washes. Take an 18" X 24" piece of gray construction paper. Draw figures similar to the Pecos pictographs in heavy black, red, and white crayon. Lightly wash with diluted brown, orange, and yellow tempera paint. After it dries, crumple the paper to give it a rock-like effect.

Karankawas:
Make an Indian necklace or bracelet. One way is to make a clay medallion and several clay beads to string on a leather strip with feathers, shells, or even pasta noodles. Another possibility is to braid three pieces of yarn into a "friendship" bracelet or necklace.

Coahuiltecans:
Use soaked corn husks (tamale wrappings) to make a fiber weaving. Soak the husks for at least thirty minutes, tear into long strips, and line up about eight strips on a piece of masking tape, leaving a little space between. Then tightly weave other strips through the "warp" you have made. It isn't beautiful, but it is gives the feeling for the difficulty of working with a natural product.

Jumanos:

I teach the children string tricks like Cat's Cradle and Jacob's Ladder. This was a common winter activity of many Indian children. I have experimented with making sand paintings, but have not perfected it yet.

Caddo:

We make clay coil pots by making long "snakes" of clay and spiraling a base and then adding coils to make the sides. You should learn how to score and slip so the product will stay together better.

Plains:

You can make a fine-looking medicine shield to hang by using a crayon resist and brown tempera paint wash on a paper plate. Let each child choose an Indian name and draw a picture representing that name on the paper plate in heavy crayon. Wash with brown tempera paint and hang three construction paper feathers from the bottom. In addition, a beautiful headband can be woven with yarn on a cardboard loom and you can crumple paper grocery bags and create a pictograph story on "bisonhide."

Assessment

Evaluate the students on how well they relate these skills to the tribes studied.

Quadrant 4—Creations

 ## Left Mode—Refine

Projects: Plan, Implement, Evaluate.

Objective

To help the student find a meaningful project on Indians to plan and implement, to evaluate the progress on that project.

Activity

Introduce the assignment to the students and let them brainstorm ideas for projects. They could: build models of Indian shelters, do research and make a poster on a different Indian tribe, write to and get information about Indian reservations in Texas, prepare a review of the Texas Indian tribes to help the class prepare for the final examination on this unit, explore the dilemma facing Native Indian cultures in modern society by reading periodical articles on the subject. Keep up with the progress of the students on their projects through journal writings and conferences.

Assessment

The choice and originality of the project, the implementation of the project.

 ## Right Mode—Integrate

Projects: Share with others.

Objective

The students present what they have learned to others.

Activity

As projects are finished, the students make presentations to their own class and to other classes. They are to communicate what they have learned to their audience. The products can be displayed in the library or in the community.

Assessment

The quality of the project and the effectiveness of the presentation.

Current Events

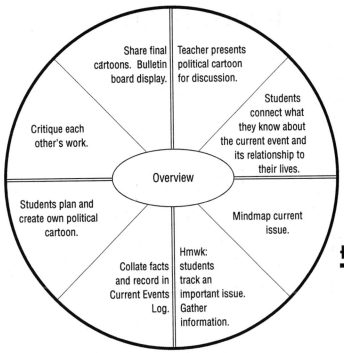

Share final cartoons. Bulletin board display.

Teacher presents political cartoon for discussion.

Students connect what they know about the current event and its relationship to their lives.

Critique each other's work.

Overview

Students plan and create own political cartoon.

Mindmap current issue.

Collate facts and record in Current Events Log.

Hmwk: students track an important issue. Gather information.

Duration
As needed

Author(s)
Nona Bock

Concept
Current Events and their Connections

Key words/Cross reference

History and Today, Current Events, Political Cartoons

Overview

Objective
To enable student to see that history is created on a daily basis in the world we live in.

About the Author
Nona Bock is a 6th grade teacher and staff developer at Pierce School, Brookline, Massachusetts. She has been involved in education for over twenty-five years. In addition to her teaching experience in several Massachusetts school districts, she has also taught in Ecuador. She is a certified 4MAT trainer.

Required Resources
Current appropriate political cartoons; current news magazines and newspapers

Author's Notes
The objective of this plan is to connect students to what is happening in the world around them, near and far; to trace present issues to their past roots, and to examine how we will be affected in the future. This unit is interspersed throughout the school year as important events occur.

Quadrant 1—Experience

 ## Right Mode—Connect

Teacher presents political cartoon for discussion.

Objective
To engage student interest in world issues and enable them to see themselves as part of what is happening in the world.

Activity
Teacher brings to class an appropriate political cartoon from current events to which students can easily relate. With students in small groups for discussion, teacher leads discussion with questions to which each group responds.

Assessment
Quality of student participation and interest.

 ## Left Mode—Examine

Students connect what they know about the current event and its relationship to their lives.

Objective
To analyze current issues raised in relation to themselves.

Activity
Teacher-led discussion focusing on what students know about the current issue presented and how they see the issue as relating to their lives.

Assessment
Quality of student participation.

Quadrant 2—Concepts

 ## Right Mode—Image

Mindmap current issue.

Objective
To broaden students' awareness of one current issue.

Activity
Mindmap one issue, first individually, then collectively as a class. Have students make connections they see on the class mindmap, with a focus on their specific observations.

Assessment
Quality of individual and class mindmaps; contributions to the group; quality of observations.

 ## Left Mode—Define

Hmwk: students track an important issue. Gather information.

Objective
To gather information on a pertinent issue.

Activity
For homework two or three nights a week, students select an issue to follow. Their task is to gather as much information as possible to build their own expertise. Suggested information sources are TV news; radio; discussion with parents and friends; and newspapers, from which they should attend to political cartoons, headlines and lead paragraphs, articles, and editorials.

Assessment
Thoroughness of information gathered.

Current Events

Quadrant 3—Applications

 ### Left Mode—Try

Collate facts and record in Current Events Log.

Objective

To collate student facts in an organized way to support their positions on issues. To expand their awareness of issues and possible effect on them. To understand the background of today's issues and to project into the future.

Activity

Students share information about issues with other students adding additional information from what they themselves know. Students record facts in Current Events Log.

Assessment

Quality of student reports and quality of class contributions to individual reports.

 ### Right Mode—Extend

Students plan and create own political cartoon.

Objective

To have students develop and present their point of view on a current issue.

Activity

Students will plan their own political cartoon. They must select an issue; decide on their message; sketch their idea, and provide any necessary verbal information.

Assessment

Quality of thought put into project.

Quadrant 4—Creations

 ### Left Mode—Refine

Critique each other's work.

Objective

To have students look critically and constructively at their own work.

Activity

Share working copies of political cartoons in small cooperative groups. Students critique each other's work for editing and improvement.

Assessment

Quality of student group contributions. Ability to critique work for substance and originality.

 ### Right Mode—Integrate

Share final cartoons. Bulletin board display.

Objective

To share and enjoy the products created. To respect different points of view.

Activity

Students present final cartoon to the rest of the class. Cartoons are displayed on a bulletin board to be shared with the school.

Assessment

Quality of completed projects, presentation, participation, and enjoyment of the learning.

Democracy

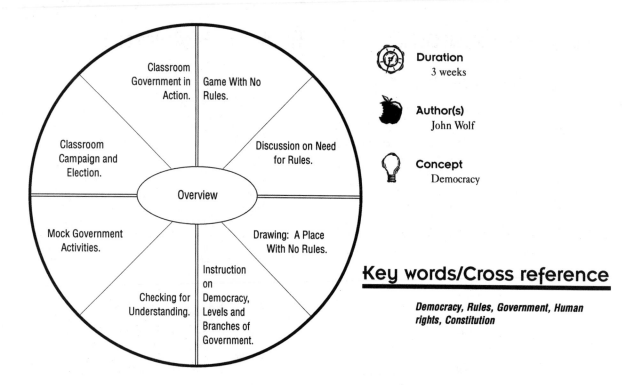

Duration
3 weeks

Author(s)
John Wolf

Concept
Democracy

Classroom Government in Action.

Game With No Rules.

Discussion on Need for Rules.

Classroom Campaign and Election.

Overview

Mock Government Activities.

Drawing: A Place With No Rules.

Checking for Understanding.

Instruction on Democracy, Levels and Branches of Government.

Key words/Cross reference

Democracy, Rules, Government, Human rights, Constitution

Overview

Objective
As citizens of a democratic republic, it is our responsibility to understand and participate in our governmental processes. Our government serves us by establishing order and justice, protecting the rights of individuals and society, and undertaking large public projects.

About the Author
John Wolf is a fourth grade classroom teacher and certified 4MAT trainer for the North East ISD in San Antonio, Texas.

Democracy

Quadrant 1—Experience

 ### Right Mode—Connect

Game With No Rules.

Objective

To create an experience in which there is no order and people's rights are not protected.

Activity

Choose five students to participate in a game. Choose several aggressive and several timid students. These students sit in a circle on the floor and the other students can stand around to watch the action. The object of the game is to have 4 of the 5 dice showing the same number. The prize is a piece of candy. There are no rules, except, when the teacher says "freeze," all action must come to an immediate stop. When the teacher puts the dice down in the middle of the circle, the game begins. The other students are to observe the behaviors of the students chosen to play the game.

Assessment

The effectiveness of the activity in showing that playing a game with no rules is not fair and could lead to disputes, possibly even to someone getting hurt
Personal Note:
I have tried this activity with three different classes and it has proved to be effective in showing that a lack of rules is inherently unfair, with the advantage going to the most aggressive. I do allow anything to happen up to the point of someone getting hurt. It is important to emphasize the "freeze" rule. My students showed predictable behaviors and did not let these get "out of hand."

 ## Left Mode—Examine

Discussion on Need for Rules.

Objective

To discuss what happened in the game and make adjustments.

Activity

Allow each student involved in playing the game a moment to express how s/he felt during the game and afterwards. Ask for observations about specific behaviors from the students not participating in the game. Allow each student who was involved in playing the game a chance to suggest changes in how the game is played. How are they going to decide which changes to make? Play the game with the changes. Discuss how the new "rules" changed the fairness of the game. Allow other students to play and make changes to the rules.

Assessment

Ability of the students to express their feelings and observations and to suggest changes and a fair way of deciding changes.

Quadrant 2—Concepts

Right Mode—Image

Drawing: A Place With No Rules.

Objective

To get the students to consider what life would be like without rules and then to express it in a visual image.

Activity

The students are asked to draw a picture of what life would be like in a place in their community if there were no laws or rules. Suggestions might include: school, a sports event, mall, grocery store, at an intersection, their neighborhood, or a park. Create a "gallery" of images by taping the drawings to the wall and allow the students to browse and quietly discuss their "gallery" pictures.

Assessment

The ideas in and the expressiveness of the drawings.

Left Mode—Define

Instruction on Democracy, Levels and Branches of Government.

Objective

To teach highlighted vocabulary and concepts to the students.

Activity

Use a variety of instructional methods, including lecture, text, and filmstrips, to teach the vocabulary and concepts that need to be presented to the students. Most curriculums and textbooks include: the idea of self-governance, the Constitution, majority/minority rule, representational government, the levels of government, the three branches of government, campaigns and elections.

Assessment

Informal verbal feedback from the students.

Quadrant 3—Applications

Left Mode—Try

Checking for Understanding.

Objective

To check for student understanding of concepts and vocabulary.

Activity

Use worksheets, chapter reviews, and quizzes to check for student understanding. Reteach when appropriate.

Assessment

Objective evaluation of work.

Right Mode—Extend

Mock Government Activities.

Objective

To allow the students to experience democracy for themselves.

Activity

Do a series of mock activities to go along with the concepts presented in the 2 Right and 3 Left steps.

Majority Rule:

Choose a controversial class problem to solve using majority rule in a secret ballot election.

Legislative Branch:

Divide the class into a House of Representatives and a Senate. Try to make the Senate smaller than the House, but retain small groups that become "committees." Each committee is to pass two bill proposals, with at least one legislator sponsoring the bill. The Constitution is represented by the rules and regulations regarding education adopted by the state, school district, and school administration. Students cannot violate these rules by trying to change dismissal times, length of recess, etc. The teacher does not interfere by autocratically dismissing any bills. After the bills pass the committee, they are presented to the whole legislative body which then discusses and votes on the bill. The bills that are passed are discussed and voted on in the other legislative body.

Executive Branch:

Since no class election may have taken place at this point, the teacher can have a drawing for "Class President for the Day." The President will take an opinion poll (thumbs up/thumbs down) from the class

Democracy

about each bill that has passed the "legislature." He or she may then choose to sign or veto the bill. If a bill is signed and the teacher questions the constitutionality of the bill, it will be challenged in the Supreme Court.

Judicial Branch:

Let the President choose nine students to act as a Supreme Court. The teacher informs the justices of their job: not to decide if they like the bill or not, but whether the bill conforms to the rules and regulations of the school as explained above. All laws must also protect the rights of the individual and of minorities. If there is not a controversial bill passed, then the teacher may make up one or two. Lawyers for both sides are allowed to prepare a case and present it to the justices.

Assessment

The knowledge of how government works that the students display in doing the activities.

Quadrant 4—Creations

Left Mode—Refine

Classroom Campaign and Election.

Objective

To hold class elections in order to set up a class government.

Activity

The students will organize a class election with the teacher moderating. Class positions can be modeled after either the federal or state government, and should include all three branches of the government. Students will campaign, register to vote, and have a secret ballot election. Each student can write a journal entry on "What a Class Government Means to Me."

Assessment

Ability of the students to organize and hold an election, the journal entry.

Right Mode—Integrate

Classroom Government in Action.

Objective

To allow the students to make certain class decisions for themselves.

Activity

Allow the student government to meet and make "laws" for the class. Begin with the legislative branch, let the President/Governor sign or veto the bills, and allow the Supreme Court to rule on controversial bills. Post the laws and allow the executive branch to take the responsibility of enacting them.

Assessment

The ability of the students to organize and run an effective class government.

Democratic Rules

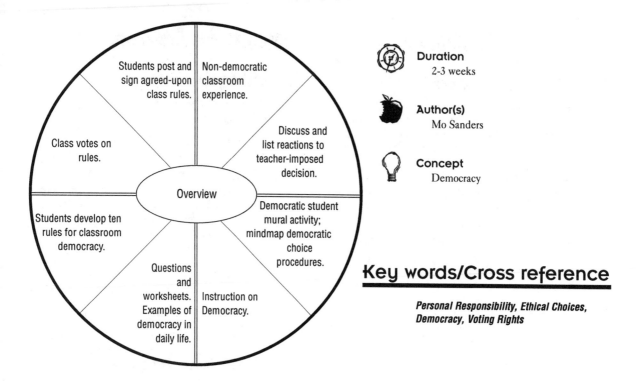

Students post and sign agreed-upon class rules.

Non-democratic classroom experience.

Class votes on rules.

Discuss and list reactions to teacher-imposed decision.

Overview

Students develop ten rules for classroom democracy.

Democratic student mural activity; mindmap democratic choice procedures.

Questions and worksheets. Examples of democracy in daily life.

Instruction on Democracy.

Duration
2-3 weeks

Author(s)
Mo Sanders

Concept
Democracy

Key words/Cross reference

Personal Responsibility, Ethical Choices, Democracy, Voting Rights

Overview

Objective
Students will understand how the concept of "democracy" affects them in their daily lives.

About the Author
Mo Sanders is a Staff Trainer for Federal Programs in the Kenai Peninsula Borough School District, Soldotna, Alaska. She has been involved in education for over twenty-five years. In addition to elementary classroom teaching experience, she also taught special education and gifted education. She is Project Leader of the Kenai Peninsula 4MAT Implementation Project as well as a Certified 4MAT Trainer.

Required Resources
Materials for class mural; appropriate film, video or filmstrip on "democracy" (optional: many good ones are available through most media centers); teacher-prepared worksheets; materials for class poster.

Author's Notes
As a continuing extension of this unit, the teacher may wish to plan several more debate/discussions as events occur throughout the remainder of the school year. For example, "Should we allow chasing on the playground? Why or why not?" "Should we enforce local litter laws at school?" Outcomes of class debate and vote could be shared with the rest of the school.

Quadrant 1—Experience

Right Mode—Connect

Non-democratic classroom experience.

Objective
To create an experience to connect students to the concept of democracy in their own lives.

Activity
The teacher presents the students with two choices, such as free time or learning centers. S/he conducts a class discussion on the merits of each choice, involving the students as much as possible, then calls for a class vote. Following the vote, s/he completely ignores its outcome and proceeds to impose a totally unrelated activity on the class as a whole. This activity should be one which is not nearly as much fun as the two choices, such as spelling practice. The teacher should impose the decision, allow for no discussion, and follow through with the imposed activity.

Assessment
Emotional involvement and reaction of students.

Left Mode—Examine

Discuss and list reactions to teacher-imposed decision.

Objective
To analyze the non-democratic experience.

Activity
After the imposed activity is completed, discuss student reactions to the teacher-imposed decision. List positive and negative reactions, and list and discuss student feelings.

Assessment
Quality of student participation.

Quadrant 2—Concepts

Right Mode—Image

Democratic student mural activity; mindmap democratic choice procedures.

Objective
To broaden students' awareness of democracy in action.

Activity
1. Students participate in the creation of a part-to-whole mural or cartoon sequence. For example, select a theme from science like "A Natural Habitat" or from health like "A Healthy School Environment." Students will first brainstorm the possible theme and design of the mural and then vote on the theme and design. They will create the mural together, and all individual efforts will contribute to the completed project.
2. Teacher-led discussion should focus on how the completed mural is like a group decision, i.e., most of us agreed on the theme and are satisfied with the outcome, though some of us may not have been supportive of the project or satisfied with the outcome.
3. Using a class mindmap for categorizing student responses, brainstorm choices which effect whole groups and ways to make group decisions which will satisfy most people.

Assessment
Participation in and contribution to the mural. Quality of discussion and accompanying mindmap.

Left Mode—Define

Instruction on democracy.

Objective
To teach the concept of democracy and define necessary terms.

Activity
Through mini-lecture, film, text assignments, and outside readings, students will overview the concept of democracy.

Assessment
Teacher observation of student attention and teacher verbal checking of understanding during instruction.

Democratic Rules

Quadrant 3—Applications

Left Mode—Try

Questions and worksheets. Examples of democracy in daily life.

Objective

To reinforce the concepts presented.

Activity

Students complete guided practice activities through questions in the textbook and teacher-prepared worksheets (close review, crossword puzzles, etc.) reviewing vocabulary. In cooperative groups students develop examples of democracy in real life: at school, at home, in the community, in the state, in the nation, and their personal responsibility in a democratic system. Group examples are shared with the whole class and collated by the teacher into a composite class chart.

Assessment

Quality of student practice sheets, group examples of democracy, and composite class chart.

Right Mode—Extend

Students develop ten rules for classroom democracy.

Objective

To apply what has been learned.

Activity

Working in cooperative groups, students will develop ten rules for democracy in their classroom. They will post their rules on a chart and illustrate the chart to portray "democracy in action."

Assessment

Quality of thought put into project; individual contributions to group effort.

Quadrant 4—Creations

Left Mode—Refine

Class votes on rules.

Objective

To evaluate the contribution of each group.

Activity

Each group will present its poster and rules. The teacher will conduct pro and con discussion with a final class vote for each rule.

Assessment

Quality of student group contributions. Ability to sensitively critique the work of others for substance and workability.

Right Mode—Integrate

Students post and sign agreed-upon class rules.

Objective

To implement what has been learned.

Activity

The final agreed-upon rules for the class are posted and signed by each student and by the teacher. The rules are adhered to by the teacher and the class.

Assessment

Student pride and sense of commitment to creating their own class code.

Exploration

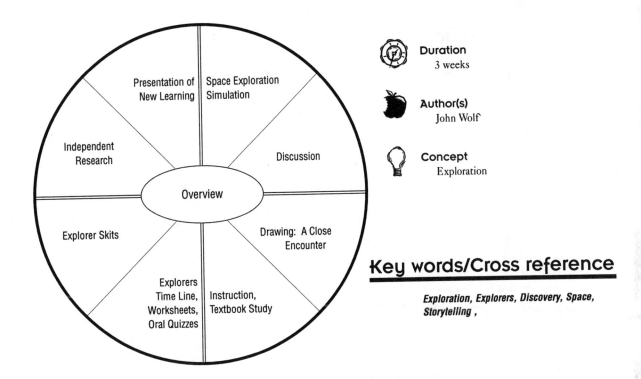

Presentation of New Learning

Space Exploration Simulation

Independent Research

Discussion

Overview

Explorer Skits

Drawing: A Close Encounter

Explorers Time Line, Worksheets, Oral Quizzes

Instruction, Textbook Study

Duration
3 weeks

Author(s)
John Wolf

Concept
Exploration

Key words/Cross reference

Exploration, Explorers, Discovery, Space, Storytelling ,

Overview

Objective
Explorers have had many different motivations for their actions, have faced extraordinary risks, hardships, and dangers, and have had significant impacts on the history of man.

About the Author
John Wolf is a fourth grade classroom teacher and a certified 4MAT trainer for the North East ISD in San Antonio, Texas.

Required Resources
Related textbook pages, worksheets, dice, art paper, crayons, index cards, yarn.

Quadrant 1—Experience

Right Mode—Connect

Space Exploration Simulation.

Objective
To simulate the excitement, risks, and dangers of exploration.

Activity
Lead a Space Simulation Game similar in spirit to this one. Each small group represents a separate space vehicle and is provided with one die to roll at critical moments during the game. Rolling a 1 has unfortunate consequences and rolling a 6 will help in rescuing other crews and in finding the resource they are looking for.

You have been gathered together here at the NASA Space Center on an urgent secret mission. Unmanned satellites have discovered a vital supply of zirconium on the surface of Io, a moon of Jupiter. It is your mission to discover the location and bring back a supply of this valuable resource. Each group must choose a leader who will make the final decisions for your space craft. (Allow students to choose leaders). Enter your space vehicles and prepare for launch.

(Countdown from 10) Roll the die, if you roll a 1 your launch is delayed and you must roll again. If you roll a 1 again, your space craft has exploded. It is now time for your rocket booster to send you into the proper orbit. If you roll a 1, your booster does not fire properly and you must try again. If you roll another 1, the mission must be abandoned and you must try to safely return to earth. You are now on course for Io, but you must safely pass through the asteroid belt. Roll the die, if you roll a 1 your craft has been hit and disabled. If you roll a 1 again, your ship is destroyed. You are now approaching Io and must try to make a safe landing. Roll the die, if you roll a 1, you have crashed on impact and your spacecraft is inoperable. If you roll another 1, you do not survive. Roll again, if you roll a 6 you have found zirconium and may start the return trip home. Suddenly, aliens appear. They look fierce and threatening. You must quickly decide what you are going to do-make peace or fight? If you fight, you must roll a 4, 5, or 6 to win.

A 1, 2, or 3 means you are captured. If you make peace, you must roll and the aliens will accept the peace unless you roll a 1. In that case, you are captured. You can free yourselves from the alien captors if you roll a 6. Other space crews can rescue you if they roll a 6. Check your food and oxygen supplies by rolling the die. You must begin your return for home after that many rolls or you will not survive. You may roll to try to find zirconium, escape from the aliens, or rescue another crew. On the way home you must safely pass back through the asteroid belt and you must not roll a 1 when landing.

Assessment
Participation in and excitement generated by the simulation.

Left Mode—Examine

Discussion

Objective
To analyze and discuss the simulated exploration experience.

Activity
The teacher moderates a discussion about the risks, the hardships, the rewards, and the importance of leadership in exploration. Ask the students to brainstorm as a class as many explorers as they can name.

Assessment
The quality of thoughts in the discussion.

Quadrant 2—Concepts

 ### Right Mode—Image

Drawing: A Close Encounter.

Objective

To create an image that captures the risks, hardships, and danger involved in exploration.

Activity

Each student draws an image from these two choices - Close Encounters: Space Explorers Meet Aliens, or Columbus: Danger in the New World. The pictures should try to capture the risks, hardships, and danger involved in exploration. Display and discuss.

Assessment

The product's ability to communicate the objective.

 ### Left Mode—Define

Instruction, Textbook Study.

Objective

To examine the explorations and historical significances of selected explorers.

Activity

The teacher uses storytelling, lectures, filmstrips and textbook readings to teach about explorers, their quests, their significance, and the historical importance of their explorations. Personal Note: In my curriculum, I teach about important Texas explorers, so I focus my attention on these men: Cabeza de Vaca and Esteban, Coronado, and LaSalle. I have had great success in presenting the information in storytelling form, followed by independent textbook reading. I stress the reasons for the exploration, the risks, hardships, and dangers encountered, and the impact on history the explorer made.

Assessment

Student feedback through informal verbal checking.

Quadrant 3—Applications

 ### Left Mode—Try

Explorers Time Line, Worksheets, Oral Quizzes.

Objective

To check for understanding through summarization and sequencing of events.

Activity

After an explorer is studied, give each student a 4 X 6 index card, lined on one side. On the lined side, the student is to summarize the story of the explorer. A title with the name of the explorer and the dates of the exploration is required. On the opposite side, the student is to draw an image of one of the most significant events in the explorer's story. After each explorer has been studied and each card has been completed, create a timeline by punching holes in the cards and connecting them with yarn. Worksheets and quizzes over the material can also be administered.

Assessment

The completeness and conciseness of the summaries, the information conveyed in the images, the ability to properly sequence the cards in a timeline, and the performance of the student on the worksheet(s).

 ### Right Mode—Extend

Explorer Skits.

Objective

To express the explorations studied in an original skit.

Activity

Divide the class into small groups to write, prepare, and present skits on the explorers studied in class. You could group by asking each student to write down his or her favorite explorer and then match accordingly. Each group is to recreate the story by acting it out for the others.

Assessment

Accuracy and completeness of information included in the skit.

Quadrant 4—Creations

 ## Left Mode—Refine

Independent Research.

Objective

To use self-directed inquiry to learn about another
explorer.

Activity

Individually, or in small groups, the students will choose
another explorer to learn about in a self-directed
inquiry. They will plan and prepare a presentation to
the whole class that will teach others what they have
learned. The presentation should be creative, informational, and entertaining. Approaches could include: simulation, storytelling, puppet shows, skits, artwork, rap,
or video. Lists of explorers can be found in almanacs.
Space and ocean exploration are especially vital and
interesting topics relevant to today. Many great explorers have left journals and books which could be read,
including John Wesley Powell, John Muir, Cabeza de
Vaca, and Coronado.

Assessment

Ability to gather information independently, and to prepare a presentation on the material.

 ## Right Mode—Integrate

Presentation of New Learning.

Objective

To communicate to others what the student has
learned.

Activity

The students share what they have learned in their
prepared presentations to the whole class.

Assessment

How successfully the student communicates what s/he
has learned.

Inventions

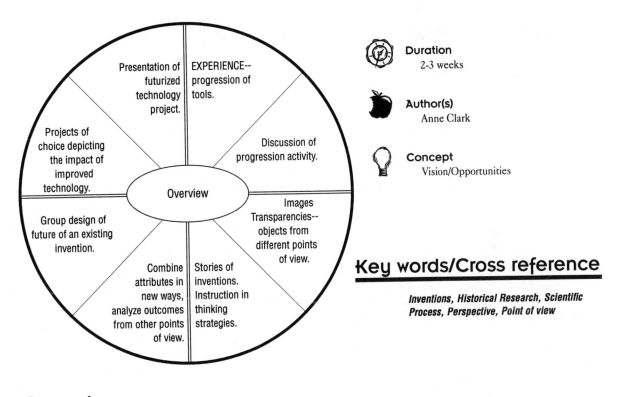

Presentation of futurized technology project.

EXPERIENCE-- progression of tools.

Projects of choice depicting the impact of improved technology.

Discussion of progression activity.

Overview

Group design of future of an existing invention.

Images Transparencies-- objects from different points of view.

Combine attributes in new ways, analyze outcomes from other points of view.

Stories of inventions. Instruction in thinking strategies.

Duration
2-3 weeks

Author(s)
Anne Clark

Concept
Vision/Opportunities

Key words/Cross reference

Inventions, Historical Research, Scientific Process, Perspective, Point of view

Overview

Objective
To help students appreciate the opportunities that problems present and to be prepared to act upon the situation with alertness perceiving new possibilities and finally to be willing to look at all ramifications before jumping to a decision.

About the Author
Anne Clark is an instructional specialist in the K-5 gifted/talented program in the North East Independent School District in San Antonio, Texas. She is a certified 4MAT Trainer.

Required Resources
Tools, such as wooden spoon, wire whisk, hand-held egg beater, and electric mixer, overhead transparencies. Copies of Escher Prints.

Bibliography
Alex Osborn's SCAMPER.

Inventions

Quadrant 1—Experience

Right Mode—Connect

EXPERIENCE—progression of tools.

Objective
To gain personal understanding of the increasing complexity of tools.

Activity
Students will produce a product, such as instant pudding, using a progression of tools working through stations. First station will use wooden spoon. Second, will use a wire whisk. Third, will use a hand-held egg beater. Fourth will use an electric mixer.

Assessment
Student participation in activity.

Left Mode—Examine

Discussion of progression activity.

Objective
To examine the similarities and differences of tools. To understand how and why improvements are made in existing tools.

Activity
Students will eat the products and analyze the different characteristics of the pudding produced at each station. Students will analyze the series of tools. Students will note the attributes of the tool and the product made at each station. Students will observe the improvement of the tool from station to station and the changing attributes of the ensuing product.

Assessment
Student participation and verbal response.

Quadrant 2—Concepts

Right Mode—Image

Images Transparencies—objects from different points of view.

Objective
To become aware of patterns and transformations in order to see how the old can be rearranged or elaborated on to become new.

Activity
Students view images via overhead transparencies showing objects from different points of view. Students will respond noting the observer's point of view in each instance. Same images changing by differing perspective. Copies of Escher Prints are shown as students note differences in perspective.

Assessment
Quality of student attention and response.

Left Mode—Define

Stories of inventions. Instruction in thinking strategies.

Objective
To develop thinking techniques and strategies—such as the Consequences Wheel and Alex Osborn's SCAMPER strategy—to empower students to solve problems. To understand the historical development of tools and the ensuing effects on a civilization.

Activity
Students will participate in directed reading activities of the stories of various everyday inventions such as the shopping cart. Students will learn of inventions that occurred by mistake, but were capitalized upon by the alertness of the inventor to possibilities. Students will generate lists of characteristics of inventors as thinkers prepared for opportunities. Students will be instructed in Alex Osborn's SCAMPER techniques and see how substitution, minification, etc. will generate new ideas for invention. Students will be instructed in ways to evaluate inventions. Students will explore problem situations from different perspectives using a consequences wheel which explores possible ramifications of solutions. Students will explore how inventors use analogies to come up with new ideas.

Assessment
Student oral and written responses throughout directed activities and completion of a consequences wheel.

Inventions

Quadrant 3—Applications

 ### Left Mode—Try

Combine attributes in new ways, analyze outcomes from other points of view.

Objective

To provide practice in analyzing objects so that specific attributes can be improved upon. To provide practice in looking at existing things in new ways.

Activity

Application of Alex Osborn's SCAMPER strategy as various classroom objects are minified, maximized, etc. Note attributes of objects so that they can be combined in new ways. In groups of four, students take ordinary objects, analyze what is the thing they find the most difficult about it, and then design an improvement, such as a tape dispenser that dispenses pieces of tape in exact lengths as programmed by a key pad. Analyze invention, such as moving belt to load the school bus. List people that might be affected. Construct a consequences wheel that projects possible consequences from all points of view.

Assessment

Student ability to work in groups and complete activities.

 ### Right Mode—Extend

Group design of future of an existing invention.

Objective

To develop an awareness that complex inventions and/or technological processes have developed from additions to simpler inventions and/or the addition or deletion of attributes. To understand the necessity for open mindedness in brainstorming possibilities and provide students with opportunity to understand that they can monitor group solutions by making intelligent decisions.

Activity

In teams of four, students will set up companies and select a current invention or technological process and do historical research to observe trends. Companies will project what that invention might be like 25 years from now. The projects must be plausible not involving magic or extraordinary powers.

Assessment

Group design of a project.

Quadrant 4—Creations

 ### Left Mode—Refine

Projects of choice depicting the impact of improved technology.

Objective

To initiate, plan, and refine a creative presentation incorporating elements of creative problem solving.

Activity

Students will project the impact of their future invention on that culture. Students will use the consequences wheel to evaluate priorities. Students will create their choice of one or any combination of newspaper or magazine advertising of the new invention, television commercials, talk shows with interviews with inventors and reactions of those affected by the new invention or any other format they may devise.

Assessment

Quality of the creative production.

 ### Right Mode—Integrate

Presentation of futurized technology project.

Objective

To provide the opportunity for students to present and imagine possible real-life applications of the learning. To help students understand that they can control solutions by making intelligent decisions.

Activity

Group presentation of futurized technology project to an audience.

Assessment

Quality of student presentation and enthusiasm of audience.

Local History

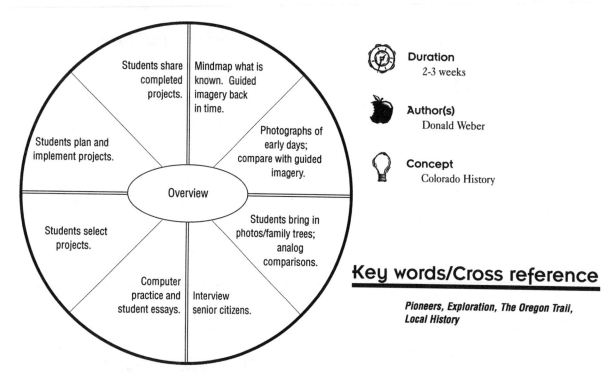

Overview

- Students share completed projects.
- Mindmap what is known. Guided imagery back in time.
- Students plan and implement projects.
- Photographs of early days; compare with guided imagery.
- Students select projects.
- Students bring in photos/family trees; analog comparisons.
- Computer practice and student essays.
- Interview senior citizens.

Duration
2-3 weeks

Author(s)
Donald Weber

Concept
Colorado History

Key words/Cross reference

Pioneers, Exploration, The Oregon Trail, Local History

Overview

Objective
To help students connect to their place in the history of the town where they live.

About the Author
Donald Weber is former principal of Georgetown and Empire Schools, Clear Creek School District, Georgetown, CO. He has been involved in education for over thirty-five years as a classroom teacher and school administrator. He is a certifed 4MAT Trainer.

Required Resources
Teacher-prepared guided imagery, "going back in time;" old photographs of the area; volunteer local senior citizen to share personal history.

Bibliography
Digerness, David. *The Mineral Belt.* Silverton, CO: Sundance Publications, Ltd., 1982.
Luchetti, Cathy, and Olwell, Carol. *Women of the West.* Berkeley, CA: Antelope Island Press, 1982.

Russell, Carl P. Firearms, *Traps, & Tools of the Mountain Men.* Albuquerque, NM: University of New Mexico Press, 1977.
Software used in Step Five:
"The Oregon Trail," (software and manual). MECC, 3490 Lexington Ave. North, St. Paul, MN 55126, 1985.

Author's Notes
Colorado History is a required course in the Colorado elementary curriculum. Living in a National Historic District with many buildings from the 1800's provides a wonderful opportunity to involve the students in this great heritage. Many other communities in this country have a similar advantage. The objective of this three-week unit is to help the students relate to not only the early days of Georgetown, but also to understand and appreciate the pioneer way of life.

Quadrant 1—Experience

 Right Mode—Connect

Mindmap what is known. Guided imagery back in time.

Objective

To acquaint students with life in Georgetown, Colorado, in the mid-1800's.

Activity

The teacher conducts a guided imagery taking students back in time. The imagery emphasizes the harsh living conditions of the time and how people of strong character emerged from these conditions. Visualization material is taken from *The Mineral Belt*, by Digerness; *Women of the West*, by Luchetti & Olwell; and Firearms, *Traps, and Tools of the Mountain Men*, by Russell.

Assessment

Engagement of students.

 Left Mode—Examine

Photographs of early days; compare with guided imagery.

Objective

To develop empathy for these pioneers and an understanding of their problems. To develop discussion techniques.

Activity

Show photographs and drawings of early Georgetown. Many of these are available from the local Historical Society. See how these photographs compare with their own images from the guided imagery. Discuss problems of the era and how the students feel about these people. Break students into small groups to make lists of pioneer problems and student feelings.

Students teams brainstorm and record in mindmap form what they already know about their local history. From their mindmap, the students prepare questions for interviewing several native senior citizens who will visit the class during this unit and share their experiences about growing up in Georgetown in another time.

Assessment

Quality of discussion and group lists.

Quadrant 2—Concepts

 Right Mode—Image

Students bring in photos/family trees; analog comparisons.

Objective

To compare life of early Coloradoans with those of the students' ancestors.

Activity

Students bring in photos, family histories, or family trees and discuss similarities and differences between their own ancestors and Georgetown pioneers discussed earlier. Draw analogs to describe comparisons.

Assessment

Quality of discussion and analogs.

 Left Mode—Define

Interview senior citizens.

Objective

To teach about the lifestyles of early pioneers and the changes in those lifestyles. To teach summarizing techniques.

Activity

Bring in several native senior citizens to tell about their memories of growing up in Georgetown, and students ask the interview questions developed in the first activity. In addition, bring in a guest speaker from the local Historical Society to share information on local Georgetown history. Students write summaries of presentations.

Assessment

Student interest during presentations and quality of written summaries.

Quadrant 3—Applications

 ## Left Mode—Try

Computer practice and student essays.

Objective
To reinforce learning about the pioneers. To reinforce research skills.

Activity
Students use the computer software *Oregon Trail* which deals with some of the problems pioneers encountered. Students select an aspect of pioneer life which interests them and write a brief paper from materials in the classroom and media center.

Assessment
Quality of student reports.

 ## Right Mode—Extend

Students select projects.

Objective
To personalize the learning by allowing students to choose a project related to their report. To form cooperative learning groups for projects.

Activity
Students groups choose from the following suggested projects:
1. Produce a skit about pioneer days.
2. Make a model of early Georgetown.
3. Write up a mock newspaper page from the period.
4. Make a model of a silver mine or sluice box.
5. Draw scenes from early Georgetown.
6. Take pictures of buildings which existed in early days.
7. A project of their own.

Assessment
Students' ability to form teams and get on task.

Quadrant 4—Creations

 ## Left Mode—Refine

Students plan and implement projects.

Objective
To help students work cooperatively. To help students plan and work systematically.

Activity
Each group will write out a plan for its project, including materials needed and time of completion. Students will conference with the teacher for approval of their plan.

Assessment
Quality of student plans.

 ## Right Mode—Integrate

Students share completed projects.

Objective
To increase student ability to work as a member of a group and to share what they have learned.

Activity
Students complete projects and share their results with the class through visual and oral presentations.

Assessment
Quality of completed projects, participation, and sharing.

Rivers

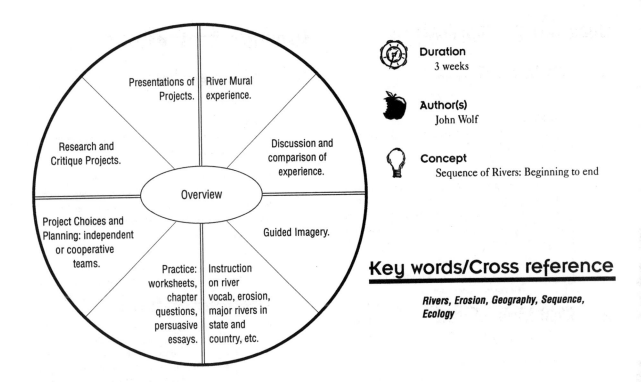

Duration
3 weeks

Author(s)
John Wolf

Concept
Sequence of Rivers: Beginning to end

Key words/Cross reference

Rivers, Erosion, Geography, Sequence, Ecology

Overview

Objective
Rivers are important resources that we need to understand and protect. They supply people with fresh water for drinking, factories, agriculture, and recreation. They have significant historical importance and are critical to our future.

About the Author
John Wolf is a fourth grade classroom teacher and a 4MAT trainer in the NorthEast ISD in San Antonio, Texas. He lives on the scenic Guadalupe River, and hopes to swim and canoe in its pristine waters for a long time to come.

Required Resources
Bulletin board paper, tape recording of *"The Moldau"* by Smetana.

Quadrant 1—Experience

 ## Right Mode—Connect

River Mural experience.

Objective

To connect with the student's perceptions of what a river is like and what it is used for.

Activity

The class will create a mural of a river showing it from its source to its mouth. The teacher outlines a river on a long piece of bulletin board paper. The children are instructed to add as much detail as they can that shows what a river is like and how people use rivers. Encourage the students to remember experiences they have had at rivers and to include what they know about rivers from television, movies and books. Discuss things that they may want to include in the mural (towns, bridges, lakes, tributaries). Have the students spread out along the length of the river and fill in all parts of the mural, discussing what they are doing with others and using cooperative skills.

Assessment

The ideas expressed in the mural, participation in the activity.

 ## Left Mode—Examine

Discussion and comparison of experience.

Objective

To examine the ideas presented in the river mural, to check for current knowledge of rivers.

Activity

Examine the mural starting at the source. Have each student explain why they chose to include what they added. Listen to river experiences and ask if anyone else has experienced the same thing. Ask if they feel anything has been left out. Allow the students to add to the mural if there seems to be a need for it.

Assessment

Participation in sharing experiences and ideas.

Quadrant 2—Concepts

 ## Right Mode—Image

Guided Imagery.

Objective

To visualize a river from its beginning to its end.

Activity

Lead the students on a guided imagery down a river. For background music, play a recording of Smetana's *The Moldau,* a famous orchestral piece that depicts the Moldau River. This should be easy to obtain from your school's music teacher. Here is a script to aid you in making your own guided imagery.

"Imagine a beautiful, warm, summer day. You are standing at the beginning of a river. Here water bubbles forth from the earth into a stream. Barefoot, you step into the water and feel it swirling around your ankles. You cup your hands and pour it over your head, feeling its icy coolness on your hot skin. Take a deep breath and smell the freshness of the countryside. Run down the stream. Other streams join in and now it is a small river. There is an inner tube waiting for you to hop on and ride the current. Feel the pull of the water as it moves you along faster and faster. Look at the banks of the river. What plants and animals do you see? The water begins to change speed and color as you enter some whitewater rapids. The river slows again. On your left another river joins this one. You're getting hot from the sun, so get off the tube and swim. How deep is the water now? The river empties into a large lake. A motorboat ties your tube onto it and races you across the lake. Leave your tube and walk down the steep dam. There a canoe waits for you. Get in, pick up the paddle and continue on your journey down the river. You go under a bridge and enter a small city. Take a deep breath and smell the city. A pipe from a factory spits water out into the river. What color is the water from the pipe? You leave the city and the river widens and deepens as you get closer to the sea. You can smell the saltwater, hear the gulls laughing, and feel the sea breeze. Beach your canoe and run into the surf. Take a deep breath and return slowly to the classroom."

Assessment

Participation in the activity.

Rivers

 ## Left Mode—Define

Instruction river vocab, erosion, major rivers in state and country, etc.

Objective
To teach vocabulary and concepts.

Activity
Use a variety of instructional methods to teach the vocabulary and concepts important in your curriculum. Suggestions include teacher lecture, textbook reading, filmstrips, and videos. Concepts that I teach in this unit to my fourth grade Texas students are:
river vocabulary (source, river basin, aquifer, bank, riverbed, current, tributary, reservoir, dam, mouth), uses of rivers, geographical location of major Texas rivers, comparison to major rivers in the United States and the World, flooding and erosion, and river protection.

Assessment
Informal verbal feedback from students.

Quadrant 3—Applications

 ## Left Mode—Try

Practice: worksheets, chapter questions, persuasive essays.

Objective
To check for student understanding.

Activity
Use a variety of standard evaluative techniques including worksheets and review questions from the textbook. An interesting assignment would be to write a persuasive paragraph on the importance (or lack of importance) of preserving and protecting our rivers. These could be sent in to local newspapers and mailed to government officials.

Assessment
Objective evaluation of work.

 ## Right Mode—Extend

Project Choices and Planning: independent or cooperative teams.

Objective
To choose and begin work on a culminating project.

Activity
Give options to the student in devising an appropriate project, including whether to work individually or in a small group. Project ideas could include: organizing and implementing a river cleanup in your local area (photograph the event), research a river and share with the class what you learn, an erosion-control project on the school campus, get involved in an environmental group's campaign to protect or preserve a local river, investigate the water quality and effects of industries on a local water source.

Assessment
Choice of projects, enthusiasm for follow-through.

Quadrant 4—Creations

Left Mode—Refine

Research and Critique Projects.

Objective
To critique and evaluate progress and importance of project.

Activity
Every third day, ask the students to write journal entries on the progress of their project. What difficulties are they encountering? Do they need additional help or support? Is their project practical?

Assessment
Honesty and insight shared in journal entries.

Right Mode—Integrate

Presentations of Projects.

Objective
To share their project experiences with others.

Activity
At the completion of the project, the student(s) present what they have done and what they have learned to their classmates and possibly to a larger audience. A bulletin board display would be a good to provide broader exposure. It is quite conceivable that the projects would be completed at very different times and it is assumed that the teacher has started the next journey around a 4MAT wheel. . .

Assessment
The quality of the project and the effect it has made on the student.

Texas Indians

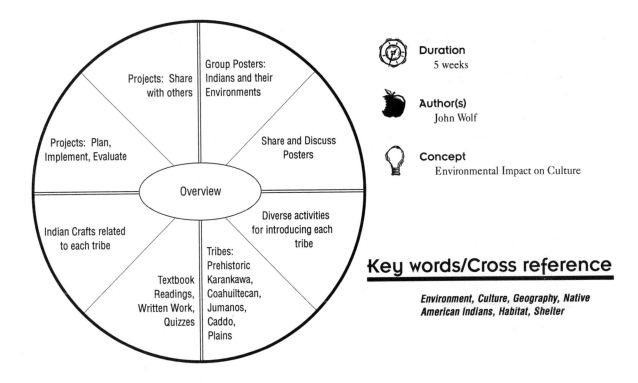

Projects: Share with others

Group Posters: Indians and their Environments

Projects: Plan, Implement, Evaluate

Share and Discuss Posters

Overview

Indian Crafts related to each tribe

Diverse activities for introducing each tribe

Textbook Readings, Written Work, Quizzes

Tribes: Prehistoric Karankawa, Coahuiltecan, Jumanos, Caddo, Plains

Duration
5 weeks

Author(s)
John Wolf

Concept
Environmental Impact on Culture

Key words/Cross reference

Environment, Culture, Geography, Native American Indians, Habitat, Shelter

Overview

Objective
The fourth grade curriculum in Texas includes studies of the Native American Indian groups that lived in Texas. These cultures were profoundly affected by the physical environment and natural resources available to them. An understanding of the relationship of the Indians to their surroundings is essential to understanding the Indians themselves.

About the Author
John Wolf is a fourth grade classroom teacher and certified 4MAT trainer for the North East ISD in San Antonio, Texas.

Required Resources
Posterboard, assorted art supplies, clay, yarn, beads, feathers, tempera paint, corn husks, paper plates.

Bibliography
Dances With Wolves. Orion films, 1990. Directed by Kevin Costner.
Warren, Betsy. *Indians Who Lived In Texas.* Dallas: Hendrick-Long Publishing Co., 1970.
Newcomb, W. W. *The Indians of Texas.* Austin: University of Texas Press, 1961.
Winrey, Dorman H., et. al. *Indian Tribes of Texas.* Waco, Texas: Texian Press, 1971.
Fields, F. T. *Texas Sketchbook.* Humble Oil and Refining Co.
Shafer, Harry J. *Ancient Texans.* Austin: Texas Monthly Press, 1986.
McDermott, Gerald. *Arrow to the Sun.* New York: Penguin Books, 1974.
Goble, Paul. *The Gift of the Sacred Dog.* New York: Macmillan, 1980.
Goble, Paul. *Buffalo Woman.* New York: Macmillan, 1984.
Goble, Paul. *The Girl Who Loved Wild Horses.* New York: Macmillan, 1978.
DePaola, Tomie. *The Legend of the Bluebonnet.* New York: G. P. Putnam's Sons, 1983.
DePaola, Tomie. *The Legend of the Scarlet Paintbrush.* New York: G.P. Putnam's Sons,
Storm, Hyemeyohsts. *Seven Arrows.* New York: Ballantine, 1972.
Warren, Betsy. *Inside a Tepee.* Austin: RanchGate Books, 1989.

Quadrant 1—Experience

Right Mode—Connect

Group Posters: Indians and their Environments

Objective

To challenge the student to think about the connection between the availability and type of resources in an environment and the way it would affect how a Native American culture would express itself.

Activity

Divide the class into five cooperative groups with 4 or 5 students in each group. Assign a leader for each group and have the leaders draw from five slips of paper with these environments written on them: coastal, desert, forest, mountains, plains. On a poster board, using markers, colors, construction paper, wooden sticks, feathers, and whatever else you have available in your art supplies, each group is to show the shelter, clothing, food, and tools of an Indian group that might live in that environment.

Assessment

Participation in the activity, thought processes used in deciding what to include in the product.

Left Mode—Examine

Share and discuss posters

Objective

The students will share, discuss, and justify what they included in their products.

Activity

Each group presents their poster to the class, explaining what they have included and why they believe an Indian group in that environment would express itself in that manner. The other students can ask questions of the presenting group and the teacher moderates the discussion.

Assessment

Quality of the thoughts in justifying or challenging what is included in the products.

Quadrant 2—Concepts

Right Mode—Image

Diverse activities for introducing each tribe.

Objective

To provide the students with stimulating experiences that lead them into an understanding of the Indian tribes they will be studying.
Personal Note: Study each tribe in a mini-wheel that follows this sequence: 2R - 2L - 3L - 3R. Then repeat the cycle with the next tribe. The following activities are the 2R pieces to these mini-wheels.

Activities

Prehistoric Indians:
Simulate an archaeological experience through the use of fantasy. Pretend you have packed your car and you are driving southwest of San Antonio, Texas to some cave shelters along the lower Pecos River. As you carefully dig for archeological evidence, pretend to find items such as: animal teeth, pottery shards, charred wood, flint points, etc.

Karankawa Indians:
Tell the story of Cabeza de Vaca and his rescue by the Karankawa Indians. A good source of information for this is the book, *Texas Sketchbook* (see the bibliography).

Coahuiltecan Indians:
Simulate a rabbit hunt on the playground using the cooperative "surround" technique. Choose three students to be "rabbits" and five students to be the "hunters." The rest of the class forms a horseshoe around the rabbits. The "hunters" are waiting to ambush the "rabbits" in the open end of the horseshoe. The "tribe" pretends to beat the bushes and begins to close in on the "rabbits." The "rabbits" run to the open end of the horseshoe and are "hunted" by being tagged. Make sure everyone knows their roles before you begin.

Jumanos Indians:
Show pictures of Anasazi Indian ruins, pueblos, pottery, and sand painting. Read aloud the children's book, *Arrow to the Sun.*

Caddo Indians:
Show the pictures on pages 6-14 in the book, *Indians Who Lived In Texas.*

Plains Indians:
Show short, appropriate sections of the popular movie, *Dances With Wolves.* I like to show the scenes when the soldier is coming into the Indian village for the first

time and when the tribe is moving to hunt the buffalo. Read aloud the children's book, *Gift of the Sacred Dogs*, by Paul Goble. I like to read aloud books by Paul Goble each day that we study the Plains Indians.

Assessment
Student participation, student interest generated by the activities.

Left Mode—Define

Tribes: Prehistoric Karankawa, Coahuiltecan, Jumanos, Caddo, Plains.

Objective
The student will learn about the major Texas Indian tribes, where they lived, and how their environment shaped their culture.

Activity
The teacher uses lectures, readings, and note-taking to convey the information needed by the students. Students should note the geographical region of the tribe and understand how the resources of that area contributed to the expression of that culture. Food, shelter, clothing, way of life, and size of tribe should all be stressed.

Assessment
Informal verbal feedback.

Quadrant 3—Applications

Left Mode—Try

Textbook Readings, Written Work, Quizzes

Objective
The student will show mastery of material on written work.

Activity
The students reread independently the text that was studied as a class and answer questions relating to the tribe. Verbal checks and short quizzes can also be used.

Assessment
Objective evaluation of written work.

Right Mode—Extend

Indian Crafts related to each tribe.

Objective
To recreate Indian skills in craft activities related to each tribe.

Activity
Follow the activity below immediately after learning about that individual tribe. Then return to the 2R piece and begin studying the next tribe.

Lower Pecos River Indians:
Recreate cave pictographs with a crayon resist and tempera paint washes. Take an 18" X 24" piece of gray construction paper. Draw figures similar to the Pecos pictographs in heavy black, red, and white crayon. Lightly wash with diluted brown, orange, and yellow tempera paint. After it dries, crumple the paper to give it a rock-like effect.

Karankawas:
Make an Indian necklace or bracelet. One way is to make a clay medallion and several clay beads to string on a leather strip with feathers, shells, or even pasta noodles. Another possibility is to braid three pieces of yarn into a "friendship" bracelet or necklace.

Coahuiltecans:
Use soaked corn husks (tamale wrappings) to make a fiber weaving. Soak the husks for at least thirty minutes, tear into long strips, and line up about eight strips on a piece of masking tape, leaving a little space between. Then tightly weave other strips through the "warp" you have made. It isn't beautiful, but it is gives the feeling for the difficulty of working with a natural product.

Jumanos:

I teach the children string tricks like Cat's Cradle and Jacob's Ladder. This was a common winter activity of many Indian children. I have experimented with making sand paintings, but have not perfected it yet.

Caddo:

We make clay coil pots by making long "snakes" of clay and spiraling a base and then adding coils to make the sides. You should learn how to score and slip so the product will stay together better.

Plains:

You can make a fine-looking medicine shield to hang by using a crayon resist and brown tempera paint wash on a paper plate. Let each child choose an Indian name and draw a picture representing that name on the paper plate in heavy crayon. Wash with brown tempera paint and hang three construction paper feathers from the bottom. In addition, a beautiful headband can be woven with yarn on a cardboard loom and you can crumple paper grocery bags and create a pictograph story on "bisonhide."

Assessment

Evaluate the students on how well they relate these skills to the tribes studied.

Quadrant 4—Creations

 ## Left Mode—Refine

Projects: Plan, Implement, Evaluate.

Objective

To help the student find a meaningful project on Indians to plan and implement, to evaluate the progress on that project.

Activity

Introduce the assignment to the students and let them brainstorm ideas for projects. They could: build models of Indian shelters, do research and make a poster on a different Indian tribe, write to and get information about Indian reservations in Texas, prepare a review of the Texas Indian tribes to help the class prepare for the final examination on this unit, explore the dilemma facing Native Indian cultures in modern society by reading periodical articles on the subject. Keep up with the progress of the students on their projects through journal writings and conferences.

Assessment

The choice and originality of the project, the implementation of the project.

 ## Right Mode—Integrate

Projects: Share with others.

Objective

The students present what they have learned to others.

Activity

As projects are finished, the students make presentations to their own class and to other classes. They are to communicate what they have learned to their audience. The products can be displayed in the library or in the community.

Assessment

The quality of the project and the effectiveness of the presentation.

Index

Index